TO RAISE UP THE SOUTH

Sunday Schools in Black and White Churches, 1865–1915

Sally G. McMillen

Louisiana State University Press
Baton Rouge

Copyright © 2001 by Louisiana State University Press
All rights reserved
Manufactured in the United States of America
First printing
10 09 08 07 06 05 04 03 02 01
5 4 3 2 1

Designer: Amanda McDonald Scallan
Typeface: Display, Brice; Text, Sabon
Typesetter: Coghill Composition Co., Inc.
Printer and binder: Thomson-Shore, Inc.

Library of Congress Cataloging-in-Publication Data

McMillen, Sally Gregory, 1944–
  To raise up the South : Sunday schools in Black and White churches, 1865–1915 / Sally G. McMillen.
      p. cm.
  Includes bibliographical references and index.
  ISBN 0-8071-2725-6 (alk. paper) — ISBN 0-8071-2749-3 (pbk. : alk. paper)
  1. Sunday schools—Southern States—History—19th century. 2. Sunday schools—Southern States—History—20th century. I. Title.
  BV1467 .M36 2001
  268′.0975′09034—dc21   2001002785

The paper in this book meets the guidelines for permanence and durability of the Committee on Production Guidelines for Book Longevity of the Council on Library Resources. ♾

to Bruce

Contents

Introduction ix
Abbreviations xvii

1 A Cure for the South 1
2 Reconstructing the South 26
3 Reclaiming Our Children's Souls 55
4 Uplift and Redemption through the Published Word 89
5 Inside the Sunday Classroom 121
6 Race and the Sunday School 163
7 The Modern Southern Sunday School 194
8 An Incomplete Cure 224

Bibliography 251
Index 289

Illustrations

following page 88

Opening Day at Log Cabin Sunday School outside Atlanta
Sabbath school in a Kentucky "cove"
Open-air Sunday school in Arkansas
Family in Mrs. Campbell's Sunday school, Burkeville, Virginia
Children's Day at a Sunday school in Blackwater, Tennessee
"The Nucleus of a Sunday School founded in April, 1899 . . ."
Original "Akron plan" for Sunday school classrooms
Floor plan for separate Sunday school facilities
Certificate of Sunday school membership
Certificate for recruiting new pupils
Nashville publishing house of the AME Church Sunday School Union
Shape-note notation in hymns
Southern Baptist mite box

Introduction

"In every age, from the time of Moses to the present, it has been universally agreed, that one of the highest duties we owe to God, is to educate the young in all the requirements of the divine law," intoned Baptist James Harvey Joiner at a Sunday school meeting in Eufala, Alabama, around 1870. "For this purpose various schemes and institutions have been organized, and in our day, the Sunday school has been established and is now regarded as the most efficient means of instructing the young in all the words of law." Nearly four decades later, the Reverend Charles C. Jacobs, a Methodist black minister and missionary, articulated similar feelings. "I think the greatest field for activity along the line of development and elevation is in the Sunday school," he asserted. "The new method of salvation is to take the child and make of him such a man as he should be. We are not aiming to get the older people, but we want to get the children." Although Joiner and Jacobs represented different generations, races, and denominations, they shared an important sentiment: the Sunday school, with its focus on educating youngsters in Christian precepts and proper morals, and leading them toward conversion and salvation, was the institution that could raise up the South.[1]

---

1. James Harvey Joiner, "Speech to the Sunday School," Eufala, Ala., c. 1870, James Harvey Joiner Papers, Southern Historical Collection, Wilson Library, University of North Carolina at Chapel Hill (hereafter cited as SHC); Charles C. Jacobs, "The Present Needs of

The Sunday school became so important to millions of southerners in the half century after the Civil War because it promised to uplift individual lives, improve behavior, and strengthen churches, denominations, and communities. To men like Jacobs and Joiner who engaged in Sunday school work, the possibilities seemed endless. In the decades after 1865, both northern and southern evangelicals believed that individuals educated in Christian principles and sound morals held the answer to the region's future; a new generation brought to God could resurrect the South and fashion a truly Christian world. Optimistically, evangelicals assumed that hundreds of thousands of adults ultimately would make a commitment to their church by volunteering to supervise or teach Sunday school, millions of children would eagerly attend class and absorb its lessons, and all would be touched by the experience and emerge the better for it. Denominations were anxious to expand their influence and increase their membership, and the Sunday school proved to be the most effective means to attract new followers to church. Religious leaders gradually recognized and accepted their responsibility to offer lessons and activities that exposed children (and later adults) to Christian teachings, biblical truths, and exemplary behavior—all of which, they believed, would raise up the South, its churches, and its citizens. As a Methodist bishop proclaimed in what would become familiar rhetoric, the "triumphs of the millennium are rocked in the cradle of the Sunday-school." Many idealistic southerners shared his belief, sensing that no institution was as remarkable or could bring about such significant changes to future generations as the Sunday school. As they trumpeted, "in moral grandeur, it stands alone."[2]

The Sunday school was especially welcome throughout the South because it touched the very heart and soul of the region. Southerners filtered

---

the Negro," in William Newton Hartshorn, ed., *An Era of Progress and Promise, 1863–1910: The Religious, Moral, and Educational Development of the American Negro since His Emancipation* (Boston: Priscilla, 1910), 61.

2. C. K. Marshall, "Committee on Sunday Schools," *Journal of the General Conference of the Methodist Episcopal Church, South, 1878* (Nashville: A. H. Radford, 1878), 184, 187; R. M. Heriges, comp., *Sunday School Legislation by the General Conference, Methodist Episcopal Church, South, 1846–1926* (n.p., n.d. [1930 typeset copy]), 30. For a study on how Protestants hoped to transform America into a truly Christian society during this period, see Robert T. Handy, *A Christian America: Protestant Hopes and Historical Realities* (New York: Oxford University Press, 1971), 65–93.

their world view through family, church, and community; as an institution that emphasized faith and family and helped to fashion a church community for youngsters, the Sunday school fit their vision. The aftermath of the Civil War had heightened southerners' concerns about the world their children would inherit, how youngsters would behave, and how the next generation would take charge of the future. Southern Sunday schools seemed to be the most appropriate—and sometimes the only—place for children to learn Scripture. There they could absorb proper morals and manners, learn about salvation, and be taught how to live according to God's word. By the late nineteenth century, Sunday schools served as a haven from devastation and sin, offering a refuge for those overwhelmed by a rapidly changing and unstable world.

Yet although southern religion and the region's denominations have attracted well-deserved scholarly attention, Sabbath schools generally have been overlooked or perhaps taken for granted. "I have always been amazed," remarked religious historian Martin Marty, "to see how little attention has been given this basic institution by historians and scholars." Perhaps its seemingly ordinary nature has caused scholars to ignore the Sunday school. While Robert Lynn has called the Sunday school phenomenon of the late nineteenth century the "last of the great religious movements in American history" and one "ripe and ready for discovery and critical examination," Gerald E. Knoff notes that most religious historians "have neglected the significance of this complex and intriguing tale." Only a handful of journal articles and brief comments in monographs suggest the Sunday school's significant role in southern churches and communities. A few articles, dissertations, and books have explored denominational efforts to create Sunday schools, with the most extensive work done on black and white Southern Baptists. Anne M. Boylan's important and well-argued study, *Sunday School,* stands as the most comprehensive recent examination of the institution. The bulk of her book explores the growth of American Sunday schools in the decades up to the Civil War. Daniel Stowell's more recent monograph, *Rebuilding Zion,* includes a chapter on the role of Sunday schools in the South's post–Civil War recovery. Overall, though, the southern Sunday school movement, which reached its zenith in the early twentieth century, has never been explored adequately. This void needs to be addressed. One cannot consider the rebirth of the South in the post–Civil War period without considering the impact of this religious institution that touched so many lives. Northerners and southerners, blacks and whites alike, came to view the southern Sunday school as central to their efforts to rebuild the region out of the ashes of the Civil War.[3]

This study explores the southern Sunday school and its development during the half century following the Civil War and the role the institution played in uplifting the region, its people, and its churches. The Sunday School was hardly unique to the South but was part of what religious historians have identified as a nationwide "Sunday school movement" during this time period, as the institution developed into a significant arm of most American denominations. The Sunday school was not, of course, new in 1865; Anne Boylan has shown that during the antebellum period, Americans founded many Sunday schools for their children. Church records and personal correspondence from the antebellum South reveal a number of people involved in Sunday schools. But it was only after 1865 that the nation, and especially the South, demonstrated unprecedented interest in this institution. It played a major role in reconstructing this war-torn region and giving hope to its people. Black and white denominations saw the Sunday school as a means to expand their numbers, power, and influence, and as a place where they could raise their children to become upright citizens. Southerners felt youngsters needed the moral guidance and spiritual regeneration that the Sunday school promised them.

This book begins by looking at the role of several northern missionary organizations and their efforts to establish Sunday schools throughout the region. Despite the split that occurred before the Civil War—when white Southern Baptists, Methodists, and Presbyterians each broke from

---

3. Martin Marty quote in Robert Wood Lynn, "The Last of the Great Religious Movements," *The Duke Divinity School Review* 40 (fall 1975): 151; Robert Lynn quote, *ibid*, 160; Gerald E. Knoff, *The World Sunday School Movement: The Story of a Broadening Mission* (New York: Seabury Press, 1979), xi (quotation); Anne M. Boylan, *Sunday School: The Formation of an American Institution, 1790–1880* (New Haven: Yale University Press, 1988); Daniel Stowell, *Rebuilding Zion: The Religious Reconstruction of the South, 1863–1877* (New York: Oxford University Press, 1998). For additional background on Sunday schools, see: Jack L. Seymour, *From Sunday School to Church School: Continuities in Protestant Church Education in the United States, 1860–1929* (St. Louis: Washington University Press of America, 1982); Boardman W. Kathan, "The Sunday School Revisited," *Religious Education* 75 (Jan.–Feb. 1980): 5–14; and Thomas W. Laqueur, *Religion and Respectability: Sunday Schools and Working Class Culture* (New Haven: Yale University Press, 1976).

their national church to form separate southern denominations—white northern churches and missionary societies worked actively in the region, retaining, and in many cases gaining, followers in the postbellum South. Their missionaries and volunteers organized Sunday schools and churches in many southern communities.

I then turn to the Sunday school in seven of the South's largest and most influential denominations—the Southern Baptist Convention, National Baptist Convention, Colored Methodist Episcopal Church, Methodist Episcopal Church South, African Methodist Episcopal Church, African Methodist Episcopal Zion Church, and the Presbyterian Church in the United States. Leaders in each denomination identified the Sunday school as the best means to expose children to the Bible and lead them toward conversion, attract new church members, strengthen their denomination, and mold the next generation into pious, purposeful adults. By focusing on these particular Protestant denominations and certain northern missionary societies, I do not intend to dismiss efforts by other religious organizations and individuals involved in the Sunday school movement. Other denominations in the South such as the Disciples of Christ, Colored Free Will Baptists, Jews, Moravians, Episcopalians, Colored Primitive Baptists, and Cumberland Presbyterians also had Sunday schools. The Catholic Church had a significant presence in many southern cities and states, reaching out to attract young members. Lutherans, Congregationalists, Quakers, and northern Methodists and Presbyterians found adherents in southern communities. But the seven denominations covered here encompass the overwhelming majority of southern black and white Protestants in the region. According to one scholar, 90 percent of all southern churches and Sunday schools were affiliated with Methodist, Presbyterian, or Baptist denominations. Most left extensive sources for the historian interested in studying the southern Sunday school.[4]

Examining an institution like the southern Sunday school raises questions and offers fresh insight into issues that scholars have long debated. While many historians argue that southerners resisted and resented northern involvement in their region after the Civil War, this study presents a different perspective. Initially, most southerners did not view Yankee missionaries as carpetbaggers but as agents seeking to uplift their

4. William Mouzon Brabham, *The Sunday School at Work in Town and Country* (New York: George H. Doran, 1922).

children through the Sunday school. For a while at least, southerners welcomed northern assistance, putting their children's future far above sectional concerns. Another issue that continues to haunt historians is the question of southern exceptionalism. In many respects, there was little difference between those Sunday schools founded by northern missionaries and those established by southerners. Northern and southern evangelicals taught similar values and often used the same classroom material and lesson plans. Yet in the late nineteenth century, as the desire for regional identity heightened, southern denominations began to recoil against northern involvement in their Sunday schools. Southern church leaders initiated efforts to create an institution that would reflect the ideas of the region and their own denominations. The question of how much the Old South influenced the New South also arises in studying the Sunday school. This institution seemed to be a bridge between the two, though its focus on traditional scriptural lessons raises the question of how "new" the region was by the late nineteenth century. Finally, an examination of the southern Sunday school helps us detect similarities and differences between southern black and white religious institutions.

A study of any institution engaged in benevolent work also raises important questions about the motivation of its leaders and volunteer workers. Never having been a particularly enthusiastic Sunday school pupil, I began my research with a wary eye, easily detecting manipulation, materialism, competition, self-interest, and racist and sexist sentiments in those engaged in southern Sunday school work. One can become cynical about the motivations of single-minded Sunday school volunteers, who often appeared to be overly directive and serious. But I also found devoted, benevolent believers involved in Sunday schools— men and women who were driven by faith and humanitarianism, and who were truly anxious about southern youngsters and the region's future.

This book has given me the opportunity to explore one of the most interesting periods in southern history. But a single monograph can only do so much. I do not intend this to be a religious history of the South, and I make few theological comparisons within the Sunday school movement except when they seem important to the task at hand. A more theoretical, comparative study of this subject is left to religious historians. I sense that sectarian orthodoxy did not become a major part of the southern Sunday school curriculum until the early twentieth century, after this study ends,

Introduction   xv

despite church leaders' dramatic rhetoric to the contrary. While southern church publishers insisted that they set themselves apart from rival denominations, their actions did not match their words. I also write this book with broad strokes, covering much of the South, seven denominations, and several northern missionary organizations that worked there. I hope this book will give readers a better understanding of an institution that was so important to the South and its future.

No book is solely the product of its author, and I owe a great deal to scores of people. The most important scholarly inspiration for this project was Sam Hill. Through letters, phone conversations, and discussions at history conferences, he challenged and probed but always encouraged me and saw the worth of this undertaking. For advice and assistance in reading this manuscript, I want to thank Elizabeth Hayes Turner, John Kuykendall, Don Mathews, Joyce Seltzer, Alisa Plant, Gerry Anders, and the anonymous readers at LSU Press. I am grateful to scholars who have commented on portions of this work at scholarly conventions, including Gail Murray, Charles Reagan Wilson, Kathleen Berkeley, Anne Boylan, Randy Sparks, Clarence Walker, and Janet Cornelius. I wish to thank three former students, Amy Howard, Rachel Newcomb, and especially Brian Luskey, as well as members of my family, for reading the manuscript and offering helpful comments. However, my thanks are by no means an effort to pass blame for errors or interpretation; that responsibility is mine.

Historical sources have been far more extensive than I ever imagined, and many collections and libraries remain untouched. Nearly every library I visited offered extensive and useful materials. I owe endless thanks to the helpful librarians and staff members at the Southern Historical Collection at the University of North Carolina at Chapel Hill; the Duke University Manuscript Collection; Emory University Libraries; the Southern Baptist Historical Library and Archives; the Presbyterian Historical Society at Montreat, North Carolina; the Presbyterian Historical Library in Philadelphia; the American Bible Society in New York City; the North Carolina Baptist History Collection at the Z. Smith Reynolds Library at Wake Forest University; the Union Theological Seminary Library in Richmond, Virginia; the Methodist Archives at Drew University; Vanderbilt University Library; Livingstone College in Salisbury, North Carolina; the Tennessee State Archives in Nashville; the Alabama State

Archives in Montgomery; the Carolina Room at the Charlotte, North Carolina Public Library; and the Southern Baptist Seminary in Louisville, Kentucky. The entire Davidson College Library staff, especially Joe Gutekanst, has been extraordinarily patient and helpful with my interlibrary loan and research requests. I am indebted to the National Endowment for the Humanities for its generous 1991–92 Fellowship for College Teachers and Independent Scholars. I am also grateful for a MacArthur Fellowship to College Teachers, for a grant from the Southern Baptist Convention, and for several summer research grants from Davidson College and Middle Tennessee State University.

It is always family and friends to whom I owe my deepest thanks. Both have been a mainstay in my life, and in this case, have thankfully pulled me away from the computer on occasion to provide perspective as well as conversation and laughter. To my children, Blair and Carrie, I am grateful for their support, enthusiasm, and the question, "Are you done yet, Mom?" To my husband, Bruce, I benefit once again from his ongoing support, as well as his exacting editing of the entire manuscript. His friendship, sense of humor, love, and patience have proven invaluable throughout this long project. It is to Bruce that I dedicate this book, for it is rare when we have an opportunity to experience a great relationship a second time around.

Abbreviations

ABHMS	American Baptist Home Missionary Society
ABPS	American Baptist Publication Society
ABS	American Bible Society
AMA	American Missionary Association
AME	African Methodist Episcopal Church
AMEZ	African Methodist Episcopal Zion Church
ASSU	American Sunday School Union
ATS	American Tract Society
CME	Colored Methodist Episcopal Church
Duke	William R. Perkins Library, Duke University, Durham, N.C.
Emory	Emory University, Atlanta, Ga.
ISSA	International Sunday School Association
KSSU	Kentucky Sunday School Union
MEC	Methodist Episcopal Church
MECS	Methodist Episcopal Church South

NBC	National Baptist Convention
NCSA	North Carolina State Archives, Raleigh
PCUS	Presbyterian Church in the U.S. (Southern)
PHS	Presbyterian Historical Society, Philadelphia
SBC	Southern Baptist Convention
SBHLA	Southern Baptist History and Library Archives, Nashville, Tenn.
SHC	Southern Historical Collection, Wilson Library, University of North Carolina at Chapel Hill
Wake	Baptist History Collection, Wake Forest University, Winston-Salem, N.C.

To Raise Up the South

1

A Cure for the South

Only a year after the Civil War ended, a disheartened Southern Baptist assessed his bleak surroundings, taking stock of what limited possibilities the future now held. "Indeed, our children are nearly all the treasures left to us," he lamented. At that juncture, it is doubtful that he understood the import of his words and the significance they would come to hold for millions of southerners. With the troubling political, economic, and social issues of Reconstruction facing the region, southerners seemed to have little left besides their offspring.[1]

Hope was in short supply. The Civil War had ravaged southern lands, torn apart black and white families, and destroyed homes, crops, and farm equipment. It had killed more than a quarter of a million of the region's white men, and had left tens of thousands of individuals destitute. Towns and cities lay in ruins, innumerable schools and churches had closed, and thousands of refugee families returned to find their farms, plantations, and communities in shambles. Credit and capital were

1. "Sunday School Literature—An Important Question," *Religious Herald*, 12 April 1866.

scarce. Former slaves gained their freedom in 1865 but lacked the land, economic resources, and job opportunities necessary to take full advantage of their liberty. Many southerners keenly understood an observer who later mourned that the Civil War and its aftermath had extinguished the "mental, spiritual, and physical life of millions."[2]

In addition, policies imposed under federal Reconstruction created uneasiness among white southerners. With the end of slave labor, the South's largely agrarian economy became dependent on sharecropping and tenant farming, offering black farmers little opportunity for economic betterment. Both blacks and whites struggled to deal with changing race relations. The passage of the Fifteenth Amendment in 1870 seemed to promise black men the right to vote and to participate in politics. Yet within a few years southern whites began to use legal and social means to remove African Americans from political and economic life and to ensure their subordination.

In the midst of such an unsettled period, it is easy to overlook the role that community institutions played both in the immediate and long-term aftermath of the Civil War. Yet while southerners despaired over their future, northerners envisioned endless opportunities in the post–Civil War South. Here lay a vast frontier to engage their attention. To their thinking, the region would rebound quickly if Yankees oversaw and guided that process. Like the thousands of northern teachers who came south to educate freedmen after the war, northern missionaries and ministers saw a region that was more than ready for them. Destitution in religious matters was apparent; the war had destroyed churches and Sunday schools, and had led to a significant decline in church attendance. With energy and determination, northern agents headed south to found Sunday schools and churches, and to distribute and sell religious literature on behalf of their sponsoring organization.

Indeed, the Sunday school would be of vital importance to the South in the half century after the war. Southerners needed to address the war's impact on their families, institutions, and communities; they soon expressed concern about the failures and frustrations of Reconstruction. Religious faith offered southerners a source of inner strength. Though certainly some men and women were indifferent toward religion, many

---

2. S. W. Melton, "The Society and the Denomination at Large," *Eightieth Anniversary of the American Baptist Publication Society* (Philadelphia: ABPS, 1904), 57.

southerners turned inward to their faith, not away from it, to help them overcome their sorrows. Religious faith had been important to the region since the late eighteenth century. The South's relatively homogeneous approach to Protestantism, which became evident by the first quarter of the nineteenth century, slowly but surely began to build a cultural norm. The church offered blacks a venue for social, cultural, and political expression; it was equally significant in southern white communities. Southerners embraced their evangelical beliefs with striking intensity. The Sunday school offered individuals, churches, and the region a place to influence the next generation by overseeing the spiritual lives of children. Youngsters needed a solid exposure to the Bible and a firm grounding in Christian morals and good manners; the Sunday school promised to address those needs and help make children into purposeful, pious adults. A sound religious education and the conversion of children "constitute the best hope of our country and our Church," insisted Southern Presbyterians in 1868. African Americans dreamed of racial uplift and the opportunity to achieve respectability, perhaps even equality, if their youngsters were exposed to Scripture and middle-class values. Both races believed that children who learned to live by Scripture, who dedicated their lives to God, could eventually raise up the South. The establishment and growth of southern Sunday schools could not have been better timed or found a needier population. The thought of southern children brought up in Sunday schools became an antidote for widespread postwar despair. In the post–Civil War era, southerners came to view the Sunday school as not merely a legitimate extension of the church, but a highly desirable institution in its own right.[3]

3. See Randy J. Sparks, *On Jordan's Stormy Banks: Evangelicalism in Mississippi, 1773–1876* (Athens: University of Georgia Press, 1994), 184–5, and Harvey J. Graff, *Conflicting Paths: Growing Up in America* (Cambridge: Harvard University Press, 1995), 187; "Narrative of the State of Religion," *Minutes of the General Assembly of the Presbyterian Church in the United States, 1868* (Columbia, S.C.: Office of the Southern Presbyterian Review, 1868), 284 (quotation); C. Eric Lincoln and Lawrence H. Mamiya, *The Black Church in the African-American Experience* (Durham, N.C.: Duke University Press, 1990); John B. Boles, *The Irony of Southern Religion* (New York: Peter Lang, 1994). Countless studies discuss the central role of religion in southern life. See C. Vann Woodward, *Origins of the New South, 1877–1913* (Baton Rouge: Louisiana State University Press, 1951), 448; Edward L. Ayers, *The Promise of the New South: Life after Reconstruction* (New York: Oxford University Press, 1992), 160–86; Frederick Bode, *Protestantism and the New South: North Carolina Baptists and Methodists in Political Crisis, 1894–1903* (Charlottesville: University Press of Virginia, 1975); Mitchell Snay, *Gospel of Disunion: Religion and*

The heightened interest in Sunday school was not an isolated southern response, but reflected wider trends in how nineteenth-century men and women regarded children. As historians have shown, childhood is as much a cultural construction as it is a biological one. Ideas shift in terms of how a society views its children. By the nineteenth century, Americans had cast aside the Puritan idea that youngsters were born in sin and needed to have their wills broken, in favor of a more sentimental view of children. Horace Bushnell's *Views of Christian Nurture,* first published in 1847, was instrumental in challenging the harsh Calvinistic approach to childrearing, articulating instead a far gentler method. He and other religious educators regarded youngsters as innocent and vulnerable rather than as miniature adults. Parents had an important role to play in socializing and guiding them as they matured. Notions of childhood changed still further between 1870 and 1930 in regard to the economic and sentimental value attached to children. As Viviana Zelizer has argued, perceptions shifted from the idea of an "economically worthless" child to an "emotionally priceless" child.[4]

Adult attitudes toward childhood were often determined by economic concerns, which fostered different ideas on how best to raise youngsters. Privileged parents often lavished affection and attention on their offspring. Some viewed childhood through a nostalgic, romantic lens and embraced the innocence and joy of youth. This idealized vision presented childhood as a magical time, especially when compared to the seemingly competitive, stressful world of adults. This notion of youthful innocence

---

Separatism in the Antebellum South (Cambridge: Cambridge University Press, 1993), 2–5; J. Wayne Flynt, "Southern Protestantism and Reform, 1890–1920," in Samuel S. Hill, ed., *Varieties of Southern Religious Experience* (Baton Rouge: Louisiana State University Press, 1982), 135–55; Samuel S. Hill, ed., *Religion in the Southern States: A Historical Study* (Macon, Ga.: Mercer University Press, 1983); William Edward Montgomery, *Under Their Own Vine and Fig Tree: The African-American Church in the South, 1865–1900* (Baton Rouge: Louisiana State University Press, 1992); Clarence E. Walker, *A Rock in a Weary Land: The African Methodist Episcopal Church during the Civil War and Reconstruction* (Baton Rouge: Louisiana State University Press, 1982); Charles Reagan Wilson, *Baptized in Blood: The Religion of the Lost Cause, 1865–1920* (Athens: University of Georgia Press, 1980).

4. Philippe Ariès, *Centuries of Childhood* (New York: W. W. Norton, 1962); Horace Bushnell, *Christian Nurture* (1847; reprint, New Haven: Yale University Press, 1950); Viviana A. Zelizer, *Pricing the Priceless Child: The Changing Social Value of Children* (New York: Basic Books, 1985), 7.

encouraged adults to educate children for purposeful, righteous activity. By contrast, parents who struggled to survive had little time to romanticize childhood; their youngsters often labored in factories or fields. Adults who tended to be skeptical of American youth emphasized another side of childhood: purportedly sinful, ill-mannered children who needed adult guidance and strong discipline. Yet whether adults saw childhood as a sentimentalized time of innocence and vulnerability, a time when children played a key role in family survival, or a period of sinful temptation and raucous behavior, they felt that Sunday schools could serve youngsters well.[5]

In the last third of the nineteenth century, as Americans became increasingly fascinated with children and how best to raise them, community institutions began to play a greater role in the character formation and the socialization process of youth. Public and Sunday school teachers were accorded some responsibility for children's upbringing and were expected to incorporate the discoveries of child experts into classroom instruction. Reverend George Smith, known as the "children's preacher," believed southern churches had no choice but to make children a target of their interest. The perfect age to absorb Christian messages was during youth, he insisted, "when the ground is comparatively free from weeds." The interest in Sunday school indicated that "childhood has been taken into its embrace, its sympathies, and yearning love," intoned a Southern Methodist. Sunday school advice books urged teachers to offer education

---

5. For thoughts on the changing views of American children, see Graff, *Conflicting Paths,* 303; Christopher Lasch, *Haven in a Heartless World: The Family Besieged* (New York: Basic Books, 1977), 5, 9, 14; Carl N. Degler, *At Odds: Women and the Family in America from the Revolution to the Present* (New York: Oxford University Press, 1980); Stephen Mintz and Susan Kellogg, *Domestic Revolutions: A Social History of American Family Life* (New York: The Free Press, 1988), 58–9; David L. Macleod, *The Age of the Child: Children in America, 1890–1920* (New York: Twayne, 1998), 22–5; T. Jackson Lears, *No Place of Grace: Antimodernism and the Transformation of American Culture, 1880–1920* (New York: Pantheon, 1981), 144–6; Gillian Avery, *Behold the Child: American Children and Their Books, 1621–1922* (Baltimore: Johns Hopkins University Press, 1994), 94; Peter Bardaglio, *Reconstructing the Household: Families, Sex, and the Law in the Nineteenth-Century South* (Chapel Hill: University of North Carolina Press, 1995), xi–xiii, 83. For perspective on childhood and a nostalgic ideal, see Sarah Burns, "Barefoot Boys and Other Country Children: Sentiment and Ideology in Nineteenth-Century American Art," *American Art Journal* 20 (1988): 24–50. For contemporary thoughts on childhood, see Peter Applebone, "No Room for Children in a World of Little Adults," *New York Times,* 10 May 1998.

in morals and Scripture early in life; to delay the process was to court disaster. "Nothing can be more dangerous to the temporal and especially to the spiritual interests of our children than to wait until false theories of life and religion have been embraced and evil habits formed before we begin to teach them the doctrines of the gospel," warned an Alabama Methodist in 1874. "In this way the weeds of depravity and sin may be choked in their budding." Childhood was the opportune time to influence character; that was when, as a Baptist noted, the "shrub is easily bent and trained to grow." Sunday school teachers were urged to awaken in every vulnerable young mind the importance of leading a Christian life. Children were a precious gift from God, and southerners had a responsibility to see that they were raised according to biblical truths and Christian doctrine.[6]

Thus the Sunday school gave adults a place where they could train youngsters in good behavior, piety, and obedience. This development was especially important in the decades after the Civil War, for youthful virtue seemed in short supply. Parents and community leaders bemoaned the shattering impact of the war on southern families, and they decried the rise of waywardness and lawlessness they perceived among undisciplined youth. During and after the war, parental control had diminished. With most fathers absent from home and mothers overwhelmed by the daily struggle to survive, many southern children had been less subject to parental discipline. By 1865, moreover, many youngsters were fatherless—some 258,000 southern men had died in the war. The men who survived often returned home physically or psychologically wounded, unable to function effectively. In this context, many southerners thought that the Sunday school could help parents and single mothers instill Christian values and good behavior into their children. Children condi-

6. Jacqueline S. Reinier, *From Virtue to Character: American Childhood, 1775–1850* (New York: Twayne, 1996), xi; George G. Smith, *Childhood and Conversion* (Nashville: Publishing House of the MECS, 1891), 72; R. M. Heriges, *Sunday School Legislation by the General Conference of the MEC, South* (typeset copy, Emory University Libraries); A. S. Andrews, "Report of the Committee on Sunday Schools," *Minutes of the Alabama Annual Conference of the MECS, 1874,* 21; J. C. B., "Plea for Sabbath Schools," *Working Christian,* July 1869. See also Edwin Barfield Chappell, *Recent Development of Religious Education in the MEC, South: An Interpretation* (Nashville: Cokesbury Press, 1935), 52–7; Wade Crawford Barclay, *The Pupil, the Teacher, and the School: First Standard Manual of Teacher Training* (Nashville: Publishing House of the MECS, 1914), 21–5.

tioned to live according to southern evangelicals' code of moral behavior in turn promised a well-behaved citizenry and real hope for the future of the South.[7]

Adult intervention and guidance were essential in order to improve and mold the next generation. Basil Manly Jr., a Southern Baptist prominent in Sunday school circles, expressed typical concerns about his offspring. "I have had to set them an example of quiet industry and honesty, of love to God and to man," he wrote, "but if they shall any of them turn out worthless my soul shall weep in secret for their folly. I trust this will never be the case." Beyond the Christian lessons he could teach them at home, Manly pointed to Sunday school as the place where young people could learn to conduct themselves properly, follow a righteous path, and seek conversion. Southern parents had to give their children the spiritual direction necessary to lead a Christian life. As he and other southern parents concluded, the Sunday school was the place to accomplish this.[8]

Growing interest in the relatively new field of child study also stimulated Americans' interest in Sunday schools. Formerly, childhood had been overlooked as a subject for psychological study because it seemed to lack "any great innate dignity or worth," according to a Southern Methodist. This old-fashioned view needed recasting. Child study experts now insisted that youngsters be placed at the forefront of human development and that childhood receive serious attention. Studies suggested that it was never too early to start the socialization process, undo bad habits, and ensure a child's perfectibility. From birth, a child's innocence could be molded according to certain guidelines. While it might be too late to alter adult behavior, proper nurturing could shape children into responsible, upstanding Christians.[9]

Another important change occurring in the nineteenth century was that the nation's churches began to take a deep interest in the young. Denominations began to identify the Sunday school as a religious institution. The National Sunday School Association made this official in 1858.

---

7. See James Marten, *The Children's Civil War* (Chapel Hill: University of North Carolina Press, 1998); David J. Pivar, *Purity Crusade, Sexual Morality, and Social Control, 1868–1900* (Westport, Conn.: Greenwood, 1973), 235, 264–5.

8. Basil Manly Jr. to John Broadus, October 1872, Georgetown, Ky., Basil Manly Jr. Collection, SHC.

9. C. K. Marshall, "Committee on Sunday Schools," *Journal of the General Conference of the Methodist Episcopal Church, South* (Nashville: A. H. Redford, 1878), 187.

By promoting the Sunday school as an important religious and educational institution, the association hoped that churches and missionary organizations would accept their obligation (beyond that of baptism) to direct greater attention toward children. Sunday school supporters saw this as a significant step, noting that for centuries, religious organizations had paid attention to adults but had generally ignored children. Here was a segment of the church population ripe for Christian education and conversion. In 1869, Alabama Presbyterians declared that it was the "strength and glory of our church that we have attached a very high value to the religious training of our children." By bringing young people into special classes and preparing them for Christian adulthood, the Sunday school would shape their future and ensure the prosperity of every church. As Baptist Samuel Greene prophesied, "The church of the future is the child of to-day." Greene believed that providing Christian education to children was a Sunday school's highest form of service. Creating religious classes for youngsters "aims at the very heart of the world's great problems. It seeks for individual regeneration, and so the regeneration of the home, the nation, the world," he added.[10]

Protestant denominations began to feel derelict if they ignored southern youth. Arkansas Baptists darkly intoned that any church that overlooked its children "neglects its future, for the children are the hope of the church as well as the hope of the world." Southern Presbyterians called children their "gold mine of the future." Children had to be saved before they became hardened adults, and difficult—if not impossible—to reach. No denomination could afford to be without Sunday classes, or it could lose potential converts and loyal members.[11]

Finally, the volunteerism and institution-building that were important components of middle-class life in the late nineteenth century also help explain the success of Sunday schools. A growing number of middle-class Americans, especially women, had both the interest and time to devote

---

10. "Narrative of the State of Religion," *Minutes of the Synod of Alabama* (Montgomery: Barrett and Brown, 1869), 15; Samuel Harrison Greene, *The Twentieth Century Sunday School* (Nashville: Sunday School Board of the SBC, 1904), 105, 104. See also Boylan, *Sunday School,* 161–4.

11. "Sunday-School and Colportage Board," *Proceedings of the 52nd Annual Arkansas Baptist State Convention, 1900* (Little Rock: Arkansas Baptist State Convention, 1900), 41; Thornton Whaling, "Young People and Lexington Assembly," *Presbyterian Standard,* 4 March 1903.

to various projects improving church and community. For some women, household responsibilities and family size began to shrink, giving them more free time to address issues beyond the domestic sphere. They engaged in community outreach projects through their church, clubs, and various institutions, sensing that their influence and dedicated efforts could make the world a better place. Women found the Sunday school a perfect place to employ their energy and talents, for this type of volunteer work pleased even tradition-minded southerners. As the effects of industrialization rippled through American society, many people feared that traditional values and gender roles would be undermined. In response, a chorus of southerners voiced traditional gender distinctions and insisted that women's rightful place was in their God-ordained sphere, focused on home and family. The Sunday school was one of the few places outside the home where a woman could shine, using her maternal, pious nature to uplift and save the region's next generation. Sunday school teaching quickly became the most popular volunteer activity available to women. Ultimately, the Sunday school movement could not have survived or thrived without so many willing volunteers.[12]

The Sunday school was especially important to the South because so many of its children had been personally affected by the Civil War. As James Marten shows in his study of children who lived through the Civil War, that conflict had sharply disrupted southern childhood. Far more southern youngsters experienced trauma and hardship during the four-year conflict than northern youth. Because nearly the entire war was

---

12. See Betty A. DeBerg, *Ungodly Women: Gender and the First Wave of American Fundamentalism* (Minneapolis: Fortress Press, 1990), 7–13, 43–50. Historians have examined women's activism in church and volunteer activities during this time period. See Elizabeth Hayes Turner, *Women, Culture, and Community: Religion and Reform in Galveston, 1880–1920* (New York: Oxford University Press, 1997); Anne Firor Scott, *Natural Allies: Women's Associations in American History* (Urbana: University of Illinois Press, 1991), 79–81; Evelyn Brooks Higginbotham, *Righteous Discontent: The Women's Movement in the Black Baptist Church, 1880–1920* (Cambridge: Harvard University Press, 1993); Lori D. Ginzberg, *Women and the Work of Benevolence: Morality, Politics, and Class in the Nineteenth-Century United States* (New Haven: Yale University Press, 1990); Glenda Elizabeth Gilmore, *Gender and Jim Crow: Women and the Politics of White Supremacy in North Carolina, 1896–1920* (Chapel Hill: University of North Carolina Press, 1996); Paul Harvey, *Redeeming the South: Religious Cultures and Racial Identities among Southern Baptists, 1865–1925* (Chapel Hill: University of North Carolina Press, 1997); Degler, *At Odds*, esp. 298–327.

fought on southern soil, many of the South's children endured first-hand the physical and psychological horrors of war. Some witnessed actual battles and saw dying or wounded soldiers. They experienced military invasion, hunger, perhaps even the destruction of their family home and resulting homelessness. Southern slave families were torn apart during the war when male slaves were impressed into Confederate service. Other slaves became refugees, forced to accompany an owner who fled to safety. Youngsters who later wrote about the Civil War invariably depicted it as the defining period in their upbringing. Because of the war, both black and white southerners had become highly sensitized to the fragility of family life. As an institution that focused on children and a brighter future, the Sunday school had enormous appeal.[13]

The founding or rebuilding of southern Sunday schools engaged the attention of thousands of northern missionaries, southern church leaders, and laypeople. With determination, hope, and perhaps a sense of guilt over the chaos that the war had visited upon children, individuals set to work to advance the cause. Northern missionaries flocked southward in order to establish Sunday schools and churches and influence the region in the name of their faith or religious institution. Southerners became profoundly interested in the role their children could play in uplifting the region. Despite the bleakness and "fearful scenes through which we have passed," southerners anticipated a time of renewal as they organized Sunday schools. "There never was a time in the history of our country when Sunday schools were more imperatively [sic] demanded," a Virginia Baptist, J. B. Watkins, reported. "The depraving influence of the War has been at work upon the youthful mind. Disease and death, during the war, have relaxed many a hand of paternal restraint." He envisioned a Sunday school in every church, and hundreds of thousands of children infused with Christian values. "The conversion of children, even very young children, should be sought for, prayed for, and expected," Watkins wrote. Though war had ravaged his state, "to every destitute family send a Colporteur. To every struggling Sabbath school send words of encouragement and books of instruction." Southern evangelicals like Watkins

---

13. Marten, *Children of the Civil War,* 168–9, 188–9. See also C. Peter Ripley, *Slaves and Freedmen in Civil War Louisiana* (Baton Rouge: Louisiana State University Press, 1976), 151; Peter Bardaglio, "The Children of Jubilee: African American Childhood in Wartime," in Catherine Clinton and Nina Silber, eds., *Divided Houses: Gender and the Civil War* (New York: Oxford University Press, 1992), 213–29.

vowed never to rest "until we see [children] able to go to Sunday school."[14]

Although the southern Sunday school had a history that predated the American Civil War, the first modern Sunday school was organized in Great Britain in the eighteenth century with the purpose of teaching urban urchins how to read and how to behave. Initially, it was not associated with a church. The Sunday school gained popularity in the United States during the colonial and antebellum periods and gradually became less secular. Savannah's Christ Church built a Sunday school for Episcopalians in that city in 1737; the first Baptist Sunday school in the South was founded in Baltimore in 1803. Anne Boylan claims that the Sunday school had become a fixture of American life by the 1830s, at least in the urban Northeast. Throughout the antebellum period, northern missionary societies sent a number of agents to the South to organize Sunday schools, distribute Bibles and Sunday school literature, and establish new churches. Usually these early schools were located in urban areas, since the region's dispersed population and limited modes of transportation made their founding difficult in rural areas.[15]

Though most antebellum southern Sunday schools served white children, classes also existed for slaves and free blacks. Some plantation owners organized Sunday schools for their slaves, believing that an exposure to Christian precepts would ensure obedience and good behavior. A plantation mistress might perform her Christian duty by drilling slave youngsters in Scripture and reading Bible stories to them. Individual churches did their part as well, such as Fairview Presbyterian Church in Greenville, South Carolina, which held a morning Sunday school for white children and an afternoon one for slaves. The Moravian Female Mission Society in Winston-Salem, North Carolina, formed a Sunday school class for that

14. Edward Brawley, "Narrative of the State of Religion," *Minutes of the Synod of Alabama, 1865* (Montgomery: Barrett and Brown, 1865), 16; J. B. Watkins, "Annual Report of the Sunday School and Publication Board of the General Association of Virginia," *Religious Herald,* 21 June 1866.

15. Boylan, *Sunday School,* 28–30; J. N. Barnette, "Sunday Schools," *Encyclopedia of Southern Baptists,* ed. Norman Wade Cox, vol. 2 (Nashville: Broadman Press, 1958), 1316. See also Anne C. Loveland, *Southern Evangelicals and the Social Order, 1800–1860* (Baton Rouge: Louisiana State University Press, 1980), 33–4; Sparks, *On Jordan's Stormy Banks,* 95; Cynthia Kierner, *Beyond the Household: Women's Place in the Early South, 1700–1835* (Ithaca: Cornell University Press, 1999).

town's slaves. Frederick Douglass taught a Sabbath class in the Baltimore home of a free black. General Stonewall Jackson conducted a Sunday school for black children in Lexington, Virginia.[16]

The central role that Sunday schools began to play in the conversion process also led to their widespread acceptance in the South. While revivals and camp meetings remained the setting where the conversion experience usually took place, after the Civil War many southerners became convinced that sustained Sunday school education was the surest path to conversion. As the cornerstone of southern evangelical faith, the conversion experience was critical. Through conversion, an individual gave visible evidence of spiritual redemption, being pardoned of sin, and being born anew with a special relationship to God. Southern churches and Sunday schools sought this goal at all costs, not only because of its important implications for individual faith but because denominations measured their success in terms of the number of new conversions and church members. Churches became increasingly competitive in these efforts. As North Carolina Sunday school workers observed, "The churches, in their commendable zeal to surpass one another in extending their power and usefulness have become convinced that one of the best methods of doing so is to enlist the young." To evangelicals, conversion was the very heart of the Sunday school. It meant another life saved from sin, confirmed the personal meaning and success of the Christian message, and, as a byproduct, enlarged church membership.[17]

The conversion experience was supposed to arise from an individual, spontaneous decision. But the Sunday school altered this approach by offering carefully crafted lessons that encouraged pupils to make this decision in a controlled group setting and as a collective—and directed—

---

16. Mary Lou Stewart Garrett, *History of Fairview Presbyterian Church of Greenville County, South Carolina* (n.p.: A. Press, 1986), 211; Frederick Douglass, *Narrative of the Life of Frederick Douglass, An American Slave* (New York: Penguin Books, 1982), 120–1; J. B. Robertson, "One Hundred Fifty Years of Sunday School History," *Raleigh News and Observer*, 31 May 1931.

17. For further information, see Boles, *Irony of Southern Religion*, 26; Samuel S. Hill Jr., *The South and the North in American Religion* (Athens: University of Georgia Press, 1980), 23–4, 71–2; Montgomery, *Under Their Own Vine and Fig Tree*, 267–75; Ted Ownby, *Subduing Satan: Religion, Recreation, and Manhood in the Rural South, 1865–1920* (Chapel Hill: University of North Carolina Press, 1990), 148–55; Christopher H. Owen, *The Sacred Flame of Love: Methodism and Society in Nineteenth-Century Georgia* (Athens: University of Georgia Press, 1998), xi, xii.

experience. By the early twentieth century, many Sunday schools held what was called Decision Day, when groups of children from various schools all underwent conversion simultaneously. Apparently all children were supposed to feel moved to convert at the same time, in a planned setting, having learned appropriate Sunday school material.

During the latter part of the nineteenth century, adults began to recognize that children, rather than adults, were the likeliest converts. Though not all southerners agreed with him, Southern Baptist minister William Hatcher actually went so far as to dismiss revivals, calling them an antiquated means to attract new members. He saw the Sunday school as the "most hopeful field of evangelistic endeavor." In his view, sound Bible instruction was the most effective means to foster conversion—far better than emotional responses hastily produced during a revival. Recurrent scriptural lessons and rote memorization would inspire lifelong habits of piety and purposeful activity, and would provide youngsters with the best preparation for giving their lives to God.[18]

Sunday school promoters soon had more than rhetoric to support their case; statistics confirmed that Sunday schools were the ideal setting to foster conversions. "The Sunday school is now regarded as one of the most efficient agencies employed by the church in winning souls to Christ," exclaimed Alabama Methodists. "It supplements parental instruction at home, provides for multitudes who are neglected, and brings under Christian influence and training thousands who otherwise would not be reached so successfully." An African Methodist Episcopal (AME) Sunday school teacher reported that "many precious and immortal souls, through the Sunday-schools, have been added to the fold of Christ this year." For evangelicals, the success of Sunday school conversion was something to celebrate. With so many youngsters converting, Southern Baptists felt that "piety, spirituality, zeal, liberality" would infuse their churches.[19]

---

18. William E. Hatcher, *The Pastor and the Sunday School* (Nashville: Sunday School Board of the SBC, 1902), 10.

19. "Report of the Committee on Sunday Schools," *Minutes of the Alabama Conference of the Methodist Episcopal Church, South, 1882* (Montgomery: Smith and Armstrong, 1883), 15; "Report on Sunday Schools," *Minutes of the Twentieth Session of the Virginia Annual Conference of the AME Church, 1886* (Atlanta: Jas. P. Harrison, 1886), 30; B. W. Spilman, "The Sunday-School Work in North Carolina," Frost-Bell Papers, Southern Baptist History Library and Archives, Nashville (hereafter referred to as SBHLA);

The rapid increase in the number of youthful conversions was apparent in both black and white Sunday schools. To church officials interested in enlarging their churches and to evangelicals who regarded conversion as the truest test of faith, this proved one of the most compelling reasons to promote the Sunday school. Statistics demonstrated that most conversions occurred among pupils eight to fourteen years old. Both AME and African Methodist Episcopal Zion (AMEZ) churches reported that 75 percent of their converts were Sunday school pupils. American Bible Society (ABS) missionary Hight C. Moore, working in North Carolina, estimated childhood conversions to be as high as 85 percent. With actual figures to demonstrate the success of childhood conversion, denominations could justify the expenditure of personnel and resources to create and promote an institution that promised such a prosperous future for their churches. Organizing new Sunday schools and drawing more pupils into the fold was perceived by evangelicals as critical to the spiritual health of the South, to say nothing of every child. The number of new church members who came out of the Sunday school must receive credit for the remarkable growth of southern churches that took place in the latter third of the nineteenth century.[20]

Sunday schools thus quickly became the best means to strengthen the region's churches and denominations, many of which had experienced a decline in members during the Civil War. Young converts promised a new generation of individuals who would dedicate their lives to the work carried on by their church. As Baptists predicted, from the ranks of their Sunday schools would come "our seminary students, our ministers, our

---

"The Ninth Annual Report of the Sunday School Board," *Proceedings of the Seventeenth Meeting of the Southern Baptist Convention, 1872* (Baltimore: John F. Weishampel Jr., 1872), 70. See also Anne M. Boylan, "Sunday Schools and Changing Evangelical Views of Children in the 1820s," *Church History* 48 (September 1979): 320–33.

20. R. C. O. Benjamin, "The Relation of the Sunday-School to the Church," *Star of Zion*, 9 February 1893; Elmer T. Clark, *Methodism in Western North Carolina* (Nashville: Western North Carolina Conference of the Methodist Episcopal Church, 1966), 123; Hight C. Moore, *The Country Sunday School* (Philadelphia: ABPS, 1906). Only Southern Presbyterians despaired over their conversion rate from Sabbath schools, which was less than 50 percent. According to A. L. Phillips, only 40 percent of all white Presbyterian converts came from the Sunday school, 35 percent below the national average. See Phillips, "Our Supreme Need," *Earnest Worker*, January 1903. Today, church officials estimate that more than 65 percent of all members enter through the Sunday school. See "Sunday School Seen As Key to Building Church Membership," *Los Angeles Times*, 19 April 1997.

missionaries, our contributors for all Christian causes." If a denomination could lead the children of one generation into Sunday school, presumably it could hold sway over adults in the next. "The unconverted children of today will be the active workers in the vineyard of the Lord 40 years hence," noted Southern Baptists. "The Sabbath School is an efficient instrumentality to bring the young to Jesus, and educate the generation of Christians who shall succeed us to be more benevolent and self-sacrificing than any who have preceded them." Every church would prosper, thanks in part to its Sunday school.[21]

Practical reasons also explain the popularity of Sunday schools. With their volunteer teachers and superintendents, minimal furnishings, and makeshift meeting places, they were far easier and less expensive to establish than new churches. In fact, missionaries often tested a community's religious commitment by organizing a Sunday school before expending significant effort and financial resources to organize an actual church. Baptist Bernard Spilman speculated that two-thirds to three-quarters of all Baptist churches in North Carolina evolved from a Sunday school. Colored Methodist Episcopal (CME) official Charles H. Phillips estimated that 65 to 70 percent of his denomination's churches grew from pre-existing Sunday schools. It wasn't unusual for a Sunday school to exist well before a church had been founded or rebuilt.[22]

Those who despaired over the desecration of the Sabbath saw the Sunday school as one means to address this problem. Dutiful Christians insisted that Sunday always be set aside as a day devoted to God, a time of self-denial and Christian reflection. For them, Sunday observance symbolized a civilized Christian society. Some inattention to the sanctity of Sabbath observance was, of course, understandable. Southerners who struggled to put food on their table could not afford to devote Sundays to formal worship or rest. But the declining sanctity of this sacred day seemed all too obvious to many. Vigilant evangelicals were dismayed to discover trains that ran on Sundays and businessmen who devoted a por-

---

21. "Report of the Committee on the Future Plans of the S. S. Board," *Proceedings of the Seventeenth Meeting of the Southern Baptist Convention, 1872*, 25; "Report of the Sunday School Board," *Proceedings of the Thirty-Eighth Session of the Southern Baptist Convention, 1893*, 40.

22. Bernard W. Spilman, "The Sunday-School Work in North Carolina," in Frost-Bell Papers, SBHLA; Charles H. Phillips, "Greatest Needs," in Hartshorn, *Era of Progress*, 404–5. See also Brabham, *The Sunday School at Work in Town and Country*, 22.

tion of their Sundays to work. Ministers reported that on Sunday mornings, children were wasting their time playing games rather than attending church or reading the Bible. Irreligious habits and rowdy, disruptive activity on Sundays had to cease. In 1878, an Alabama layman urged fellow Baptists to organize Sunday schools to entice children away from sinful or frivolous activities. "A Sabbath school in every church," he insisted, "breaks up the marble yard, the fishing gang, the lounging group, the gadding rabble and other viler associations of the young on the day of the Lord." Attending Sunday school would prevent "our young people and children from roving around on the Sabbath and thereby disregarding the holy day," insisted CME minister G. W. Spearman. Sunday classes provided an important service by keeping children occupied and out of trouble on the day of the Lord. In fact, purists initially opposed Sunday schools because they met on a day that was to be free of secular activity. Such rigidity quickly vanished, and former critics began to regard Sunday classes as a benefit. Without them, the "devil finds work for idle hands," warned South Carolina Baptist W. A. Pearson. The Sunday school could serve as an antidote to excessive leisure. Children could avoid sinful temptation and consign their hours to Christian activity, and the Sabbath could retain its sacred meaning.[23]

Southerners also worried about the decline in family worship and Christian nurturing at home, and they saw the Sunday school as a place to address this problem. In their minds, the Civil War seemed to have undermined the tradition of domestic religion; one could no longer count on parents to give children the spiritual lessons they needed. As several historians have shown, many southern parents prided themselves on close family relationships and the attentive nurturing of their children. To southern evangelicals, these now seemed threatened. Too many parents were absent from home or too busy, indifferent, or worried to tend to their children's spiritual lives. A female reformer claimed that modern fathers were too busy to pay attention to their offspring and mothers too involved in "ceaseless household cares" to be constantly "aglow with spiritual thoughts." Methodist Henry Cope, an ardent Sunday school

23. W. Wilkes, "Report of Committee on Sabbath Schools," *Proceedings of the Fifty-Fifth Annual Session of the Alabama Baptist State Convention, 1878* (Marion, Ala.: Commonwealth Job Print, 1878), 10; G. W. Spearman, "Children's Day Address," *Christian Index*, 23 August 1890; W. A. Pearson, "Sunday School Convention," *Working Christian*, 12 August 1875. See also Handy, *A Christian America*, and Ownby, *Subduing Satan*.

supporter, felt that parents had abandoned their commitment to domestic religious instruction. He insisted that home was the place and infancy was the time to secure salvation; to prolong or ignore that effort was to court disaster. The perceived decline of domestic religion was a serious issue, or at least provided another argument to promote the Sunday school. By the late nineteenth century, statistics citing rising rates of divorce, alcoholism, gambling, prostitution, and other social ills confirmed what uneasy evangelicals had suspected: parental indifference to Christian education was leading to the decline of the family and undermining traditional values. Only the Sunday school, they insisted, could provide neglected children with the spiritual lessons they failed to receive at home.[24]

One of the most important duties southern Sunday schools undertook in the immediate post–Civil War years was to teach blacks and whites how to read. In the antebellum South, the Sunday school sometimes provided basic literacy to poor children (usually white) who attended them. Ministers felt that if the poor were to take their place in society, they needed to know how to read the Bible. After 1865, the South's four million freed people, most of whom had been denied schooling under slavery, eagerly sought a rudimentary education. The Freedmen's Bureau and some fifty other secular and religious associations undertook southern black education, establishing weekday schools and Sunday schools to teach reading and writing to freed people. Agents of the American Tract Society (ATS) in North Carolina reported on their educational work

---

24. Marianna Catherine Brown, *Sunday-School Movements in America* (New York: Fleming H. Revell, 1901), 177; Henry Frederick Cope, *Religious Education in the Family* (Chicago: University of Chicago Press, 1915), 52. For information on past ideas of child nurture and domestic religion, see Bernard Wishy, *The Child and the Republic: The Dawn of Modern American Child Nurture* (Philadelphia: University of Pennsylvania Press, 1968); Bushnell, *Christian Nurture*. For thoughts on the affectionate relationship southern parents developed with their children during an earlier period, see Jane Turner Censer, *North Carolina Planters and Their Children, 1800–1860* (Baton Rouge: Louisiana State University Press, 1984); Daniel Blake Smith, *Inside the Great House: Planter Family Life in Eighteenth-Century Chesapeake Society* (Ithaca: Cornell University Press, 1980); Jan Lewis, *The Pursuit of Happiness: Family and Values in Jefferson's Virginia* (Cambridge: Cambridge University Press, 1983); Sally McMillen, *Motherhood in the Old South: Pregnancy, Childbirth, and Infant Rearing* (Baton Rouge: Louisiana State University Press, 1990) and "Antebellum Southern Fathers and the Health Care of Children," *Journal of Southern History* 40 (1994): 513–32.

among black children, noting that they "depend entirely on these Sabbath-schools for instruction." Individuals who organized and maintained these schools often had charge of both a weekday and a Sunday school. Several northern organizations like the American Missionary Association (AMA) hired teachers to reach blacks through religious instruction. In fact, it often was difficult to distinguish between lessons taught in day schools, which exposed students to Christian and moral precepts, and Sunday schools, which taught reading and writing.[25]

Firsthand accounts confirm the fact that the Sabbath school was often the first place former slaves received an education. As John W. Alvord, Inspector of Schools for the Freedmen's Bureau and later General Superintendent of Schools for the Bureau, commented in 1866, "Sabbath schools among freedmen have opened throughout the entire South; all of them giving elementary instruction, and reaching thousands who cannot attend the week-day teaching." He witnessed children on the Sabbath, "sometimes . . . many hundreds, dressed in clean Sunday garments, with eyes sparkling, intent upon elementary and Christian instruction." AMA

---

25. American Tract Society, *44th Annual Report of the American Tract Society, 1869* (New York: ATS, 1870), 86 (quotation). For background on teaching African Americans to read during Reconstruction, see Henry Allen Bullock, *A History of Negro Education in the South from 1619 to the Present* (Cambridge: Harvard University Press, 1967); Robert C. Morris, *Reading, 'Riting, and Reconstruction: The Education of Freedmen in the South, 1861–1870* (Chicago: University of Chicago Press, 1981); Henry Lee Swint, *The Northern Teacher in the South, 1862–1870* (Nashville: Vanderbilt University Press, 1941); Jacqueline Jones, *Soldiers of Light and Love: Northern Teachers and Georgia Blacks, 1865–1873* (Athens: University of Georgia Press, 1992). For the educational role of the Sunday school, see William Bean Kennedy, *The Shaping of Protestant Education, 1789–1860: An Interpretation of the Sunday School and the Development of Protestant Educational Strategy* (New York: Association Press, 1966); Robert A. Crandall, "The Sunday School As an Instructional Agency for Religious Instruction in American Protestantism, 1872–1922" (Ph.D. diss., University of Notre Dame, 1977); Seymour, *From Sunday School to Church School*; Karen L. Zipf, "'Among These American Heathens': Congregationalist Missionaries and African American Evangelicals during Reconstruction, 1865–1878," *North Carolina Historical Review* 74 (April 1997): 111–34; James D. Anderson, *The Education of Blacks in the South, 1860–1935* (Chapel Hill: University of North Carolina Press, 1988); Kenneth Moore Startup, *The Root of All Evil: The Protestant Clergy and the Economic Mind of the Old South* (Athens: University of Georgia Press, 1997), 103. Startup may overstate the case for southern Sunday school education during the antebellum period, claiming that the schools dispensed "a desperately needed rudimentary education to hundreds of thousands of southerners."

teacher Sarah Jane Foster taught reading in her Sunday school for black children and noted that "with quite a number, Sunday school affords their only chance to read." American Sunday School Union (ASSU) missionaries observed numerous black Sunday schools where children were learning to spell and read. These filled a real void; many African Americans had never seen a book, much less a Bible.[26]

The number of southerners who required or desired basic schooling was staggering. The region had no state public school systems in place until well after the Civil War, and southern states were ill-prepared to meet children's educational needs. By the 1870s many state legislatures had made commitments to build schools and to provide universal education, yet the shortcomings of the South's school systems made basic education in Sunday school a necessity. Public schools were few in number, were open only for an abbreviated school year, and were widely dispersed, which meant that a number of pupils had to walk miles in order to attend class. Missionaries and colporteurs working in the South discovered thousands of destitute children who could not read because their parents were illiterate or because they had no school nearby. Youngsters who labored six days a week on a farm or in a factory had little free time to acquire a basic education. Even by 1880, the AME church pointed out that while southern states contained only a third of the nation's population, three-quarters of the country's illiterate people lived in the South. In his study on southern education, Edgar Knight categorized the region's schools before 1900 as "poor beyond comparison." Due to widespread poverty, a low tax base, and southerners' traditional resistance to taxation, southern states had little tax money to support public schools. Since southern families tended to be large, the number of taxpayers compared

---

26. Alvord quoted in James D. Anderson, "Ex-Slaves and the Rise of Universal Education in the New South, 1860–1880," in Ronald K. Goodenow and Arthur O. White, eds., *Education and the Rise of the New South* (Boston: G. K. Hall, 1981), 8–9; Sarah Jane Foster, *Sarah Jane Foster, Teacher of the Freedmen: A Diary and Letters*, ed. Wayne E. Reilly (Charlottesville: University Press of Virginia, 1990), 46. See also Anderson, *The Education of Blacks in the South*; Lincoln and Mamiya, *The Black Church in the African-American Experience*, 251; Katie C. Warren and Jo M. Bevington, "The Contributions of Children to Southern Baptists," *Baptist History and Heritage* 25 (October 1990): 4. For comments from ASSU missionaries, see H. Safford to Maurice A. Wurts, 6 November 1867, Greensboro, N.C., and R. B. Smith to Alexander Kirkpatrick, 1 August 1867, Union Point, Ga., both in ASSU Correspondence, Presbyterian Historical Society, Philadelphia (hereafter cited as PHS).

to per capita spending needed to educate the region's children was low. Financing the education of a large number of children put a strain on state budgets. In some states, school monies were mismanaged. And many elected officials were as reluctant to spend money for education as southerners were unwilling to be taxed for it.[27]

As a result, southern state school systems often faced severe fiscal exigencies, which in turn necessitated dramatic action. When states depleted their annual school budget—a common occurrence—they simply closed their schools before the end of a term. Between 1876 and 1889, the school year in the South lasted 88 to 95 days, half the length of northern schools. By 1900, when the average number of school days in the United States was 145, North Carolina's schools met for 70 days; Louisiana's and Virginia's schools were in session 119 days. In part, the academic year was abbreviated in order to accommodate the needs of an agrarian society; yet it was often clear that the professed commitment of southern states to universal public education was little more than lip service.[28]

Maintaining a segregated educational system in southern states added to the financial burden of schooling children, despite the fact that black schools received disproportionately little of any budgeted school funds. Many whites resented black schools, claiming that white tax dollars should not be used for African American education (though recent studies show that black tax monies helped to support white schools). Other whites were upset that former slaves were learning to read and write, insisting that there was no reason why the South's principal labor force had to be literate. An education might spoil them and make them feel the equal of whites, they argued. Southern states ignored dilapidated black school buildings, textbooks that were hand-me-downs from white schools, and African American teachers who earned only a fraction of what white instructors made. African American communities that wanted their children to enjoy decent facilities often had to

27. Benjamin Arnett, "The Perils of the Nation: The Illiterate Population of the Nation in 1880," *The Budget of the AME Church* (Xenia, Ohio: Torchlight,1881), 179–82; Edgar W. Knight, *Public Education in the South* (Boston: Ginn, 1922), 415–20; Edgar Gardner Murphy, *Problems of the Present South* (New York: MacMillan, 1904), 43; Knight, *Public Education in the South*, 419; Bullock, *History of Negro Education*, 47–9; Ayers, *Promise of the New South*, 45–6.

28. Knight, *Public Education in the South*, 420; Murphy, *Problems of the Present South*, 43; Amory D. Mayo, *Southern Women in the Recent Educational Movement in the*

raise money and upgrade their own school buildings through citizen involvement.[29]

The Sunday school therefore often became the best means—and perhaps the only one—for blacks to acquire basic literacy. For many, it was a pragmatic issue; Sunday might be their only free day to attend school. But even a minimal exposure helped. As Carter Woodson observed, "Many of these Negroes often learned more on a single Sunday than the average student acquired in a day school during the week." Sunday schools that offered lessons in reading and writing allowed blacks to become literate and gain spiritual knowledge through Christian education.[30]

Some rural southern white children also learned to read in Sunday classes. "A large proportion of the children of our country have now no means of learning to read but in the Sunday school, and experience has shown that they can there readily learn both to read and write," noted delegates to the 1866 Southern Baptist convention. North Carolina Methodists concurred, commenting that "they are the only available schools to many of our people." Alabama Baptists discovered Sunday schools in the backwoods, often with people of all ages learning to read, spell, and memorize the catechism. The Sunday school gave some rural poor white southerners their initial exposure to education.[31]

Teaching secular lessons in Sunday school was not always easy. One problem was finding suitable material to teach the basics. ASSU missionary T. H. Legare discarded the Sunday school books he had brought South and asked Philadelphia headquarters to send him "very elementary books" to teach his pupils how to read. North Carolina black Baptists used Webster's speller, instead of the Bible, as their basic Sunday text. Other classes used a "blue-back spelling book, the bible, and perhaps a Catechism," noted one observer. The American Baptist Publication Soci-

---

South (1892; reprint, Baton Rouge: Louisiana State University Press, 1978); Ayers, *Promise of the New South*, 45–6, 417–20.

29. Leon F. Litwack, *Trouble in Mind: Black Southerners in the Age of Jim Crow* (New York: Alfred A. Knopf, 1998), 88–99, 107; Ayers, *Promise of the New South*, 417–9.

30. Carter Godwin Woodson, *The History of the Negro Church*, 2nd ed. (Washington, D.C.: Associated Publishers, 1921), 268. See also Lincoln and Mamiya, *The Black Church*, 251.

31. 1866 quote in Warren and Bevington, "The Contributions of Children to Southern Baptists," 4; William Mouzon Brabham, *A History of Sunday School Work in the North*

ety (ABPS) met freedmen's needs with its *First Reader for Freedmen,* which included a picture alphabet and spelling and reading lessons covering both scriptural and moral subjects.[32]

As the number of public and Sunday schools in the South increased, literacy rates rose as well, lessening the need for Sunday schools to teach reading. AMEZ minister R. C. O. Benjamin of Birmingham, Alabama, expressed pleasure with his congregation's growing literacy, for this meant that his denomination's Sunday schools could focus more attention on the Bible and less on ABCs. Yet Benjamin's response was premature. Illiteracy among southern blacks and poor rural whites remained high; by the turn of the century, roughly half the southern black population still could not read or write. Many southern families who depended on their children's labor could not afford to let them attend weekday school. Some landowners forbade sharecroppers' children from attending public school, especially during harvest time. In such instances, Sunday schools remained the only avenue to acquire any education.[33]

Southern parents also welcomed Sunday school lessons because they were beyond the reach of government control. Before the Civil War, Bible lessons and prayers had been a normal part of southern education. Religion—conveyed through prayers, hymns, exhortations, and classes—was an accepted component of the daily schedule. State-supported education after the war, however, enhanced the possibility of outside influence. Rarely comfortable with state or federal imposition, southerners distrusted government dictates concerning education.[34]

By the late nineteenth century, a few states nationwide forbade teach-

---

Carolina Conference, MEC, South (Greensboro, N.C.: Christian Advocate, 1925), 22; "A Sabbath School 20 Years Ago," *Alabama Baptist,* 14 June 1877.

32. T. H. Legare to Maurice A. Wurts in John McCullagh, "The South," *57th Annual Report of the ASSU* (Philadelphia: ASSU, 1881), 25; "Children's Recorder" advertisement, *Christian Recorder,* 16 May 1871; "President's Annual Address," *Proceedings of the 11th Annual Baptist State Sunday School Convention of North Carolina (Negro)* (Raleigh: Caesar Johnson, 1882), 25; Lemuel Call Barnes, Mary Clark Barnes, and Edward M. Stephenson, *Pioneers of Light: The First Century of the American Baptist Publication Society, 1824–1924* (Philadelphia: ABPS, [1924]), 245.

33. R. C. O. Benjamin, "The Relation of the Sunday School to the Church," *Star of Zion,* 9 February 1893; G. S. Dickerman, "Negro Literacy and Illiteracy," *Southern Workman* 31 (Sept. 1902): 474–5. At the turn of the century, Louisiana, Alabama, South Carolina, and Georgia had more than a 50 percent illiteracy rate.

34. "Public School Concerns," *Working Christian,* 17 June 1875; Walter L. Hervey, "Moral Education in the Public Elementary Schools," *Religious Education* 2 (August 1907): 81–5.

ing the Bible in public schools; others let individual school districts or teachers determine whether or not to use the Bible. This messy situation argued for Sunday school classes that could provide unadulterated scriptural lessons corresponding to the faith of one's choice. In Sunday school, children could be inculcated in orthodox lessons without outside interference. As a Southern Baptist urged in 1896, his denomination's Sabbath schools had to counter the "inevitable defects of state education" and the "dangers which emerge from the general secularization of education which is now in progress in this country." It wasn't until 1905 that the International Sunday School Association (ISSA) took a stand on this issue, concluding that the "secular school limits itself to the preparation of the child for performing the functions of the life that now is, while the Bible or Sunday-School has always striven to prepare it both for the present life and the life that is to come."[35]

The southern Sabbath school offered other educational and social benefits. Southern Baptist minister Lansing Burrows identified it as a place to present factual material that a preacher might overlook in his sermons. Ministers had little time, he argued, to "say it all." For children who regularly attended church, Sunday school lessons could provide background information to help them better understand the sermon. A few classes offered a truly intellectual experience, such as a Sunday school class in Greenville, South Carolina, that conducted its lessons in Greek. Arkansas Baptists saw the wide-ranging benefits of Sunday classes. Here, children would be taught to obey the law, ultimately reducing the population in poorhouses and penitentiaries and lowering taxes. Similarly, Southern Presbyterians promised that their Sunday lessons would offset sin and improve all southern communities. "Comparatively few of those who have been regularly trained in the Sabbath school, perish afterwards in the bar-rooms, brothels, and gambling halls of our

---

35. "The Divorce of Education and Religion," *Kind Words*, September 1896; James Atkins, *The Kingdom in the Cradle* (Nashville: Publishing House of the MECS, 1905), 296; A. R. Taylor, "The Relation of the Sunday-School to the Public School," in the Eleventh International Sunday School Convention, *The Development of the Sunday-School, 1780–1905* (Boston: ISSA, 1905), 186. See also Donald E. Boles, *The Bible, Religion, and the Public Schools* (Ames: Iowa State University Press, 1961), 31; Ralph E. Luker, *The Social Gospel in Black and White: American Racial Reform, 1885–1912* (Chapel Hill: University of North Carolina Press, 1991), 148. Atkins states that 11 states required Bible reading and 2 prohibited it; 38 states had schools where children read the Bible and 7 states had schools in which children did not.

cities," they boasted. The Reverend Bernard Spilman, whose livelihood depended on the success of the Sunday school, exulted that it "does more to make men better citizens than all the law makers and executive and judicial officers in the State." Others celebrated the mental discipline that resulted from memorizing Scripture, which was the standard pedagogical approach used in Sunday school. There were psychological benefits to Sunday school as well. Pupils could enhance their social development by interacting with other children and overcoming shyness. By attending class, they would sever close ties to home and be introduced "to the best society, in its best aspect," claimed Methodist J. A. Lyon.[36]

Southern Sunday school promoters expressed high expectations for the institution and what it could achieve. They were convinced that a Sunday school managed by a competent supervisor and classes led by inspiring teachers could work wonders, molding youngsters into faithful churchgoers and outstanding citizens. Here, every youngster would learn to distinguish right from wrong. Lessons would erase character flaws that typified paupers and criminals, and instead fashion children into model citizens who lived by Christian ideals and the highest morals. Students would learn to respect law and order, according to a Louisianian, for religion is a "source of good citizenship and right living." Its messages would improve children's personal character and ultimately affect an entire community—and the region—by curbing crime and fostering civil conduct.[37]

The Sunday school became a significant institution throughout the South—critical to family, church, and community—and one for southerners to promote and celebrate. Those with a broad vision and a desire

---

36. Lansing Burrows, "The Triumphs of the Sabbath School Work," Lansing Burrows Papers, SBHLA; Crafts, "The Sabbath-School As a Factor in Public Education," 586–90; "Greenville Baptist Sunday School," *Baptist Courier*, 15 January 1881; E. Glenn Hinson, *A History of Baptists in Arkansas, 1818–1978* (Little Rock: Baptist State Convention, 1979), 117–8; "The Influence of the Sabbath School," *Earnest Worker*, 10 August 1871; Spilman, "The Sunday-School Work in North Carolina"; J. A. Lyon, *The Sunday School and Its Methods: A Practical Treatise for Earnest Workers in This Department of the Church of Christ* (Nashville: Publishing House of the MECS, 1895), 58. For children's social development in Sunday school, see Brown, *Sunday-School Movements in America*, 176–9. For a discussion of antebellum Sunday schools in one southern state, see John W. Quist, "Slaveholding Operatives of the Benevolent Empire: Bible, Tract and Sunday School Societies in Antebellum Tuscaloosa County, Alabama," *Journal of Southern History* 62 (August 1996): 519–20.

37. John M. Rankin quoted in Atkinson, *Value of the Sunday School*, 24.

to see the region bury past misunderstandings hoped that the Sunday school would become a means to bind the country together. Some even believed that through Sunday school, the South could adopt a global outlook. As the Reverend Martindale of Newnan, Georgia, envisioned, the Sabbath school could truly become a "world affair." The South held an important place in God's world, and its Sunday schools portended the possibility that enhancing the faith of all children would ensure the region's and the nation's future.[38]

To many southerners, the Sunday school, with its focus on the faith of children, could uplift and save a destitute, war-weary South. By instilling Christian doctrine and sound behavior in youngsters, Sabbath instruction could mold the next generation—and ultimately the entire South—into an exalted state. Sunday schools gave southern churches the opportunity to scrutinize and regulate family life and to indoctrinate children with the traits necessary to regenerate the region and its churches. "The salvation of the world, which is the great mission of the Church, depends upon the religious training of the young," proclaimed Southern Baptists. "The minds which receive their first training in spiritual things in our Sunday schools will become the leaders of our people. In the next generation they will fill the pulpits, conduct our business enterprises, and if filled with the Spirit of Truth, manage wisely, and act efficiently for the world's conversion." Southern Sunday schools promised to create spiritually and morally regenerated citizens. Perhaps North Carolinian Robert Gray said it best, predicting that those who attended Sunday school would "become ornaments to the church, bright and shining lights that add lustre to the temple. . . . Religious ideas once instilled into the mind of a child, religious devotion once implanted there, can never be wholly eradicated or extinguished." Pupils who faithfully attended Sunday school would become adult workers in the church and upstanding citizens in the community. Through their faith, they would contribute to family, church, and region. To evangelicals, Sunday school pupils would almost inevitably become model citizens who could raise up the South.[39]

38. C. O. Martindale, "The Sunday School of World Import," *Presbyterian Standard* 46 (1 August 1906): 12.
39. "Sunday School Board," *Baptist Courier,* 16 April 1891; Robert T. Gray, "Opening Address," *Proceedings of the North Carolina State Sunday School Convention, 1878* (Raleigh: Edwards, Broughton, 1878), 5. On Sunday schools regulating family behavior, see Stephanie Coontz, *The Social Origins of Private Life: A History of American Families, 1600–1900* (New York: Verso, 1988), 263.

2

Reconstructing the South

Neither "state lines, nor sectional hatreds, nor complexion of man," declared a northern Sunday school missionary in 1866, would prevent his organization from working in the South. Here was a region desperate for Christian uplift, needing the assistance and aid that northerners believed they could best provide. A savvy John McCullagh, district supervisor of the ASSU, felt he understood how to win southerners. "By no mode can the hearts of parents be so easily and quickly won," he observed, as "by interest manifested towards their children and by securing *their* affections." While politicians vacillated over how best to reunite North and South and reconstruct the former Confederate states, missionaries were unambiguous. Northern agents believed that the key to rebuilding the South was to found churches, Sunday schools, and day schools, in order to expose the region's children to God. In this way, the North could win the goodwill of the South and spritually elevate the region.[1]

---

1. "Annual Report of the Executive Board: The South," ABHMS, *34th Annual Report of the American Baptist Home Mission Society, 1866* (New York: ABHMS, 1866), 21; John McCullagh, "The Southern District," *42nd Annual Report of the ASSU* (Philadelphia: ASSU, 1866), 68. As Nina Silber has argued, northerners felt that they had to develop mu-

It may seem surprising that some of the initial success of the southern Sunday school movement was due to enterprising Yankees who represented various northern religious associations and denominations. Yet immediately after the Civil War, these determined, hard-working missionaries began to descend upon the South, ready to initiate or renew evangelical efforts. These agents saw the region as fertile ground to be refashioned and improved on northern terms. Northern clergymen also hoped that many white southerners, trapped by circumstance or wrongly led into a southern denomination, would be eager to rejoin their respective national denomination.[2]

It is impossible to overstate the excitement these northern missionaries felt as they looked southward, exclaiming over the possibilities the region offered them. The Reverend Schenck of the ATS rejoiced over the huge "field of labor . . . presented by the freedmen of the Southern country." Missionaries saw no problem "invading" a region so recently deemed enemy territory and anticipated that southerners would exhibit "manifest joy" over their appearance. Northerners seemed fearless in facing the challenges ahead, for they saw their task as God's will—a calling—and assumed that southerners would embrace them. They had little trouble justifying their presence, believing they had a God-given right to labor in the South; faith knew no regional or racial boundaries. To northern missionaries, the South appeared more than ready for divine, or at least Yankee, intervention.[3]

The most influential and successful among the many northern reli-

---

tual respect and understanding with southerners through emotional ties, rather than through force of arms or new laws. See Nina Silber, *The Romance of Reunion: Northerners and Southerners, 1865–1900* (Chapel Hill: University of North Carolina Press, 1993), 2, 23, 45, 56; Stowell, *Rebuilding Zion;* Zipf, "'Among These American Heathens,'" 111–34.

2. Stowell, *Rebuilding Zion,* 54. Paul H. Buck also argues that northern churches had their sights set on reuniting the Baptist, Methodist, and Presbyterian churches into one. While I found evidence of this among northern church officials, it was a goal that missionaries rarely expressed. See Buck, *The Road to Reunion, 1865–1900* (Baton Rouge: Louisiana State University Press, 1937), 62–3.

3. "Rev. Dr. Schenck," and "Rev. G. L. Shearer, Richmond," both in the *41st Annual Report of the American Tract Society* (New York: ATS, 1866), 8. William Preston Vaughan argues that Yankee schoolteachers who came south after the Civil War also saw the freedmen as a vast new field for their endeavors. See Vaughan, *Schools for All: The Blacks and Public Education in the South, 1865–1877* (Lexington: University Press of Kentucky, 1974), 1.

gious organizations engaged in southern Sunday school work was the American Sunday School Union of Philadelphia. Based on a similar organization that began in London in 1803, the ASSU was founded by a group of Philadelphia businessmen in 1824 to promote union, or nondenominational, schools, and to circulate and sell the organization's literature. It enjoyed financial support from individual donors and northern denominations, especially the Episcopal Church and the Presbyterian Church of the U.S.A. The ASSU first began its work in the South in 1833. By the 1870s, it claimed to be the only true national missionary society serving neglected children in areas of the country it perceived to be devoid of Christian influences.[4]

While the ASSU was only one of many religious organizations working in the South, it was the one most singularly focused on Sunday schools. The fact that it tried to organize union schools often worked to its advantage. Southerners who had difficulty accepting an institution affiliated with a single denomination, or who saw sectarian divisiveness as an impediment to Christian faith, welcomed the ASSU's inclusive approach. If there was to be only one Sunday school in a community, southerners often accepted a union one. This frequently was the case in rural, hard-to-reach areas of the South, where the organization sent many of its missionaries. A nondenominational approach was appealing to communities divided by religious loyalties.

The ASSU's southern district encompassed nine states under the jurisdiction of its energetic regional supervisor, John McCullagh, who served in this capacity from 1867 to 1884. McCullagh's achievements in the southern Sunday school movement became legendary; during his career, he organized more than a thousand Sunday schools and brought some 66,000 pupils into his classes. Of Scottish heritage, McCullagh trained

---

4. For background on ASSU missionary work in the antebellum South, see John W. Kuykendall, *Southern Enterprize: The Work of National Evangelical Societies in the Antebellum South* (Westport, Conn.: Greenwood Press, 1982); Barbara Sokolosky, *ASSU Papers, 1817–1915: A Guide to the Microfilm Edition* (Sanford, N.C.: Microfilming Corporation of America, 1980); James H. Smylie, "The American Sunday School Union Papers, 1817–1915," *Journal of Presbyterian History* 58 (winter 1980): 372–6; Boylan, *Sunday School,* 29, 69–70; Edwin Wilbur Rice, "Union Sunday Schools," vol. 3, *Encyclopedia of Sunday Schools and Religious Education,* ed. John T. McFarland et al. (New York: Thomas Nelson and Sons, 1915), 1121–2; Rice, "Sunday School Union, American," vol. 3, *Encyclopedia of Sunday Schools,* 1042–4.

for the ministry but found his real calling to be the Sunday school. After laboring among the poor in New York State for several years, he settled in Louisville, Kentucky, in 1839 and began to organize Sunday school classes—a task he continued for the next forty-five years. He was determined to place at least one ASSU missionary in every southern district. His aggressive spirit, coupled with his overriding fear that rivals might move in before the ASSU could act, led him to labor tirelessly for the cause.[5]

Like other religious organizations, the ASSU hired missionaries and colporteurs, assigning them to particular districts where they were to organize new Sunday schools, strengthen preexisting ones, and distribute and sell ASSU literature. Strictly defined, the work of a missionary and that of a colporteur were different. Missionaries helped communities organize new churches and Sunday schools and brought the word of God to the destitute. Colporteurs sold or gave away Bibles and religious tracts. Out in the field, however, responsibilities often overlapped, and no one seemed too concerned if missionaries sold books and colporteurs organized churches and Sunday schools. The duties of each might include missionary and evangelistic work such as preaching, home visiting, and converting the faithful.[6]

Aiding the ASSU's approach was that, in the immediate aftermath of the Civil War, many southerners felt only lukewarm (if any) loyalty to a particular denomination, especially when it came to Sunday schools. Those parents eager to expose their children to Sunday school lessons welcomed missionaries or ministers representing any denomination or religious society without fretting over particularities. This was especially true of rural southerners, who often attended a church without a permanent minister and who took advantage of any itinerant preacher, what-

5. Smylie, "The American Sunday School Union Papers"; McCullagh, "The Southern District," 68; Joseph H. McCullagh, *"The Sunday-School Man of the South": A Sketch of the Life and Labors of the Rev. John McCullagh* (Philadelphia: ASSU, 1889). Nine states comprised the southern district: North Carolina, South Carolina, Georgia, Florida, Alabama, Mississippi, Louisiana, Kentucky, and Tennessee.

6. For information on colporteurs and their work in the South, see James T. Siburt, "Tennessee Colporteurs: Flatboat Evangelism," *Tennessee Historical Quarterly* 47 (1988): 227–33; Ernest Trice Thompson, *Presbyterians in the South,* vol. 2, *1861–1890* (Richmond, Va.: John Knox Press, 1973), 336–8; Martin L. Massaglia, "Colporter Ministry: The Transitions of Power," *Foundations* 24 (Oct.–Dec. 1981): 328–41.

ever his faith. Often a single building served several denominations, and itinerant ministers took turns using it for worship service. Initially, the same held true of Sunday schools, which, though racially segregated, welcomed all children, regardless of faith.[7]

The ASSU's success in the South was due not only to its inclusive approach and aggressive leadership. The ASSU had financial resources, expertise in organizing Sunday schools, an extensive list of publications, and a dedicated, determined force of salaried workers. Many northern businesses had reaped huge profits from the Civil War, and religious organizations like the ASSU began to benefit from philanthropic industrialists who underwrote some of their missionary efforts. These contributions enabled the ASSU to pay field workers a decent salary and to distribute free or inexpensive materials to new Sunday schools. The ASSU also understood the wisdom of hiring local men as agents, sensing that they could gain people's trust more readily than outsiders could. Southerners found the message more palatable if one of their own delivered it. Due to his southern background, ASSU missionary C. W. Charlton believed he was more credible and had more influence than some agents. W. L. Ellington also found that his southern heritage worked to his advantage, even though strong prejudice against Sunday schools existed in his Missouri district. "But having been *born* and *raised* in one of these counties," he wrote, "I can much more successfully overcome these prejudices than could one from abroad." On the other hand, South Carolinian Edwin Bolles, an agent for the ABS, responded bitterly to his situation. He complained that southern clergymen in his church had "persecuted" him for some fifteen years because "I went to the north and got myself appointed agent of a Yankee Bible Society for the South." Here, southerners resented a minister who, in their eyes, was a turncoat.[8]

---

7. James Mallory of Talladega County, Ala., mentioned attending not only his own Baptist church between the 1840s and the 1870s, but services at various Methodist churches, a Southern Presbyterian Church, a Cumberland Presbyterian Church, and even the African Church. See Mallory, *"Fear God and Walk Humbly": The Agricultural Journal of James Mallory, 1843–1877,* ed. Grady McWhiney, Warren O. Moore Jr., and Robert F. Pace (Tuscaloosa: University of Alabama Press, 1997).

8. C. W. Charlton, 7 November 1867, Caledonia, Mo., and W. L. Ellington, 30 April 1867, Sturgeon, Mo., both to Maurice A. Wurts, in ASSU Correspondence, PHS; Edwin A. Bolles to W. J. R. Taylor, 27 August 1866, Columbia, S.C., ABS. See also Rice, "Union Sunday Schools," 1121–2.

Other northern religious organizations and missionary societies committed resources and personnel to spread the faith by distributing literature and founding Sunday schools and churches throughout the South. Within a month after the Civil War ended, the American Baptist Home Missionary Society (ABHMS) had 68 missionaries working among freedmen in 12 southern states. In 1867, the ATS turned its attention to the South. Northern Presbyterians had 179 missionaries working in the region by 1868. The ABPS, which had enjoyed substantial success in the South both before and during the Civil War, made a real commitment to southern colportage in 1867. With its focus on publishing, the ABPS sought to spread the Baptist faith by selling its books and religious tracts and by organizing new Sunday schools. By 1870, the ABPS had 29 colporteurs working in the South; it later opened several branch offices to improve the distribution of Sunday school publications throughout the region. As late as the 1880s, northern Baptists spent almost three times as much as Southern Baptists on missionary work in the South. Northern Methodists were also aggressive, reaping their greatest success in the border states and areas where slavery had been scarce. All this activity created a highly charged, competitive field of evangelistic work. In fact, exasperated ABS agent A. M. Jones felt that the number of missionaries had gotten out of hand. He found that in Alabama, a "great many preachers" were distributing so much literature that the "people have more Bibles now than they have bread and meat."[9]

9. "Missionary Table," ABHMS, *34th Annual Report of the American Baptist Home Missionary Society* (New York: ABHMS, 1866), 21; A. M. Jones, *Quaint Characters, or Colportage Sketches* (Nashville: Publishing House of the MECS, 1890), 60. See also Stephen Elmore Slocum Jr., *The American Tract Society, 1825–1975: An Evangelistic Effort to Influence the Religious and Moral Life of the United States* (New York: New York University Press, 1975), 143; George A. Peltz, "Report on Associational Colportage," *44th Annual Report of the American Baptist Publication Society* (Philadelphia: ABPS, 1868), 13; ABPS, *64th Annual Report of the American Baptist Publication Society* (Philadelphia: ABPS, 1888), 27; James A. Hoyt, "Committee on Colporter Work," ABPS, *71st Anniversary of the American Baptist Publication Society* (Philadelphia: ABPS, 1895), 41–4; S. W. Melton, "The Society and the Denomination at Large," ABPS, *80th Anniversary of the American Baptist Publication Society* (Philadelphia: ABPS, 1904), 55–9; John H. Bentley, *After Eight Decades: The Story of the American Baptist Publication Society* (Philadelphia: ABPS, 1908); Ralph E. Morrow, *Northern Methodism and Reconstruction* (East Lansing: Michigan State University Press, 1956), 29, 96; Harvey, *Redeeming the South*, 22; Owen, *Sacred Flame of Love*, 117–9. For the number of missionaries representing various religious

Both the AME and AMEZ churches also sent agents to the South. These two black denominations needed and wanted to expand their influence nationwide, and their missionaries worked tirelessly to recruit southern blacks into their Sunday schools and churches. Their missionaries saw an almost endless number of potential converts—four million former slaves—who they assumed would be eager to join a well-established black denomination. Like whites, they saw the Sunday school as the most effective evangelical agency to achieve these goals.[10]

While humanitarianism and faith often motivated these dedicated individuals, their sponsoring religious organizations had an agenda—they wanted to attract southern followers and build an audience for their material. Sunday schools were important consumers of products these organizations marketed. To the ABPS, the founding of new Sunday schools was critical, for new schools meant more readers who would purchase its literature and absorb its message. Children were now consumers of religious material, and this market had to be tapped before it fell into the hands of rivals. As missionaries opened new Sunday schools, they often donated free materials until the schools became self-sustaining, hoping that this initial generosity would translate into organizational loyalty as the schools grew and prospered.

The ABPS worked through both black and white state Baptist associations, distributing literature in various states and paying a portion of the salary of a state Sunday school evangelist. For instance, in a situation duplicated elsewhere, the ABPS gave five hundred dollars annually to the Tennessee Baptist State Convention to help support a Sunday school missionary. This subsidy yielded tangible benefits to the ABPS. Once hired by the Convention, the new missionary promised to assist his northern sponsor by selling ABPS publications "incidentally as he passed from place to place." For years, black Baptists depended on financial aid and advice from white religious organizations in the North, including the ABPS, which helped to fund black Sunday school conventions and missionaries in fifteen southern states. For instance, the ABPS supported the

---

organizations, see H. Shelton Smith, *In His Image, But . . . : Racism in Southern Religion, 1780–1910* (Durham, N.C.: Duke University Press, 1972).

10. According to H. Shelton Smith, AME and AMEZ missionaries were not welcome in the South before 1861 and were actually barred from some areas. See Smith, *In His Image, But . . .*, 225; Milton C. Sernett, *Bound for the Promised Land: African American Religion and the Great Migration* (Durham, N.C.: Duke University Press, 1977), 88.

Alabama Negro Baptist Sunday School Convention's Sunday school agent, R. T. Pollard, who traveled throughout the state, organizing new Sunday schools, raising standards in existing ones, and supplying classes with material published, of course, by the ABPS.[11]

Missionaries submitted periodic reports to their home office, describing their experiences, successes, and failures. Some organizations simplified the task and had agents merely fill out a questionnaire that requested statistical information, including the number of new Sunday schools and pupils in a district, the number of books sold, and the number of miles traveled. In addition to this, ASSU agents submitted descriptive accounts each month. These reports provide fascinating insights into Sunday school work and northern responses to conditions in the postwar South. However, one must interpret them with care. Agents had their biases; they experienced frustrations and hardships. Some northerners' negative responses to the South—such as their references to southerners as illiterate, backwards, and misguided, or to African Americans as a filthy, inferior race—were little more than crude Yankee stereotypes.

But grueling conditions and physical exhaustion could and did provoke strong responses. When tempers flared, tired workers might release a torrent of anger on paper about those whom they were supposed to aid and uplift. Without adequate rail transportation or roads in many parts of the rural South, missionaries often traveled by horse or foot. Being far from home for weeks or months at a time, agents could become lonely and disheartened. Missionaries were mere mortals, not saints. One man was accused of fraud; another was dismissed from his post and brought to trial. Missionaries frequently exaggerated the negative or positive aspects of their job to serve their own interests. To convey the importance of their work to the home office and justify demands for continued sympathy and financial support, field workers sometimes emphasized the problems they encountered, making them more dire or dramatic than

---

11. "Reports of Auxiliary Committees," *Minutes of the 10th Annual Baptist State Sunday School Convention of North Carolina (Negro)* (Raleigh: African Expositor Printing, 1881), 19–20; R. T. Pollard, "Report of R. T. Pollard, Sunday School Missionary of the ABPS and Alabama Baptist State Convention," *Minutes of the 22nd Annual Alabama Colored Baptist State Convention, 1889*, 18; *Minutes of the Proceedings of the Seventh Annual Session of the Baptist State Convention of Tennessee, 1881* (Chattanooga: Baptist Printing, n.d.); W. E. B. DuBois, *The Negro Church* (Atlanta: Atlanta University Press, 1903), 40. Both the AME and AMEZ churches made significant strides once they came South.

was actually the case. George Sharp, after presenting a lengthy list of complaints and describing the resistance he had overcome, closed his monthly report by noting, "But this so much more shows the importance of my work." On the other hand, an agent might report positive comments and enumerate tangible results in order to demonstrate that his work was reaping impressive results. To ensure ongoing support for their missionary efforts, incumbents had to walk a fine line between noting their accomplishments and describing the ongoing challenges.[12]

As these reports show, the physical condition of the region proved daunting—sometimes even shocking—to missionaries who ventured South. Especially during the early years of field work, agents often expressed alarm over the South's physical and spiritual condition and the way that southerners lived. Northern missionaries universally characterized the area and its people as "destitute," referring both to the appalling levels of poverty and to the hundreds of thousands of southerners lacking any Christian influence. As ABS agent Calvin H. Wiley noted of his efforts in Corinth, Mississippi, "The people are in a dreadful condition and it will be many years before they recover the losses, religious as well as pecuniary, sustained during the war." Others observed impoverished families without adequate food, farm animals or tools, or even a Bible. Missionaries found rural families crowded into decrepit cabins and filthy shacks. Adults and children often had little, if any, formal education.[13]

Missionaries also were appalled by the number of southerners who pursued sinful pleasures, apparently ignorant of Christian morals or any concept of decent manners. ASSU representative W. B. Graves was disheartened to have found not a single church or Sunday school in one Tennessee valley. In his view, this explained why the children in his classroom were unlike any he had met, a "wild, rude, wicked, uncultivated set of youngsters," who needed discipline and a grounding in Scripture. "It is a

---

12. D. B. Nelson, 26 February 1868, Forks of Pigeon, N.C., and George W. Sharp, 22 July 1880, Kirksville, Mo., both to Maurice A. Wurts, ASSU Correspondence, PHS. Unsolicited letters seeking employment as a Sunday school missionary suggest that this was an employer's market, especially during the economic depressions of the 1870s and 1890s when many people were out of work.

13. Calvin H. Wiley to W. J. R. Taylor, 3 November 1865, Memphis, Tenn., Calvin H. Wiley Collection, ABS. These missionaries were hardly alone in facing such conditions. See the comments of northern school teachers who ventured South after the War in Swint, *The Northern Teacher in the South*, 77–80.

back region where ignorance dwells, and where nearly all the vices are indulged in by a large proportion of the people," he observed. From Kentucky, Isaac Emory found much of the South totally "bankrupt" of religious influence, especially in its mountain regions. "One can form no conception of the deplorable ignorance, bigotry and prejudice until he mingles with the people," he stated, adding that such problems were "enough to discourage the most hopeful." On a prior occasion, a 200-mile trip into the mountains had left him "sick at heart. I never realized the importance of the Sunday school cause or of the value of a Sunday school missionary so fully before," he wrote. "In this trip I passed over 30 churches and not a school in them—ignorance, prejudice and superstition abounds." C. W. Charlton minced no words: "I have never seen, in all my life, a more destitute section. It is absolutely distressing to think of it. No intelligence—no refinement, and as stupid as ignorance can make them."[14]

Northern missionaries apparently felt no need to be discreet or to disguise a sense of superiority in their reports home. With almost one voice, they proclaimed that southerners were ignorant, ill-mannered, and ungrounded in Christian principles. Because agents purposely ventured into some of the most impoverished areas of the South, it is little wonder that such scenes hit them hard. And the condition of the South's poor undoubtedly shocked the middle-class sensibilities of many of these missionaries.

Though agents often found their work discouraging, the daily challenges they faced also emboldened their spirit and heightened their determination. Distressing circumstances offered them a constant reminder, as they ventured into areas lacking Christian influences or modern amenities, that their work could reap positive results. In their eyes, the only direction the South could go was up. The Appalachian region in particular appeared untouched by outsiders and more than ready for religious uplift. Colporteurs traveling through mountain highlands discovered people who had never visited a town or seen a buggy, and families living without candles, mirrors, or combs. Mountain children who smoked or chewed

14. W. B. Graves to John McCullagh, 24 December 1870, Lee Valley, Tenn.; Isaac Emory to Maurice A. Wurts, 31 May 1875 and 30 August 1870, both from Knoxville, Tenn.; C. W. Charlton to John McCullagh, 19 May 1867, Patterson, Mo., all in ASSU Correspondence, PHS.

tobacco, drank, and swore tested northern agents' patience. Southern preachers could be as ill-bred as members of their congregations. A few ministers were known bigamists; others preached while drunk. Some were illiterate and did not even own a Bible. Northern missionaries realized that the need to civilize and Christianize these people went hand in hand.

Obtaining support for a Sunday school from impoverished and unenlightened southerners could be difficult. Fed up with the excuses he heard from locals who had no use for a Sunday school he founded, ASSU missionary James C. Buchanan wrote despairingly, "it is very difficult to arouse the spirit of benevolence and sacrifice in the hearts and minds of a people that have never been trained to give to the support of missionary effort." T. H. Legare in South Carolina was less gracious: "The people whom I am expected to observe are the very farthest of all natural beings who live in a Christian country."[15]

Missionary work required superhuman effort, endless patience, and a healthy constitution. One Methodist minister seemed the perfect candidate for the post because "he is used to swimming rivers and sleeping under the trees and can easily pick out a trail for miles through the forest." Notwithstanding the jocular tone, this assessment contained more than a kernel of truth. All agents commented on the grueling nature of their job. One colporteur reported traveling nearly twenty thousand miles in a year; others routinely journeyed ten to fifteen thousand miles annually. This meant venturing hundreds of miles each month into frontier areas while carrying personal supplies, books, and Bibles by horseback, carriage, train, steamboat, flatboat, or on foot. Poor weather brought additional challenges and complaints of snow, rain, flooded rivers and streams, high winds, or relentless heat.[16]

15. James C. Buchanan, 23 December 1869, Campbellsville, Ky., and T. H. Legare, 5 November 1880, Orangeburg, S.C., both to Maurice A. Wurts, ASSU Correspondence, PHS. For missionary efforts in the mountains, see Henry D. Shapiro, *Appalachia on Our Mind: The Southern Mountains and Mountaineers in the American Consciousness, 1870–1920* (Chapel Hill: University of North Carolina Press, 1978); Samuel Hunter Thompson, *The Highlanders of the South* (New York: Eaton and Mains, 1910); H. Paul Douglass, *Christian Reconstruction in the South* (Boston: Pilgrim Press, 1909), 303–66.

16. Joseph C. Buchanan, 23 December 1869, Campbellsville, Ky.; Isaac Emory, 6 January 1870, Knoxville, Tenn.; G. S. Jones, 19 January and 14 March 1870, Hendersonville, N.C.; all to Maurice A. Wurts, ASSU Correspondence, PHS.

Travel conditions tested the health and patience of even the strongest constitution. Two Presbyterian missionaries described the summer they spent covering eleven counties in western North Carolina. As was often the case, in order to save money—and lacking any alternative—they depended on the hospitality of local families. Northern agents reportedly ate coarse, half-cooked food served on dirty dishes and slept on filthy beds crawling with insects. Not everyone could tolerate these conditions. A few missionaries quit from exhaustion or loneliness; a handful became ill and died on the job. Missionaries' pleas to improve their working conditions usually fell on deaf ears, or at least on the ears of organization officials with limited resources and no means to alter the situation. S. R. Chadwick, an ABS agent in East Texas, tried to improve his situation by convincing his home office that a new buggy would help him immeasurably. He complained of being "constantly exposed to the heat and the cold, the wet of the rain, the fatigues of long rides, the troubles of high waters, the hardships of bad accommodations, and dangers of life from the highwayman. It is only for the sake of the great and goodness and not for the money that there is in it, that we take our lives, as it were, in our hands, and go forth, sacrificing ease and comforts, forgoing the pleasures of home and society of loved ones, exposing our lives and wasting our energies in constant labor." Despite his impassioned, long-winded request, the Society did not send him $350 for a carriage.[17]

Not everyone was suited for the job. As Sunday school agent Frank Whildren reported from South Carolina, "I have never undertaken any work with which I am so dissatisfied with the result, and I feel that it is in no small measure due to the fact that I am not cut out for this style of work." He asked to be replaced, adding that southerners seemed more interested in politics than in either the Sunday school or the state of their souls.[18]

---

17. S. R. Chadwick to T. Ralston Smith, 17 February 1870, Huntsville, Tex., S. R. Chadwick Collection, ABS; "Mission Work among 'The Mountain Whites' in Asheville Presbytery, North Carolina," Papers on Presbyterianism, Montreat, N.C., 1–11. Alex G. Brown mentioned two colporteurs out of nine hired who died on the job in Virginia. See Brown, "Colportage," *Minutes of the 109th Session of the Virginia Annual Conference of the Methodist Episcopal Church, South, 1891* (Richmond: J. W. Fergusson and Son, 1891), 60.

18. Frank Whildren, "Report of Statistical Secretary," *Minutes of the South Carolina State Sunday School Convention, 1891* (Spartanburg: Spartanburg Herald Print, 1891), 10.

Despite the challenges, missionaries and colporteurs tackled the tasks before them, determined to bring the word of God, as well as civilization and good manners, to southerners. Many seemed to operate in a race against time, fearful that a soul might be lost forever or, more likely, that a rival society or denomination might prevail against them. The enemies were not only the devil and unenlightened southerners, but rival missionaries. Agents wanted to be the first to organize a community Sunday school, for they believed that school members then would remain loyal to the founding organization and to its publications. Almost as soon as the Civil War ended, the ABHMS urged its agents to push ahead without hesitation. "If we move promptly, we can establish our churches in their villages, can gain their sympathy and support, can win souls, and thus upbuild the cause of Christ. We must act promptly," insisted one ABHMS official. "The delay of a year now is the delay of a generation in securing the final triumph of truth." This urgency was about more than the triumph of Christianity. Yankee missionaries were a competitive lot, far more so than southern recipients of their goodwill and largesse. Agents rushed as quickly as their horse, carriage, or feet would carry them, determined to establish a Sunday school in the name of their institution or denomination.[19]

Missionaries who went South arrived neither as conquerors nor as enemies. Certainly they encountered some resistance. Skeptical parents questioned whether any institution could do anything to uplift and Christianize their children. Local ministers and laypeople sometimes looked askance at religious instruction that took place beyond home and pulpit; some even regarded the Sunday school as a sinful enterprise. Religious traditionalists questioned an institution without any scriptural justification. For that reason, a minister in Kentucky refused to allow anyone to organize a Sunday school in his community. "They ain't once mentioned in the Bible," he insisted. "The Sunday school is a thing of the devil and I'll have none of it in my churches." A pastor at the Pleasant Valley Church in Weyers Cave, Virginia, deemed the Sabbath school sinful and forbade the formation of one in his church. Others argued that Sunday classes usurped traditional worship service. A disheartened Tennessee Baptist missionary quietly commented, "There is not the enthusiasm or

19. "Report of the Executive Board: The Importance of Present Activity," ABHMS, *34th Annual Report*, 11.

enterprise in Sunday school work which the necessities of the times demand." Some conservative sects, such as the Primitive Baptists, recoiled against the very concept of the Sunday school and never allowed any in their churches. Missionaries on the frontier had to deal with the frustrating and unique problem of a restless population. Without warning, migration could deplete an entire school. After opening a new Sunday school one day, a missionary wrote that he might awaken the next morning to discover that the "thing may go off in a covered wagon." An inherent streak of southern independence often challenged what northerners depicted as their well-intentioned benevolence. Some parents, especially in rural areas, found missionaries pretentious for trying to instill middle-class values and good manners in their children. Other southerners distrusted anything that appeared in the guise of Yankee benevolence. Finding needy southerners proved easy; having them accept missionaries' convictions that Sunday schools based on a northern model would enhance their children's lives proved a greater challenge.[20]

Even if community residents agreed that a Sunday school was needed, they often disagreed over which one would best serve their children. Though many southerners were comfortable with a nondenominational approach, others, especially church leaders, insisted that children remain faithful to their denomination. Southern Presbyterians, who had a strong sectarian streak, labeled the union approach "tawdry" and without substance, no doubt fearing the loss of potential members for its congregation. Among those who felt a sectarian identity was essential to faith, union Sunday schools evoked powerful resistance. To take one example, ASSU missionary G. W. Ryan, working in Rose Hill, Mississippi, faced enormous opposition; the local minister threatened to expel church mem-

20. Quote in David Sumner, "Sunday Schools Started Interchurch Work in Kentucky," news release, Kentucky Council of Churches, 2 May 1980, Lexington, Ky.; Minor C. Miller, *These Things I Remember* (Philadelphia: Dorrance, 1968), 86–7; *Minutes of the Proceedings of the Ninth Annual Tennessee Baptist Convention* (Nashville: Committee of Publication, MECS, 1883); "Mission Work among 'The Mountain Whites'"; and Edwin Wilbur Rice, *The Sunday School Movement, 1780–1917 and the ASSU, 1817–1917* (1917; reprint, New York: Arno Press, 1971), 409. Paul Buck claims that northern missionaries came south "as conquerors." See Buck, *The Road to Reunion*, 62. Daniel Stowell claims that northern missionaries were almost universally shunned. I found less resistance to these men except among church leaders and southern missionaries who began to compete for youngsters. What is striking is how successful northern missionaries were in setting up Sunday schools and attracting local children to attend. See Stowell, *Rebuilding Zion*, 132.

bers if they joined Ryan's union Sunday school. The minister delivered several sermons that were, according to Ryan, a "tirade of abuse and bitter invecting against the Union Schools," accusing the ASSU of sending "infidells and unbelievers" who were "goten up for the sole purpose of braking the church down." In a series of exchanges, the minister sent Ryan a direct "chalenge" to defend his honor and position in the community by engaging in a formal duel. Ryan was unable to pass up the opportunity, although he admitted that as a missionary for the ASSU he should not have accepted the challenge, coming as it did from a man who Ryan felt lacked character. As he later explained, "in order to defend my personal and Christian character," he had to defend the ASSU against such aspersions. Reason or cowardice eventually prevailed, for the minister found excuses to delay the confrontation, which Ryan interpreted as merely a "bluf game." Days passed, and Ryan fashioned this situation into one of biblical proportions. Here was his opportunity to "slay Goliath the Philistine champion." As he wrote, "I had my sling and pebbles ready, and that I intended to continue to pray that the God of Israle might direct the pebble of truth to the heads and hearts of all opposers to truth." Probably both men were relieved that blood was never shed. Instead of a duel, they met to debate the merits of union Sunday schools; naturally Ryan felt that he emerged triumphant. According to his account, his Sunday school ultimately gained new members, and the minister lost ground.[21]

Uncooperative pupils offered other challenges. Missionaries had high standards for the behavior they expected of Sunday school students, and disappointment was inevitable when restless, ill-mannered children and adolescents did not conform to their expectations. Chaos was the order of the day in William Bulkley's Louisville Sunday school; he described his pupils as "boys and girls of the roughest type." Whistling, talking, playing, shouting, and shooting spit wads characterized one class. Bulkley stationed a policeman outside the door, which he locked in order to keep his pupils in and troublemakers out. When the teacher could not control the class, Bulkley had to intervene. He admitted that the situation was the worst he had ever witnessed; for the first time in his thirty-five years of Sunday school work, he could not command his students' attention.

21. G. W. Ryan to the ASSU, 30 May, 18 July, and 28 July 1870, Rose Hill, Miss., ASSU Correspondence, PHS. The original spelling is retained.

Realizing that further effort was fruitless, he unbolted the classroom door, and the students rushed "pell mell out of the room." Yet Bulkley was not discouraged. In fact, he "felt a stronger inducement to labor the more worthless the subject." After several weeks, the pupils began to settle down and learn their lessons. Missionaries usually assumed that such unruly students came from homes with inept or uncaring adults, or parents who regarded the Sunday school merely as a place to deposit their kids once a week.[22]

Financial matters played a key role in defining how and where an organization conducted its Sunday school work, reflecting the central role that economic concerns played in the Sunday school movement. ASSU reports and letters reveal how contributions affected the number of missionaries in the field and where the organization focused its attention. Although purportedly acting in the name of God and reaching out to uplift the religiously destitute, missionary associations and churches also had to find opportunities to raise money and sell more publications. Like other religious groups working in the region, the ASSU continually sought additional funding to support its efforts. Necessary expenditures—missionaries' salaries and travel expenses, the rent or mortgage on office space, and the cost of printing and distributing free or inexpensive Sunday school literature—could drain a budget.

District Secretary John McCullagh proved a master at raising money. In fact, financial issues appeared to be foremost on his mind, or at least foremost in his correspondence. He constantly solicited donations and bequests to aid his district. Due to his efforts, for example, Mrs. Henrietta Parker of Connecticut willed two hundred dollars to the ASSU to organize Sunday schools for freedmen in Georgia and to supply them with Bibles and testaments. McCullagh envisioned the South as a place with great potential for contributions, despite the fact that so many southerners were impoverished. He ably masked economic concerns behind a guise of Christian goodwill, confining mercenary comments to his private correspondence. In describing the ASSU's work among southerners, McCullagh wrote, "I am into their hearts by helping them in this cloudy and dark day, and after a while we will get into their purses, *no doubt of that.*" The very basis of Sunday school work was a bet on future

---

22. William Bulkley to Maurice A. Wurts, 1 October and 1 November 1870, Louisville, Ky., ASSU Correspondence, PHS.

rewards, and McCullagh believed that with patience, he could eventually mine the South for significant financial support.[23]

Any opportunity to raise money influenced McCullagh's actions. He even joined missionaries in the field when he saw an opportunity to solicit funds. In 1867, McCullagh traveled to North Carolina to help ASSU missionary Jonathan Marsh raise money for Sunday school work. Before he began his trip, McCullagh described his philosophy of fund raising. To "make people feel a permanent interest in any good cause you must get them to *feel in their pockets*," he wrote. "We always think *more* of what we pay for." The possibility of receiving financial assistance from a particular area dictated where he positioned his missionaries, causing McCullagh at one point to defend a seemingly hasty decision to place an agent in Texas. "One very important point is that money is plenty in Texas now," he responded to someone who questioned his action. When McCullagh discovered a Kentucky minister promoting denominational Sunday schools, he made him an honorary member of the ASSU in order to "hold him" and obtain a hundred-dollar donation from his church. In 1875, upon learning that wealthy New Yorkers were settling in east Tennessee, McCullagh suggested sending missionary Isaac Emory there because, as a former New Yorker, Emory could readily solicit contributions by relating personally to potential benefactors. In another instance, a widow's substantial contribution was promised for union Sunday schools in Virginia. This prompted McCullagh to relocate John Legare, who was doing excellent work in a South Carolina district, to the Old Dominion. Unfortunately, the woman withdrew her support, and McCullagh fumed that she "has been *trapped* into denomination work for the South, and is now hopelessly lost."[24]

Patience and sensitivity were essential to fund raising. McCullagh spent ten years wooing another wealthy widow, Mrs. Lapsley, who finally agreed to pay the annual salary of an ASSU missionary in the South. In return, she asked to read that individual's monthly field reports. Perhaps due to a shortage of experienced missionaries, McCullagh had no choice but to pick Brother Barry, despite the poor quality of his written

23. John McCullagh to Maurice A. Wurts, 14 August 1867, Henderson, Ky., ASSU Correspondence, PHS.

24. John McCullagh, 14 August 1867, Henderson, Ky.; John McCullagh, 7 June 1875, Louisville, Ky.; John McCullagh, 9 November 1870, 28 January, 2 February 1869, Henderson, Ky.; all to Maurice A. Wurts, ASSU Correspondence, PHS.

correspondence. McCullagh announced that he would send Barry's comments to Mrs. Lapsley, but only after they were "revised, remodeled or in other words, a good letter made out of each." As he wrote a colleague, "I positively *forbid* their *being sent until they were so prepared.*" McCullagh saw Barry's appointment as a temporary solution, and hoped to find a "better man for her." Careful action was critical, for his desire was to "get her interested in our work so as to secure a legacy from her some day."[25]

Budgetary matters affected not just the ASSU, but all northern religious organizations as they expanded their influence and conducted Christian work in the South. To take one example, the ATS "Instructions of the Executive Committee" debated whether to sell or distribute free copies of its literature to individuals and Sunday schools. Not surprisingly, the organization decided that charging for books was the preferred path, but it disguised any profit motive by claiming that books "are usually more valued than when given." It urged agents to use "all proper means" to effect more sales. ATS missionaries were never to give away expensively bound books and were to refrain from "lavish or unwise distribution." If any book was to be given away gratis, it should only be a "small volume."[26]

Financial issues also affected missionaries in the field. Tennessee ASSU agent Isaac Emory grumbled that southerners in his district usually opened their arms to him whenever they wanted a new Sunday school and free publications, but "if they have a dollar to spend for books, they will buy only their own denominational books." Several months later, he fretted that more generous missionaries were attracting customers and cutting into his profits. Nevertheless, dispensing advice and free or inexpensive literature to needy southerners gave northern organizations an edge. Jaded ASSU field worker Adam Reeder knew how to account for his success in the South. "There is but few in this part of the Country of the common people," he wrote his supervisor, "that knows or cares much about what sort of Sunday school they have [just] so it will keep their children off from home on Sunday so that they won't bother them,

---

25. John McCullagh, 18 October 1867, Louisville, Ky., to Maurice A. Wurts, ASSU Correspondence, PHS.

26. American Tract Society, "Instructions of the Executive Committee, 1868," *The American Tract Society Documents, 1824–1925* (New York: Arno Press, 1972), 40.

that is, if it does not cost any thing." Effective Sunday school work demanded dedicated workers and an organization with deep pockets.[27]

Northern missionaries, like Yankee schoolteachers who came South, made major efforts to recruit freed people and organize Sunday schools for them. The task was obvious—to educate and uplift the South's black population, using Yankee expertise and resources. Many agents saw freed people as "sheep without shepherds," and they knew exactly who those shepherds should be. Northerners assumed that they could be more effective in dealing with blacks than could former slaveholders, many of whom had difficulty accepting the idea that blacks were legally free and equal under the U.S. Constitution. Moreover, the hundreds of thousands of black children in the South offered seemingly infinite opportunities for missionary work. Northerners didn't question the assumption that most African Americans lacked the religious guidelines and the middle-class values necessary to function effectively in a free world. Sunday school was the place to help them develop character, learn good manners, and gain a grounding in Scripture. African American youngsters who attended their Sunday lessons faithfully might be able to fashion their own future, become respectable citizens, and occupy a meaningful place in the South.[28]

By the 1870s, thousands of black and white preachers, lay teachers, and missionaries went to the South to organize churches, day schools, and Sunday schools for freed people. Driven by duty, guilt, and Christian benevolence, well-intentioned agents sought to prepare freed people for life in the South. However troubled northern missionaries were by the appalling living conditions of blacks, or by the acts of racism and violence perpetrated by southern whites against blacks, they never encouraged freed people to come North and begin life anew. The idea was to

---

27. Isaac Emory, 2 March 1867, 1 August 1867, Knoxville, Tenn., both to Maurice A. Wurts; Adam Reeder to John McCullagh, 19 January 1875, Barbourville, Ky.; all in ASSU Correspondence, PHS. For background on northern philanthropy and missionary work, see Henry Farnham May, *Protestant Churches and Industrial America* (New York: Harper, 1949; reprint, New York: Octagon Books, 1963). For information on the ASSU and its financial concerns, see Boylan, *Sunday School*, 61–77.

28. As an example, see the Rev. G. Wilson McPhail to H. A. Boardman, 26 December 1867, Davidson, N.C., McPhail Correspondence, North Carolina State Archives, Raleigh, N.C. The work of missionaries and teachers often overlapped. See Jones, *Soldiers of Light and Love*; Peter Kolchin, *First Freedom: The Responses of Alabama Blacks to Emancipation and Reconstruction* (Westport, Conn.: Greenwood Press, 1972), 112–5.

improve their lives in the South. By focusing on ideas of racial uplift and Christian ideals, Sunday schools seemed a promising means to reach and influence southern blacks—on home turf.

Initially, northern missionaries working among former slaves faced little competition from white southerners, who exhibited less interest in the faith of freed people than they had before the Civil War. Since African Americans were no longer their property, most southern whites felt little responsibility for their souls. Many whites welcomed their departure from white churches after the Civil War. Though white southerners waxed enthusiastic about the importance of Sunday school and its role in exposing blacks to Christian ideals and in creating a more godly society, they had more pressing problems to handle than their former slaves. As an ASSU missionary in Texas observed in 1869, whites in his district avoided any involvement in the secular and spiritual instruction of blacks. "Since they have been freed no one troubles themselves about them," he wrote; "the prejudice against teaching them is so great that my heart faints at the thought of undertaking the work." His endeavors on behalf of black Sunday schools apparently created hardly a stir. Though his comment may have been somewhat self-serving, other whites expressed similar sentiments. Arkansas Baptists admitted that they had been too preoccupied with their own problems to help blacks establish their own churches or Sunday schools. Northern Methodist Erasmus Fuller claimed that southern blacks now appeared "waylaid, beaten and left beaten and half dead," for "scarcely a Samaritan hand has been extended to bind up their wounds or alleviate their distresses." Such a dramatic assessment may have encouraged others to come to their rescue.[29]

Northern missionary organizations and churches became actively involved in organizing and supporting hundreds of black Sunday schools. As black and white missionaries tried to assist former slaves, competition grew rapidly. Beyond teaching reading and exposing children to the Bible, missionary societies supported schools by donating money, Bibles, books, lesson plans, and periodicals, and by assisting officers and teachers as they set about their work. By 1872, white northern Methodists had

---

29. H. Bell to Maurice A. Wurts, 15 April 1869, Chambers Creek, Tex., ASSU Correspondence, PHS; "Negro Work," *Proceedings of the 52nd Annual Meeting of the Arkansas Baptist State Convention, 1900,* 47; Erasmus Fuller, "Our Southern Field," *Methodist Quarterly Review* 60 (April 1878): 228.

more than seventy-five missionaries working in southern states, with many focusing their attention on African Americans. Among the various denominations, the northern Methodist Episcopal Church (MEC) made by far the greatest effort to work with both races and welcome blacks into its churches and Sunday schools. ASSU missionary W. H. Ruffner was delighted that his own organization was working among this "most suffering field," since he felt that few black people were "competent to take any part in the conduct of colored Sunday schools." Though Ruffner's sense of racial superiority was evident, he nonetheless urged the ASSU to cooperate with other missionary groups and to organize black Sunday schools, a concept that apparently garnered little support. AMA and ABHMS agents traveled throughout the South to establish weekday and Sunday schools, as well as churches, for blacks. For a while at least, the field seemed crowded with northern field workers. Thomas W. Stringer, an AME missionary working in Mississippi and Louisiana, felt overwhelmed by the number of individuals engaged in this work. "The Mississippi Valley is now thronged with agents of other churches, who are leaving no stone unturned to unsettle the minds of our people concerning our Church," he fussed.[30]

African Americans initially welcomed the assistance of white northern missionaries. And northerners rightly assumed that blacks appreciated their help. An ATS agent assured his home office that southern blacks "are very grateful to the Society for the books." This assistance sustained

---

30. W. H. Ruffner to Maurice A. Wurts, 21 December 1875, Richmond, Va., ASSU Correspondence, PHS; Thomas W. Stringer, "Missionary Work in the South-West," *Christian Recorder*, 6 April 1867. For background on northern Methodists, see Henry Fox, "Our Work at the South," *Methodist Quarterly Review* 56 (January 1874): 29–45, and Morrow, *Northern Methodism and Reconstruction*, 127–35. See also Loren Schweninger, "The American Missionary Association and Northern Philanthropy in Reconstruction Alabama," *Alabama Historical Quarterly* 32 (fall and winter 1970): 129–56; Larry Wesley Pearce, "The American Missionary Association and the Freedmen in Arkansas, 1863–1878," *Arkansas Historical Quarterly* 30 (1971): 123–44; Charles Lincoln White, *A Century of Faith* (Philadelphia: ABHMS by the Judson Press, 1932), 105–6; J. A. Whitted, *A History of the Negro Baptists of North Carolina* (Raleigh: Edward and Broughton, 1908), 24–32; James D. Tyms, *The Rise of Religious Education among Negro Baptists: A Historical Case Study* (New York: Exposition Press, 1965), 148–51; Joe M. Richardson, *Christian Reconstruction: The American Missionary Association and Southern Blacks, 1861–1890* (Athens: University of Georgia Press, 1986). Christopher Owen argues that negative responses from southern whites and debate within the Northern Methodist church caused it to disband its biracial endeavors. See Owen, *Sacred Flame of Love*, 128.

many black Sunday schools well into the twentieth century, often fostering the very loyalty that northern whites sought to maintain. A number of black Baptists remained loyal to the ABPS long after they established their own publishing house and denomination. Though African Americans may have been wary of white intentions, they needed help and wasted little time worrying where it came from. AME Bishop Ward was grateful for everything his denomination received. "Many thousands of our white friends are doing all they can to atone for the past," he observed, and saw no need to question such largesse.[31]

Many southern blacks welcomed AME and AMEZ missionaries and were delighted to join a well-established black denomination and send their children to its Sunday schools. Yet others were cautious. While on the surface there might seem to be good reasons to trust northern representatives of their own race, some blacks were wary. Indeed, problems arose to undermine that initial trust. Some northern blacks, having lived as free people and having achieved greater prosperity than recently freed slaves, couldn't help but express a superior attitude toward their destitute, less mannerly brethren in the South. When southern blacks tried to establish their own churches and Sunday schools, they found themselves competing with northern black denominations. Some AME and AMEZ agents considered anything fair game, and the strong-armed tactics they used to confiscate southern black church properties left freedmen feeling betrayed. Leaders of both churches were anything but charitable toward the newly formed CME church because it retained close ties to white Southern Methodists and was less political and more rural in character. Southern blacks viewed some AME and AMEZ missionaries as overly aggressive for laying claim to their resources, church properties, and the souls of their children. Though race united them, each black denomination seemed determined to dominate southern church and Sunday school life.[32]

While white northern missionaries regarded Sunday school work

31. "The Colored Population," *47th Annual Report of the American Tract Society, 1872* (New York: ATS, 1872), 69; Bishop Ward, "Our Condition in the South," *Christian Recorder*, 16 October 1873.

32. Joe M. Richardson, *Dark Salvation: The Story of Methodism As It Developed among Blacks in America* (New York: Doubleday, 1976), 193–8; William J. Walls, *The African Methodist Episcopal Zion Church: Reality of the Black Church* (Charlotte, N.C.: AMEZ Publishing House, 1974), 185; Sernett, *Bound for the Promised Land*, 92.

among freedmen as an important endeavor, they soon discovered that by working among African Americans, they undermined their relationship with southern whites and jeopardized their position in the white community. Many Yankee missionaries naively assumed that they could work amicably with both races, unaware of, or indifferent to, southern white racial sentiments. Northerners found themselves walking a fine line between meeting the needs of blacks and not offending whites. As ASSU missionary James Buchanan warned, "Wherever you begin work among the Negroes, you lose *your influence* among the whites." ASSU missionary John Eastman reported that a Methodist minister from Maine, who was preaching to southern blacks and boarding in their homes, found that local white ministers shunned him completely, claiming his intimacies went too far. In another instance, after several blacks in Little Rock, Arkansas, begged ASSU missionary Samuel Stevenson to organize a Sunday school for their children, he initiated efforts to do so. More astute than most of his colleagues, Stevenson first consulted a white community leader about the project, only to report that he was "grossly" insulted and ordered "to go and attend to your own business." Female missionaries faced a more delicate situation, as AMA missionary Sarah Jane Foster discovered. She taught in both a public school and a Sunday school in Martinsburg, West Virginia, and became close friends with some of her black male pupils. After one walked her home after class, tongues began wagging about her inappropriate behavior. The AMA hastily transferred Foster to another location.[33]

Other reasons help explain northern success in founding southern Sunday schools. An organization's involvement in the South prior to the Civil War eased northern efforts in the postwar period, for southerners then had tangible proof that Sunday school missionaries were interested in spreading God's word and doing good work. Representatives of northern religious organizations like the AMA, ASSU, ATS, and ABS had peddled religious material during the antebellum and Civil War periods and had proselytized their Christian message. Another reason was the apolitical stance adopted by northern missionary organizations. Aware of white

---

33. James Buchanan, 15 October 1875, Elkton, Ky.; John Eastman, 29 July 1875, Newnanville, Fla.; Samuel Stevenson, 14 July 1868, Little Rock, Ark.; all to Maurice A. Wurts, ASSU Correspondence, PHS; Foster, *Sarah Jane Foster,* xii, 80. Some missionary organizations began to appoint more black teachers to freedmen schools.

southern sensitivities toward Yankees after the Civil War, northern officials insisted that their agents adopt an impartial, apolitical stance to avoid negative reactions. This approach served them well and enabled agents to work in the South without arousing much suspicion. ASSU missionary C. W. Charlton claimed that his society's neutrality during the Civil War "was one of its crowning glories, and did more to commend itself to the sympathy and confidence of the southern people than anything in all its past history." Waxing passionate, he continued, "with this unsullied prestige, it was in a condition to weep over those desolate and dispirited states and to soothe and calm the perturbed elements of that crushed and broken-hearted people." During the antebellum period, northern missionaries working in the South had skirted the volatile subject of slavery. Now they ignored issues that might remind southerners of the war's outcome.[34]

In fact, northern religious organizations censured their agents if public utterances stirred local passions or appeared unduly critical of the South and its people. One missionary noted that he never used the word "freedmen" when speaking to white southerners. Agents were cautious in uttering any critical remarks about the South, though an 1867 article in the ASSU's *Sunday School World* mentioned an unfortunate incident during the Civil War that unleashed a spate of southern outrage. When ASSU District Supervisor John McCullagh learned about the article, he exploded: negative comments should not have found their way into an ASSU publication. Editors were supposed to scrutinize all printed material before publication to ensure that they did not offend southerners. As McCullagh reminded his superior following this incident, "We must be wise as serpents and harmless as doves" and treat southerners with care. During the unsettled years of Reconstruction, the ASSU had to "pour oil" on potentially volatile issues. McCullagh urged his agents to work with southerners in a "loving, forgiving, and forgetting spirit." Repayment would come, he felt, when southerners realized that the ASSU was their best friend. Sectional bias or condescending remarks could undo all its good work and make it impossible for missionaries to penetrate the South.[35]

34. C. W. Charlton to Maurice A. Wurts, 7 November 1867, Caledonia, Mo., ASSU Correspondence, PHS. See also Avery, *Behold the Child,* 113; Boylan, *Sunday School,* 83.
35. W. P. Paxson, 21 October 1867, St. Charles, Mo., and John McCullagh, 18 October 1867, Louisville, Ky., both to Maurice A. Wurts, ASSU Correspondence, PHS. The article that upset McCullagh was "Gleanings from the Sunday School Field" in the October

Even the most skeptical southerner must have sensed the dedication and enthusiasm that many Yankee missionaries brought to their job. A black missionary in Virginia, William Harris, instructed some 225 students in two Sunday schools each week; his brother Robert assumed similar duties in North Carolina. Agents could scarcely hide their excitement when their efforts benefited needy communities, especially those that had been untouched by any Christian institution. In one report, Isaac Emory described his two-year effort that finally resulted in the opening of a union Sunday school. His hard work paid off, and the school soon boasted nearly a hundred pupils. Other missionaries pointed to Sabbath schools they founded that now had three to four times as many pupils as when the doors first opened. The growing number of youthful conversions among Sunday school pupils seemed to be tangible evidence that southerners were becoming pious and civilized. Many northern missionaries and colporteurs labored for decades in the field and truly enjoyed their work. During his tenure in Missouri, ASSU missionary Stephen Paxson claimed to have organized some 1,300 Sunday schools that welcomed 60,000 new pupils. Isaac Emory worked in Tennessee for thirty years, opening 1,010 schools and attracting as many students as Paxson. A hearty soul in Georgia, T. W. Dimmock, labored as a missionary for four decades.[36]

Earning the gratitude of a community cheered a missionary and proved that his work had made a difference. It was heartening to bring God's message to the needy. "At no time have I seen so much interest manifested as is now being manifested on the subject of Sunday schools," reported a delighted A. E. Jenkins in 1868. ASSU missionary C. W. Charl-

---

1867 issue of *Sunday School World*. Gaines Foster also argues that many southerners were quite gracious toward Yankees if northerners treated them with some respect—which many did. See Gaines Foster, *Ghosts of the Confederacy: Defeat, the Lost Cause, and the Emergence of the New South, 1865–1913* (New York: Oxford University Press, 1987), 33.

36. Earle H. West, "The Harris Brothers: Black Northern Teachers in the Reconstruction South," in Donald G. Nieman, ed., *African Americans and Education in the South, 1865–1900*, vol. 10, *African-American Life in the Post-Emancipation South* (London: Garland Publishing, 1994), 394–406 (quote on 399); Isaac Emory to Maurice Wurts, 8 October 1870, Knoxville, Tenn., ASSU Correspondence, PHS; Belle Paxson Drury, *A Fruitful Life: A Narrative of the Experiences and Missionary Labors of Stephen Paxson* (Philadelphia: ASSU, 1882), 160. Rice includes a list of missionaries who founded at least 1,000 Sunday schools. Most of them worked in the South. See Rice, *Sunday School Movement*, 461–2, 477.

ton observed a "glowing spirit of enthusiasm" among those with whom he worked. G. S. Jones, traveling through the mountains of western North Carolina, encountered people who met him with open arms. "I find a welcome wherever I go," he gushed. Though unable to hide a sense of superiority, the Reverend W. J. W. Crowder expressed enormous pleasure in his work, for he was "kindling gospel light in the sun-darkened hearts and dismal hovels in North Carolina."[37]

Northern missionaries proved effective messengers, especially when they overcame sin or convinced known skeptics to send their children to Sunday school. An ATS agent, "R. T. J.," heard rumors about a community filled with wickedness, and he was warned to stay out unless armed. Instead of carrying a gun, he armed himself with tracts and Bibles, distributed them to local citizens, and organized a Sunday school and church. Soon he presided over a large, sober congregation, proving to him that Christianity could overcome the devil himself. Even better was G. S. Jones's report on the situation two months later. Jones wrote, "I am pleased to know that although heretofore the current seemed to run strongly in the *sectarian* channel, there is now a manifest tendency towards the *ASSU*." G. Harrison Gray, working in Atlanta, reported that he founded a Sunday school in the midst of a neighborhood of Hardshell Baptists. Despite that sect's opposition to Sabbath schools, one father admitted to Gray that his children were quietly attending and benefiting from Sunday lessons. Missionaries found deep satisfaction in overcoming opposition or convincing parents that a Sunday school was in their children's best interest.[38]

In light of these challenges, it may seem surprising that northern Sunday school missionaries achieved success in the post–Civil War South. Southerners could have treated all Yankees with outright hostility and driven northern agents from their community. Considering white southerners' antipathy toward northerners—sentiments strengthened by the

37. A. E. Jenkins, 3 August 1868, Halifax County, N.C.; C. W. Charlton, 17 June 1868, Caledonia, Mo.; G. S. Jones, 8 October 1868, Hendersonville, N.C.; all to Maurice Wurts, ASSU Correspondence, PHS; "Richmond Agency," *44th Annual Report of the American Tract Society, 1869* (New York: ATS, 1869), 81.

38. "Extreme Cases Reached," *47th Annual Report of the American Tract Society, 1872* (New York: ATS, 1872), 66; G. S. Jones, 14 December 1868, Hendersonville, N.C., and G. Harrison Gray, 5 March 1869, Atlanta, Ga., both to Maurice A. Wurts, ASSU Correspondence, PHS.

war and Reconstruction—missionaries did remarkably well. Their efforts, in some respects, resembled the work of others who came South after 1865 to engage in the economic, social, and political reconstruction of the region. Yet unlike some politicians and businessmen, Sunday school missionaries were not labeled "carpetbaggers," or at least this was not noted in their correspondence. Nor did many face the social ostracism and insults that northern schoolteachers experienced. And unlike the comments found in letters and reports from Yankee teachers who worked among freedmen, most Sunday school missionaries made little mention of outright opposition to their work. Though agents sometimes were victims of southerners' disparaging words or indifference, the majority carried on Sunday school work with surprisingly little hassle.[39]

It is easy to assume that a conflict as divisive and bloody as the Civil War fostered such a deep southern hostility toward northerners that it would take decades to erase. But the founding of southern Sunday schools illustrates an instance of how victors can treat the vanquished with magnanimity, and how the defeated respond to offers of charitable help. In this case, missionaries saw the South as a golden opportunity to spread the Christian faith and create a market for their religious literature. Most southerners welcomed, not resisted, Yankee efforts to found Sunday schools because the institution brought so many benefits to the region. Southern church leaders might decry northern involvement in the region's faith, but those most directly affected by Sunday schools felt otherwise. They wanted and needed what northern missionaries brought them. As historian Gaines Foster states, "most white southerners . . . were far too realistic to let bitter memories get in the way of rebuilding their society." In the immediate postwar period, southern churches were unable to provide all that people needed. The success of northern agents also reflected the fact that individuals, North and South, embraced simi-

---

39. Henry Swint argues that northern teachers who came south encountered sneers, social ostracism, and insults from white southerners. Teaching blacks to read and write was a more threatening endeavor than uplifting youngsters through Sunday schools. Southern whites feared that in day schools, Yankees could easily influence southern blacks. Unlike Yankee teachers, missionaries were constantly on the move. Once they established a Sunday school, they set out for new territory. This worked in their favor since their presence had little time to generate much antagonism. And when opposition mounted, they could leave the community and work where they were welcome. See Swint, *The Northern Teacher*, 95, 106–7.

lar dreams, and many shared common religious values, making it less difficult to transcend divisiveness in the aftermath of war. Southerners knew a good thing for their children when they saw it.[40]

Northern missionaries were welcome because they offered what churches and communities needed: advice, organizational skills, free or inexpensive Bibles and Sunday school literature, financial support, and inspiration. Outside resources were essential to uplift their children's lives; many southerners were too exhausted, depressed, or impoverished to undertake extensive Sunday school work on their own. The Christian institutions that northerners established in the South were far more palatable than most of the legal, political, and economic changes imposed under federal Reconstruction. African Americans felt that missionaries often had their interests at heart and were sympathetic to their situation. Southerners who desired a Christian education for their children concluded that it was more important to have their offspring in Sunday school than quibble over who was conducting this good work.[41]

Northern missionaries actually likened their endeavors to a spiritual reconstruction of the South. In confronting this destitute region and trying to uplift it, agents saw themselves as emboldened ambassadors and were convinced that Christianity was the triumphant force that would heal sectional wounds and reunite the nation. As ABS missionaries insisted, "Providence has plainly ordered that we shall be one people, with one government, one civilization, one Bible, one Christian faith and destiny." ABS agent Edwin Bolles, aware of deep divisions between northern and southern denominations, believed his organization could resolve these misunderstandings. "Thank God the American Bible Society is doing all it can to unite Northern and southern Christians," he wrote. The institution that would best deliver this Christian message and help reunite North and South by healing the gaping wounds born of their conflict was the Sunday school.[42]

---

40. Foster, *Ghosts of the Confederacy*, 5; Silber, *Romance of Reunion*, 45, 56. Northern denominations hoped to reunite their churches after the Civil War, but southern church leaders rejected the idea. See Buck, *Road to Reunion*, 61–2.

41. My findings support Gaines Foster, who sees southerners as realists not allowing bad memories to stand in the way of rebuilding their lives. See Foster, *Ghosts of the Confederacy*, 5, 22, 33, and Stowell, *Rebuilding Zion*, 57.

42. Joseph Holdich and William J. R. Taylor, "The American Bible Society and the South," *American Bible Society History* (New York: ABS, 1865); Edwin A. Bolles to W. J. R. Taylor, 20 April 1869, Columbia, S.C., Edwin A. Bolles Collection, ABS.

To northern missionaries, their efforts were far more effective than any political or economic endeavors. "For in what so hopeful way can our efforts for the restoration of harmony and union between North and South be directed, as in these Christian labours for the children of the South by the American Sunday School Union?" intoned John McCullagh in 1866. He and others well understood southerners' anxieties about their children. "The only hope I have in this great work of reconstruction," added Isaac Emory, "is in reaching after the young and educating them to fully understand their obligations to government; both civil and *Divine.*" Northern missionaries hoped—even expected—that white southerners would accept their views and institutions, recognize the errors of their past, and seek an end to the schism that had divided the three major white Protestant denominations since before the Civil War. The ultimate goal was to put all youngsters in the hands of God. The religious rebirth of the South, especially of its children, seemed possible under the guidance of its former enemy.[43]

Whatever the agenda, northern efforts made a difference, providing the impetus that initiated the southern Sunday school movement and set the South in a direction to restore and strengthen its sense of faith. Some southerners recognized these religious benefits. As a former North Carolina governor commented about the ASSU, "One missionary has done more for the true interests of our State, than has been accomplished by all the politicians in and out of the state legislature since the close of the War." Missionaries' approach during the years of Reconstruction, with their focus on faith, community, church, and Sunday school, was an important—and certainly one of the more successful—northern response to this difficult and chaotic period. Southerners were needy enough to allow Yankees to intervene in and influence their religious lives, at least for now.[44]

---

43. John McCullagh, "The Southern District," *42nd Annual Report of the ASSU* (Philadelphia: ASSU, 1866), 68; Isaac Emory to Maurice A. Wurts, 26 February 1868, Knoxville, Tenn., ASSU correspondence, PHS. On the South as a frontier for missionary work, see Luker, *The Social Gospel in Black and White;* Richardson, *Christian Reconstruction;* Stowell, *Rebuilding Zion.*

44. Quote by G. S. Jones in John McCullagh, "Southern District," *50th Annual Report of the ASSU* (Philadelphia: ASSU, 1874).

3

Reclaiming Our Children's Souls

Like northern missionaries, southern evangelicals were convinced that Sunday schools were vital to uplifting their children's lives and enhancing the region's future. In the immediate post–Civil War period, however, southern churches lacked both the institutional framework and the financial support to undertake Sunday school work on a widespread scale. This meant that for several years after the war, southern individuals, churches, and communities usually acted on their own to organize Sunday schools, with little advice or support from regional religious organizations.

As a result, southerners' efforts to establish Sunday schools during the immediate postbellum years were often personal and informal. Typically, an enterprising individual organized a class, devising his or her own teaching methods and purchasing or borrowing classroom materials. Some Sunday schools started with only a handful of students; others boasted several dozen youngsters on opening day. The meeting place depended on whatever available space a teacher could find, and he or she selected the lesson topic and Scripture readings.

Southern women played a major role in founding many of these Sunday schools. Postwar conditions spurred them to take action. As one woman queried, "Shall we, the women of the South, the descendants of noble Christian matrons, sink in listless despondency or waste our years in vain lamentations?" Apparently not. Many southern women gathered together their own children and neighborhood youngsters for weekly Bible lessons. Like the work they undertook in other benevolent endeavors, they felt responsible for improving their homes and communities. Their social and volunteer efforts moved them beyond the traditional domestic sphere and into the public arena. Organizing Sunday schools was a natural outlet for their energies, because the work earned public approval by falling within the acceptable parameters of southern women's pious and maternal concerns. In fact, female involvement in Sunday schools reinforced southerners' perception of women as Christian nurturers of the young. Females organized hundreds, if not thousands, of southern Sunday schools.[1]

Examples of southern female initiative abound. Every summer, Mrs. Jenkins of Caton's Grove, Tennessee, held a Baptist Sunday school in her home for some forty destitute children. She taught the class and recruited her husband to open the weekly sessions with a prayer. An African American servant, Jane Glenn, wrote thanking her former mistress for giving her a Bible and teaching her to read. "I have in sunday school eight schoolers last Sunday. I will have mor to me I can tech them all," Glenn wrote proudly. At the age of thirteen, Esther Trevino, niece of a San Antonio evangelist, organized a Sunday school for Mexican children and single-handedly raised money to purchase classroom chairs and Sunday school literature.[2]

As a natural and beneficial outgrowth of their Sunday school work, female teachers also tackled social ills. A Texas woman found that the

---

1. Quote in Beth Barton Schweiger, "The Transformation of Southern Religion: Clergy and Congregations in Virginia, 1830–1895." (Ph.D. diss., University of Virginia, 1994), 362. Female benevolence during this period has received wide scholarly attention. See Turner, *Women, Culture, and Community;* Scott, *Natural Allies;* Janette Thomas Greenwood, *Bittersweet Legacy: The Black and White "Better Classes" in Charlotte, 1850–1910* (Chapel Hill: University of North Carolina Press, 1994); Ginzberg, *Women and the Work of Benevolence;* Higginbotham, *Righteous Discontent.*

2. Mrs. Jenkins reported by W. B. Graves to John McCullagh, 24 December 1870, Lee Valley, Tenn., ASSU Correspondence, PHS; Jane Glenn to Miss Mattie, 29 May 1869, Calvin Henderson Wiley Collection, ABS; E. Trevino, "In the San Marcos Field," *Missionary Survey* (March 1914): 188.

Sabbath class she started had a positive effect on her entire community, for the "keeper of a grog-shop (or doggery) in the vicinity of the Sunday school, has been induced to abandon his business and engage in farming." When her husband died, Mrs. V. K. Glenn of Ironaton, Alabama, organized a Sunday school for her two sons. She worried when other boys asked to join because many of them were known gamblers. With the aid of a CME minister, a determined Glenn set to work and soon boasted that her pupils had discarded their former bad habits and "all those sinners were added to the different churches." Women also set up mission Sunday schools to reach the region's neediest, and their actions sometimes resulted in the founding of a new church. Laura Haygood of Atlanta organized two mission Sunday schools in that city, and both developed into thriving Methodist churches.[3]

Southern men also organized Sunday schools, usually in their official capacity as a minister or missionary. Ministers or male volunteers might travel miles to seek advice from a northern missionary on how to establish and run a community Sunday school. During his seventy-four years as a Methodist minister, James V. M. Morris organized countless Sunday schools for both black and white pupils. During his itinerant ministry in rural Georgia, John Baker founded Sunday schools and taught individual classes for sixteen years. This work brought special rewards to ministers, for it promised them a steady supply of potential church members as young Sunday school pupils grew up. As a church expanded and became more powerful, its minister ultimately reaped the benefits.[4] Like northern missionaries, southern laypeople, missionaries, and ministers assumed that anyone would benefit from the scriptural and moral edification provided in Sunday schools.

Sunday schools also were flexible in terms of their actual physical set-

3. "Sunday School Intelligence," *Earnest Worker*, 23 November 1871; Mrs. L. D. McAfee (Sara J.), *History of the Woman's Missionary Society in the Colored Methodist Episcopal Church* (1934; reprint, Phenix City, Ala.: Phenix City Herald, 1945), 81; Oswald Eugene Brown and Anna Muse Brown, eds., *Life and Letters of Laura Askew Haygood* (Nashville: Publishing House of the MECS, 1904), 68.

4. James V. M. Morris Diaries, 2 and 18 March, 27 July 1866, 17 June 1867; John W. Baker Diary, passim 1877–84, both in the Manuscript Department, Special Collections, Woodruff Library, Emory University (hereafter referred to as Emory). See also David M. Tucker, *Black Pastors and Leaders: Memphis, 1819–1972* (Memphis: Memphis State University Press, 1975), 8–9.

ting; almost any available spot would do. Mountain missionaries gathered children on grassy hillsides, in mountain shacks, under trees, or in open fields. One black Sabbath school met in a potato house throughout the summer and fall but had to disband when it was time to harvest and store the crop. A latitudinarian approach had its advantages, though it sometimes meant less than ideal conditions for both teachers and pupils. An AME Sunday school in Magnolia, Georgia, met in the brush, even though its 250 pupils shivered on cold days. Most often, classes met in the sanctuary or basement of a church, or in a private home, public schoolroom, or building in town. To committed evangelicals and needy communities, the presence of a Sunday school was too important to quibble over its precise location.[5]

Southerners founded Sunday schools wherever they felt the population warranted one. A Sunday school could be established almost anywhere—in town and country, in jails, penitentiaries, convict labor camps, schools for the deaf and blind, military training and mining camps, colleges and academies, mill towns, and orphanages. Penal institutions and orphanages proved to be especially popular settings. The Virginia Bible Society distributed religious tracts and supported Sunday schools in several state prisons. Hoping to expose convicts to Scripture and win them over to Christianity, the Virginia State Penitentiary established a Sunday school for inmates, and apparently its teachers witnessed several conversions. Orphanages were seen as a perfect setting for a Sunday school, since the children there lacked parental guidance and domestic religious instruction. College students throughout the South participated in Sunday school both as teachers and pupils, and many academic institutions mandated that students attend each week. If the South was to become a truly Christian region, no community or individual could be ignored.[6]

By the turn of the century, many mill villages throughout the southern Piedmont boasted at least one Sunday school. Where mill owners showed interest, missionaries and church agents found it easy to organize a school, since these communities had a well-defined population and a captive audience. The North Durham Pearl Cotton Mill had a Sunday school

---

5. Kirk Mariner, *Revival's Children: A Religious History of Virginia's Eastern Shore* (Salisbury, Md.: Peninsula Press, 1979), 160; R. H. W. Leak, "Church News," *AME Church Review* 2 (1885): 73; Moore, *The Country Sunday School*, 16–8.

6. "A State Institution," *Earnest Worker*, 28 June 1877; J. B. Link, *Texas Historical and Biographical Magazine, Designed to Give a Complete History of the Baptists of Texas*, vol. 2 (Austin: J. B. Link, 1892), 364.

for young female workers, thanks to outreach efforts by the minister and members of the First Church of Durham, North Carolina. At Cannonville, North Carolina, a Sunday school organized by a local preacher eventually led to the formation of a community church and the construction of a Sunday school building for its 220 members. Mill owners who supported and funded these schools believed that Sunday lessons exposed workers to Christianity and mitigated the grind of tedious labor. The financial investment was, in fact, negligible when compared to the benefits, for the presence of a Sunday school and public school in a mill village proved to be a strong draw to families to settle and work there.[7]

Mill owners also hoped that the lessons taught in Sunday schools would acculturate pupils and instill in them the character traits that would make them better laborers, including obedience, productivity, punctuality, and self-discipline—in short, a model workers' ethos. The thinking was that young workers who attended Sunday school would be more dutiful, honest, and God-fearing than those who did not. Yet mill owners did not encourage the foundation of Sunday schools out of mere self-interest. Certainly some owners saw the Sunday school as one means to fashion a more compliant labor force, but we also must remember that many parents desired similar behavior in their offspring. Mothers and fathers in mill towns wanted their youngsters to learn Scripture and absorb middle-class values, which were woven into the fabric of the Sunday school. Both mill owners and parents in southern mill villages saw the Sunday school as a positive influence on children.[8]

---

7. Mrs. James Day to James Marion Frost, 21 September 1897, Durham, N.C., Frost-Bell Correspondence, SBHLA; W. F. Stroud, Haw River Circuit, *Minutes of the North Carolina District Conference Reports of the MECS, 1884,* Duke.

8. Cathy McHugh calls this "profit maximizing behavior." See McHugh, *Mill Family: The Labor System in the Southern Cotton Textile Industry, 1880–1915* (New York: Oxford University Press, 1988), 57. See also Jacquelyn Hall et al., *"Like a Family": The Making of a Southern Cotton Mill World* (Chapel Hill: University of North Carolina Press, 1987), 124–6, 177–8; Boylan, *Sunday School,* 37–8; E. P. Thompson, *The Making of the English Working Class* (New York: Pantheon, 1964), 375–9; David L. Carlton, *Mill and Town in South Carolina, 1880–1920* (Baton Rouge: Louisiana State University Press, 1982), 183. Jennings J. Rhyne, who surveyed southern mill villages in the late 1920s, found that the majority of mill workers were religious: 70.9 percent of all mill workers over 14 years old were church members; 12 percent more women than men belonged to a church; 55.3 percent of all mill parents and 52 percent of all single persons 14 and older attended Sunday school. See Jennings J. Rhyne, *Some Southern Cotton Mill Workers and Their Villages* (Chapel Hill: University of North Carolina Press, 1930). Punctuality and time-

Town and village residents, convinced that the presence of a Sunday school would infuse their youngsters with spirituality and deliver an important message about their community's commitment to Christian living, sometimes undertook efforts to found one collectively. In May 1866, James Mallory met with other Talladega County, Alabama, residents to organize what became a thriving neighborhood Sunday school. Citizens of Georgia's Log Cabin Community outside Atlanta gathered to create a nondenominational Sunday school for their youngsters. "I knew it would never do to raise our children without the influence of a Sunday school," declared Mrs. O. B. Logan, one involved parent. Families there had tried to send their youngsters to Sunday school in nearby Smyrna but found the train schedule too erratic. At a community meeting, residents set up the Log Cabin Union Sunday School. They appointed a superintendent and teachers, drew up a constitution, and purchased a melodeon. The school opened with great fanfare. So successful was this undertaking that local citizens raised money and constructed a Sunday school building seven years later.[9]

Gradually, however, southerners' motivations for founding Sunday schools began to shift, or at least respond to what they increasingly saw as a troubling concern. Southerners were no longer anxious simply about their children's religious beliefs and behavior per se but worried that their children might fall into the hands of a "wrong" church. Southern adults believed that children were naively vulnerable to new ideas and thus could easily be attracted to a rival faith. It became imperative that southern churches establish their own Sunday schools to represent their own faith. As Texas Methodists cautioned, the church should never "turn the lambs over to strange shepherds." Only a denominational Sunday school would do, for "teaching which is not denominational is no teaching at all," warned North Carolina Baptist R. H. Griffith. Most children's exposure to Sunday school was no more than an hour or two a week, yet adults believed that the lessons children learned in Sunday school and the religious literature that they read there had lifelong ramifications. South-

---

consciousness, concepts associated with industrialization and a corporate mentality, have an interesting history in the antebellum South. See Mark M. Smith, *Mastered by the Clock: Time, Slavery, and Freedom in the American South* (Chapel Hill: University of North Carolina Press, 1998).

9. Mallory, *"Fear God and Walk Humbly"*, 361; "Log Cabin Community Sunday School: Memories of Twenty-Five Years," 1937, Emory.

ern evangelicals became convinced that they had to found and control their own Sunday schools and redeem the next generation on their own terms.[10]

In some places, religious rivalries seemed to overwhelm southern states. Missouri gained the reputation as a hotbed of competitive Sunday school work, as northern missionaries flocked there to labor on behalf of their various organizations and as southern denominations now began to establish a network of schools. Stephen Paxson, ASSU representative for Missouri, claimed that competition in that state was getting "hotter" and that sectarianism was "rampant." As he explained, "The spirit of sectarianism is growing so fast that any institution not connected with the 'church' is simply not tolerated. All the denominations here seem to be engaged in a general steeple chase after the most money, the most members, and influence and want all the funds their members have to carry out 'church' schemes in our little town." Disagreements divided denominations as well as communities, fostering uncharitable remarks and bad feelings, as hope for an inclusive, open spirit in Sunday school work in the South began to fade.[11]

Southerners' desire to control their children's spiritual lives was part of a larger context of redemption, as southern whites sought to drive northerners out of the South and reclaim their region. The last federal troops officially withdrew from the South in 1877, signaling an end to federal Reconstruction. Yet many southerners felt that this was not enough; they also had to deliver the region from northern religious influence. By founding Sunday schools on behalf of southern denominations, they could more effectively direct their children's religious upbringing. At the same time, some northern religious organizations (though by no means all), began to lose interest in the South and leave, turning their attention to more promising areas, such as the West. Other northern missionaries were finally beaten down by southern indifference, poverty, and growing resistance to outside help. This trend cut across color lines; northern white agents found that as freed people became more self-suffi-

---

10. "The Sunday School Board," *Minutes of the 25th Annual West Texas Northwest Conference of the Methodist Episcopal Church, South, 1890*, Duke; R. H. Griffith, "Sunday School Work in North Carolina," *Minutes of the Baptist State Sunday School Convention of North Carolina, 1874* (Raleigh: Edwards, Broughton, 1874), 31.

11. Stephen Paxson to Maurice A. Wurts, 14 September 1867, St. Louis, and 2 November 1869, St. Charles, Mo., ASSU Correspondence, PHS.

cient, some began to shun outside assistance and take charge of their own religious institutions.[12]

The spectacle of so many northern missionaries swarming through the South began to upset southerners, who saw these agents as outsiders trying to "steal" their children's souls. North Carolina Baptists spared neither language nor fury to denounce the enemy, labeling these agents as "wolves" and "false teachers" who were spreading "their pernicious and damnable heresies openly and blasphemously." Some of this invective undoubtedly reflected unresolved tensions over larger political, economic, and social issues that had long divided North and South. Yankee missionaries' success and self-righteousness may have intensified the backlash against them. The dramatic rhetoric of southern evangelicals drew people together against a common enemy and offered a compelling argument for southern Sunday schools. As denominations strengthened, a chorus of southerners insisted that their own churches undertake steps to found Sunday schools.[13]

The growing rivalry with and denouncements of northern missionaries moved beyond a struggle among Protestant faiths. Catholics and Mormons were also making a bid for southern children. As millions of immigrants—many of them Catholics from southern and eastern Europe—flocked to the United States in the late nineteenth century, Protestant Americans feared the newcomers' growing numbers. Though most immigrants settled in the North, Catholics were enough of a presence in several southern states to arouse hostility. In many places, Catholics aggressively engaged in evangelical work to recruit potential parishioners. Southern Protestants, who associated the Catholic Church with superstition and magic, railed against this Catholic assertiveness; they charged that Rome planned to extend its nefarious influence to the nation's political and social life. Virulent anti-Catholic sentiments surfaced. Southern evangelicals were determined to keep their region—especially their churches and Sunday schools—pure and Protestant. Impressionable young minds could be led astray by a Catholic just as easily as they could be attracted to another Protestant denomination.[14]

12. Harvey, *Redeeming the South*, 23; Stowell, *Rebuilding Zion*.
13. "Report on Sunday Schools," Eastern Baptist Association, *36th Annual Session of the Baptist Association of North Carolina* (Raleigh: Edwards, Broughton, 1880), 10.
14. See Randall M. Miller and Jon L. Wakelyn, eds., *Catholics in the Old South: Essays on Church and Culture* (Macon, Ga.: Mercer University Press, 1983), 18. Karen G.

For evangelicals, this fear of Catholicism served a useful purpose by energizing Sunday school workers and hastening efforts to prevent the papacy from capturing southern souls. ASSU District Supervisor John McCullagh could scarcely contain his fear of Catholicism. While he celebrated his own organization's efforts to educate southern children, he condemned Catholics who were engaged in similar pursuits, denouncing their determination to "possess the sunny South" as they lured youngsters into their churches and parochial schools. McCullagh urged his ASSU agents to outperform Catholic missionaries who were "making a *desperate* effort to get the whole system into their hands." An article in the *Tennessee Outlook* dubbed Catholics "America's great enemy" and warned readers of "crafty priests" who were engaged in a "gigantic political conspiracy" to kill all political and religious freedom. Americans needed to awaken to this "remorseless and sleepless enemy to God and man." To troubled evangelists, Roman Catholics were no idle threat.[15]

Yet many Sunday school workers seemed to worry more about Catholics' influence on blacks than on whites—or at least this concern generated more inflammatory rhetoric. An ABHMS missionary in the South warned that the Catholic Church planned to "draw to its fold the entire African race on the continent." ASSU missionary G. S. Jones urged his organization to do more work among southern blacks, for "if we can keep an open Bible in their hands, we may defy the efforts of Romanism." White Southern Baptists expected to see an army of priests and nuns teaching African Americans the "wretched superstitions and most mischievous dogmas of Rome." Protestant missionaries perhaps believed that blacks—unlike whites—were too naive to judge what faith best served their needs, and thus—like youngsters—were especially vulnerable to the lure of Catholicism. Yet, to the wary Protestant eye, there was solid evidence that Rome was gaining ground. Thousands of southern blacks attended Catholic churches. Catholics in southern cities like New Orleans, Mobile, Baltimore, and St. Augustine initiated education pro-

---

Zipf has argued that a goal of the AMA was to protect freedpeople from Roman Catholics. See Zipf, "'Among These American Heathens,'" 117–8.

15. John McCullagh, "The South," *57th Annual Report of the ASSU* (Philadelphia: ASSU, 1881): 19; John McCullagh to Maurice A. Wurts, 15 November 1870, in Texas, ASSU Correspondence, PHS; "America's Great Enemy," *Tennessee Outlook*, 4 February 1897.

grams aimed at African Americans, and by 1900 were training a handful of black men for the priesthood.[16]

Black ministers also resented Catholic efforts to attract their children. Some felt that Catholic endeavors were eating away at their constituency. An AME member urged his church to organize Sunday schools for black youths in order to save them "from the superstition, mimmeries and bigotries of the Roman Catholic Church." He characterized the Catholic Church as a vulture, "scenting its prey, far off" and swooping down to steal innocent souls from Protestant churches. In 1890, Colored Methodists uncovered what they called a grand Catholic strategy—priests trying to ensnare African Americans into their faith. The specter of the papacy prompted black evangelists to intensify efforts to establish their own Sunday schools for children before they were lost to Rome forever.[17]

Mormons also proved worrisome, though anti-Mormon rhetoric never reached the fevered pitch that southern evangelicals used to denounce Catholics. In part, this was due to the fact that only a few thousand Mormons lived or worked in the South. Nonetheless, they were perceived as a problem because of their unusual beliefs and because their dedicated, energetic male missionaries competed directly with Sunday school workers in the field. Mormon missionaries went door-to-door, spreading their message, handing out literature, and seeking converts. Tennessee Baptists worried about the four hundred Mormon missionaries in their state. One Sunday school report noted that Mormons had left their "cunningly devised literature" in southern homes and planted an influence that was becoming the "most threatening foe to the peace of

16. American Baptist Home Mission Society, "Roman Catholicism and the Colored People" (January 1884), in Una Roberts Lawrence Collection, SBHLA; G. S. Jones to Maurice A. Wurts, 27 June 1868, Hendersonville, N.C., ASSU Correspondence, PHS; Philanthropos, "The Future of the Colored Race," *Religious Herald,* 1 November 1866. For information on Catholic work among southern blacks, see Morris, *Reading, 'Riting, and Reconstruction,* 79–80; Sernett, *Bound for the Promised Land;* J. B. Slattery, "Should We Advise the Raising of the Standard Ordination for the Negro Clergy?" in Southern Society for the Promotion of the Study of Race Conditions and Problems in the South, *Race Problems of the South: Report of the Proceedings of the First Annual Conference . . . at Montgomery, Alabama* (Richmond, Va.: B. F. Johnson, 1900; reprint, New York: Negro Universities Press, 1969), 135.

17. "The Roman Catholic Church and the Colored People of the South," *Christian Recorder,* 27 October 1866; "Roman Catholicism and the Negro," *Christian Index,* 18 January 1890.

society." As Tennesseans moaned, "It will take nearly 20 years to counteract the evil they have already wrought in this state." G. E. Mize of Marion, Alabama, shared similar worries; Mormons were leaving their literature everywhere and, worse yet, people were actually reading it. Baptist Annie Armstrong called Mormons an "Octopus or Devil Fish," with their long arms trying to lay claim to innocent souls.[18]

The southern Sunday school movement, which initially had seemed relatively open to all, became much more competitive by the 1880s. Southern parents were told, often vehemently, that their children had to eschew all other religious institutions and attend only the Sunday school attached to their church. As early as 1869, Georgia Presbyterians organized a state Committee on Sabbath Schools to oversee Sunday school work, for they recognized the "impropriety and the inconsistency of committing the religious instruction of the children to voluntary associations outside the Church." North Carolina Baptists feared competitors and urged their members to "awake from our long sleep" and pursue evangelistic efforts throughout the state.[19]

Lay members of various southern denominations undertook greater efforts to found Sunday schools on behalf of their churches. Some did this the easy way by appropriating an existing Sunday school and stamping it with their denomination's identity. Apparently some individuals who founded Sunday schools felt little compunction, for instance, in adopting an ASSU school as their own, after convincing local officers and parents that it was in their best interests to affiliate with a church. Such tactics, whether guileless or intentional, understandably angered northern missionaries who had worked hard to establish schools on behalf of their organization. ASSU missionary William Bulkley complained that a former supporter was bribing his Sunday schools to become Methodist.

18. George A. Lofton, "Annual Report of the State Board: Mormonism," *24th Anniversary of the Tennessee Baptist Convention, 1898* (Paris, Tenn.: Wear's Printing Works, 1898), 18; G. E. Mize, 5 August 1897, Marion, Ala., to James Marion Frost, Frost-Bell Correspondence, SBHLA; Annie Armstrong to Miss Coker, 18 February 1899, Baltimore, Md., Annie Armstrong Correspondence, SBHLA. The 1906 Federal Census of Religion revealed some 16,000 Mormons in thirteen southern states, hardly a number to frighten anyone. See U.S. Department of Commerce and Labor, Bureau of the Census, *Special Reports: Religious Bodies, 1906*, vol. 1 (Washington, D.C.: Government Printing Office, 1910), 270.

19. "Report of Board of Missions and Sunday Schools," *Proceedings of the 39th Annual Session of the Baptist Convention of Western North Carolina (1895)* (Waynesville, N.C.: Courier Job Print, 1895), 16.

"His large grants to Sunday school has [sic] injured me greatly," he grumbled.[20]

Proponents of the Sunday school who saw sectarian rivalry as a detriment to faith often engaged in Sunday school work through a state association or convention. This statewide approach played a significant role in northern Sunday school work but never proved as successful in the postwar South.[21] The purpose of these organizations was to establish and promote Sunday schools and encourage more children to attend them, no matter what Protestant denomination a school represented. For instance, the North Carolina State Sunday School Convention sought to promote "the union of all Christians for the Salvation of all others." From its Raleigh headquarters, the Convention published its own paper, the *Sunday School Beacon,* and organized periodic regional Sunday school meetings to share information and inspire volunteers. It hired an agent to travel throughout the state, organizing and promoting Sunday schools. Both South Carolina and Georgia residents also set up state Sunday school conventions, though they failed to generate much interest or financial support. This nondenominational effort was more appealing to whites than blacks, most of whom focused on denominational Sunday school work.[22]

20. William H. Bulkley to M. M. Merrill, 9 and 16 October 1869, Louisville, Ky., ASSU Correspondence, PHS.

21. By the late nineteenth century, these statewide organizations benefited from assistance of the International Sunday School Association of Chicago. Only four southern states—Georgia, Florida, Alabama, and South Carolina—sustained interdenominational black Sunday school organizations. According to Boylan, these conventions played a major role in Sunday schools in the antebellum North and became a counterforce to the power of the ASSU. Both the ASSU and the convention movement were weaker in the South, where denominational involvement prevailed. See Boylan, *Sunday School,* 60–100.

22. Stationery of the North Carolina State Sunday School Association,1884, in Charles Duncan McIver Papers, Special Collections, Walter Clinton Jackson Library, University of North Carolina at Greensboro; *Minutes of the Sunday School Convention of the State of Georgia,* Emory; E. A. Ebert, "Address to the Sunday School Workers of North Carolina," *Proceedings of the North Carolina State Sunday School Convention, 1879* (Salem: L. V. and E. T. Blum, 1880), insert; H. N. Snow, "The Work in This State," *Proceedings of the Ninth Annual North Carolina State Sunday-School Convention, 1890* (Raleigh: Edwards and Broughton, 1890), 9–15; "Annual Report," *Minutes of the South Carolina State Sunday School Convention, 1891* (Spartanburg, S.C.: Spartanburg Herald Print, 1891), 14; Knoff, *The World Sunday School Movement,* 44; C. L. Fike, "Report," *Minutes of the South Carolina State Sunday School Convention, 1891,* 4.

The most active of these nondenominational state Sunday school associations in the South was the Kentucky Sunday School Union (KSSU), organized shortly after the Civil War. It sought to ensure that every child in the state attended a Sunday school. The southern identity of the KSSU and its interest in promoting both union and denominational Sunday schools proved key to its success, as did its effort to remain independent of the ASSU. The KSSU hired its own field workers, including C. M. Arnold, who saw nondenominational work as one answer to Kentucky's Sunday schools. In his travels, he came upon a mountain village torn by sectarian rivalry, where each church was determined to control the community's single Sunday school. Arnold claimed to have saved the day by overcoming the rival factions and patiently organizing a nondenominational school. He exhibited less patience when only a small crowd gathered for a Sunday school meeting he had organized. He denounced the flashy attractions of "Barnum's great show" and a simultaneous lecture at the Court House, which apparently had attracted much larger audiences. Like other single-minded missionaries, Arnold displayed little tolerance toward those who failed to put Sunday school matters at the top of their list.[23]

The various projects that KSSU members undertook suggest that a good deal of self-promotion and activity was essential to the organization's survival. In 1893, some eight hundred KSSU members conducted a "House-to-House Visitation" survey of Louisville, Kentucky, accumulating data on Sunday attendance and inviting more youngsters to come to their Sunday schools. Organizers felt rewarded by their effort, although their survey yielded unexpected results. Some parents assumed their children were faithfully attending Sunday school, only to discover that their progeny were out on the streets and spending their weekly offering on personal pleasures. Nevertheless, volunteers felt that they had raised community interest, and they vowed to carry out a similar campaign the following year. The KSSU also published its own newspaper, the *Ken-*

---

23. C. M. Arnold, "C. M. Arnold for Western District," *Minutes of the 25th Annual Session of the Kentucky Sunday School Union* (Louisville: John P. Morton, 1890), 33–5; "The Specific Purpose and Work of the Kentucky Sunday-School Association," *Kentucky Sunday School Reporter* 9 (December 1900): 2. See also Sumner, "Sunday Schools Started Interchurch Work." The Union changed names several times. It began as the Kentucky Sabbath School Association; in 1876 it became the Kentucky Sunday School Union, and in 1898 it became the Kentucky Sunday School Association.

tucky Sunday School Reporter. By the late nineteenth century the KSSU sponsored special institutes and conventions to improve Sunday school teaching.[24]

As southern denominations became more actively involved in Sunday school work, they organized their efforts on both a local and a statewide basis. White Southern Baptists conducted early Sunday school work through their state conventions, appointing an evangelist and a volunteer Sunday school board to oversee these efforts. In the 1870s, for instance, Alabama Baptists began to worry about competition from northern organizations and southern denominations alike, in part because their own Sunday schools were in such a sorry state. In a pattern typical of other states, the Alabama Baptist State Convention set up a Sunday school association and appointed a Sabbath School Executive Committee to oversee the work. The committee then hired Thomas Cooper Boykin as its first state Sunday school evangelist. Taking advantage of the state's improved railroad system (which began to ease the work of all colporteurs and missionaries in the South), Boykin traveled throughout the state, visiting communities, organizing new Sunday schools, and collecting his salary from donations. After only a year, the number of Baptist Sunday schools in Alabama had increased substantially. Boykin then left to conduct similar work in Georgia, leading to the establishment of more Baptist Sunday schools than churches in that state.[25]

At their 1866 General Conference, white Southern Methodists made the Sunday school an official arm of their church and appointed special

---

24. W. H. Miley, "The Race, the Mark, the Prize in Sunday School Work," *Minutes of the 28th Annual Session of the Kentucky Sunday School Union* (Louisville: John P. Morton, 1893), 19, 24; "Constitution," *Kentucky Sunday School Reporter* 9 (December 1900): 4.

25. T. C. Boykin, "Sunday School Committee Report," *Minutes of the Alabama Baptist State Convention, 1872* (n.p., 1872), 11; Robert G. Gardner et al., *A History of the Georgia Baptist Association, 1784–1984* (Atlanta: Georgia Baptist Historical Society, 1988), 227–8. ASSU missionary J. S. Houston showed annoyance with Boykin's success, commenting that his work "will furnish many persons with an excuse to withhold their subscriptions from us." J. S. Houston to Maurice A. Wurts, 2 February 1875, Macon, Ga., ASSU Correspondence, PHS. Histories of Baptist work in various southern states reveal that results varied widely, and many Baptist state conventions were not as successful as those in Georgia. See R. L. Robinson, *History of the Georgia Baptist Association* (Union Point, Ga.: n.p., 1928); John T. Christian, *A History of the Baptists of Louisiana* (Shreveport: Executive Board, Louisiana Baptist Convention, 1923); Hinson, *A History of Baptists in Arkansas.*

boards to oversee and promote Sunday schools in each annual conference. Methodists celebrated their built-in approach to evangelistic fieldwork: itinerant ministers who organized, oversaw, and promoted Sunday schools as they traveled their circuit. This may help explain why Methodists seemed reluctant to hire an official to organize and oversee Sunday school work on a state- or conference-wide basis. Kentucky Methodists did not appoint a state agent until 1891; the Louisiana Methodist Conference hired its first Sunday school agent in 1910. The use of itinerant ministers seemed to guarantee numerous workers in the field and led to remarkable success in the number of new Sunday schools the denomination founded.[26]

But to compete with well-organized, well-funded religious organizations from the North demanded more than individual and statewide initiative. While some successes were evident, a number of state or convention organizations floundered and did little to advance the Sunday school cause. Gradually, the larger southern denominations began to organize, centralize, and expand their Sunday school work. Yet even as denominations began to invest more time, money, and personnel in Sunday schools, initial efforts were often halting and inconsistent; what appeared as official policy in print did not necessarily translate into effective change.

As a first step, church leaders usually appointed a Sunday school board or special committee, hired men to conduct fieldwork, and upgraded and expanded their Sunday schools. Each southern denomination then weighed the idea of consolidating all their regional Sunday school work under a single entity to direct efforts on behalf of the entire denomination. Not only would this enhance the Sunday school cause, supporters argued, but a single organization could strengthen the denomination by articulating a unified approach. A centralized Sunday school board could

26. Heriges, *Sunday School Legislation*, 12; J. E. Edwards, "Report on Sunday School," *Journal of the General Conference of the MEC, South* (Nashville: A. H. Redford, 1866), 13; "On the Instruction of Children," *The Doctrines of Discipline of the Methodist Episcopal Church South* (Nashville: A. H. Redford, 1866), 100; "Sunday-School Board," *Minutes of the 71st Session of the Kentucky Annual Conference of the MECS* (Harrodsburg, Ky.: Democrat Printing, 1891), 48; "Report of the Sunday School Board," *Minutes of the 66th Session of the Louisiana Annual Conference of the MECS, 1910* (n.p., n.d.), 26; "Report of the Sunday School Board," *Journal of the 68th Session of the Louisiana Conference of the MECS, 1913* (New Orleans: New Orleans Christian Advocate, 1913), 25.

foster greater adherence to the faith, set standards for teachers and officers, and select appropriate materials for the classroom.

Many church leaders and members touted the wisdom of this approach; yet most denominational Sunday school boards did not exist or function effectively until the end of nineteenth century. One reason for the delay was strong opposition by vocal minorities in each denomination. Most southerners valued local control and resisted any large entity trying to assert power over their lives and institutions. Others resisted a centralized structure that would oversee an institution that they felt was unnecessary in the first place. Some volunteers were already committed to Sunday school work at the local or state level and had no desire to relinquish control to a single board. Northern missionary societies naturally opposed this approach, for it would increase competition and cut into their book profits. Southerners who were loyal to Yankee enterprises insisted that northern money, advice, and inexpensive, well-written Sunday school materials had served them well so far. There seemed little reason to centralize or create competition for structures soundly in place.[27]

Southern Baptists expressed the greatest objection to the idea of a centralized Sunday school board, which would necessarily entail a loss of church autonomy that was at the heart of Southern Baptist faith. As an Alabamian stated, the relation of his church to any centralized enterprise was a "peculiar and delicate" issue. "Where others have nothing at stake in external organism, Baptists have all to risk," he warned. I. T. Tichenor, who was organizing Sunday schools in Louisiana, was frustrated by the "hopeless disorganization" among church members there. As he described the situation, Baptists "will do as they please, and, sometimes, purposely do wrong, in order that they may show that they are at liberty to do so."[28]

---

27. William Link, *A Hard Country and a Lonely Place: Schooling, Society, and Reform in Rural Virginia, 1870–1920* (Chapel Hill: University of North Carolina Press, 1986), 5–7; Walter B. Shurden, *The Sunday School Board: Ninety Years of Service* (Nashville: Broadman Press, 1981), 17–24; Lynn E. May, "The Emerging Role of Sunday Schools in Southern Baptist Life to 1900," *Baptist History and Heritage* 18, no. 1 (1983): 6–17.

28. W. Wilkes, "Report of Committee on Sunday Schools," *Minutes of the 55th Annual Session of the Alabama Baptist State Convention, 1878* (Marion, Ala.: Commonwealth Job Print, 1878), 10; I. T. Tichenor to Annie Armstrong, 13 September 1898, Frost-Bell Correspondence, SBHLA. The formation of the Southern Baptist Sunday School Board has received more scholarly attention than other southern denominations. See Robert Andrew Baker, *The Southern Baptist Convention and Its People, 1607–1972* (Nashville:

These objections, among others, led supporters of a Sunday school board to reformulate their argument, claiming that centralization actually promised greater independence for the denomination. According to this line of reasoning, if Southern Baptists had their own board, they could control their own Sunday schools and ensure that all Baptist children in the South absorbed an orthodox Baptist message. Rather than leaving others, such as the ABPS, to establish and oversee Sunday schools, Southern Baptists themselves would take charge of the schools. A single board responsible for organizing, managing, and promoting Sunday schools throughout the entire Southern Baptist Convention (SBC) would foster religious and regional identity, ensuring Southern Baptist independence.

The SBC ultimately created what many religious historians have seen as the most powerful, centralized Sunday school structure among the denominations studied here. Several respected Baptist leaders feared dire consequences if the SBC failed to act, for Sunday school work in several southern states was lagging. Statistics indicated that only a third of all Baptist children attended Sunday school; far more effort was needed to bring others into the classroom. Competition from northern missionary organizations and southern denominations was increasing. In a dramatic moment at the SBC Convention of 1891, delegates voted to establish a single Sunday school board to oversee all Baptist Sunday school work. At least one historian has called the formation of the Southern Baptist Sunday School Board the most significant step in the recent history of that church.[29]

Broadman Press, 1974) and *The Story of the Sunday School Board* (Nashville: Convention Press, 1966); William Wright Barnes, *The Southern Baptist Convention, 1845–1953* (Nashville: Broadman Press, 1954); Lynn E. May Jr., "A Brief History of Southern Baptist Sunday School Work," 1 June 1964, pamphlet in Sunday School file, SBHLA; "The Emerging Role of Sunday Schools," 7–17, and "The Sunday School: A Two-Hundred-Year Heritage," *Baptist History and Heritage* 15, no. 1 (1980): 3–11. For background on James Marion Frost (1848–1916), secretary of the Southern Baptist Sunday School Board, see Sam Hill, ed., *Encyclopedia of Religion in the South* (Macon, Ga.: Mercer University Press, 1984), 275–6; James L. Sullivan, "James Marion Frost," *Encyclopedia of Southern Baptists*, vol. 1, 512–3.

29. For information on the founding of the SBC Sunday School Board, see Baker, *The Story of the Sunday School Board*, 3–25; Shurden, *The Sunday School Board*, 11–16; Prince Emanuel Burroughs, *Fifty Fruitful Years, 1891–1941: The Story of the Sunday School Board of the Southern Baptist Convention* (Nashville: Broadman Press, 1941); Clifton J. Allen, "Sunday School Board," *Encyclopedia of Southern Baptists*, vol. 2, 1315–39;

White Southern Presbyterians approached centralized Sunday school work with their typical intellectual vigor and endless debate. Never known to act precipitously, the General Assembly moved more cautiously than its rhetoric would suggest. Members were of one mind in wanting to educate youngsters in their own Sunday schools, but articulating a plan and carrying it out were two different matters. Presbyterians created a Standing Committee on Sabbath Schools in 1869, but it made little headway; a decade later Presbyterians learned that they were far behind other denominations in Sunday school work. Officials warned of irreparable harm if the church failed to reach all Presbyterian children. In order to upgrade efforts and work more efficiently, in the 1880s the General Assembly coordinated its colportage and Sabbath school work, appointing a single officer to oversee both activities.[30] Not until the 1890s did Southern Presbyterians feel that they had made progress. In 1901, the church hired its first General Superintendent of Sabbath Schools and Young People's Work, Alexander L. Phillips, who devoted his full attention to this work. Under Phillips's energetic leadership, Presbyterians felt they had developed a sound approach to Sunday school work.[31]

Though the Methodist Episcopal Church, South (MECS) failed to centralize Sunday school work through its ministers and district conferences, the church began to develop a unified regional effort. Comparing two editions of the church's *Doctrines and Discipline* suggests how far the Methodists advanced in less than fifty years. In the 1866 edition, Sunday school guidelines occupied little more than three pages. The 1914 edi-

---

Lynn E. May Jr., "A Brief History." See also Archibald Thomas Robertson, *Life and Letters of John Albert Broadus* (Philadelphia: ABPS, 1901), 393–4; V. L. Stanfield, "John Albert Broadus," *Encyclopedia of Southern Baptists,* vol. 1, 195.

30. "Standing Committee on Sabbath Schools," *Minutes of the General Assembly of the Presbyterian Church in the U.S., 1869* (Columbia, S.C.: Office of the Southern Presbyterian Review, 1869), 379; H. Moseley et al., "Report of the Standing Committee on Sabbath Schools," *Minutes of the General Assembly of the Presbyterian Church in the United States, 1879* (Wilmington: Jackson and Bell, 1879), 59–60; Henry W. Smith, "Standing Committee on Publication," *Minutes of the General Assembly of the Presbyterian Church in the United States, 1888* (Richmond: Presbyterian Committee of Publications, 1888), 394–5.

31. F. H. Gaines, "The Sabbath-School Cause and the Question of a General Secretary," *Presbyterian Quarterly* 10 (1896): 222–36; Thompson, *Presbyterians in the South,* vol. 3, 144–6.

tion, in contrast, devoted an entire chapter and several additional pages to Sunday school. It not only discussed the importance of Sunday school education but detailed the duties of the General Sunday School Board, which now oversaw all MECS Sunday school work, including the hiring of a Sunday School Field Secretary. By the early twentieth century, the MECS boasted a well-coordinated regional Sunday school organization.[32]

African American denominations also recognized the importance of centralizing and strengthening Sunday school work. As Benjamin Tanner of the AME church pointed out, too few of their youngsters attended a denominational Sunday school and thus missed lessons that could influence their lives forever. "If we would raise up a generation of pious, staunch African-Methodists, we must train them in our Sunday schools," he insisted. Like whites, blacks worried that competitors were trying to entice their children into rival Sunday schools; yet black church leaders were also eager to free themselves from white control. By founding and managing their own churches and Sunday schools, southern blacks could control their own religious lives, raising their children according to church doctrine and also exposed to issues critical to their race.[33]

Unlike southern white churches, African American denominations did not worry about regional identity, for they sought members nationwide. But they understood the importance of locating a Sunday school board where it could serve the most members. In 1872, the AME church established a Committee on Sabbath Schools; a decade later, it formed what became known as the Connectional Sabbath School Union of the AME church, with its headquarters in Nashville. One church leader heralded this step as a "citadel of light and inspiration to young African Methodists in all lands and in all cities." The AMEZ church organized its Sunday school board in Charlotte, North Carolina. This became an effective gov-

---

32. "On the Instruction of Children," *The Doctrines and Discipline, 1866*, 101–3; "Sunday Schools," *The Doctrines and Discipline of the Methodist Episcopal Church, South, 1914*, ed. Gross Alexander (Nashville: Publishing House of the MECS, 1915), 94–109.

33. Benjamin Tucker Tanner, "Publishing Department Report," in *4th Annual Budget of the AME*, ed. Benjamin W. Arnett (Xenia, Ohio: Torchlight Printing, 1884), 119–20. For background on African Americans' efforts to form their own religious institutions, see Eric Foner, *Reconstruction: America's Unfinished Revolution, 1863–1877* (New York: Harper and Row, 1988), 88–99; Litwack, *Been in the Storm So Long*, 465–71.

erning agency in 1884, when the church established its Sunday school publishing firm in the same city. The CME church, with close ties to white Methodists, for years depended on that denomination for advice and assistance about Sunday school matters. But with the formation of its own book concern in Jackson, Tennessee, the CME church assumed greater control over its Sunday school work.[34]

Like northern organizations, southern denominations hired Sunday school missionaries and book agents, and they, too, found their labors uplifting and demanding. Though more accustomed to the people, climate, and situations than were Yankee agents, the work proved challenging to them. Southern missionaries made it clear that they represented a particular denomination, an affiliation that might clash with community sentiments. In rural areas that could support only a single school, founding one that appealed to the majority of residents could prove divisive. Some Baptist sects, as well as many rural southerners, opposed any Sunday school and tried to impede missionary efforts. Baptist L. J. Lancaster encountered resistance in a Hardshell Baptist community, and he unleashed his frustration on paper. "I find some people that are almost heathen, and so ignorant are they that they do not know that Jesus is the Saviour," he complained. "The greater part of this ignorance is attributable to hardshell influence." Yet with persistence, he was able to organize a Sunday school there. And community opposition could provide just the motivation a man needed. H. N. Quisenberry met resistance when organizing a Baptist Sunday school in Liberty, Virginia, but he refused to give up. When he finally opened his school, he claimed that the packed house heralded a "new era in the history of this church."[35]

---

34. W. F. Dickerson, "Quadrennial Address," *Journal of the 18th Session of the General Conference of the AME Church, 1884*, ed. Benjamin W. Arnett and M. E. Bryant (Philadelphia: AME Publishing House, 1884), 119–20; George Lincoln Blackwell, "Report of the Publishing House," *Daily Proceedings of the 21st Official Journal of the Quadrennial Session of the General Conference of the AMEZ Church* (York, Pa.: Dispatch Print, 1901), 196; *The Doctrines and Discipline of the Colored Methodist Episcopal Church in America* (Byhalia, Miss.: E. Cottrell, 1883), 113–4.

35. L. J. Lancaster, "Forty-Ninth Annual Report of the Sunday-School Bible Board," *Minutes of the 64th Annual Session of the Baptist General Association of Virginia, 1887* (Richmond: Dispatch Steam Printing, 1887), 33; H. N. Quisenberry, "Report of the Sunday School and Bible Board," *Minutes of the 63rd Annual Session of the Baptist General Association of Virginia, 1886* (Richmond: Dispatch Steam Printing,1887), 20. See also "Mission Work among 'The Mountain Whites'."

Southern Sunday school missionaries also complained of physical hardships. Traveling into remote areas and dealing with rural southerners' primitive ways might have disheartened less determined men. "Ticks and bed bugs; fleas and rattle snakes! This is a hard region . . . looking glasses and wash pans are luxuries here," reported Methodist minister William Henry Wills as he journeyed through Stanly County, North Carolina. Though shocked to see so many barefoot women, he was relieved to have slept without encountering a single bedbug. "I get on very well and feel thankful that my health allows me to submit to some inconveniences," Wills related. He was not about to give up on his God-given duty to expose children to Sunday school.[36]

In traveling to remote areas for the first time, religious destitution and sinful behavior startled southern ministers and missionaries. Like their northern counterparts, they were surprised to discover entire communities without a hint of religious conviction. From Albemarle, Virginia, J. W. Johnson wrote, "I have found great need of the gospel in the mountains—children twelve and fourteen years of age that had never heard a prayer." He organized Sunday schools in communities that had never had a church. J. J. Ancott found residents near Fork Union, Virginia, who had never heard a prayer or a sermon until he appeared. Immoral behavior proved equally unsettling. A Southern Methodist working in South Caswell, North Carolina, reported that the "obstacles to the progress of Methodism in this section are Calvinism, whiskey, and in some corners, ignorance," and he saw little hope for the Sunday school cause there. Though startled by such backward ways, these serious-minded men remained convinced that their fellow southerners needed the civilizing effects of the Sunday school.[37]

Indifference among the people they were trying to reach also proved frustrating; it was hard to excite those who evidenced no interest in Sunday schools whatsoever. A disheartened Methodist reported that he was

---

36. William Henry Wills to his wife, 23 June 1869, Albemarle, Stanly County, N.C., William Henry Wills Collection, SHC.

37. J. W. Johnson, "Report of the Sunday School and Bible Board," *Minutes of the 63rd Annual Session of the Baptist General Association of Virginia,* 17; J. J. Ancott, "Forty-Ninth Annual Report of the Sunday School and Bible Board," *Minutes of the 64th Annual Session of the Baptist General Association of Virginia,* 34; "Missionary Report," South Caswell Circuit, Hillsboro District, N.C., *Minutes of the North Carolina District Quarterly Conference Reports of the MECS, 1884,* Duke.

unable to develop a "Sunday school conscience" in youngsters in Goldsboro, North Carolina, whom he found "lacking in zeal." Only a half dozen aggressive and "thorough going Christians" there belonged to any church. Methodist minister George G. Smith was upset with Georgia residents who could not understand the importance of the Sunday school and failed to send their children to the classes he had organized.[38]

Because evangelicals envisioned their undertaking to be God's work and the Sunday school to be central to every youngster's future, their contemporaries' indifference and opposition demanded an explanation. Unlike northerners, these agents could not attribute their setbacks to regional flaws. Some blamed their reverses on the behavioral characteristics of those whom they tried to serve—depravity, ill manners, and alcoholism were likely culprits. Underhanded tactics by rival religious organizations also worked against these evangelicals. Unruly children and disrespectful parents might cause a Sunday school to close or force a teacher to dismiss an entire class. Sectarianism could prevent a denomination from making headway. Presbyterians blamed Methodists; Methodists blamed Baptists. Family and community feuds in mountain areas further impeded missionary work. And when all other explanations failed, Satan himself seemed to have taken hold of a community, making it impossible to found a Sunday school. Of course, the depraved, indifferent, inebriated, sinful, and religiously destitute were the very individuals whom southern missionaries most needed to reach. A majority of agents recognized and accepted the challenges; a few, however, gave up.

As southern denominations centralized and took control of their Sunday school work, a number of related issues emerged. Like northern missionary associations, southerners found financing Sunday school work to be a major concern, for resources were limited. Children's weekly donations were hardly adequate to support Sunday school needs. Many rural southern churches served congregations whose impoverished members could do little to support a Sunday school. White southerners had never been in the habit of giving their money to charitable causes; most had little to give away anyway. Until church publishing houses became profitable, Sunday school boards depended on the contributions they re-

38. St. Paul's, Goldsboro, New Bern District, *Minutes of the North Carolina District Quarterly Conference Reports of the MECS,* July 1895, Duke; George G. Smith Diary, 23 January and 30 June 1887, 20 February 1888, in George G. Smith Papers, Emory.

ceived from members and donors. They often operated on tight budgets and encouraged schools to make do with less.

While the endeavors of northern and southern missionaries were similar in many respects, their approach to Sunday school work and the issues they each had to address were somewhat different. Unlike northern missionaries, who seemed bent upon imposing their ideas and institutions on a needy South, southerners demonstrated greater concern with the ongoing success and life of each Sunday school. There was to be nothing temporary about the schools these men organized; southern evangelicals were not detached outsiders whose sojourn in the region was usually brief. While northern missionaries often saw the Sunday school as a force in reconstructing the region and perhaps in unifying the nation, only a few southerners gave much thought to reuniting the country or its churches through the Sunday school—or through any institution, for that matter. Instead, southerners envisioned the Sunday school as the place to lead children to conversion and salvation.

To that end, southern boards and missionaries worked tirelessly to ensure that each Sunday school succeeded. In areas where competition for youngsters was keen, church officials took a competitive approach, urging agents to rush to a particular community and be the first to lay claim to lost souls. Sunday school work assumed the trappings of a virtual race. Virginia Baptists, for example, exhorted their missionaries to "possess the field" and gain adherents before rival denominations took over the state. These competitive tactics bothered some Sunday school officials, who felt that missionaries were losing sight of their larger purpose and merely trying to enhance their reputations by submitting impressive statistics rather than creating sound schools. Hastily formed Sabbath schools that resulted purely from missionary zeal were fragile and likely to die once an agent left a community. As Southern Presbyterians described one of their shaky Sunday schools, "Its going is wobbly and its life is uncertain. It needs to be carefully nurtured." To address this situation, southern Sunday school officials insisted that their missionaries periodically revisit every school they founded and assist those that were floundering. Effective Sunday schools had to be durable and long-lived.[39]

39. J. M. Pilcher, "Report of the Sunday-School and Bible Board," *Minutes of the Sixtieth Annual Session of the Baptist General Association of Virginia, 1883* (Richmond: Dispatch Steam Printing House, 1884), 27; "Spiritual Values in Sunday School Extension," *Missionary Survey* (September 1913): 819.

Southern Sunday school workers wrestled with some issues that northern missionaries rarely took time to consider. One was the Sunday school's long-term relationship with the minister of its sponsoring church. The number of ministers who opposed or were indifferent to the Sunday school surprised field agents and missionaries. Although northern missionaries sometimes confronted ministers who wanted nothing to do with a Sunday school, opposition to northern missionaries was rare or short-lived, since most agents moved on when they were not wanted or needed. Southerners seemed undone by a preacher's indifference. In the mid-1870s, Southern Baptists wailed that no more than a quarter of their clergy participated in Sunday school activities. A North Carolina Baptist called apathetic preachers "*obstacles* in the way of the progress of Sunday schools." Presbyterian C. O. Martindale denounced a preacher who failed to sympathize with the school's purpose and acted more like a "bundling hinderer" than a helper.[40]

We can only speculate about what prompted ministers' indifference or resistance to Sunday schools. While preachers in sects like the Primitive Baptists had no use for any Sunday school, jealousy on the part of some ministers may have been a factor, especially as the Sunday school movement began to enjoy some success. Illiterate or poorly educated ministers in some Baptist and Methodist churches may have resented the Sunday school missionaries' efforts to teach reading and middle-class values to children. Preachers may have been uneasy with lessons that seemed pretentious or paternalistic. Even some ministers who had themselves gone to Sunday school as youths, or had taught one as adults, sensed a loss of personal prestige and power; advocates of Sunday schools credited their beloved institution with attracting the majority of new church members. Schools that retained a degree of autonomy, thanks to financial support from an outside organization, also might upset a minister. A successful school was a thorn in the side of those who regarded preaching, rather than teaching, as the best means to entice the flock into the fold.[41]

---

40. I. W. Thomas, "Missionary Report, Brier Creek," *Minutes of the Baptist State Sunday School Convention of North Carolina, 1874* (Raleigh: Edwards, Broughton, 1875), 8; C. O. Martindale, "The Gospel Ministry and the Sunday School," *Presbyterian Standard*, 22 August 1906.

41. Kevin K. Gaines, *Uplifting the Race: Black Leadership, Politics, and Culture in the Twentieth Century* (Chapel Hill: University of North Carolina Press, 1996), xv, 2–3.

As the most important individual in a church—and often in a community—a minister's attitude and actions could make or break a Sunday school. Apparently a good many ministers chose the latter course. In part, this reflected the fluctuating and unclear relationship of the Sunday school to the parent church. Since the Sunday school historically began as a secular organization, some ministers felt that it had no right to claim an association with any church. While the Sunday school lacked ministerial authority, it did prepare youngsters for conversion—a situation that must have upset some clergy. Even after denominations embraced the Sunday school as the place for children to acquire a Christian education, some ministers refused to mention the Sunday school in the same breath as the church, regarding it both as an inferior appendage to the church and as a rival to their authority.[42]

To address this problem, Sunday school boards tried to delineate a meaningful role for the minister within the Sunday school. Some officials gently reminded preachers of their duty to foster any institution associated with the church. Others encouraged ministers to participate in weekly classroom proceedings by welcoming Sunday school pupils, teaching a class, visiting children and their parents at home, or promoting the institution in their sermons. Still others urged ministers to assume more challenging tasks, such as disciplining children and stemming the tide of backsliders who abandoned both church and Sunday school. Unfortunately, advice of this kind was part of the problem. Most ministers felt that Sunday school officers had no right to dictate their activities; as head of the church, preachers should determine their own agenda.[43]

Another important problem that southern Sunday school leaders debated was how to balance the role of the Sunday school with the duty of parents. This issue centered on determining whether parents or the Sunday school ultimately had responsibility for the Christian nurture of children. By the latter third of the nineteenth century, the appearance and expansion of various institutions like public and Sunday schools, kindergartens, juvenile homes, asylums, and prisons raised similar questions among Americans nationwide, who debated how best to educate, reha-

---

42. Boylan, *Sunday School,* 160; M. Isaac Myers, "The Relation of the Sunday-School to the Church," *AME Church Review* 6 (1889–1890): 134.

43. W. M. Parker, "A Letter from Wilmington, N.C.," *Sunday School Magazine* 3 (1873): 3; A. L. Phillips, "The Pastor and the Sabbath School Day," *Presbyterian Standard,* 19 September 1906.

bilitate, and uplift youngsters. Public school educators had to respond to critics who claimed that public education was challenging parental authority and falling into the clutches of the state. Historian Stephanie Coontz has argued that this situation created a troubling paradox in the late nineteenth century, for the "increasing emphasis on the family as sole source of personal support and class identity was accompanied by a growth of public institutions that took over many traditional family functions."[44]

Here, the issue was the primacy of home and domestic religious nurture versus the role of the Sunday school. As historians of the family have shown, throughout much of America's early history, parents—and especially mothers—were deemed guardians of their children's spiritual lives. The maternal role grew in importance during the nineteenth century as the productive duties of many women diminished, due to the availability of more consumer goods in an expanding market economy, men's changing work roles due to industrialization, and for many mothers, the birth of fewer children. Yet on a more spiritual level, women's domestic role was enhanced and elevated by their increased devotion to all aspects of their children's lives. In particular, mothers were expected to guide their children down a righteous path.[45]

Thus the growing number of institutions that catered to children—the Sunday school among them—both presented new possibilities and raised pressing questions for parents. In general, southerners embraced the sanctity of their homes and families, and feared that a proliferation of schools and other institutions would lead mothers to forsake their duties. Most southern clergy and Sunday school advisors insisted that nothing should ever come between a mother and her children that would mitigate her sacred responsibility for their welfare. Southern preachers took up the cry for domestic nurturing, constantly reminding mothers that their

---

44. Coontz, *Social Origins of Private Life*, 272.

45. For background on the American family and the role of mothers, see Degler, *At Odds;* Mintz and Kellogg, *Domestic Revolutions*. For background on family life in the South, see Smith, *Inside the Great House;* Lewis, *Pursuit of Happiness;* Censer, *North Carolina Planters and Their Children;* Elizabeth Fox-Genovese, *Within the Plantation Household: Black and White Women of the Old South* (Chapel Hill: University of North Carolina Press, 1988); McMillen, *Motherhood in the Old South;* Steven Stowe, *Intimacy and Power in the Old South* (Baltimore: Johns Hopkins University Press, 1987).

most important duty was to raise their youngsters in a loving, Christian environment. A mother should "excel" at her duties, intoned Southern Baptists, for "the brightest jewels in the mother's immortal crown will be her sainted children." Methodist Atticus Haygood labeled the home a school and parents "divinely appointed teachers." Mothers were "nature's ordained instructors of the children," echoed Virginia AME members. While most southern clergymen admitted that Sunday schools put children in the hands of teachers well-versed in Scripture, they nonetheless proclaimed that parents retained the ultimate responsibility for Christian nurture of their young. Every day, parents had the opportunity to instruct by example and to emphasize righteous moral behavior. Methodist preacher George Smith concluded that southerners had their priorities straight, especially when compared to northerners. "Thank God, our favored southern land is a land of homes," Smith asserted, "and in these sacred castles the father and mother are chief rulers." Nothing could or should supersede Christian lessons learned in the home.[46]

Those men who insisted on the primacy of domestic nurturing assumed, of course, that most parents fulfilled their religious duties to perfection and that the home environment was a happy place. Some used their own upbringing as proof, fondly recalling their Christian childhood home and their loving parents. CME minister Charles H. Phillips remembered his parents' piety with lifelong gratitude. "The example and home life of my parents brought me, quite early, into the most vital relations with the Church and Sunday School," he wrote. In a survey of 120 white Baptist ministers, a hundred of them claimed that their mothers had led them to Christ. Reverend Theodore Cuyler stated that no Sunday school in the world could have given him what his mother had provided. "Bunyan and the Catechism were the dairy that supplied the 'sincere milk' of our childhood; it was fed to us by a praying, loving mother's hand," he reminisced. In such ideal settings, dutiful Christian parents lovingly

---

46. "Motherhood," *Baptist Courier*, 10 May 1883; "The Training of Children," *Working Christian*, 9 October 1879; Atticus G. Haygood, *Our Children* (St. Louis: Advocate Publishing House, 1884), 110; Robert Davis et al., "Report on Sunday School Work," *Journal of the Virginia Annual Conference of the AME Church, 1897* (Richmond: n.d.), 49; Smith, *Childhood and Conversion*, 114. See also Lyon, *The Sunday School and Its Methods*, 52–9.

urged their children to read their Bible, always attend Sunday school, say their prayers, and lead a moral life.[47]

Yet although the majority of evangelicals insisted upon the primacy of mother love, many also realized that parents were hardly perfect. Especially in poverty-stricken rural areas, parents seemed to have little concept of proper childrearing and often raised their youngsters with little Christian guidance. Domestic violence, alcoholism, or severe want defined the home lives of many children. Even middle-class families had problems. Too many parents now seemed indifferent to a duty they presumably had once taken seriously. Missionaries and clergy sensed a decline in Christian piety in the home. They accused parents of being too apathetic or too busy to carry out their spiritual duties. In his gloomy treatise *The Great Evil and Its Remedy,* Southern Methodist Reverend Samuel W. Cope blamed widespread social problems on mothers who failed to carry out their family responsibilities. Still other writers felt that in an increasingly complex, sinful world, with a bewildering array of childrearing methods, even the most devoted parent faced unprecedented problems in carrying out his or her tasks. How could an adult keep abreast of the latest child studies and scientific theories? Could parents possibly know how to teach a child by using modern methods? Some observers warned against the mistake of entrusting religious instruction to "those of the preceding generation who have made no special study either of the subject-matter, or of the art of teaching."[48]

A growing number of evangelicals were convinced that the best means to educate and mold youngsters into good Christians was to accord the Sunday school an active role in teaching them the Bible and leading them to God. No one suggested that Sunday school should supplant all domestic religious instruction; rather, it should be an auxiliary to what children learned at home. "The Sunday school is an ally which God has provided for carrying forward the work begun in Christian homes," wrote J. A. Lyon, "and for inaugurating a work impossible in unchristian ones." Sunday school volunteers often were more knowledgeable about Scrip-

---

47. Charles H. Phillips, *From the Farm to the Bishopric: An Autobiography* (Nashville: Parthenon Press, 1932), 27; Fay Mills, "Motherhood," *Baptist Courier,* 12 March 1892; Theodore Cuyler, "Christianity in the Home," *Baptist Courier,* 29 January 1891.

48. Samuel W. Cope, *The Great Evil and Its Remedy, or Parental Responsibility in the Moral and Religious Training of Children* (Nashville: Publishing House of the MECS, 1889), 62.

ture than parents, for they had access to lesson material and training manuals. KSSU officials suggested that parents contribute to the Sunday school effort by providing financial support and reviewing children's Sunday lessons at home. The combined power of parents and Sunday school would surely assure the future of every southern child. Southern Methodists concurred, insisting that the best plan was to have both parents and the Sunday school commit to Christian education. "When home and Christ are in intelligent accord in their efforts to bring up a child in the nurture and admonition of the lord, success is almost certain," one concluded. To enhance this relationship, advisors urged Sunday school teachers to visit each pupil's home and discuss Christian nurturing with parents. Yet Sunday school leaders also urged caution, for if the institution did an extraordinary job of implanting religious values in youngsters, parents might forgo their responsibilities altogether. Probably to drive the point home, some leaders suggested that if parents became lax and too dependent on the Sunday school for children's Christian nurturing, churches should abandon the Sunday school altogether.[49]

This issue of the primacy of home versus the role of institutions would become increasingly important by the early twentieth century. In the South, the decades following the Civil War witnessed the simultaneous expansion of both common schools and Sunday schools. Their growing presence in towns and rural areas meant that more children spent more time away from home and beyond parental control. As schools began to exert greater influence on youngsters, the singular importance of parental instruction began to decline. Neither common schools nor Sunday schools yet occupied a central role in the life of southern youngsters, and certainly parents did not place as many expectations on these institutions as they do today. Nevertheless, the rapid growth of schools was troubling for many parents, who worried about the pernicious influence of outsiders on their children.

Related to this issue, but more disquieting to public school officials than to Sunday school leaders, was the role that public school should play in religious and moral education. Offering Bible study and prayers as standard fare in weekday schools was not necessarily the answer, be-

49. Lyon, *The Sunday School and Its Methods*, 57–8; Rev. R. J. Deering, "What Should Parents Do for the Sunday-School?" *Twenty-First Annual Convention of the Kentucky Sunday School Union* (Louisville: Courier Journal, 1886), 42.

cause many evangelicals feared the dilution of religious thought that would be necessary to please the numerous constituencies in public school. Parents worried that if a particular religious doctrine was emphasized in public school, it might conflict with their own. This led to fears of religious tyranny, in which the largest denominations in the state would try to control public school lessons. In Virginia, the issue created lengthy debate. Officials who wanted to maintain the separation of church and state insisted that the home and Sunday school assume responsibility for Christian education, while public schools concentrate on academics. By the 1880s, as fewer Sunday schools were teaching reading and spelling, some people argued that public schools should give up any effort to provide a religious education. In contrast, those supporting religious education in public school pointed to states in the Northeast that had legislated an end to prayers and Bible reading, declaring that this had led to the demise of all civil and Christian behavior. They insisted that the Bible was the most suitable textbook for children. Ultimately, there was no happy resolution to this issue. Virginians settled into an uneasy compromise, leaving some decisions to local school districts and letting private and parochial schools teach as they saw best. Sunday school officials seemed unruffled by these public school debates, probably feeling that children could never acquire too much of a good thing.[50]

Poor or irregular attendance was another problem that troubled Sunday school workers. Pressure from church officials and parents was the best means to ensure a youngster's presence in Sunday school, but practical problems often prevented a child's weekly appearance. A major hindrance to regular attendance was the periodic closing of rural churches. Those that depended on an itinerant minister usually met only once a month, with the Sunday school following a regular service. Frustrated officials argued that this made no sense. The Sunday school should never have to close since local volunteers staffed it, and their presence did not depend on a minister's appearance. Sunday school leaders proposed that one way to keep a church functioning, with or without a permanent minister, was to create "evergreen" Sunday schools, which stayed open year round. All southern Sunday schools, especially in rural areas, would thus be able to meet regularly throughout the year.

50. Sadie Bell, *The Church, the State, and Education in Virginia* (1930; reprint, New York: Arno Press, 1969), 411–31, 446–52; Handy, *Christian America*, 102.

But attendance was often beyond human control. Bad weather and dilapidated buildings caused pupils and teachers to stay home. Rural churches that were not winterized had no means to warm the sanctuary. Hastily built or run-down churches might have leaky roofs, unchinked walls, and drafty doors and windows. ASSU missionary D. B. Nelson described such a scene in the North Carolina mountains. "Think of a Sunday school in a house with cracks a cat could jump through without stove or fire place, a roof that admits half the rain and sometimes no floor but old Mother Earth," he wrote. Heavy winter and spring rains made roads and bridges impassable, making it impossible for children to get to school. Hot weather also caused problems. ASSU missionary John Eastman in Cedar Key, Florida, explained that he could not attract children to Sunday school in summertime, for they could not tolerate the hot sand on bare feet as they walked to class. In urban areas, children's interest in Sunday school waned in summer, when fishing, playing outdoors, or vacationing with parents was more appealing. To entice youngsters, advisors suggested that Sunday schools enliven their proceedings with more social outings and public readings, livelier hymns, and games with the stereopticon.[51]

Weather aside, poverty often stood in the way of southern children attending Sunday school. Youngsters often went barefoot nine months of the year but found a long walk to Sunday school without a pair of shoes too painful. Others felt ashamed to appear without shoes. Yet ASSU missionary J. F. Marsh described three pupils who wrapped their feet in rags and children who ran around half naked even in winter. Mothers also were ashamed when they could not dress their children properly and many refused to send them to Sunday school or church in ragged attire. Attending Sunday school called for a decent set of clothes, often an impossible goal for destitute families.[52]

Such problems help explain why some children were not in Sunday school, but they did not appease advocates of the institution. North Carolina Baptist W. W. Holden claimed that bad weather was no excuse to avoid Sunday school. "The Devil is as busy in Winter as he is in Sum-

51. D. B. Nelson, 30 September 1867, Forks of Pigeon, N.C., and John Eastman, 21 June 1875, Cedar Keys, Fla., both to Maurice A. Wurts, ASSU Correspondence, PHS.

52. J. F. Marsh to Maurice A. Wurts, 22 October 1867, Brevard, N.C., ASSU Correspondence, PHS.

mer," he warned. Methodist J. A. Lyon depicted the situation in equally dire terms. Closing Sunday schools, he insisted, created a "season of pernicious idleness, furnishing the amplest liberty and leisure for mischievous associations and doubtful pursuits." Atticus Haygood undertook a one-man campaign to ensure that all Methodist Sunday schools stayed open year round. "Scores of miserable huts, that we call 'churches' in Georgia, are an insult to the almighty," an impatient Haygood wrote. He decried run-down Sunday schools that closed due to ill-repair, and he urged every church member to get to work and chink wall cracks and fill holes. A savvy Texan chided parents whose children managed to attend public school in winter but found excuses to avoid Sunday school, stating forcefully that every church had to hold year-round Sunday school. Ultimately, the situation did begin to improve. Better roads and modern modes of transportation made rural churches more accessible. As churches and Sunday school buildings became more comfortable, concern over evergreen Sunday schools quieted.[53]

Yet what often seemed like hindrances to the Sunday school movement proved a boon in some circumstances. Sometimes, heightened rivalry actually helped local schools, especially those with few resources on hand. Savvy superintendents and teachers took advantage of their situation by shifting their loyalty among different religious organizations as the situation warranted. In seeking financial aid or inexpensive or free books from a Sunday school board or publisher, for example, officers and teachers might reveal the number of new Bibles or Sunday school aids donated by a rival religious society or denomination. Women seemed especially adept at getting what they needed. Miss Wallie M. Morgan of Morgansville, Kentucky, was only one of many teachers who acquired free books from the Southern Baptist Sunday School Board. She wrote the board, carefully noting that the ABPS already had donated ten dollars worth of books to her school, and hoping that her own Sunday School board would emulate this "noble example." Teachers hinted that the generosity extended by others had surpassed donations from their own denomination. Thanks to a clever superintendent or teacher who

53. W. W. Holden, "Organization of the Sunday School Work in North Carolina—Its Practicability & Necessity," *Minutes of the Baptist State Sunday School Convention of North Carolina, 1874,* 17; Lyon, *The Sunday School and Its Methods,* 436; Atticus Haygood, "Our Annual Hibernation," *Sunday School Magazine* 1 (July 1871): 234–5; Haygood, "Our Children" and "Winter Quarters," *Texas Christian Advocate,* 3 July 1872.

played on denominational competition, individual Sunday schools often did quite well.⁵⁴

In a larger sense as well, competition was beneficial to the Sunday school cause. Scholars who study the history of American religion have explained the vitality and strength of American religions by the nation's relative openness to various faiths. Sociologists Roger Finke and Rodney Stark have described American religion as a "free market religious economy," in which each denomination's success depends on competitive endeavors and where the unchurched, or at least the uncommitted, are up for grabs. R. Stephen Warner has characterized American religions as "distinctly competitive." As he wrote, "Pluralism and especially competition are the reasons that American religion is more robust than religion in almost any other advanced society." The same could be said of the southern Sunday school movement, where so many different religious organizations fought to attract new members. Rather than seeing chaos in this religious reconstruction of the South, it makes more sense to see competition as enhancing and advancing the Sunday school cause. As Finke and Stark argue, pluralism strengthens, rather than weakens, faith. The presence of so many different religious organizations kept the Sunday school movement alive, allowing no one to be lazy or indifferent toward the work at hand. The perception of an external enemy, whether it was a Northern Methodist or Southern Baptist, generated some cohesiveness within a denomination and strengthened a missionary's sense of purpose and determination. Competition motivated missionaries and ministers to travel farther and to be the first to reach a particular community and establish a Sunday school before a rival moved in. Though officials expressed alarm and disgust at the situation, those being served by the institution ultimately benefited from it.⁵⁵

Southern evangelicals, individually and collectively, were of one mind in wanting to expose their youngsters to the Bible, instruct them in proper morals and manners, and foster their conversion and salvation.

54. Miss Wallie M. Morgan to James Marion Frost, 16 September 1897, Morgansville, Ky., Frost-Bell Correspondence, SBHLA.
55. R. Stephen Warner, "Work in Progress toward a New Paradigm for the Sociological Study of Religion in the United States," *American Journal of Sociology* 98 (March 1993): 1055–6; Ellen C. Coughlin, "A Market Perspective on Religion," *Chronicle of Higher Education* (17 May 1996), A12; Stowell, *Rebuilding Zion,* 95; Finke and Stark, *The Churching of America,* 18–9.

But changes in southern Sunday school work were evident. By the late nineteenth century, southern denominations were determined to establish and control their own Sunday schools. Their efforts, coupled with competition among various religious organizations in the North and South, created a lively field of action that led to significant growth in new southern Sunday schools. Sunday school promoters were determined to stamp a denominational identity on their institutions and pupils. By the late nineteenth century, black and white southerners celebrated their Sunday school work, feeling that youngsters were headed in the right direction, overseen by those who knew and loved them best.

Montage of Opening Day, June 2, 1912, at the Log Cabin Community Sunday School outside Atlanta

Courtesy Special Collections Dept., Woodruff Library, Emory University

Sabbath school in a Kentucky "cove," pictured in the December 1911 *Home Mission Monthly*
Courtesy Presbyterian Historical Society, Montreat, N.C.

Open-air Sunday school in Arkansas, *Home Mission Monthly,* April 1897
Courtesy Presbyterian Historical Society

Family in Mrs. Campbell's Sunday school, Burkeville, Virginia, April 1911
Home Mission Monthly
Courtesy Presbyterian Historical Society

Children's Day at a Sunday school in Blackwater, Tennessee, *Home Mission Monthly,* December 1906
Courtesy Presbyterian Historical Society

"The Nucleus of a Sunday School founded in April, 1899, from which the Hancock Street Chapel, with 450 pupils, developed."

Hartshorn, ed., *Era of Progress*, 235

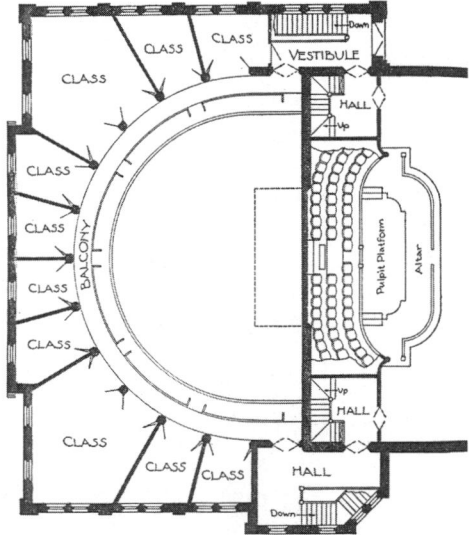

As churches grew, they required new means of allocating space for Sunday school. The original "Akron plan" deployed classrooms—separated by temporary partitions—in a semicircle around the main worship area.

Lawrance, *Housing the Sunday School*, 88

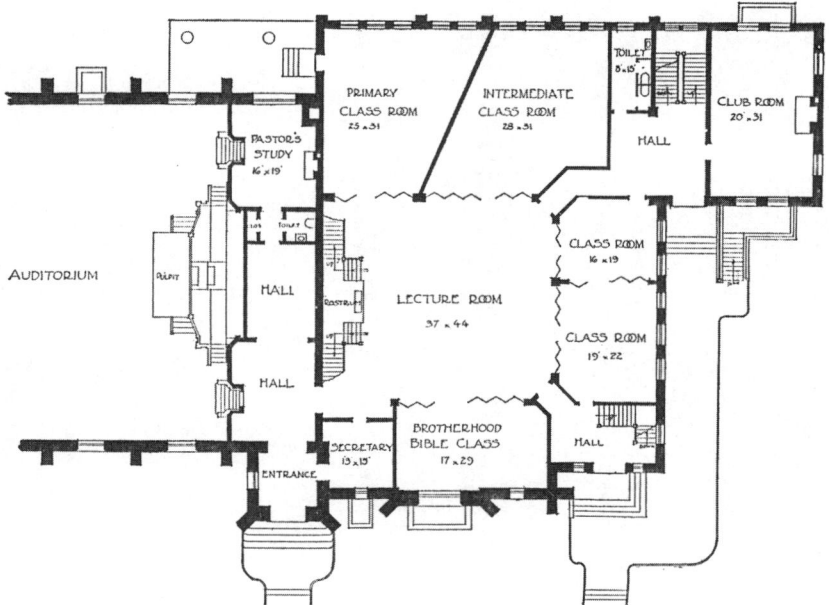

With increasing specialization in their endeavors, Sunday schools moved to larger facilities set apart from the main sanctuary, as in this Louisville Presbyterian church.

Lawrance, *Housing the Sunday School*, 46

Elaborate certificates of membership, like this one from the Edenton Street MEC,S in Raleigh, North Carolina, emphasized the importance of Sunday school in the eyes of pupils and parents alike.
Courtesy Rare Book, Manuscript, and Special Collections Library, Duke University

A certificate testifies to the value placed on recruiting pupils for Sunday schools.
Courtesy Presbyterian Historical Society

The Nashville publishing house of the AME Church Sunday School Union. Black denominations founded their own publishing ventures in part to end their reliance on white-published materials that ignored or demeaned African Americans.
Courtesy Tennessee State Library and Archives, Nashville

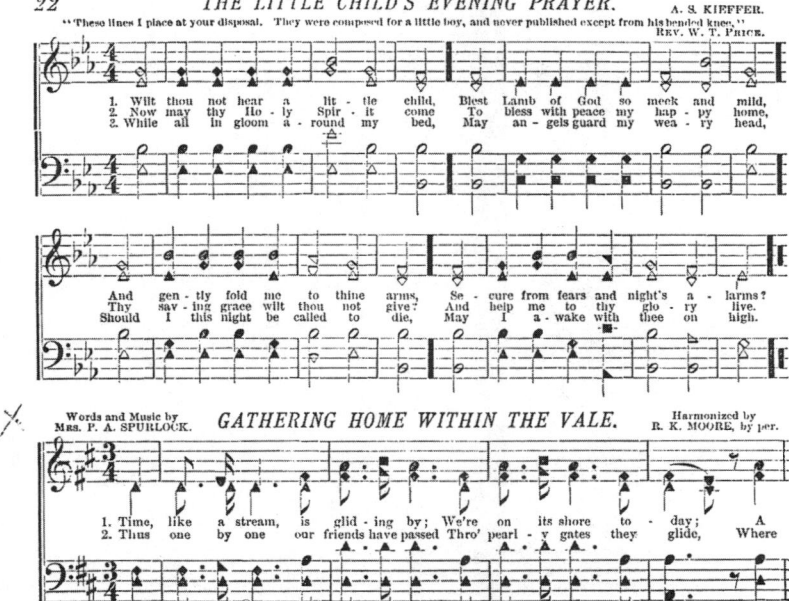

For musically unsophisticated singers, some hymnals used shape-note notation, in which each tone of the octave had its own distinctive form.

Glenn and Kieffer, eds., *New Melodies of Praise*, 22

A Southern Baptist mite box provided edification for the child who folded it to enclose his or her penny contribution.
Frost-Bell Correspondence, Southern Baptist Historical Library and Archives, Nashville

4

UPLIFT AND REDEMPTION THROUGH THE PUBLISHED WORD

In 1894, the AME church opened its publishing firm in downtown Nashville. The Reverend Charles Smith, chief spokesman for the publishing venture, set the tone for the grand occasion. Determination and hard work had "placed us in possession of a most magnificent building on the public square of a leading Southern city," he boasted. AME bishop A. Grant declared that publishing Sunday school literature allowed the AME church "to control our children and to take care of their best interest in the future." Numerous church officials, Nashville's mayor, and several white politicians—as well as hundreds of church members and bystanders—witnessed an event that AME leaders saw as a watershed moment in their church history. After the luminaries had delivered their speeches, perfumed water was sprinkled copiously throughout the building and over the gathered crowd. One proud AME member exulted that his church would now produce Sunday school literature that was the "product of our own hands, heads and hearts."[1]

---

1. C. S. Smith, "Dr. Smith's Speech," in C. S. Smith, ed., *Dedicatory Services at the Publishing House of the A. M. E. Church Sunday School Union* (Nashville: Publishing

The AME venture into publishing was not an isolated occurrence. As southern Sunday schools proliferated and as centralized boards emerged to direct their work, religious denominations made a major commitment to Sunday school publishing. Church officials realized that in order to instill the right lessons in children—including loyalty to a particular church—they had to produce their own literature for classroom and home use. Self-reliance was key. By the turn of the century, publishing became an important activity for southern denominations, putting financial issues in the forefront of Sunday school efforts.

Southerners' involvement in Sunday school publishing paralleled a period of increased literacy among American children and adult concern about what children read. Virginia Methodist James Moss identified the late nineteenth century as a "reading age" and noted that young readers were at the perfect age to attend Sunday school. Publishing houses thus could take advantage of a growing number of youthful consumers who would purchase their materials. With a larger, more literate audience for their products, those involved in denominational publishing foresaw a rosy future.[2]

The demand for children's reading material had exploded by the middle third of the nineteenth century, and an astonishing number of new journals and books were published to meet that need. According to Gillian Avery, more than 130 children's journals were launched between 1840 and 1870; another 105 titles were in print before 1900. In the United States and Europe, authors wrote numerous books for young readers, including such classics as *The Wizard of Oz*, the *Uncle Remus* stories, *Alice in Wonderland,* and *Peter Rabbit*. Sentimental tales of virtue—such as the Horatio Alger novels that celebrated courage, duty, honesty, honor, and good manners—were extremely popular in the late nineteenth century. Sunday school books and religious tracts also made up a significant portion of what American youngsters read.[3]

House of the AME Church Sunday School Union, 1894), 37–88; A. Grant, "Bishop Grant's Speech in St. Paul Church," in Smith, *Dedicatory Services,* 40–9 (quote, 41).

2. James O. Moss, "Publishing Interests," *Minutes of the 109th Session of the Virginia Annual Conference of the Methodist Episcopal Church, South, 1891* (Richmond: J. W. Fergusson and Son, 1891), 63; Higginbotham, *Righteous Discontent,* 11.

3. Avery, *Behold the Child,* 146. For interesting comments on children's literature from an earlier period see Joanna Gillespie, "Schooling through Fiction," *Children's Literature* 14 (1986), 62–81, esp. 62–4. R. Gordon Kelley states that the decade after the Civil War

Yet a growing number of publishers produced a seemingly endless stream of "trash" literature for both children and adults. Moralists across America were shocked by the lurid tales and sensational stories available to the public. Among the most prominent of these critics was New York reformer and crusader Anthony Comstock. For years, Comstock made a name for himself and his vice squad by trying to eradicate all pornographic and obscene material from newsstands and the U.S. mail. Sleazy books and magazines undermined Comstock's definition of a proper moral order, and he and his followers were determined to set things right. White southern evangelicals were equally—if not more—outraged by modern literature.[4]

Nothing seemed to generate more passionate reactions from southern evangelicals than what they perceived as the horrifying state of the literary scene. Their emotional responses, which may strike the modern reader as rather histrionic, were heartfelt. Critics lashed out against popular literature, voicing their concerns in essays, letters, and sermons. Reformers condemned the "moral poison for children" they found in books and sensational newspapers. Lurid headlines in some of the nation's papers confirmed the sorry state of what came to be known as yellow journalism. Shocking words and scandalous ideas in dime novels and crime tales could corrupt the young. Outraged Southern Presbyterians denounced a particularly seedy magazine, *Star Spangled Banner,* which they discovered being sold at a newsstand near an elementary school. Its

---

was "perhaps the richest in the history of American children's periodicals." Kelley, ed., *Children's Periodicals of the United States* (Westport, Conn.: Greenwood Press, 1984), xxii. For information on children's book publishing, see Avery, *Behold the Child,* 5–8, 121, 146; Margaret Nancy Cutt, *Ministering Angels: A Study of Nineteenth-Century Evangelical Writing for Children* (Wormley, England: Five Owls Press, 1979); Daniel T. Rodgers, "Socializing Middle-Class Children: Institutions, Fables, and Work Values in Nineteenth-Century America," in *Growing Up in America: Children in Historical Perspective,* ed. N. Ray Hiner and Joseph M. Hawes (Urbana: University of Illinois Press, 1985), 123. For thoughts on adults' desire to control children through the literature they read, see Anne Scott MacLeod, *American Childhood: Essays on Children's Literature of the Nineteenth and Twentieth Centuries* (Athens: University of Georgia Press), vii.

4. Ownby, *Subduing Satan,* 3–4. See also Boyer, *Urban Masses and Moral Order in America,* 44, and *Purity in Print: The Vice-Society Movement and Book Censorship in America* (New York: Charles Scribner's Sons, 1968). MacLeod says that American publishers did produce a great deal of "trash" literature during this period. MacLeod, *American Childhood,* 4, 121.

"hotly spiced romance and adventure" fostered a "compound of the passions and appetites." Should it fall into children's hands, it could inflame their emotions and harden their hearts. "The pestilent publications swarm upon the land like the frogs upon Egypt," these Presbyterians raged, noting that the *Star Spangled Banner* was merely one of many equally shocking examples.[5]

The Presbyterians were hardly alone. Methodists also decried the "baneful effects of the vicious literature that teems from the press in the most attractive forms that depraved ingenuity can devise." Only the "creation and culture of a pure literary taste" could save the young. Fiction was especially suspect. Historical novels were "filling the minds and hearts of our young people with evil suggestions, slurs on religion, and altogether false ideas of life, and its aims." Too many contemporary books and newspapers lacked any redeeming value whatsoever. Children's stories had become absurd, insisted William Leftwich; dime novels were pure trash and "ought to be legislated out of existence." Rarely did critics cite specific titles or authors when venting their anger; specific facts were immaterial when warning Americans of the evils of contemporary publications. A world awash in trashy literature could be the undoing of all that evangelicals held sacred.[6]

If southern evangelicals were to educate children in Christian ideals and lead them toward salvation, more than a weekly visit to Sunday school was necessary; ongoing exposure to sound, orthodox Christian literature was essential. The church had to prevent youngsters from "devouring vicious books" and instead provide them with an "ample supply of healthful, helpful ones." Methodists seemed determined to spare neither resources nor personnel to promote Sunday school publishing. "It is of vital importance that the Church should have a pure literature to educate and sanctify the taste," they insisted, "a sound literature to enlighten the judgment, a divine literature to convert the heart, and a faithful litera-

---

5. "Moral Poison for Children," *Earnest Worker,* 22 January 1874.
6. "Report of the Executive Committee on Sunday Schools," *Journal of the Tenth Session of the General Conference of the Methodist Episcopal Church, South,* (Nashville: MECS Publishing House, 1886), 51; William Leftwich, *The Child in the Midst; or, The Sunday-School of To-Day* (Nashville: MECS Publishing House, 1882), 99. See also Ownby, *Subduing Satan,* 103–4; MacLeod, *American Childhood,* 121.

ture to mold the character and life of the young." Churches and Sunday schools had to assume responsibility for everything children read.[7]

In part, these dramatic comments reflected southerners' larger apprehensions about modernity and a changing world. Daily newspapers available in southern communities brought tales of sin and immoral behavior into the home, making people all too aware of widespread social ills. The secular press tended to popularize the sensational, with its "marvelous cheapness and lamentable corruption." Adults feared that gullible youngsters were likely to mimic anything they read and to occupy their reading hours with worthless, even harmful, material. The written word could easily affect a child's character, for better or worse. Middle-class reformers—ministers, businessmen, parents, moralists, and especially editors of Sunday school material—insisted that all books and magazines aimed at children had to uplift their moral development.[8]

But the moralists' dramatic remarks and censorship campaigns were also self-serving; they had found a useful enemy. In the face of declining American morals, it was not enough to eradicate scandalous and immoral publications. Sound literature—chock-full of messages that adults wanted children to absorb—had to replace the dross. A denomination or religious publishing house could produce wholesome Christian material to counter tasteless reading material. Parents and Sunday school volunteers needed to understand that literature produced by a church firm could help to ensure every child's redemption. Eventually, moralists' denunciations proved effective in banishing scandalous material from the market and replacing it with sound religious literature. Armed with material from a church publishing firm, Sunday school teachers could more easily mold southern children into morally upright Christians.[9]

Southern Sunday school officials also worried about northern publishers and rival denominations whose publications might influence their

---

7. Cope, *Religious Education in the Family*, 114; "Report of the Executive Committee on Sunday Schools," *Journal of the Tenth Session Methodist Episcopal Church, South, 1886*, 51. See also Ruth Miller Elson, *Guardians of Tradition: American Schoolbooks of the Nineteenth Century* (Lincoln: University of Nebraska Press, 1964), 1–6.

8. "Publications," *Proceedings of the 47th Annual Session of the Arkansas Baptist State Convention, 1895*, 14.

9. Alison M. Parker, *Purifying America: Women, Cultural Reform, and Pro-Censorship Activism, 1873–1933* (Urbana: University of Illinois Press, 1997).

children. For years, northern religious organizations and private publishers had produced most of the literature that southern Sunday schools used. Southerners began to find fault with this material, demanding that their own denominations publish literature suitable both for Sunday school and home consumption. Authoritative material was needed that presented an orthodox approach to Scripture and that taught lessons that southerners valued. Kentucky Methodists, for example, expressed uneasiness with the "foreign" publications used in their Sunday schools. They wanted their church, with its keen interest in education, to produce its own Sunday school literature for members to purchase and read. Similarly, E. Thompson Baird, editor of the Presbyterian publishing house, demanded that church members reject all "foreign" influences. Baird argued that it made little sense to found and run southern Sunday schools if children continued to purchase and read northern material. Only southern denominational literature would ensure purity of thought and sound doctrine, uplift youngsters on southern terms, and control the messages they read.[10]

Vigilant adults began to scrutinize northern publications with a critical eye. Southern Baptists discovered ABPS publications with "allusions to northern glories" and books dedicated to northern heroes like Abraham Lincoln and Ulysses S. Grant—tributes that offended former Confederates. Alabama Presbyterians objected to the "cheap, purchasable literature" and Sunday school texts with "indefinable doctrinal bases" that were produced by a private northern firm. Virginia Baptists condemned northern Sunday school publications as "prejudicial to our political, social and religious sentiments." Lacking their own publishing firm at this juncture, they appointed a special committee to create a catalogue listing only those ABPS Sunday school materials they deemed acceptable.[11]

10. "Report of the Committee on Books and Periodicals," *Minutes of the Fifty-Sixth Session of the Kentucky Annual Conference of the Methodist Episcopal Church, South, 1876,* 21; E. Thompson Baird, "Ninth Annual Report of the Executive Committee of Publication," *Minutes of the General Assembly of the Presbyterian Church in the United States, 1870* (Columbia, S.C.: Presbyterian Publishing House, 1870), 563.

11. "Sunday School Literature—An Important Question," *Religious Herald,* 12 April 1866; "Narrative of the State of Religion," *Minutes of the Synod of Alabama* (Montgomery: n.p., 1900); Baptist General Association of Virginia, *Catalogue of Sunday School*

Such worries were similar to those expressed about textbooks used in southern public schools, the majority of which were published and written by northerners. During the Civil War, loyal Confederates were dedicated to the idea of producing school books on home turf—textbooks that reflected southern beliefs and values. Similar sentiments emerged during Reconstruction, as southern states established public school systems and oversaw the content of classroom lessons. As early as 1874, Virginians worried about the textbooks their children used, wanting youngsters to learn facts without a northern bias. To that end, the state legislature introduced a bill to eliminate all "immoral, irreverent, false, unpatriotic" statements from schoolbooks.[12]

African Americans seemed less troubled by the state of contemporary literature than white evangelicals, or at least they spent far less energy and ink venting indignation over the state of modern books and newspapers. Several factors may help explain this disparity. First, fewer blacks than whites could read. Endemic poverty among blacks also prevented their purchase of popular books and magazines, perhaps causing them to be more accepting of any literature that came their way. Initially, no struggling Sunday school could afford to be too choosy about the literature used in its classrooms. And African Americans had far larger concerns to address; they generally seemed to be less horrified by modernity and changing morality than were whites.

There were nonetheless sound arguments for Sunday school publishing. Advocates insisted that religious literature could counter what seemed to be growing parental indifference to religious home instruction. Too few parents seemed to pay attention to what their children read in Sunday school or at home. As a black Baptist bemoaned, "many boys' and girls' prospects are blighted for life for the want of this care on the part of parents." While adults might subscribe to and read two or three daily newspapers to keep abreast of national news, he noted, they often avoided reading a church paper. Without a Sunday school newspaper,

---

Books Approved by the Sunday School and Publishing Board of the Baptist General Association of Virginia (Richmond: Starke and Ryland's Book Store, 1867), preface. Baptists complained that Jefferson Davis was highlighted in these dedications, suggesting that they feared a secular element infiltrating Sunday school books.

12. Bell, *The Church, the State, and Education in Virginia*, 408–9. The bill did not pass.

Methodists insisted, children in their church were growing up in ignorance. A denominational publishing house could tackle both indifference and ignorance by producing material for its members.[13]

African Americans had compelling reasons to engage in Sunday school publishing. "We can more successfully bestir our people by persuading them to properly cultivate race pride by inaugurating enterprises of their own than in any other way," insisted Elias Camp Morris, an ardent supporter of National Baptist Convention (NBC) publishing. AME bishop J. P. Campbell urged his church to publish literature that would be the "product of our own hands, heads, and hearts, adapted to the wants and necessities of our schools." Setting up and managing this business became an issue of race pride, displaying blacks' capabilities to the world.[14]

African Americans were also troubled by the fact that most of their Sunday schools purchased and used material produced by and for whites. White publishers invariably ignored African Americans in their Sunday school material. If present at all, blacks usually appeared as field laborers or domestic servants. For instance, Northern Methodists, in conjunction with the ATS, produced the Sunday school magazine *Good Tidings,* "designed specifically for the colored people in the South." Its stories and illustrations solely depicted white situations and culture. Though the ABPS and ASSU sought out black Baptist subscribers, neither organization produced material directed at African American readers. In response to complaints, the ABPS hinted that it would hire black writers and include their material in its magazines. White southerners got wind of this idea and strongly objected; the ABPS backed down. Southern African Americans also deplored the fact that their purchases supported white enterprises and writers rather than their own. Unfortunately, this was not

---

13. "Religious Literature," *Journal of the Proceedings of the 12th Annual Session of the Western North Carolina Association* (n.p., 1897); "Report of the Committee on Books and Periodicals," *Minutes of the 51st Session of the Kentucky Annual Conference of the Methodist Episcopal Church, South, 1871* (Cincinnati: Applegate, Youngsford, 1871), 24.

14. Elias Camp Morris, "The Demand for a Negro Baptist Publishing House," in *Sermons, Addresses and Reminiscences and Important Correspondence* (Nashville: National Baptist Publishing Board, 1901); J. P. Campbell, "Address by Bishop J. P. Campbell," *Journal of the 17th Quadrennial Session of the General Conference of the AME Church, 1880* (Xenia, Ohio: Torchlight Printing, 1882), 89. See also James Melvin Washington, *Frustrated Fellowship: The Black Baptist Quest for Social Power* (Macon, Ga.: Mercer University Press, 1985), 163–6; Lincoln and Mamiya, *The Black Church,* 242–3.

a unique situation; public school textbooks were equally remiss in addressing race issues and black history. The hand-me-down texts that African American children used in day school were created for white children and selected by white boards of education.[15]

Many African Americans believed that owning and managing their own publishing houses would promote racial identity and race pride. Church leaders wanted youngsters to read literature written by and about blacks and their concerns, which was impossible as long as whites dominated religious publishing. As a National Baptist writer insisted, his race had to stand among other progressive peoples and "have its names and its deeds fully and accurately recorded in history, [and] must make a literature that is *distinctly* and peculiarly its own." The right materials had to be put before children. "We want to read race literature and have a little more race pride," concurred Bishop Grant. "If other races can be proud of themselves, we must learn to be proud of our development." African Americans controlled their own churches and Sunday schools; they also needed to control the messages taught there. With Sunday school boards in place, publishing houses were the next logical step for black denominations.[16]

For several of these denominations, Sunday school publishing was not a new undertaking. The AME church had a long-established publishing firm in Philadelphia, which first produced material in 1817. After the Civil War, as the denomination founded more churches and Sunday schools, the AME publishing business grew so dramatically that it had to divide its church and Sunday school publishing into two separate businesses. As a result, in 1882 the AME church established a separate Sun-

15. Litwack, *Trouble in Mind*, 17–8; "Some Facts Concerning the Sunday School Union of the Methodist Episcopal Church," in *The Centennial Budget of the AME Church, 1887–1888*, ed. Benjamin William Arnett (Philadelphia: AME Publishing House, 1888), 414. See also Harvey, *Redeeming the South*, 70–1; Marie Elizabeth Carpenter, *The Treatment of the Negro in American History School Textbooks* (Menasha, Wis.: George Banta, 1941), 70–5.

16. "Negro Literature an Absolute Necessity," *National Baptist Union*, 17 October 1903; Grant, "Bishop Grant's Speech," *Dedicatory Services*, 42. See also W. E. B. DuBois, *The Negro Church*, 115. For an overview of black publishing, see Penelope L. Bullock, *The Afro-American Periodical Press, 1838–1909* (Baton Rouge: Louisiana State University Press, 1981), esp. 68–98. Black pupils were often well aware of the "whiteness" of their schoolbooks and the lessons that ignored race and black history. See Litwack, *Trouble in Mind*, 71–80.

day school publishing house in Bloomington, Indiana, where it remained for a few years before moving to Nashville in 1886.[17]

The AMEZ church opened its book concern in New York City in 1841. For years, its Sunday schools purchased and used literature produced by white Northern Methodists, with the AMEZ book concern adding its own imprint. Desiring more independence, the AMEZ General Conference set up a publishing firm in Montgomery, Alabama, in 1888. After briefly relocating to Livingstone College in Salisbury, North Carolina, the AMEZ publishing firm was reorganized by the Board of Bishops, who combined church and Sunday school publishing under a single roof. This business opened in Charlotte, North Carolina, in 1896. City fathers dubbed the AMEZ's impressive new headquarters Charlotte's first "Negro skyscraper." In 1911, after some major struggles, editor Robert Blair Bruce was able to claim that years of "dark and impending clouds" had given way to "words of praise and good cheer." As they had done with their Sunday school boards, both the AME and AMEZ churches purposely chose a southern location for their publishing firms in order to better serve their members, 80 to 90 percent of whom now lived in the South.[18]

Sunday school publishing was a new undertaking for Colored Methodists. After a group of blacks left the Methodist Episcopal Church,

17. For information on AME publishing, see J. P. Campbell, "Address by Bishop J. P. Campbell," *Journal of the 17th Quadrennial of the General Conference, AME Church, 1882,* 89; "Historical," *Dedicatory Services,* 7; "A Mammoth Purchase," *AME Bicentennial, 1887–1888,* ed. Benjamin William Arnett (Philadelphia: AME Publishing House, 1888), 416–8; J. C. Embry, "Publishing Department," *Journal of the 19th Session and 18th Quadrennial Session of the General Conference of the AME Church, 1888* (Philadelphia: AME, 1888), 170.

18. For information on AMEZ publishing, see Walls, *The African Methodist Episcopal Zion Church,* 284–6, 290, 335; "Report of the General Agent of Book Concern," *Daily Proceedings of the 16th Quadrennial Session of the General Conference of the AMEZ, 1880* (New York: William Knowles, 1880), 60; "Report on Sabbath Schools," *Daily Proceedings of the 18th Quadrennial Session of the General Conference of the AMEZ, 1888* (Wilmington, N.C.: Jackson and Bell, 1888), 96; G. L. Blackwell, "Report of the Publishing House," *Official Journal of the Daily Proceedings of the 21st Quadrennial Session of the General Conference of the AMEZ Church* (York, Pa.: Dispatch Print, 1901), 199–200; Robert Blair Bruce, "Sunday School Department" and "Report of the Publishing House," in *Official Journal of the 22nd Quadrennial Session of the General Conference of the AME Zion Church* (New York: AMEZ Book Concern, 1904), 137–8, 306–8; Sernett, *Bound for the Promised Land,* 36.

South (MECS) and formed the Colored Methodist Episcopal Church (CME) in 1870, they set up a book concern at their Jackson, Tennessee, headquarters. For years, this served as a clearinghouse to purchase and distribute Sunday school material acquired from other firms. This dependency began to bother CME members, who wanted their children reading "unadulterated" doctrine. "We have been too careless," one member warned, for "enemies are taking advantage of our membership." He urged the denomination to engage in its own Sunday school publishing. By the end of the century, the CME church had purchased a printing press and was producing some of its own material.[19]

Several southern white denominations had engaged in Sunday school publishing during the antebellum and Civil War periods, but the war interrupted or ruined most of these businesses. At their 1866 general conference, Southern Methodists expressed their determination to rebuild their Nashville house and publish Sunday school material. The firm overcame significant hurdles, including a debt estimated by some to be as high as $100,000. By tightening its belt and charging higher prices for its publications, the MECS finally eliminated this debt. By the early twentieth century, Methodists began to exhibit confidence in their business. In 1908, the church constructed a four-story building in Nashville to house publishing operations. Vanderbilt University's dean Wilbur Tillett boasted, "Never, in all its long history, has the church produced such splendid literature as it is sending forth today." Methodist material was "unsurpassed by that of any other of our American churches," he proclaimed.[20]

19. "Sunday School Literature of the CME Church," *Christian Index*, 13 September 1890; Lakey, *The Rise of "Colored Methodism"*, 103. For background on the CME church, see Lincoln and Mamiya, *The Black Church*, 60–4; Gravely, "The Social, Political and Religious Significance of the Formation of the Colored Methodist Episcopal Church (1870)," *Methodist History* 18 (1979): 3–25; Charles Henry Phillips, *The History of the Colored Methodist Episcopal Church in America: Comprising Its Organization, Subsequent Development, and Present Status* (Jackson, Tenn.: Publishing House of the CME, 1925). The CME later changed its name to the Christian Methodist Church.

20. Wilbur Fiske Tillett, *Theological Seminaries and Teacher Training: A Discussion of the Preachers' Relation to the Sunday School and the Young Life of the Church* (Nashville: Smith and Lamar, 1910), 10. See Stowell, *Rebuilding Zion*, 112, 115; Harold W. Mann, *Atticus Greene Haygood: Methodist Bishop, Editor, and Educator* (Athens: University of Georgia Press, 1965), 83–5; "75 Years of Progress: A Story of Growth of the Publishing House, Methodist Episcopal Church, South," (Nashville: Lamar and Whitmore, 1930), 4–6; "Address of the Bishops," *Journal of the Eleventh General Conference of the Methodist Episcopal Church, South* (Nashville: Southern Methodist Publishing House, 1890), 36;

The Presbyterian Church of the United States (PCUS) also experienced checkered success in publishing. The war left the church's Richmond publishing firm in ruins, but the General Assembly voted to rebuild the enterprise. Due to unsound, perhaps unethical, business practices by one editor, the firm compiled a debt of $31,000. By reorganizing and adopting cost-cutting measures and more aggressive sales tactics, the situation improved. By the early twentieth century, Presbyterians had their business on a sound financial footing. In 1904, the PCUS dedicated its handsome new brick headquarters in Richmond's finest downtown neighborhood and opened a branch depository to serve members in the Southwest.[21]

The movement of white and black Southern Baptists into Sunday school publishing deserves a somewhat lengthier discussion, in part because of the issues involved but also because scholars have studied them in more detail. White Southern Baptists had engaged in various Sunday school publishing efforts before the Civil War, but few ventures had experienced lasting success. For years, Baptist Sunday schools purchased material produced by the ABPS. Not until the 1890s and the formation of the Southern Baptist Convention (SBC) Sunday school board was there adequate support for establishing a regional publishing house. But there was also a good deal of opposition to such a plan, especially from Baptists who feared the possible power and influence of a single publishing house to serve all white Southern Baptists. Others were content to rely on the ABPS for Sunday school literature. Supporters of the enterprise were fortunate to have the energies and commitment of James Marion

---

"The Publishing House," *Journal of the Fifteenth General Conference of the Methodist Episcopal Church, South* (Nashville: Publishing House of the MECS, 1906), 35. Stowell says the debt was $71,000, but some contemporary sources note the higher figure of $100,000.

21. "Executive Committee of Publication," *Missionary Survey,* 230; "The Children's Friend," *Minutes of the General Assembly of the Presbyterian Church in the United States, 1867* (Columbia: Southern Presbyterian Review, 1867), 196; "Abstract of the Annual Report of the Executive Committee of Publication," *Minutes of the General Assembly of the Presbyterian Church in the United States, 1868* (Richmond: Presbyterian Committee of Publication, 1868), 297; "Twelfth Annual Report of the Executive Committee of Publication," *Minutes of the General Assembly of the Presbyterian Church in the United States, 1873* (Richmond: Presbyterian Committee of Publication, 1873), 371; Thompson, *Presbyterians in the South,* vol. 2, 332; "The New Home of the Presbyterian Committee of Publications," *Presbyterian Standard,* 10 February 1904.

Frost, who served as secretary of the Sunday School Board from 1891 to 1893 and 1896 to 1916. In Frost's eyes, a regional publishing house was the best means to unify and strengthen the denomination. "Make the Convention stronger and larger in its facilities, and you will add to the greatness of its mission, and the glory of its destiny," he urged. To gain support, he authored two pamphlets for his fellow Baptists, exploring the prospects and potential influence of a publishing house. "Everyone recognizes that the power of the printed page is hardly second to any of the forces that influence men," he wrote, "and why should not the SBC, representing as it does over a million and a half Baptists, have under its power and control all the advantages which come from conducting a great publishing interest?"[22]

To Frost and like-minded supporters, a publishing firm would allow all Baptist Sunday schools to instill the "right" church principles in their members and end their dependence on others. Frost depicted northern organizations such as the ABPS as enemies of "exceeding shrewdness" that wanted "to capture and hold the South"—a strategy which he believed was completely untenable. He argued that a southern publishing firm would allow Baptists to achieve greater autonomy, both in the literature they used and in the way they conducted their Sunday school work. Under Frost's leadership, the Sunday School Board began to publish a variety of materials, including an inexpensive Bible, which it introduced in order to undercut a bestseller of the ABPS. Its doctrinally correct material began to win over former critics. In 1913, the Convention built a multi-storied building in Nashville for its publishing business, which today houses some of the operations of the SBC Sunday School Board.[23]

22. James Marion Frost, "The Convention As Viewed from Its Sunday School Board," *Seminary Magazine* 12 (May 1899): 383, and *A Word and a Plea Made with Those Not Using the Sunday School Periodicals Issued by the Southern Baptist Convention* (Nashville: SBC, 1903), 10. The other pamphlet was *The Sunday School Problem and What Can Be Done with It* (Nashville: SBC, 1903). See also Ethel Harrison Grice, "The History of the Sunday School Work in the Southern Baptist Convention" (M.A. thesis, Vanderbilt University, 1929), 27–33; Joe Wright Burton, *Road to Nashville* (Nashville: Broadman Press, 1977), 37–46; Hill, *Encyclopedia of Religion*, 275; William Preston Clemmons, "The Development of a Sunday School Strategy in the Southern Baptist Convention, 1896–1926" (Ed.D. diss, Southern Baptist Theological Seminary, 1971), 170–3; Shurden, *The Sunday School Board*, 23–6.

23. May, "The Emerging Role of Sunday Schools in Southern Baptist Life to 1900," 6–16 (quote, 6), and "The Sunday School: A Two-Hundred Year Heritage," 3–11; James Marion Frost, *The Sunday School Board: Southern Baptist Convention, Its History and*

The National Baptist Convention (NBC) organized its publishing house following the denomination's official creation in 1895. For years, members had debated the wisdom of producing Sunday school and religious literature for black Baptists. A church leader, Elias Camp Morris, urged members forward. As a strong proponent of racial uplift, black enterprise, and self-help, Morris worried that black scholarship was "going largely unexercised and unremunerated." It took little persuasion to convince the enterprising head of the new NBC Sunday School Union, Richard H. Boyd, that a publishing firm was important, and the company soon began producing NBC literature. NBC Sunday school literature soon carved out a significant market, thanks to Boyd's savvy business sense, aggressive marketing, and a large, rapidly growing denomination. Boyd swiftly expanded NBC publications and merchandise—whatever seemed marketable caught his eye. Black self-help was his promotional theme, and Boyd pointed to his own success as an example of what blacks could achieve. Most church members regarded this firm as the official church publishing house. Boyd saw it as his personal enterprise.[24]

Boyd's business (as well as all these publishing houses) reflected much about the New South. Many business leaders began to encourage greater industrial and commercial development by the late nineteenth century. In 1898, Boyd incorporated his firm under Tennessee law and copyrighted material in his own name. Using property he purchased in downtown Nashville, Boyd built a publishing house with modern presses and spacious storerooms. By 1905, his firm had done $2.4 million in business; by 1910, it employed more than 150 blacks. He saw his business as the "largest and most complete printing, binding, stereotyping and engraving plant in the world owned and operated exclusively by negroes."

Work (Nashville: Sunday School Board, 1914), 7; Burton, *Road to Nashville,* 87–91; Harvey, *Redeeming the South,* 30.

24. Morris, "The Demand for a Negro Baptist Publishing House," 56; "The New Sunday School Commentary in Demand," *National Baptist Union,* January 1904. See also Joseph Harrison Jackson, *A Story of Christian Activism: The History of the National Baptist Convention, U.S.A., Inc.* (Nashville: Townsend Press, 1980), 66, 71–8, 94–101; Washington, *Frustrated Fellowship,* 180–1; Montgomery, *Under Their Own Vine,* 239, 335–6. Paul Harvey calls Boyd another "unsung hero of the urban black middle class." See Harvey, *Redeeming the South,* 243–7. Contemporary opinion was less flattering and widely divergent about this brash, outspoken, and successful man.

Historian Loren Schweninger has called Boyd's firm "one of the most successful black enterprises in the South." Boyd also welcomed white support; to that end, he developed a close working relationship with James Frost and sought SBC assistance when needed.[25]

Sunday school publishing houses had a critical purpose: to produce instructional material that would expose Biblical truths, teach moral lessons, supplement the weekly lesson plan (which became known as the uniform lesson), and see that children read acceptable literature. This meant not catering to a "youthful, morbid appetite for fiction" in order to sell books merely for the sake of profit, insisted one editor. Virginia Methodists promised that only inspiring literature would roll off their presses, for too many publications "have no more solidarity than a soap bubble—are not good for the soul." In language that rural southerners well understood, publishing houses had to produce appropriate titles "as carefully as a farmer selects his seed corn."[26]

These firms published instructional literature appealing to children but meeting adults' standards and delivering an appropriate message. Apparently the supply of writers exceeded the demand, for one jaded South Carolina Baptist seemed overwhelmed by the amount of material being written for children. "The Sunday school is the most convenient subject of the day," he observed. "It has served as a kind of safety valve to more young writers in letting off literary steam than perhaps any other subject." Sunday school literature was a handy outlet for budding authors and writers seeking a venue to express their faith as well as their talent. Though contributors may have been plentiful, an editor like Atticus Haygood preferred to produce much of his own copy. Other editors sought contributions by holding competitions for new tales and

---

25. Owen D. Pelt and Ralph Lee Smith, *The Story of the National Baptists* (New York: Vantage Press, 1960), 103–4; Sernett, *Bound for the Promised Land*, 97–8; Loren Schweninger, *Black Property Owners in the South, 1790–1915* (Urbana: University of Illinois Press, 1990), 219. NBC officials discovered that profits from the firm and its related businesses were not funneled into church projects but into Boyd's pocket. By 1907, anxious NBC leaders insisted on examining the books. Boyd refused, and feelings on both sides grew hostile. In 1915, Boyd parted ways with the NBC, and his publishing business became the nucleus of a new religious body, the NBC, Unincorporated.

26. E. M. Peterson, "Sunday-Schools," *Minutes of the One Hundred and Twelfth Session of the Virginia Annual Conference of the Methodist Episcopal Church, South* (Richmond: J. W. Fergusson and Son, 1894), 49.

poems. In 1873, the Methodists offered a $300 prize for the best original story.[27]

Women produced a goodly percentage of Sunday school literature, including poems, moral tales, hymns, and religious essays. Mrs. F. M. Smith won the Methodists' $300 prize for the best original story. For three years, Mrs. E. H. Morse wrote "delightfully entertaining" stories and poems that appeared in the Presbyterian *Children's Friend.* Female novelists included Sarah Myers, who wrote *Our Kate,* and Mrs. McConoughly, who produced *The Widow's Sewing Machine.* The *AME Review* printed several women's essays, including "The Colored Women in Verse" and "The Women of Our Race Worthy of Imitation." Baptist women wrote "Grace and her Stepmother" and "Quince, and How the Lord Led Them." Other female writers included Alice Hartland, author of "Bessie's Handkerchief," and Mary Bradley, who wrote "Kiss and Make Up." A few women eventually moved into editorial positions, usually overseeing the publications that served young pupils. Mrs. Allen Preston, a regular contributor to several Presbyterian publications, became editor of *Children's Friend* and *Pearls for Little Ones;* in the early twentieth century, Mrs. W. C. Edmondson became editor of the Presbyterian *Primary Quarterly.*[28]

To aid superintendents and teachers in selecting the best literature for their Sunday schools—and to hawk their own products—publishing firms used self-promotion and extensive advertising. Like Sunday school missionary work, publishing was a cutthroat business, and church firms scrambled to secure a market. Editors had to generate demand in the marketplace, for no one could be assured of loyal fans. With Sunday school publishers expanding their publication lists, undercutting prices, and sending book agents far afield, competitors had to pursue and foster

---

27. "Sunday School Literature," *Working Christian,* 11 February 1875; "Miscellany," "Our Prize Series," and "Prize Winner," *Sunday School Magazine* 3 (1873): 137, 168, 298.

28. Schweiger, "Transformation of Southern Religion," 374; "Death of Mrs. E. H. Morse," *Children's Friend,* 16 October 1880; "The Children's Friend," *Children's Friend,* January 1910; *Alabama Baptist,* 3 May 1883; Charles R. Nisbet, "Standing Committee on Publications and Sabbath Schools and Young Peoples' Societies," *Minutes of the General Assembly of the Presbyterian Church in the United States, 1905* (Richmond: Presbyterian Committee of Publication, 1905), 52. Because bylines were rare or listed only as initials, it is difficult to determine gender. For background on female writers during this period, see Jane Benardete and Phyllis Moe, eds., *Companions of Our Youth: Stories by Women for Young People's Magazines, 1865–1900* (New York: Frederick Ungar, 1980).

customer loyalty. To this end, full-page advertisements for Sunday school publications littered local and church newspapers. Church presses printed and distributed price lists of their publications, complete with purchasing instructions, specially discounted items, and glowing comments touting their literature. To assist buyers, the publishing house of the MECS published a catalogue listing all its publications and even spelled out recommendations for prospective buyers. For instance, a small Sunday school with five dollars to spend should purchase two copies of the denomination's *Sunday School Magazine,* ten lesson papers, ten copies of *Our Little People,* twelve *Little Hymn Books,* six Southern Methodist Primers, and a dozen Capter's Catechisms. Larger, more prosperous classes should buy additional copies of these publications, as well as subscriptions to *Monthly Visitor, Wesleyan Catechism,* and the *Amaranth Song Book.* Errors undoubtedly fell on the side of oversupply, for firms were eager to sell as many books and magazines as possible.[29]

As publishers became more competitive, however, editors adopted more aggressive marketing techniques and advertising—some even heavy-handed—to sell their material. They touted their products in church newspapers and convention programs. Mail order catalogues, which became popular in the late nineteenth century, helped to increase sales. To handle a growing mail order business, white Southern Methodists and Presbyterians set up satellite offices across the South. Editors and publishing boards shamelessly demanded members' loyalty. Sunday school readers were to purchase only denominational material. An AME member was clear on this point: "The law makes it the duty of every Sunday school to use our own literature," he insisted. The Methodist *Doctrines and Discipline* urged every Sunday school to adopt only denominational books and periodicals.[30]

The most profitable best-sellers were Sunday school hymnals. Until the mid-nineteenth century, few hymnbooks targeted children, but the popularity of Sunday schools created a golden opportunity to capture an audience of young singers. Southern Methodists were prolific publishers in this area, and several of their popular, if pricey, children's hymnals

29. "Catalogue and Price List of the Publishing House of the Methodist Episcopal Church, South" (Nashville: MECS Publishing House, 1885).
30. "Report on Sunday Schools," *Journal of the Virginia Annual Conference of the AME Church* (1887), 42; "Kind Words Series of S. S. Publications of the Southern Baptist Convention," *Our Home Field,* August 1888.

helped the publishing house eradicate its debt. The firm even hired its own music editor, R. M. McIntosh, who was associated with it for thirty years. These tactics did not escape notice. Southern Presbyterians sniffed at the Methodists, commenting that they had "put such a price on their Hymn Book as made it an immense source of revenue to their house." Hymnals also gave composers and amateur song writers an opportunity to express their musicality, gain an audience, and earn money composing original hymns. Sunday schools provided the demand, and publishing houses and musicians happily met the need.[31]

The sheer number of children's hymnals produced by private and church presses during this period is astonishing. One music scholar estimates that in the late nineteenth century, thousands of copies of Sunday school and church hymnals were sold annually. This profusion reflected not only growth in Sunday schools but attested to the important role that music played in the Sunday classroom. At times the market seemed flooded with children's hymnals. Song books varied from the simple to the sophisticated, but were usually small in size to minimize cost and fit easily into a child's hand. Some contained only a few pages stitched inside a cardboard cover, while others were bound and included several hundred hymns. Publishers usually included a few popular tunes as well as perennial favorites like "My Country 'Tis of Thee," though serious-minded editors incorporated only sacred and traditional hymns in their songbooks.

When it came to marketing their musical compilations, editors were hardly subtle. Despite the similarity of various hymnals, each promised something unique. *Pure Songs for Sunday-Schools* claimed to be filled with songs of "rare merit" based on the parables and miracles of Jesus Christ and other verses from Holy Scripture. Low cost could also be a selling point. Basil Manly Jr. touted his *Manly's Choice* as being "cheap and of convenient size; it contains no trash and no unreal sentiment or unsound doctrine." Asa Hull and D. R. McAnally Jr. boasted that most of the songs in their hymnal were new and copyrighted. The NBC published several hymnals, including its popular *Celestial Showers* and *Pearls*

---

31. "Abstract of the Fifteenth Annual Report of the Committee of Publication," *Minutes of the General Assembly of the Presbyterian Church in the United States, 1876* (Richmond: Whittet and Shepperson, 1876), 261. See William Jensen Reynolds, *A Survey of Christian Hymnody* (New York: Holt, Rinehart, and Winston, 1963), 99–101.

of *Paradise,* and sought to meet every need with the *National Baptist Hymnal,* which contained 531 songs. Editors encouraged Sunday school instructors to buy only hymnals produced by the appropriate publishing house, pointing out the importance of having Sunday school pupils sing denominationally approved songs.[32]

The most widely read publications, however, were Sunday school magazines. These appeared with some regularity and usually contained the uniform lessons, Bible stories, questions on Scripture, and a smattering of fiction, essays, poems, illustrations, and a golden text. Over time, publishing houses responded to their expanding and changing Sunday school population by producing special magazines for differently aged pupils. Southern Baptists' most enduring publication was their children's magazine *Kind Words,* which first appeared in 1866. In 1878, the church inaugurated *The Child's Gem* for older youngsters. The MECS revived its periodical for older children, *Sunday School Visitor,* in 1869, while its publication *Our Little People* focused on younger pupils. A single lesson sheet for toddlers, *Leaf Cluster,* contained one or two simple stories and an illustrated lesson. By the early twentieth century, with more adults and infants in Sunday school, the MECS produced *The Adult Student* for officers and teachers who had charge of older pupils and *The Primary Teacher* for instructors of young students. The AME Sunday School Publishing House also produced a variety of periodicals, including *The Scholar's Quarterly* for intermediate pupils, *The Juvenile Lesson Paper* for youngsters, *The Gem Lesson Paper* for primary children, and *Lesson Pictures* for toddlers.[33]

A profusion of advice books and periodicals addressed to teachers, su-

---

32. Atticus Haygood and R. M. McIntosh, *Pure Songs for Sunday-Schools* (Macon, Ga.: J. W. Burke, 1889), preface; Basil Manly Jr., *Manly's Choice: A New Selection of Approved Hymns for Baptist Churches* (Louisville, Ky.: Baptist Book Concern, 1892); Asa Hull and D. R. McAnally Jr., *The Royal Favorite: A Choice Collection of Original and Selected Hymns* (St. Louis: Advocate Publishing House, 1877). White Southern Baptists did not publish any hymnals until the twentieth century. Their Sunday schools used hymnals produced by other firms.

33. "The Lesson Papers," *Sunday School Magazine* 6 (January 1876): 13; James E. Fitch, "Major Thrusts in Sunday School Development since 1900," *Baptist History and Heritage* 18, no. 1 (1983): 18–9; "Report of Sunday School Board," *Journal of the Forty-Second Annual Session, Northwest Texas Conferences, Methodist Episcopal Church, South* (Fort Worth: Keystone Printing, 1907), 43; "Publications of the AME Church Sunday School Union," *AME Church Review* 19 (April 1903), frontispiece.

perintendents, and parents also poured forth from religious presses. Writers spelled out tips on how to ensure that every Sunday class was well organized and appealing, and editors urged Sunday school volunteers to purchase these practical manuals. Southern Presbyterians' *Earnest Worker* targeted volunteers and parents with its "spirited, concise" articles to advise and inspire. A weekly column, "Sunday School Intelligence," described activities undertaken by Presbyterian Sunday schools throughout the South. One pastor complimented the paper for its "potent influence . . . in exciting or in promoting revivals of religion." The *AME Teacher's Quarterly* presented both practical and miscellaneous information, including advice for instructors, the annual budget, obituaries of prominent church officials, weekly lessons, and illustrated Bible stories. The Methodists' *Sunday School Magazine* offered a variety of tips to superintendents and instructors, including how to run evergreen Sunday schools, the proper attire for teachers, ways to stimulate pupils, and how to select appropriate texts. The SBC Sunday School Board began publishing the *Superintendent's Quarterly* in 1905 to publicize the latest methods in Sunday school work and to convey its philosophy. Editors tried to provide varied Sunday school material and a standardized approach.[34]

Despite widespread criticism hurled at popular fiction, short stories and allegorical tales were an important feature in Sunday school literature. Editors had to please children in order to retain youthful readers, and fiction proved an appealing means to deliver a moral truth. But lest parents worry about the fiction their children read, editors insisted that the stories in their literature paralleled "real life" and would not offend readers. As Presbyterian E. Thompson Baird explained, his firm tried to avoid the sensational and instead "give life and practical point to the truths presented." He rejected any material that "would excite the young mind to a morbid thirst after the marvelous." The circumstances of the tale, not its form, apparently made the difference.[35]

Publishing houses also produced children's books for the Sunday

---

34. "The Earnest Worker," *Earnest Worker*, 5 October 1870; "Tenth Annual Report of the Executive Committee of Publication," *Minutes of the General Assembly of the Presbyterian Church in the United States, 1871* (Columbia, S.C.: Presbyterian Publishing House, 1871), 67; Fitch, "Major Thrusts," 18–9.

35. E. Thompson Baird, "Eleventh Annual Report of the Executive Committee of Publication," *Minutes of the General Assembly of the Presbyterian Church in the United States, 1872* (Richmond: Presbyterian Committee of Publication, 1872), 200–1.

school library. The library was an important component of every successful Sunday school, giving children an opportunity to borrow books to read at home. It is easy to forget how few southern families actually owned many books in the second half of the nineteenth century. If they had a book in their home, it was likely to be a Bible. Benjamin Mays's family was more fortunate than most, owning a Bible, a dictionary, works by Booker T. Washington, Paul Laurence Dunbar, and Frederick Douglass, and Sunday school and common school texts. In the late-nineteenth-century South, public libraries were rare. The Sunday school library filled a gap; it was often the best, and only, place to borrow books. Many southerners regarded the library as an invaluable part of the Sunday school and an enhancement of home life. "How glad the children and young people and teachers would be," rhapsodized a Presbyterian, "each one to have a good book to carry home every Sabbath, and how much it would add to the profit and delight of the Sabbath evening around the fire-side and in the home circle." Publishing houses could supply children with "pure, moral, and religious" material to read at home.[36]

Determining what books to put on library shelves demanded vigilant adults. They were not about to see children's minds sullied by trashy books and magazines. Sunday schools appointed volunteers to library committees to oversee the collection, and committee members assumed the responsibility for selecting appropriate titles, discarding useless and tasteless material, and raising money for new purchases. To promote sound reading habits in all their Sunday schools, Presbyterians created a list of suitable selections, which included Bible commentaries, church

36. "Letter to Editor," *Presbyterian Standard*, 26 February 1902. See also Benjamin E. Mays, *Born to Rebel: An Autobiography* (New York: Scribner, 1971; reprint, Athens: University of Georgia, 1987), 20; Julius D. Dreher, "Public Libraries as a Means of Popular Education," in The Southern Society for the Promotion of the Study of Race Conditions and Problems in the South, *Race Problems of the South: Report of the Proceedings of the First Annual Conference . . . at Montgomery, Alabama* (1900; reprint, New York: Negro Universities Press, 1969), 101; "If the Children Are Saved, the Parents Must Help," *Christian Advocate*, 23 January 1886. Dreher reported that in 1900, of 7,184 libraries in the U.S., the 13 southern states had 806; of 34.6 million volumes in this country, 2.7 million were in southern libraries. Both New York and Massachusetts had two times as many books as the entire South (p. 100). Elizabeth Nesbitt argues that Sunday schools were often the best source for children's books. See Nesbitt, "A Rightful Heritage, 1890–1920," in *A Critical History of Children's Literature: A Survey of Children's Books in English*, ed. Cornelia Meigs (London: Macmillan, 1969), 384–6.

histories, doctrines of grace, Christian biographies, and annals of mission work. Whether youngsters enjoyed such weighty tomes was immaterial; adults selected the books as they saw fit.

Some Sunday school library committees sought to ban fiction entirely, arguing that children who read novels would carry this wasteful habit into adulthood. Novel reading could weaken the mind, diminish a taste for reading history books and the Bible, and generate a "morbid and unnatural craving for excitement," according to one horrified Baptist. C. O. Trapp discovered novels in his children's Sunday school library and demanded their removal; the only acceptable work of fiction, he announced, was John Bunyan's *The Christian Pilgrim*. Presbyterian S. F. Tenney insisted that his church exert more control over the material that it published and avoid the business of selling novels. He objected to one list of recommended books that included fiction. "It is well known that one of the evil effects of novel-reading is to create a distaste for solid, and Christian literature," he lamented. Atticus Haygood was distressed to find "trashy" books on Methodist library shelves. "The amount of mere rubbish—the quantity of dreary platitudes and of shallow twaddlings—neatly boxed up and labeled 'Sunday School library'—by enterprising publishers who pay small prices for cheap brains—is absolutely appalling," he wrote. No one could be too careful when it came to monitoring children's reading habits.[37]

Yet even the most watchful committee could not ensure the suitability of every book. Ideally, all volumes that filled the Sunday school library came directly from the appropriate denominational firm. The need to keep shelves well stocked with material, however, meant that some schools accepted almost anything. Donations came from church members, and northern churches sent secondhand books. When committee members failed to peruse every donation and unfiltered material found its way into the library, criticism inevitably followed.[38]

Sunday school library books covered a variety of subjects, but all were supposed to convey a moral lesson. Southern Presbyterians tried to entice and stimulate children with such tales as *Our Kate, or the Grateful Or-*

37. C. O. Trapp, "Fiction As a Medium of Instruction," *Working Christian,* 9 September 1875; S. F. Tenney, letter to editor, *Presbyterian Standard* 45 (8 April 1903): 14; "What Constitutes a 'Good Library Book'?" *Presbyterian Standard* 45 (21 January 1903): 11; Haygood quote in Mann, *Atticus Greene Haygood,* 74.

38. "Sunday School Libraries," *Sunday School Magazine* 4 (October 1874): 289–90.

phan; The Widow's Sewing Machine, or What a Helping Hand Did for a Poor Family; The Jewess and Her Daughter, or Light Shining Out of Darkness; and *The Sapling and the Tree, or Results of Early Training.* These examples, their content self-evident from the title and all aimed at young readers, usually had between sixty and a hundred pages and often were illustrated.[39]

The Southern Methodists' "Catalogue and Price List" for 1885 reveals books and pamphlets approved and printed by that church. Its lengthy list included Sunday school textbooks, hymnals, catechisms for different ages, questionnaires covering books of the Bible, Gospel commentaries, and attendance record books. To entice buyers, publishers packaged several volumes with a common theme into inexpensive sets. The "Village Library" included ten books selling for $3.65, with such titles as *The Village Blacksmith, Religion in Common Life,* and *Wayside Flowerets.* The "Buds and Blossoms Library" included *Fifty Beautiful Ballads, Fifty Fine Poems,* and two volumes of *World of Waters.* The firm also sold a "Heroes Library," a "Famous Cities Library," and a "Bible Christian Library."[40]

In order to increase profits, some enterprising editors moved their publishing houses into more commercial ventures, producing or selling a panoply of products, or "Sunday school helps." These included maps, organs, chalkboards, stereopticons, classroom furniture, encyclopedias, holiday greeting cards, and classroom rewards and prizes. Firms sold special notebooks for recording classroom statistics. Presbyterians printed and sold colored attendance tickets for superintendents to hand pupils as they arrived in class, with different colors designating promptness or tardiness. Special envelopes and mite boxes were sold to ease weekly giving and ensure privacy. The Methodist Publishing House marketed stationery, marriage and birth certificates, baptism records, and preachers' licenses. Richard Boyd's NBC firm sold classroom banners, bells, and maps of the Holy Land. Presbyterians offered special binders for preserving copies of favorite Sunday school magazines. All publishing firms printed programs for their Sunday school celebrations and conference proceedings. Some businesses even sold items that seemed to have little to do with the Sunday school. Boyd's enterprise established a savings

39. Baird, "Eleventh Annual Report," *Minutes of the General Assembly, 1872,* 200.
40. Methodist Episcopal Church, South, "Catalogue and Price List of 1885," 46–51.

bank, sold sewing machines, and owned a factory that manufactured black dolls—all important money-makers.

Despite the growing insistence on denominational identity and doctrinal orthodoxy, the classroom materials produced by these different firms were, in fact, surprisingly similar. This suggests that although southern Sunday school officials and instructors avowedly were bent upon introducing southern and sectarian themes into their lesson materials, this phenomenon proved to be far more evident in rhetoric than in practice. One of the most striking things about Sunday school literature was its universal message, which undermined the concept of southern exceptionalism or religious sectional identity. Southern publications aimed at Sunday schools taught Scripture and middle-class values in ways that were similar to most Protestant Sunday schools nationwide. At least until the early twentieth century, book editors and publishing committees seemed to be of a similar mind when considering how to meet the needs of their Sunday schools and what would most appeal to pupils and adults.

Few major differences distinguished the contents of one Sunday school magazine from another, except what might suit a particular age of pupil. In general, Baptist publications such as *Child's Gem* seemed a bit more austere, with fewer illustrations than the Methodist and Presbyterian children's magazines. Baptist stories often focused narrowly on the Bible, while Methodists and Presbyterians used more fiction and lifelike experiences to teach a moral. Stories and essays ran the gamut from the entertaining to the banal, with allegory always a popular means to teach a lesson. Morality, piety, obedience, honesty, and the need to lead a Christian life were universal themes rather than strong sectarian messages. Publishers seemed more intent upon instilling moral values and teaching the Bible than worrying about orthodox church doctrine. Each publishing house's insistence on denominational loyalty was thus primarily an attempt to corner the market.[41]

In fact, at this juncture, denominations seemed largely untroubled by the absence of doctrinaire lessons. Southern Baptists initially depended

---

41. Anne Boylan found a similar trend in her study of Sunday schools, stating that literature before 1880 "was hardly sectarian in content." Boylan, *Sunday School,* 80. In his study of religious reconstruction, Daniel Stowell argues that the content of Sunday school publications upheld southern denominationalism and the memory of the Confederacy. He cites only two examples from *Kind Words* in 1866. I found few sectarian or orthodox messages in the many Sunday school materials I read. Stowell, *Rebuilding Zion,* 121, 108.

on Southern Methodists to handle their printing needs. The Methodist imprint on Baptist Sunday school lessons seemed to leave even a loyal Baptist like Annie Armstrong unruffled. "I have for years received much aid from others outside our own denomination and propose to continue making use of a good thing whenever I find it," she wrote in 1897. Baptist J. N. Hall of Dresden, Tennessee, admired his denomination's publications, "not because I think they are more Baptistic, but because they are southern" and because they helped to support the SBC. Orthodox belief seemed to be a secondary consideration to the desire for a successful southern religious publishing firm.[42]

This universality in Sunday school literature probably made sense. Issues of debate among church officials and academics, or the distinctions between dominations—such as the appropriate age and timing of baptism, the pros and cons of an educated ministry, and particular interpretations of Scripture—were not appropriate for Sunday school. Youngsters had no interest in such concerns, and until a certain age, would not have understood them anyway. Sunday school lessons were to be simple, direct, and inspiring. Emphasizing faith in God and the inerrancy of the Bible, proper behavior, good manners, and sound morals were important lessons for the South's next generation. Sunday school literature offered children a fairly catholic approach to Christian faith.

One reason for the similarity of many Sunday school materials was the degree of borrowing or outright plagiarism that took place among different publishers. The fact that this habit did not elicit complaints, at least not from Sunday school publishing firms, suggests that it was a commonplace practice, and that American copyright laws were either imprecise or lax. African American publishing houses openly expressed gratitude for material they borrowed from other firms. Generally, each house added its own imprint before reselling it to its own Sunday schools. Publishing houses often sold stories, poems, illustrations, and entire books to one another; in other cases, editors used or borrowed material with or without permission. For instance, the AMEZ paid the Northern Methodists two hundred dollars for the use of their engraved plates to illustrate the AMEZ hymnal, *An Offering of Praise*. AME editor Benjamin T. Tanner boasted that the beautiful illustrations embellishing one

---

42. Annie Armstrong, 1 July 1897, Baltimore, Md., and J. N. Hall, 7 December 1897, Dresden, Tenn., both to James Marion Frost, Frost-Bell Correspondence, SBHLA.

AME magazine were from stereotype plates of the London Tract Society. Under editor Thomas O. Summers, the MECS publishing house reissued books that either the denomination or another firm had produced years earlier, with no credit given to the original publisher.[43]

Though denominations did not present the sectarian message that editors promised, publishing had a profound effect on the southern Sunday school movement and on church identity. The commitment to publishing not only intensified competition among denominations and religious organizations. It also lent a more commercial, economic character to the Sunday school movement. By the early twentieth century, there was more to consider than exposing Sunday school pupils to the Bible and teaching good behavior. Editors had a business to run, one that would reap profits for their church. This is solid corroborating evidence for historians and sociologists who claim that economic interests often drove denominational activity. Although editors and publishing boards continued to profess a desire to teach morality and salvation, convention reports and personal correspondence suggest a somewhat different story. Church officials began to see Sunday school publishing as an end in itself. A successful firm became key to a denomination's survival and a visible means to enhance the status of a church. Producing Sunday school materials and doing so profitably demonstrated what a denomination could achieve and where it stood in relation to others.[44]

Profits from the sale of Sunday school materials became critical to each denomination. Some editors made no apologies for this economic focus. I. J. Van Ness was clear on this. Sunday schools were the "best

---

43. "Report on Hymnal," *Proceedings of the General Conference of the AMEZ Church, May 2, 1888* (n.p., n.d.), 85; B. T. Tanner, "Editor's Report," *Journal of the 18th Session of the General Conference of the African Methodist Episcopal Church* (Philadelphia: AME Publishing House, 1884), 231. Well-established firms such as the London Religious Tract Society often loaned plates and materials to struggling firms; such assistance aided several African American enterprises. Southern Methodists also borrowed material. For instance, they printed *London in the Olden Time* in 1855, a reprint of an earlier London Religious Tract Society book. When it was reissued again, the editor gave no credit to the Tract Society. See the Methodist Archives, Drew University, Madison, N.J.

44. See Roger Finke and Rodney Stark, *The Churching of America, 1776–1900: Winners and Losers in Our Religious Economy* (New Brunswick, N.J.: Rutgers University Press, 1992), and R. Stephen Warner, "Work in Progress toward a New Paradigm for the Sociological Study of Religion in the United States," *American Journal of Sociology* 98 (March 1993): 1044–93.

business getters we could have, for more Sunday schools, larger Sunday schools, and better Sunday schools mean more business for the publishers." Editors monitored their markets and added their voices to those who demanded more Sunday schools and more pupils. Firms began to keep careful records of annual expenditures and profits, as well as the circulation figures of each serial and book they produced. They introduced new publications to attract more readers and eliminated those that showed declining circulation. By the early twentieth century, publishing businesses experimented with new layouts for their magazines and new illustrations for the mastheads. To enhance the appeal to children, editors added special pages with sections for cut-outs and coloring, scrapbooks, dioramas, and pictures. Profits from these ventures went back into the business to purchase modern presses and hire additional employees. Publishing house profits also supported foreign and home mission work, supplemented missionaries' and ministers' salaries, paid for the construction of church facilities and Sunday school buildings, and purchased additional real estate—all things that reflected positively on a denomination's image.[45]

Yet the the growth of religious publishing houses and the desire of denominations to make money had negative consequences as well. Advertisements that literally filled entire pages of Sunday school magazines and church newspapers made the focus on profits all too apparent. Many advertisements bore little relationship to faith, betraying a firm's desire to rake in revenue. Advertisements marketed wood stoves, home organs and pianos, furniture, hair straighteners, clothing and shoes, European imports, and medical and quack remedies for every conceivable ill. Commercialism sometimes overwhelmed a publication, such as an ad for a huge textile sale that covered the entire front page of several issues of the *Christian Recorder*. James Frost tried to deflect any criticism of extensive advertising, insisting that denominational publishing and marketing efforts had a higher goal than crass profits. "It is something more than buying and selling periodicals," he argued, "it is a union of hearts and efforts to bring in the kingdom of God's dear Son." Though critics may have

---

45. I. J. Van Ness, "What Southern Baptists Are Attempting in Sunday School Work," *Sunday School Magazine* 39 (October 1909): 634; Robert Blair Bruce, "Sunday School Department," *Official Journal of the 22nd Quadrennial Session of the General Conference of the AMEZ Church* (Charlotte: G. L. Blackwell, 1904), 306.

had trouble detecting the union of hearts that Frost envisioned, who could argue with such uplifting thoughts?[46]

As one might expect, the move to Sunday school publishing did not please everyone. Some church members feared that the infusion of printed literature would drive the Bible right out of the classroom. Increasingly visible competition and a greater emphasis on materialistic concerns alarmed traditionalists. Many rural southerners worried as their denominations created more bureaucratic structures, erected fancy buildings, and ran their churches with an eye on the bottom line. To these men and women, publishing was an aspect of modern church life that seemed to alter the very meaning of Christianity. Aggressive marketing tactics ran counter to Christian ideals and the need to save souls. Critics insisted that Sunday schools and publishing houses teach youngsters sound morals, expose them to Scripture, and lead them toward conversion—but do no more. The Methodists seemed well aware of such complaints. Publicly, church officials underplayed any economic motive to their publishing efforts, insisting that financial interests were always secondary to Christian concerns. "A publishing house conducted by the Church is not a mercantile, but chiefly a moral, scheme. It must be conducted on business principles, but for religious ends," stated one editor in order to silence potential critics.[47]

Yet not all critics were silent. Some southern skeptics labeled publishing the "devil's work," pointing out that a church's success had never depended on publishing. Others were perfectly satisfied with local and state publications or those sold by northern religious societies and saw no need for a large centralized church publishing firm. Many church members objected to this move toward bureaucratization. Some black Baptists worried about committing to an enormous, risky business venture when so many of their churches were struggling to survive. Those Southern Baptists attracted to the ideas of the antimission movement in the Baptist church denounced all efforts to centralize. Older, conservative

46. See *Christian Recorder*, 31 October and 7 November 1903; James Marion Frost, *A Word and a Plea Made with Those Not Using the Sunday School Periodicals Issued by the Southern Baptist Convention* (Nashville: n.p., 1903), 5.

47. Owen, *Sacred Flame of Love*, 150–3; "Report of Bishops," *Journal of the General Conference of the Methodist Episcopal Church, South, 1882*, ed. W. P. Harrison (Nashville: MECS Publishing House, 1882).

laypeople argued that a publishing house would undermine black Baptists' longstanding, friendly relationship with white Northern Baptist organizations, and they feared the end of Yankee goodwill and generous support.[48]

The fact that several church publishing houses operated in the red during their early years may have quieted some who protested what they saw as growing materialism. Most firms initially tried to employ judicious business practices in order to balance their budget or eliminate debt, giving editors an effective defense to counter complaints. They depicted their financial struggles in terms of self-sacrifice and Christian fortitude.

Yet even as readership and book sales increased, editors and book committees rarely seemed satisfied. Using emotionally charged sales pitches—of despair, guilt, or boundless enthusiasm—they pressured members to buy more material. The AMEZ Board of Publications even suggested that all preachers and superintendents be required to subscribe to the *Star of Zion*. Book committees were clear: loyalty to the faith meant loyalty to the publishing house and its Sunday school literature.[49]

Various marketing techniques tried to boost sales and outsell competitors. Editors promised free samples, hoping that new subscriptions and additional purchases would follow. Some firms advertised holiday gifts; the Southern Methodists specifically created books and periodicals for Christmas giving. Some firms slashed prices to undercut their rivals. For a while, white Methodists gave preachers and wholesale dealers a 25 percent discount on all new magazine subscriptions. In order to compete, the Southern Presbyterians offered a 20 percent discount on their books and periodicals. They also began to mail sample copies of *Children's Friend* and *Earnest Worker* to entice new subscribers and advertisers. Southern Methodists used some of their own publications to good effect, such as two inexpensive pamphlets, "Reasons for Not Joining the Baptist Church" and "Why I Am Not a Baptist." Though the growth of Sunday

---

48. Burton, *Road to Nashville*, 52–3; Pelt and Smith, *The Story of the National Baptists*, 92–8; Harvey, *Redeeming the South*, 28–30. The antimission movement was begun in the 1830s by Southern Baptists who resisted social and religious innovation, including missionary work, Sunday schools, and state conventions.

49. See Owen L. W. Smith, "A Neglected Child," *Star of Zion*, 25 June 1893; Robert Davids, "Report on Sunday School Work," *Journal of the Thirty-First Session of the Virginia Conference of the AME Church* (n.p., 1897), 48.

schools throughout the South created an expanding market, publishers could not take anything for granted.[50]

Southern publishing houses continued to depend on a network of colporteurs and book agents, and appointed dozens of new field workers to sell more material. Colporteurs began to confine their sales solely to denominational literature. Southern Methodists eventually found that itinerant preachers could no longer handle the demands of the ministry and also sell Sunday school literature. The church hired Sunday school agents, purchased special colporteur wagons to carry men and books far afield, and made greater use of the region's railroad system to cover assigned turf. Sunday school boards tried to improve efficiency and increase profits by reorganizing and streamlining their operations. In 1888, Southern Presbyterians merged their Sunday school and colportage boards to cut costs and increase sales. Baptists turned to an underutilized source to sell material: Baptist women, especially Sunday school teachers. "I earnestly hope that our women will turn their attention to helping forward the circulation of the books of the Sunday-School Board," wrote James Frost in a letter he addressed to all Southern Baptist women. He claimed to be seeking female assistance not for increasing profits, but for advancing Christian education.[51]

Loyalty to a publishing house, of course, could work two ways. Even as denominational firms produced various publications, many southern Sunday schools continued to purchase what they needed from northern firms. Defending their stance, some instructors claimed that southern businesses lacked the know-how to produce quality literature. Initially there was some truth to this claim. Unfilled or delayed orders often typified a southern firm's early years. Workers new to the field sometimes had little understanding of proper business practices and lacked the skills for publishing work. Many areas of the South had no rail service or decent roads, which meant that literature sent to rural areas might be delayed. Sunday school teachers, who depended on the timely arrival of dated ma-

---

50. "For Christmas" advertisement in *The Tennessee Methodist*, 10 December 1896; "10th Annual Report of the Executive Committee of Publication," *Minutes of the General Assembly, 1871*, 67.

51. Alex G. Brown, "General Agent of Colportage," *Minutes of the 108th Session of the Virginia Annual Conference of the Methodist Episcopal Church, South, 1890* (Richmond: J. W. Fergusson and Son, 1890), 52; James Marion Frost, "The Sunday-School Board, Our Women's Work," *Religious Herald*, 4 September 1902.

terial, rightly complained when lesson plans arrived after a particular lesson had been taught. Virginia Methodists defended their decision not to purchase denominational literature because the MECS publishing house seemed so poorly run. Some black Sunday schools also put quality over denominational loyalty, continuing to purchase white publications rather than those that their own church produced. AMEZ Reverend L. W. Smith admitted that white publishers produced better material than his own firm, but he explained that whites could afford talented writers, better paper and ink, and finer illustrations than his business. Nevertheless, he asked members' indulgence, noting that African Americans had had only a quarter of a century to learn sound business practices.[52]

Changing from one firm to another was often an uncomfortable and contested decision for a Sunday school. The choice of classroom literature, for example, could divide a church. D. S. Snodgrass warned James Frost that publishing rivals, such as the ABPS, were trying to undermine Southern Baptist endeavors. "There are preachers here in Texas who will watch our S. S. literature, eager to find objections to it, and help to displace it with the 'Society's' publications," he wrote. Practical concerns could also affect loyalty to certain firms. Sunday schools ran on a tight budget, and officers and teachers understandably wanted the highest quality and lowest priced literature available. Northern publishers that had been in business for years knew how to produce good literature at low cost. Southern publishing houses struggled to compete and shame members into purchasing their material. Yet to a Sunday school, price and quality were always critical concerns.[53]

As firms began to operate in the black, public complaints focused on the end product and the materialism that seemed to be creeping into the church. Publishing may have been depicted as a Christian enterprise, but mere mortals produced Sunday school material, and it was impossible to please everyone. Traditionalists complained that their denominational firm produced too much superfluous material and insisted that only the Bible and catechism were worthy publications. Individuals criticized the content of books and magazines—the slipshod lessons, inappropriate

---

52. A. Coke Smith, "Publishing Interests," *Minutes of the 111th Session of the Virginia Annual Conference of the MECS* (Richmond: J. W. Fergusson and Son, 1893), 55; L. W. Smith, "A Neglected Child," 1.

53. D. S. Snodgrass to James Marion Frost, 31 August 1892, San Antonio, Tex., Frost-Bell Correspondence, SBHLA.

stories, and poor illustrations. People, including children, wrote and complained when they discovered mistakes in the Sunday lesson. Pictures in a child's newspaper shocked at least one white Southern Baptist. Lidd Robinson could hardly contain his fury over a "vicious impression" of Christ and his apostles that appeared "on cheap paper, which is flawed and repulsive." What troubled him most was a darkened depiction of Christ's face, making him seem "far more like Barabbas than our Redeemer. I shudder when I place such into a little child's hands for I know not what contempt may be sown in this little head by such a picture of our Saviour," he fumed. To Robinson, a lily-white Christ was the proper rendering.[54]

Despite the grumbling, the creation of denominational publishing houses had an enormous impact on the southern Sunday school movement and on these denominations. Publishing gave denominational Sunday school boards and editors greater control over classroom messages. Publishing allowed African Americans to promote racial interests, organize and oversee their own businesses, and have a venue for their own writers, poets, artists, and musicians. Publishing gave southern evangelicals yet another way to diminish the influence that outsiders had over their children. And last but hardly least, Sunday school publishing profits became a significant factor in advancing and empowering a denomination.

What began as an effort to uplift and influence the minds and behavior of young Christians, promote good reading habits, and expose children to sound religious ideas and moral concerns became, to some degree, an end in itself. Certainly religious stories, poems, and hymns reinforced Sunday school lessons and inspired pupils at home and in the classroom. But by the early twentieth century, publishing had become a major business for the major southern denominations and pivotal to their future success. More denominational Sunday schools were needed to attract new pupils into the classroom who, as consumers, would purchase material. These commercial, competitive enterprises influenced and altered the southern Sunday school and the goals of each denomination involved in this Christian enterprise.

54. Lidd B. Robinson to James Marion Frost, Mobile, Ala., 11 April 1898, Frost-Bell Correspondence, SBHLA.

5

INSIDE THE SUNDAY CLASSROOM

Despite the expressed desire of Sunday school officials to stamp a denominational identity on Sunday schools, the actual lessons in Sunday classrooms—like Sunday school publications—would become surprisingly similar. Perhaps this is because the Sunday school was, first and foremost, what Anne Boylan has called an "agency of cultural transmission," and the values it taught were those that most southerners deemed important. Other than insisting on loyalty to one's church, southern Sunday schools at this juncture did little to differentiate themselves. They all adopted similar lesson plans and taught values embraced by most middle-class Americans. Whatever their denomination, evangelicals were of like mind on issues such as exposing youngsters to the Bible, molding character, and saving souls. They saw the Sunday school as the most meaningful, uplifting event of a child's week. They also agreed that a good Sunday school had to be appealing and well organized. To that end, they structured it according to well-defined guidelines. The first task was to adopt a constitution that outlined structure and goals. Every Sunday school needed a competent manager, capable instructors, enthusiastic pupils, effective lessons, and engaging activities to ensure its success.[1]

The superintendent managed the Sunday school and ultimately was responsible for its proper functioning. Ideally, this was a capable, skilled male volunteer who commanded respect and accepted responsibility. Above all, he was to have a take-charge attitude. "The man who can properly govern a Sunday school can command an army," one Sunday school advisor asserted. Others likened a supervisor to a railroad or factory manager. Everyone agreed that an energetic, dedicated supervisor was indispensable to a well-run Sunday school.[2]

Many denominations spelled out in detail the desirable qualifications of a superintendent. He should be responsible, pious, organized, inspirational, and stay abreast of modern Sunday school methods. AME leaders wanted their superintendents to possess energy, perseverance, self-control, tact, and geniality. One man with a proclivity for alliteration felt that a superintendent should be "pious, prayerful, patient, punctual, persevering." This was not a job for the faint-hearted, at least according to Sunday school advisor James Axtell, who felt that the office demanded the "highest courage." While most people accorded the position considerable status, Axtell added that a superintendent also had to serve as "janitor, factotum, and general drudge." Naturally not everyone lived up to these ideals. Some evangelicals complained that too many "quacks" volunteered for the post, craving honor but lacking the training and personal skills to do a good job.[3]

Despite a superintendent's visibility in the community, finding an ideal candidate—or any candidate, for that matter—was not always easy, and Sunday school supporters often scrambled to find a man willing to serve. There were rare men like the Reverend McCormick who found superintendents wherever he went. According to William P. Paxson, McCormick could "manufacture a Superintendent of the poorest possible material of any man I ever knew; he just prays it right into them." More typically, organizers often had to relax their standards and accept almost any vol-

1. Boylan, *Sunday School*, 33.
2. James Harvey Joiner, paraphrasing Dr. J. W. Alexander, "Speech to the Eufala Sunday School," c. 1870, SHC.
3. Jonathan M. Taylor, "Requirements of the Sabbath School," *AME Church Review* 17 (July 1900): 166; James Wickleff Axtell, *The Organized Sunday School: A Working Manual for Officers* (Nashville: Publishing House of the MECS, 1902), 11, 64.

unteer, but not without first getting a second opinion. A troubled George T. Ware requested a "scriptural view" from the Alabama Baptist Sunday school board to determine whether a man living in sin and who was not a member of the church should be allowed to hold the job. Truly desperate Sunday schools turned to women to fill the post.[4]

James Axtell's remark about courage contained a kernel of truth, for the job was demanding. Duties ranged from administrative oversight to tasks such as airing the Sunday school building. The superintendent was expected to set the tone for the institution and keep the school running smoothly. A superintendent had to select instructors and teaching materials, ensure that teachers and pupils were prompt and prepared, stimulate community interest, and reprimand ill-behaved pupils. His authority did not, however, extend to dispensing corporal punishment; a loving environment was to prevail in the classroom. The Sunday school was to be a welcoming place where children's needs came first. Yet the superintendent was also expected to maintain an orderly school and not allow his pupils to pull hair, throw paper, or roughhouse. A superintendent often kept unruly students in check by using a long stick to point to restless or inattentive children. In each week's opening assembly, the superintendent was supposed to present a brief, stimulating speech before leading pupils in prayer and song. When Sunday school boards began to demand weekly records, it was the superintendent who recorded and submitted these statistics.[5]

Although women comprised the majority of church and Sunday school members, superintendents were usually male, especially in white Sunday schools. In the South, where traditional gender ideology prevailed, most whites never considered women suited for such an elevated public position. Most southerners assumed that a man could more readily gain and hold people's attention and respect than a woman could. As head of the Sunday school, he could act on an equal plane with the

---

4. William P. Paxson to Maurice Wurts, 7 June 1867, St. Charles, Mo., ASSU Correspondence, PHS; George T. Ware to James Marion Frost, 2 June 1898, Partridge, Ala., Frost-Bell Correspondence, SBHLA.

5. B. Franklin Maulden, "Can the Interest in the Sunday School Be Kept Up and Increased?" *Baptist Courier,* 10 September 1891; "Sunday School As Woman's Place," *Working Christian,* 11 November 1880; "How They Succeed in Macon City, Mo.," *Sunday School Magazine* 11 (1881): 324.

minister—an important consideration when dealing with preachers who had little use for a Sunday school in their church.

On occasion, women became superintendents when no male could be found to do the job. Northern missionary organizations sometimes appointed white women to oversee the black Sunday schools they established, perhaps because mission schools had little status and women were more willing to manage them than were men. ASSU missionary N. H. Downing observed "northern ladies" supervising six mission Sunday schools for freedmen in his district. Pragmatic needs often elevated women to this role. When Methodist minister Fenner Pigott found that his itinerant duties interfered with Sunday school administration, he appointed his wife to serve as superintendent. A few select women were actually deemed best qualified for the post. In 1892, Frances Louisa Goodrich, a Presbyterian missionary and educator working in the North Carolina mountains, was surprised to find herself elected head of the local Sunday school. She had attended a community meeting to help residents organize a new school, and tensions mounted when the group had to choose one of two men for superintendent. A man in the audience stood up, and as Goodrich recalled, he "made a speech and said he was a woman's suffrage man they all knew and that he was in favor of their having a lady." The group promptly elected Goodrich, she delivered her acceptance speech, and Sunday school plans moved forward.[6]

Goodrich was the exception, however. Southern whites believed that women were well suited to teach in Sunday schools, not to direct them; females were too delicate to fill such a demanding post. James Axtell felt that men made better superintendents than women due to the "onerous character of the duties, which is sometimes a severe tax on one's personal strength." However, he admitted that females who held the position invariably outperformed men. "Observation goes to show that in the comparatively few instances in which women are working as superintendents, their success is of a higher order than that of the other sex," he observed. Axtell suggested that if a woman wished to become a Sunday school officer, she first serve as a supervisor's assistant. Had he seen Mrs. Lilly

6. N. H. Downing to Maurice A. Wurts, 25 November 1868, Warrenton, N.C., ASSU Correspondence, PHS; Levi Woodbury Pigott, *Scenes and Incidents in the Life of a Home Missionary, with a Biographical Sketch of Fenner S. Pigott* (Norfolk, Va.: n.p., 1901), 29; Frances Louisa Goodrich Diary, 20 November 1892, Duke.

Morehead of Leaksville, North Carolina, in action, he surely would have commended her for organizing and running an outstanding Sunday school. Though Morehead's official title was assistant superintendent, locals credited her with the school's success. As one observer noted, "she is doing nearly all the work."[7]

Most white southern women accepted society's view of their limitations, and were content to be less visible than men. Trained from childhood to accept their secondary status, white southern women believed that men were best suited to hold administrative positions. The female sphere was domestic, and that was where women were supposed to shine. Annie Armstrong, secretary of the Baptist Woman's Home Missionary Society, protested that it was "sheerest nonsense" to think that women could perform men's work. "Our brethren are the God-appointed leaders," she stated, feeling that physical and mental limitations circumscribed the amount of work that most females could perform. Armstrong failed to consider, of course, the influential and visible position she had held for years.[8]

While the superintendent was the overall figure of authority in the Sunday school, teachers were key to its ongoing success. Typical of those heralding the importance of Christian education was W. G. E. Cunnyngham, who believed Sunday school teaching "has come to stand alongside the ministry of the gospel preacher." Sunday school leaders, always on the lookout for additional volunteers, claimed that no area of service did more to uplift humankind than teaching Sunday school. By having a direct, personal impact on the pupils in their charge, instructors had an awe-inspiring task. Methodist Howard Hamill, whose profession was to train Sunday school teachers, naturally made much of this role (which he inaccurately associated with men). "Out of a whole week he has 30 golden minutes in which to teach the greatest and hardest of all books," Hamill asserted. The instructor had to inspire each child, mold his or her

---

7. Axtell, *The Organized Sunday School*, 64; R. H. Griffith, "Banner Sunday School," *Minutes of the Baptist State Sunday School Convention of North Carolina* (Raleigh: Edwards, Broughton, 1875), 11.

8. Annie Armstrong to James Marion Frost, 24 July 1896, Baltimore, Md., Annie Armstrong Correspondence in Frost-Bell Correspondence, SBHLA. See also Boylan, "Evangelical Womanhood in the Nineteenth Century," and Anastatia Sims, *The Power of Femininity in the New South: Women's Organizations and Politics in North Carolina, 1880–1930* (Columbia: University of South Carolina Press, 1997).

character, and lead an entire class toward conversion. Some advisors saw the Sunday school teacher as being as influential in the life of children as a parent, especially for youngsters from "godless homes." The teacher was a spiritual guide and, in some cases, the only one a child might have.[9]

According to Sunday school advisors, a model teacher had to possess a nearly flawless character. He or she was to be intelligent, pious, creative, humble, and multitalented. Knowledge of the Bible was essential. A teacher should know how to sing, or at least how to direct others to do so. One observer suggested that young women who sang to gentlemen callers also should "consecrate their vocal powers to the cause of the dear Redeemer." If they could sing during courtship, he opined, they could teach Sunday school and inspire pupils with their vocal skills. Sunday school advisors urged instructors to be clean and wear modest clothing so that a child's attention would not wander from Scripture to a fashionable outfit. Teachers were to be grave in deportment and display exemplary manners. They should avoid late nights, especially on Saturdays, so they would be alert for Sunday class. No man or woman who "engages with the world in a frolic" was suited to teach Sunday school and serve God, Baptists insisted. Every Sunday school teacher had to serve as a model of moral rectitude.[10]

These qualifications probably reflected more rhetoric than reality, for an ongoing problem that all denominations faced was a paucity of instructors. Finding capable, pious, serious-minded teachers to serve the growing number of children in Sunday school proved a challenge. The dearth of teachers to serve eager children confounded supporters, and they despaired over the shortage. Finding enough teachers to serve a growing number of new Sunday schools inevitably demanded compromise. A Crockett, Texas, Sunday school's standards for instructors allowed for considerable latitude. Its guidelines merely suggested that a

---

9. W. G. E. Cunnyngham, *The Sunday School: Its History and Management* (Nashville: Barbee and Smith, 1902), 11; Howard Hamill, *Sunday School Teacher-Training* (Philadelphia: Sunday School Times, 1904), 8; Strange, "Sunday School Work," 341. See also Howard Hamill, *The Sunday School Teacher* (Nashville: Publishing House of the MECS, 1906).

10. "A Teacher," *Religious Herald*, 4 October 1866; R. Q. A. Teague, "A Word on Sunday Schools," *Biblical Recorder*, 14 September 1870. See also Bishop M'Tyeire, "Punctuality in Sunday-School Teachers" and "The Teacher's Dress," *Sunday School Magazine* 1 (1871): 1, 8.

teacher be at least fifteen years old, have attended Sunday school for three years, and have exhibited promise on a general exam. Perhaps reflecting the desperation of some schools, a number of young teenagers served as Sunday school teachers.[11]

Though officials continually insisted on denominational loyalty, they frequently overlooked this in order to meet Sunday school needs. When a troubled reader wrote the *Baptist Courier* asking whether a Sunday school teacher in his church could belong to another denomination, the editor claimed that church membership was not a consideration. "We have never felt scruples about encouraging any serious minded person to take part in helping children to read the Bible or to memorize hymns and passages of Scriptures," he asserted. Alabama Baptists reached a similar conclusion, noting that in cases when a church member could not be found, it was "better [to have] any moral and upright person than none." One Georgia Baptist Sunday school could not find a single Baptist volunteer, so it appointed a male Methodist to serve as superintendent and two female Methodists as teachers. Individuals living in areas with only a single Sunday class had no choice but to accept the faith of its teacher. Southern laypeople found denominational identity far less important than saving their children's souls.[12]

Other issues typified the Sunday classroom. The most common pedagogical approach was rote memorization, which had both detractors and supporters. James Robinson excelled in Sunday school but recalled nothing challenging about this technique. "It was a simple matter to parrot theological doctrine back to them without understanding it," he recalled. Yet other pupils relished this straightforward method and made a point of memorizing everything assigned to them. Time was another issue for teachers. Whatever lesson they taught and whatever style they used, instructors were never to waste a precious moment. "What you dear teachers do for them must be done quickly," insisted AMEZ member James Tyson, "or while we are deliberating what and how, they will be out of our reach." Many teachers made do with little. In her run-down Appalachian school, Elizabeth Hooker's pupils sat on homemade benches as she

11. S. F. Tenney, "A Sabbath School in Texas," *Kind Words,* 27 March 1873.
12. Query and response in the *Baptist Courier,* 2 July 1885; "Report on Sabbath Schools," *Minutes of the 59th Annual Session of the Alabama Baptist Association, 1878* (Montgomery: Daily Mail Power Press, 1878), 4; W. A. Pickering to Southern Baptist Sunday School Board, 22 March 1897, McBean, Ga., Frost-Bell Correspondence, SBHLA.

read to them from her Bible, drilled them aloud on their weekly lessons, and questioned them on the text. For children who could not read, storytelling was an ideal method to absorb Bible tales and moral truths. To capture the attention of their pupils, some instructors displayed a flair for the dramatic. For her temperance lesson, Mrs. C. M. Carnahan mimicked a drunken man, reeling around the classroom to demonstrate the evils of alcohol, and warning her pupils that they would not go to heaven if they ever entered a saloon.[13]

Gender was also an issue for Sunday school teachers. Though a number of southern men taught Sunday school in the immediate postwar years, women quickly came to dominate the field. For instance, the Union Methodist Church Sunday School in Goldsboro, North Carolina, had an equal number of male and female teachers in 1868; by 1871, eight of its eleven teachers were female. Records from the First Presbyterian Church of Greenwood, South Carolina, indicate that by 1892, sixteen of its twenty-one white teachers were women. Such female dedication was appreciated. As a Presbyterian gratuitously observed, "some of the most competent and efficient teachers of the Bible to youths and young men have been intelligent, patient and gracious women."[14]

This preponderance of female Sunday school teachers paralleled two related trends: a majority of female members in southern churches and a growing number of women teaching public school in the South. As Don Mathews notes in his study of antebellum southern religion, approximately two-thirds of church members were female, a trend that continued after the Civil War. (In fact, throughout the history of the United

---

13. James H. Robinson, *Road without Turning: The Story of Reverend James H. Robinson, An Autobiography* (New York: Farrar, Straus, 1950), 52; James A. Tyson, "Children, Sunday Schools and Parents," *Star of Zion*, 22 May 1885; Elizabeth R. Hooker, *Religion in the Highlands: Native Churches and Missionary Enterprises in the Southern Appalachian Area* (New York: Home Missions Council, 1923), 86–7; Mrs. C. M. Carnahan, "The Primary Teachers' Conference," *Minutes of the 28th Annual Session of the Kentucky Sunday School Union* (Louisville: John P. Morton, 1893), 67. Few first-hand accounts of teaching methods exist; these offer a sampling of various approaches.

14. St. Paul's Church, Goldsboro, *Minutes of the District Conference Reports of the North Carolina Methodist Episcopal Church, South, 1894*, Duke; Lois Johnson Grier, ed., *The First Presbyterian Church of Greenwood, South Carolina, 1883–1958* (privately printed by Carolina Engraving, 1958), 68; "Woman's Position As Teacher in the Church," *Presbyterian Standard* 44 (12 March 1902): 13. Females dominated northern Sunday schools several decades earlier than in the South. See Boylan, *Sunday School*, 114–6.

States, American women—regardless of race, class or region—have been more likely to join a church and participate in religious activities than men.) During this time, society began to identify public school teaching (at least in the elementary grades) and Sunday school teaching as feminine occupations. With the creation and expansion of public school systems in the South, school boards began to hire more women, as northern states had been doing for years. School systems actually preferred to hire women because they were cheaper than men and thus saved school districts a good deal of money. Officials also saw women as more compliant workers than men. The growing number of female Sunday school instructors also reflected the fact that women's sphere of activity was widening beyond the home. To many tradition-minded southerners, teaching Sunday school was a perfect fit; pious women could be both mothers and teachers, raising Christian children at home and in Sunday school.[15]

Whether married women retained their position as Sunday school teachers depended on circumstance as well as need. Some young women relinquished their post when they married and returned to it when they no longer had youngsters underfoot. Many mothers with young children would have been hard pressed to keep up their teaching duties and care for home and family. This volunteer work demanded preparation and commitment. Interestingly, marriage did not seem to be an impediment to men's work in Sunday school. "How can he better prepare himself to become the perception of the little circle, that may one day surround his own fireside, than by acquiring the art of instruction among the sons and daughters of the stranger," asked an ASSU teachers' guide. Apparently Sunday school teaching was excellent preparation for fatherhood. This

---

15. Don Mathews, *Religion in the Old South* (Chicago: University of Chicago Press, 1977), 47–8; Roger Finke, "Demography of Religious Participation: An Ecological Approach, 1850–1980," *Journal for the Scientific Study of Religion* 28 (1989): 49; Boylan, *Sunday School,* 115–6; Schweiger, "The Transformation of Southern Religion," 374. Michael Kimmel states that in 1870, two-thirds of all schoolteachers nationwide were female; by 1910 women held four-fifths of all teaching positions. See Kimmel, *Manhood in America: A Cultural History* (New York: Free Press, 1996), 121. The feminization of teaching in the South took longer. See Glenda Elizabeth Gilmore, *Gender and Jim Crow: Women and the Politics of White Supremacy in North Carolina, 1896–1920* (Chapel Hill: University of North Carolina Press, 1996), 157; DeBerg, *Ungodly Women,* 80; James L. Leloudis, *Schooling the New South: Pedagogy, Self, and Society in North Carolina, 1880–1920* (Chapel Hill: University of North Carolina Press, 1996), 73–8.

plaintive query also suggests that the ASSU was seeking more male teachers. Obviously, there were no hard and fast rules.¹⁶

Church officials went to great effort to flatter and encourage female teachers. Like many southern ministers, Baptist Lansing Burrows was an open fan of female Sunday school teachers. He viewed Sunday school work as a golden opportunity for women to expand their commitment to Christian nurturing, while accepting their submissive, though meaningful, role as servants of the church. In a series of sermons, Burrows exhorted women to avoid the rough and tumble of the public sphere and work quietly for the salvation of the young. "No Christian woman is guiltless who seeks not assiduously the conversion of her children, who prays not, labors not, entreats not to this end," Burrows thundered. He believed that women were blessed to have both home and Sunday school as an outlet for their Christian duties. Teaching youngsters was a glorious means to serve God. Yet Burrows worried that too few women took advantage of this opportunity. "It is more frequently the case that she herself shrinks from it than that she is driven away from the work," he grumbled. Trying to stir enthusiasm, Burrows admonished women to "estimate the importance of the task—its nobility—its grandeur—its undying influence, and bring back to Christ in this manner the native moral estimate, the natural influence, the inherent patience, hope and tenderness with which He has graciously endowed you." No other task compared to the "dignity and rewards" of teaching Sunday school. Whether Burrows was gratefully acknowledging women's participation, lobbying for more Sunday school volunteers, or reminding females of their assigned role is not clear. Probably it was all three.¹⁷

Burrows was hardly alone. Southern evangelicals believed that teaching Sunday school gave women the perfect opportunity to engage in purposeful, benevolent activity beyond the home. J. K. Ryan claimed that southern women could no longer complain of boredom or a lack of opportunity. "Those days of ignorance and donothingness are past," he stated. Certainly most southerners preferred to see women teaching Sun-

---

16. J. A. James, *The Sunday School Teacher's Guide* (Philadelphia: ASSU, n.d.), 41. White female public schoolteachers often quit when they married, while many black public schoolteachers, both male and female, were married. See Gilmore, *Gender and Jim Crow*, 157.

17. Lansing Burrows, "The Woman of Samaria," Sermon #152 (1872), and "Priscilla," Sermon #160 (1872), in Lansing Burrows Papers, SBHLA.

day school than engaging in more assertive behavior. When two Arkansas women tried to be seated at the 1885 Baptist State Convention, male delegates dismissed them, removed the disruption from the minutes, and shuddered at its possible repercussions. "We all insist upon women teaching in our Sabbath schools, and in higher branches of scholastic learning; but we rule her out if she desires to meddle with the affairs of church polity," one man fumed. Women's place in the social order was self-evident. Teaching Sunday school was the apex of a southern woman's position within the church. And unlike the radical female reformers in the Northeast who were demanding women's suffrage and equitable marital laws, southern women must shun the limelight of mob protest. Instead, they should inspire and heal, reign over the home from a secluded position, and elevate youngsters by teaching Sunday school. As a writer for the *Working Christian* sighed, "We shudder when we think what a change would be wrought in society were these notions of woman's rights to prevail. May God preserve our sunny South from such a curse."[18]

The influence that women had on the Sunday school and the church was profound. Men may have been officially in charge of the institution, but women shaped the direction of Sunday school education. Women's involvement in various causes—teaching Sunday school, raising money to beautify church sanctuaries, and tending church cemeteries—gave a feminine touch to these endeavors. Female teachers, for example, brought a gentle, maternal approach to the classroom. Sunday school advisors celebrated this, recognizing that pupils could not be dragged reluctantly to class; instead "their hearts must be won, and this can be done [more easily] by a gentle, Christian woman, than by any other." The language used to describe the Sunday school experience reflected a feminine, innocent character. Pupils were described as "lambs" or "buds" that were "blossoming." Sunday school poems and hymns celebrated female

---

18. J. K. Ryan, "Her Mission and Work," *Alabama Baptist*, 25 January 1877; M. G. H., "Woman's Work," *Working Christian*, 25 November 1875; "Southern Baptist Convention, Augusta," *Baptist Courier*, 14 May 1885; "Woman's Right to Speak in Public," *Baptist Courier*, 23 July 1885. See also Leon McBeth, *Women in Baptist Life* (Nashville: Broadman Press, 1979) and "The Changing Role of Women in Baptist History," *Southwestern Journal of Theology* 22 (fall 1979): 84–96; Sarah Frances Anders, "Woman's Role in the Southern Baptist Convention and Its Churches," *Review and Expositor* 72 (winter 1975): 31–9.

teachers: "She came amidst her children like sunshine 'mongst the flowers, Cheering with love's soft radiance, Those blessed Sabbath hours." Some women literally transformed their classroom. "Woman's never failing but delicate taste for decoration greeted our eyes," wrote one delighted observer as he visited a Saluda, North Carolina, Sunday school. The Sunday school was a sphere where women felt capable and comfortable, and where a feminine language and setting reflected their influence.[19]

Yet it is important to consider whether southern women effectively were co-opted into this selfless volunteer activity by the proclamations and urgings of their male contemporaries. At least one sociologist has argued that the more a woman identifies with organized religion, the less she identifies with feminism. Did Sunday school work, then, deter southern women from adopting more assertive behavior or engaging in reform issues similar to those that attracted some northern women? In the South, tremendous social pressure argued for women to expend their energies in a quiet but influential role in Sunday school. Southern men celebrated it; church officials urged them to serve; and women's very upbringing reinforced the importance of their maternal role. It is little wonder that women responded enthusiastically to a job that fit so well into southern women's culture, where they learned to "make the best of their historical circumstances," as R. Stephen Warner has argued. He added, "Religion has long provided moral leverage to American women when other power resources were lacking." Certainly this was true during the late nineteenth century. Most women relished Sunday school teaching and saw it as an inspiring task to bring the word of God to innocent souls and try to save them.[20]

With personnel in place, Sunday school advisors focused attention on the most critical part of the day: the weekly lesson. Each lesson had one overriding purpose, which was to expose pupils to the Bible and teach them to know and love God. The hope was that each child would experience conversion and make a permanent commitment to the church, theo-

---

19. Turner, *Women, Culture, and Community,* 40–74; "The Influence of Women in the Church," *Working Christian,* 11 November 1880; "Report on Sabbath School," *Minutes of the 62nd Annual Session of the Alabama Baptist Association, 1881* (Selma: John L. West, 1881), 7; "The Sunday School Maid," *Pearls for Little Ones,* 8 March 1896; "Saluda Baptist Sunday School Institute," *Working Christian,* 31 July 1879.

20. Warner, "Work in Progress toward a New Paradigm," 1071, 1073.

retically thus ensuring his or her bright future. To begin this education when youngsters were open to new ideas was essential. "The conversion of children, even very young children, should be sought for, prayed for and expected," intoned Southern Baptists.[21]

Nothing seemed more rewarding to Sunday school workers than seeing youngsters convert as a result of their Sunday school education. Black Baptists in a Tennessee church were thrilled when twelve children joined their church. "How many of these conversions are due mainly to the teaching in Sunday school it is impossible to say," they noted, "but it is a matter for thanksgiving and a source of great encouragement to teachers and officers." North Carolina Methodists were overjoyed that at "every revival meeting some of the Sunday school children are brought into the church." Delighted Baptists learned that at a recent revival, a quarter to a third of the pupils in one Sunday school "were converted to the service of Jesus." Conversion was the goal of every Sunday school. Because the number of conversions was so easy to quantify, it gave schools a means to judge their success and compare themselves to others.[22]

The importance of the conversion experience resonated with laypeople and clergy alike, who endlessly reiterated its importance. With childhood conversion, declared Methodist A. S. Andrews, the "weeds of depravity and sin may be choked in their budding." Adults who had never converted were the object of some suspicion and derision. "Nothing can be more dangerous to the temporal and especially to the spiritual interests of our children than to wait until false theories of life and religion have been embraced and evil habits formed before we begin to teach them the doctrines of the gospel," Andrews continued breathlessly. For evangelicals, the Sunday school was the primary place to effect youthful conversions.[23]

---

21. "Annual Report of the Sunday School and Publishing Board of the General Association of Virginia," *Religious Herald*, 21 June 1866; Boylan, *Sunday School*, 141–4.

22. Immanuel E. S. Baptist Church, Tennessee State Archives, Nashville; New Bern District, Hancock Station, *Minutes of the District Conference Reports of the North Carolina Methodist Episcopal Church, South, 1893–1909*, Duke; J. B. Watkins, "The Blessed Fruits of Some Sunday Schools during the Past Year," *Religious Herald*, 23 August 1866.

23. A. S. Andrews, "Report of the Committee on Sunday Schools," *Minutes of the Alabama Conference of the Methodist Episcopal Church, South, 1874* (Selma: James P. Armstrong, 1875), 21–2. Methodists had formerly believed that conversion was appropriate for

In order to convert, children had to know and understand the Bible and learn to live according to God's word. Thus, an exposure to Scripture was at the heart of the Sunday school lesson. "The Sunday school is the world's greatest institution for popularizing the world's greatest book," observed Methodist Wade Barclay. Officials insisted that every Sunday school lesson focus on the gospel. Nothing was more important than the time a class spent absorbing the Bible, reading its stories and learning Scripture. Teachers should encourage pupils to memorize Scripture and the catechism and accept God's word as a matter of faith.[24]

Sunday school officials soon began to feel the need to exert more control over the lesson. Though their institutional goals seemed clear, officials were uneasy over the varieties of classroom instruction and different lesson plans in Sunday schools. There was no guarantee that all teachers were accomplishing their goals. Evangelicals fretted that a haphazard, inconsistent approach to Christian learning could ignore important material and even prove counterproductive. Sunday instruction was too important to leave to chance or in the hands of a bad instructor. Studying the Bible had to be handled in an orderly fashion. Thus, interest developed in creating what scholars have called a "common language," or uniform lessons, for Sunday schools nationwide.[25]

The concept of a uniform lesson system had been tried well before the Civil War. In 1841, the Sunday School Union of London produced a common lesson plan for all member schools. British communities gradually accepted this concept, and the idea subsequently attracted interest in the United States. A few American denominations began to develop a single lesson plan for their Sunday schools. In 1867, for instance, Reverend Basil Manly Jr. began producing his *Little Lessons for Little People* for Southern Baptists, which included teacher guidelines, simple texts representing only the "choice and precious fruit of the Bible," and easy questions for pupils to answer.[26]

---

mature, rational adults but now declared their former prejudice against early conversion to be outdated.

24. Barclay, *The Pupil, the Teacher, and the School*, x; R. C. Hiden, "Speech to the Southern Baptist Sunday School Institute, Macon, Georgia, 1869," *The Baptist*, 29 January 1870.

25. Robert Wood Lynn, *Protestant Strategies*, 102; Boylan, *Sunday School*, 98.

26. Basil Manly Jr., *Little Lessons for Little People* (St. Louis: National Baptist Publishing, 1867), 2. See also Basil Manly Jr., 19 July 1871, Greenville, S.C., and T. J. Earle,

Methodist John H. Vincent was the individual most responsible for encouraging Protestant denominations in the United States to create a national, unified Sunday school lesson plan. The variety of lessons produced by denominations and private publishers troubled him, as did the many teachers who devised their own approach to Sunday school classes. Responding to his concerns, five representatives from different northern denominations met to create the first series of uniform lessons. Delegates at the 1872 National Sunday School Convention established a permanent committee of clergymen and laymen to develop weekly uniform lessons that systematically covered the entire Bible every few years. Under this plan, children would be well versed in the Bible by the time they matured.[27]

The timing of these uniform lessons was especially propitious for the South. In the wake of the Civil War, northern church leaders saw the creation and adoption of uniform lessons as not only critical to the future of the Sunday school but as a gesture with important political implications. With youngsters nationwide learning the same lessons, the Sunday school could serve as a vehicle to help restore national harmony. Even though white Southern Baptists, Methodists, and Presbyterians had split with their northern counterparts and formed their own denominations years earlier, and even though churches in the South were racially segregated, all youngsters taught from a uniform plan would learn the same Sunday school lessons. In the eyes of some Sunday school advocates, this was something to celebrate.[28]

Yet uniform lessons did not gain immediate acceptance in the South. Some denominations and individual Sunday schools took years to approve the idea; others never did. Southern Presbyterians officially

---

30 June 1870, Youngsville, S.C., both to John Broadus, in the John Albert Broadus Collection, James. P. Boyce Centennial Library Archives, Southern Baptist Theological Seminary, Louisville, Ky.; Clarence Benson, *A Popular History of Christian Education* (Chicago: Moody Press, 1943), 188; Boylan, *Sunday School*, 98–9.

27. Boylan, *Sunday School*, 150.

28. For background and history on uniform lessons, see Mary Jo Osterman, "The Two Hundred Year Struggle for Protestant Religious Education Curriculum Theory," *Religious Education* 75 (Sept.–Oct. 1980): 528–38, esp. 533–7; J. R. Sampey, "Uniform Lesson System," *Encyclopedia of Sunday Schools*, vol. 3, 1114–20; Robert Wood Lynn and Elliott Wright, *The Big Little School: Two Hundred Years of the Sunday School*, 2nd ed. (Birmingham, Ala.: Religious Education Press, 1980); Grant, "The Sunday School Movement in America." Osterman calls the period from 1872 to 1908 the "Uniform Lesson Period."

adopted the lessons in 1875; some (but not all) AMEZ Sabbath schools used uniform lessons for several years before the church officially endorsed them in 1880. A single influential individual could impede the acceptance of the uniform lesson plan. Atticus Haygood insisted that Methodist Sunday schools use only their own questions and lesson outlines that he had created and published in the *Sunday School Magazine*. Southern Methodists only officially adopted uniform lessons in 1878, when a new editor took over the magazine.[29]

Opponents to uniform lessons voiced several complaints. Some disliked them because they put southerners in the uncomfortable position of being dependent on outsiders. If southerners were to express distinctiveness of faith, critics argued, they should not depend on lesson plans created by northerners. Other critics hated the thought of different denominations offering the same lesson each Sunday. If all schools taught the same material in Sunday school, so their thinking went, some people might demand a uniform worship service or question the need for different denominations. Some felt that it was premature to assume that cordial relationships could develop between northern and southern churches based on shared lessons. A long-winded Kentuckian complained that the next step would be a national religion. "The best thing which our people can do is utterly to ignore all that kind of Sunday school literature and put themselves to work to build up within our own Church what we actually need for the defense and propagation of the faith once delivered unto the saints," he wrote. To Methodists, uniform lessons left little opportunity to focus on important issues such as missionary work, temperance, and church precepts. North Carolina Baptists feared that they gave teachers an easy out—an "opportunity to make the teacher indolent"—for instructors did not need to spend hours poring over their Bible each week to develop their lesson plan. Others objected to the manner in which National Sunday School Convention delegates adopted the plan. Southerners scoffed at these so-called "national" lessons, for no one from the South had attended the initial meeting to discuss them or had voted to adopt them. "This kind of unity is more fanciful than real," sniffed Southern Presbyterians.[30]

---

29. Atticus Haygood, "Uniform Lessons," *Sunday School Magazine* 6 (1876): 12; Stowell, *Rebuilding Zion,* 119.

30. Sampey, "Uniform Lesson System," 1116–7; W. H. Pace, "The One Lesson System," *Minutes of the Baptist State Sunday School Convention of North Carolina, 1874,* 35; Thompson, *Presbyterians in the South,* vol. 2., *1861–1890,* 338. See also R. K. S., "The National Sabbath School Lessons," *Earnest Worker,* 2 May 1872.

What is more surprising and significant, however, was the degree of southern support for the lessons. Many southerners came to view the acceptance of uniform lessons as an important step in overcoming national tensions. In Sunday school, the focus could be completely on the universal importance of God's word, bypassing regional, racial, and sectarian divisions. Though northerners initially created the lessons, most southern denominations eventually adopted them. Southern resistance to a uniform lesson plan crumbled significantly in 1878 when Southern Baptist John Broadus became part of the committee that created the lessons.[31]

Teachers' responses also played a role in southern reaction to the lessons. While some Sunday school teachers objected to the slipshod appearance of the first set of lessons and the evident haste with which they were written, most seem to have been enthusiastic. We have no way of knowing how many teachers actually used the uniform lessons, but instructors surely welcomed assistance in preparing their weekly lesson. Creating a Sunday school lesson had often been a time-consuming task. Now, by simply following a prescribed outline printed in a Sunday school magazine, pamphlet, or local newspaper, a teacher could use pre-existing lessons and add supplemental material as he or she saw fit. In one instance, teachers pressured their denomination to accept uniform lessons. Fearing the loss of their particular theological viewpoint, Southern Presbyterian officials had hesitated to adopt the new system, but Presbyterian Sunday school teachers saw the matter differently. When the Presbyterian publishing house failed to print the lessons in its Sunday school magazines, teachers purchased rival publications that included them. The General Assembly, hearing of their journals' declining circulations and their teachers' rising protests, finally agreed to uniform lessons.[32]

Southerners' desire for quality teaching and the uniform lessons' emphasis on the Bible outweighed uneasiness and silenced critics. Evangeli-

---

31. Robertson, *Life and Letters of John Albert Broadus*, 332; James Henry Thayer, "Southern Baptists in Sunday School Work" (Ph.D. diss., Southern Baptist Theological Seminary, 1910), 132. Broadus described his work on this committee as "two days of very hard work."

32. E. Thompson Baird, "Ninth Annual Report of the Executive Committee of Publication," *Minutes of the General Assembly of the Presbyterian Church in the United States, 1870* (Columbia, S.C.: Presbyterian Publishing House, 1870), 563; "Abstract of the Fourteenth Annual Report of the Committee of Publication," *Minutes of the General Assembly of the Presbyterian Church in the United States, 1875* (Richmond: Presbyterian Committee of Publication, 1875), 64.

cals felt comfortable knowing that every lesson centered on Scripture, for each six- or seven-year lesson cycle covered the entire Bible. Baptist officials pointed to the positive impact they would have, "particularly with backward and undecided teachers," for they worried that many instructors did not understand or use the Bible correctly. With experts writing the lessons, they believed that content and quality could be assured and teaching would improve. Content became much more important by the late nineteenth century as biblical criticism and controversial scientific ideas—such as Darwin's theory of evolution—challenged traditional religious beliefs. As a white Methodist wrote, uniform lessons were the "best antidote to the skeptical tendencies and abounding iniquity of the times," and he praised their creation.[33]

The eventual adoption of a single set of Sunday school lessons for most Protestants nationwide was an unprecedented and extraordinary step. A year after their initial appearance, one southerner called them the "greatest mile-post in the ascending path of Sunday school progress." Two decades later, J. Allen Viney, speaking at the Texas Annual Conference of the AME, also applauded this accomplishment. "The idea of the Declaration of Independence, conceived and formulated by the Hon. Richard Henry Lee, was in no way grander in its purpose and design than the notion of a uniformity of lesson helps to be coextensive with the Sunday schools of the world," he grandly intoned. By 1890, it was estimated that some ten million pupils benefited from their use. One writer has guessed that by 1904, 90 percent of all Sunday schools nationwide used the lessons. A historian has called them "one of the greatest accomplishments in the history of Sunday schools."[34]

While teaching the Bible was paramount, Sunday school lessons also served more pragmatic purposes. Woven into the religious material used in Sunday school and read outside class were lessons in behavior, as well as moral and social values that evangelicals held dear. The Reverend J. C. Hiden, among others, insisted that good behavior would flow naturally from a weekly exposure to the gospel. "If we can succeed in bringing

---

33. Rev. M. Stone, "Organization of Sunday Schools," *Minutes of the Baptist State Sunday School Convention of North Carolina, 1874*, 20; "Uniform Lessons," *Sunday School Magazine* 1 (1871): 35.

34. J. Allen Viney, "Sunday-Schools," *AME Church Review* 7 (1891): 311; A. E. Dunning, "The Sunday School As a Factor in Education," *Educational Review* 27 (February 1904): 135; Benson, *A Popular History of Christian Education*, 188.

the children to Christ, we may rest confident that their manners and general behavior will not be very far from right," he observed. The topics of Sunday lessons thus reveal what southerners regarded as critical issues for the uplift of the South and the creation of a morally sound, well-behaved citizenry.[35]

Children absorbed their first messages merely by attending Sunday school and interacting with superintendents, teachers, and other pupils. It was easy to grasp the importance of punctuality. Sunday classes started and ended at a set time, and punctual students were rewarded with a colored ticket or commendation from their teacher. Children who brought a Bible and a weekly donation—thus demonstrating that they understood the importance of responsibility—might win a gold star. Perfect attendance for an entire year might earn children a Bible. The need to be clean and to wear decent clothes were not only important hygienic attributes, but a way of showing respect toward God that teachers might reward with a smile or compliment.

One of the most important lessons drilled into pupils was God's omnipotence in the world, his eternal wisdom and power, and his love for everyone. Children learned that they could never escape God's all-seeing eye, and therefore always had to be good. Sunday school stories featured young heroes or heroines who underscored the importance of obedience—God was always vigilant, especially when adults were absent. By obeying God, youngsters would find a path to salvation; disobedient children would suffer the consequences.[36]

Children learned that as Christians, they could save others. Sunday school tales often depicted youngsters redeeming adults, in a reversal of what one might expect. In a typical story, a young girl attended Sunday school despite her parent's objections, for she knew it was the right thing to do. The parents threatened to turn their disobedient child out of the house, but she persisted in going each week. One Sunday, her parents secretly followed their daughter, and they were so pleased with her Sunday school that they welcomed her home with open arms. The child saw this as an opportunity to teach her parents a lesson, and she refused to

---

35. Rev. R. C. Hiden, "Delivery to the Southern Baptist Sunday School Institute, Macon, Ga.," *The Baptist,* 29 January 1870. For historical background on proper manners and behavior, see John F. Kasson, *Rudeness and Civility: Manners in Nineteenth-Century Urban America* (New York: Hill and Wang, 1990).

36. Avery, *Behold the Child,* 4, 8, 104.

cross the threshold until they promised to attend church. Naturally they did, and as a result, "their religious convictions deepened." Children who read this story were meant to understand the power they acquired as good Christians who attended Sunday school.[37]

While irreligious adults needed redeeming, Sunday school lessons taught that church-going parents were endowed with God-given authority and knew what was best for their young. Children always needed to respect their parents, or they would face dire consequences—possibly even eternal damnation. Sunday lessons, like much of the literature directed at middle-class American children, celebrated close family relationships. The ideal family was intact and loving. Christian parents were invariably wise and affectionate. Story illustrations depicted scrubbed, well-dressed children joyfully huddling around their father's knee, or leaning over their mother as she read them a Bible story in front of a toasty fire. In one illustration, a father led his family in prayer—an activity that promised to keep alive the "flame of Christian love" and bind the family together under God. Middle-class homes were invariably depicted as clean and tidy. Happy homes were the center of Christian nurturing. The darker side of home life was not deemed appropriate for Sunday school lessons.[38]

Mothers received much attention in Sunday lessons. Mary Washington, mother of George, was presented as "one of the most honorable characters in modern history" for raising such a remarkable son. Youngsters were instructed that their mothers' word should engender respect. In one story, a young boy ignored his mother's warnings not to go sledding; during his forbidden outing, his sled overturned on a steep slope, and he broke his arm. As a consequence, he suffered for weeks in bed, where he read copies of his Sunday school magazine and learned that obedience pays. The moral was obvious: children should obey Christian mothers who knew what was best. And children should always love their mothers. "You will never meet an eye as tender, a hand as gentle, or a heart as kind as hers," wrote the author of one honeyed tale. Mothers turned their sons away from gambling, smoking, and drinking, and reprimanded children who strayed from a righteous path. Wayward children

---

37. "The Little Daughter," *Children's Friend*, 7 April 1883.
38. "Giving the Heart," *Good Tidings*, 14 May 1885. Many Americans credited their moral and religious training to their mothers. See Avery, *Behold the Child*, 165–8.

in Sunday school stories ultimately always repented. "What do I not owe to my Mother!" exclaimed a character in one story. Silas Floyd, in his children's book, *Floyd's Flowers,* recalled his "sweet and patient" mother, whose words and prayers would always "be the brightest of all the joys that shall light up the evening of my life."[39]

Children's stories and hymns praised good behavior and taught youngsters the evils of smoking, swearing, gambling, lying, stealing, and mixing with bad company. A typical didactic message in a poem entitled "Dare to Say No!" told children that sinful temptations were to be avoided at all cost. "When tempted to do wrong, oh! Yield not an inch," it read. When poems and stories presented various courses of action, the straight and narrow path was always correct.[40]

Faithfully attending Sunday school was another common theme of classroom literature. Such lessons emphasized the sacredness of the Sabbath, for Sunday observance was an essential part of being a good Christian. Writers described children joyfully learning their lessons, and they used positive reinforcement to convince everyone, but especially a reluctant or ill-behaved child, that this was the best place to spend every Sunday. Youngsters were told never to miss Sunday school; a week lost was a lesson not learned and perhaps a soul not saved. Backsliders and absentees learned of dire consequences if they skipped class.[41]

Weekly Sunday school lessons also exposed children to many contemporary social concerns. Among these, evangelicals saw alcohol abuse as the region's most widespread social problem, for it affected family life, fostered crime and violence, and undermined productivity. Since the 1820s, ministers and middle-class reformers had engaged in a temperance crusade to end alcohol abuse. These reform efforts were interrupted by the Civil War but gained renewed vigor in the postbellum years. By the 1870s, Virginia Baptists had launched a new campaign to eradicate alcohol, urging "all Christians to put far from them the intoxicating cup." Southerners began to pass local and state ordinances to curb the produc-

---

39. "Story of Mary," *Kind Words,* 8 July 1873; "Susy and Johnny," *Children's Friend,* 5 February 1887; "Mothers," *Kind Words,* 25 June 1873; Silas X. Floyd, *Floyd's Flowers, or Duty and Beauty for Colored Children* (Atlanta: Hertel, Jenkins, 1905), 325.
40. "Dare to Say No," *Children's Friend,* 20 August 1881.
41. "The Sunday School Maid," *Pearls for Little Ones,* 8 March 1896. See also Link, *Paradox of Southern Progressivism,* 54–5.

tion and sale of alcohol, well before the Eighteenth Amendment became federal law in 1919.⁴²

Southern states led the way in temperance and prohibition activity, and Sunday schools played a central role in these efforts. The Women's Christian Temperance Union (WCTU) initially selected Sunday schools, rather than public schools, as the place to spread its message. The organization managed to convince national Sunday school leaders to incorporate temperance as an issue in the 1880 series of uniform lessons. The following year, under its president, Frances Willard, the WCTU embarked on a southern campaign. The speeches Willard delivered in the South emphasized moral issues and the need for southern women to protect their home and family by promoting temperance.⁴³

Influential figures in leading southern denominations also actively urged Sunday schools to address prohibition and temperance issues. As they saw it, demon alcohol was causing a demise in civilized behavior and a breakdown of the social order. Mississippi Methodist W. C. Black blamed half of all crimes on alcohol. Children "must fortify the character against the assaults of the liquor-demon," he insisted. His own children set an example by attending both regular Sunday school and temperance Sunday school. In the latter, they sang temperance hymns "with great gusto," learned about the physiological effects of alcohol, and memorized Bible passages that denounced this evil. These special lessons allowed his children to embrace temperance principles, and Black urged all churches to make greater efforts to teach temperance lessons and publish more temperance songs and stories before secular institutions like the WCTU took over. "The Church is unquestionably losing by relegating this work to outside agencies," he warned. Children needed to learn the message that his youngsters had absorbed, and Sunday school was the best place to do this. Legal restrictions could only go so far; it was impor-

---

42. J. C. Hiden, "Preamble and Resolutions," *Minutes of the Baptist General Association of Virginia, 1866* (Richmond: Dispatch Steam Presses, 1866), 22; Maud Junkin Baldwin, *The Juniors: How to Teach and Train Them* (1916; reprint, Nashville: Baptist Sunday School Board, 1924), 71–81. See also Loveland, *Southern Evangelicals and the Social Order, 1800–1860*, 130–58, for background on earlier temperance activity.

43. A. R. Wells, "Temperance Teaching in the Sunday School," *Encyclopedia of Sunday Schools*, vol. 3, 1094–6. See Avery, *Behold the Child*, 148; Ruth Bordin, *Women and Temperance: The Quest for Power and Liberty, 1873–1900* (Philadelphia: Temple University Press, 1981), 54–5; Silber, *The Romance of Reunion*.

tant to address individual behavior. But young people could be saved before bad habits had crystallized. If they were taught to eschew liquor forever and to make vows of abstinence, reformation would occur within a generation, leaving a sober citizenry to do God's work.[44]

In a variety of ways, lessons warning of the evils of alcohol rapidly became integrated into the southern Sunday school curriculum. Temperance Sunday, a celebration started in Great Britain in 1881, became an annual celebration in southern Sunday schools. Denominations organized special temperance committees to stay abreast of the issue and had them present their findings at Sunday school conventions. Pupils memorized temperance verses, sang temperance hymns, and learned about liquor's damaging effects on body and mind. Relevant stories appeared in Sunday school magazines, and temperance lessons used Scripture verses such as Proverbs 20:1—"Wine is a mocker, strong drink is raging"—to good effect. Prayers in *Good Tidings* had black children reciting: "A barrel of headaches, of heartaches, of woes; A barrel of curses, a barrel of blows." Special temperance maps hung in classrooms, highlighting states that had enacted blue laws. Apparently such lessons had some impact. Aggrey Lancaster recalled that after a WCTU agent visited her Sunday school in 1914, she returned home vowing that she would never let alcohol or tobacco touch her lips. Though temperance could be a highly charged political issue, few critics attacked these lessons as too secular or political. Teaching children the dangers of drink was essential in order to ensure a moral southern citizenry.[45]

Some Sunday school lessons brought direct rewards to the church. One of the most important outreach efforts in the late nineteenth century was mission work, both abroad and at home. Ministers encouraged every church member to aid and uplift the less fortunate and bring to them the

44. W. C. Black, "A Seed Thought," *Christian Advocate*, 20 March 1886. Ted Ownby sees the temperance crusade as a means to purify the region. See Ownby, *Subduing Satan*, 170.

45. "Temperance Lesson," *Our Little People*, September 1906; "Beef Tea Better Than Wine," *Our Little People*, February 1906; "Temperance Lesson," *Children's Friend*, 3 March 1883; *Good Tidings*, 19 November 1887; "Us Boys," *Our Little People*, 23 March 1890; "A Barrel of Whiskey," *Good Tidings*, 20 May 1893. For the Lancaster quote, see Gilmore, *Gender and Jim Crow*, 156. See also A. R. Wells, "Temperance Teaching in the Sunday School," *Encyclopedia of Sunday Schools*, vol. 3, 1094–6; Nancy A. Hardesty, "The Best Temperance Organization in the Land: Southern Methodism and the W.C.T.U. in Georgia," *Methodist History* 28 (April 1990): 187–94.

benefits of Christianity and middle-class values. By incorporating mission work as a theme in Sunday schools, church leaders sought to interest youngsters in this endeavor and to stimulate their knowledge and curiosity about different cultures. Sabbath school magazines included lessons in world geography, with maps and stories focusing on lands in the Bible and areas of the world where missionaries labored. As the home mission movement gained popularity at the turn of the century, Sunday school literature focused more attention on native American cultures, while making clear which people were worthy of concern. Native Americans and foreigners overseas deserved attention; African Americans apparently did not. Tales such as "A Baby Tomb in China" and "A Scene on the Ganges" emphasized exotic cultures rather than a race of people whom white southerners regarded as ordinary.[46]

Church leaders also hoped to interest children in the mission cause so they would increase donations to help support it and perhaps devote a portion of their adult lives to spreading Christianity at home and abroad. By the late nineteenth century, the United States was showing more interest in nations overseas. American influence abroad was growing through increased trade and military involvement, as well as missionary work. Taking advantage of what they saw as a vast field of non-Christians who might be attracted to a Protestant faith, southern denominations began to send agents abroad. Workers were needed to fill the ranks of these religious ambassadors. As Presbyterians predicted, the "youths of today will be the warriors of tomorrow in the mission cause." Baptist James Frost urged all Sunday schools to celebrate Missionary Day, a special event to honor the cause and raise money for Baptist missions. This celebration would "get hold of the minds of children and young people and lodge in them the great mission thought and awaken with them an ambition for the mission life," he predicted.[47]

It is hardly surprising that a sense of superiority toward non-Christian

---

46. See "A Missionary Preaching the Gospel to the Heathen," *Pearls for Little Ones*, 6 September 1896; "Some People of Jerusalem," *Our Little People*, n.s., 2 (1909): 29; M. E., "What a Mite Box Did," *Children's Friend*, 16 August 1890. For an interesting interpretation of benevolence and missionary work in the antebellum South, see Startup, *Root of All Evil*, 100.

47. "The Necessity of Training Our Young People in Missionary Work," *Presbyterian Standard*, 5 August 1902; James Marion Frost; "On Missionary Day Education," *Missionary Messenger*, September 1898.

and foreign cultures permeated these mission lessons. To modern eyes and ears, the comments and illustrations in Sunday school stories are startling to see and read today, but they reflected the attitudes of most Americans during the late nineteenth century. Sunday school writers referred to Indians as "degraded" and "ignorant people," and dubbed the Japanese "Japs." Illustrations showed well-dressed white missionaries sitting among veiled foreigners who had to stand before them. A caption noted that dedicated American agents worked among "heathen people" to make them "good and happy by the blessed lessons from God's holy book." These tales conveyed the idea that both Christianity and the American way of life were far superior to anything that foreigners experienced, and, moreover, that Protestant missionaries could civilize and uplift unfortunate people. Sunday school children were socialized to believe that their religion and their nation were far better than anything encountered overseas.[48]

Weekly lessons in systematic benevolence reflected the important economic role of the Sunday school. From the moment children first entered Sunday school, they were taught to contribute money selflessly. The idea was to sacrifice for the greater good by sharing one's worldly gifts with God. Training children in the importance of generous giving was essential to help secure the financial position of a church and denomination, both of which were dependent upon the generosity of members. In one sense, churches were in the business of raising money in order to accomplish lofty, often expensive, goals and to assert their position in society. Sunday school lessons accordingly emphasized the need for generous, regular giving to the church.

This emphasis on benevolence also demonstrated how Americans measured success—by status and financial position. Making benevolence such an important part of the Sunday school lesson reflected not only the needs of churches; it revealed an increasingly acquisitive and materialistic national culture. It was a message that filtered down to the smallest Sunday school and the youngest pupils. Tradition-minded church members objected to this growing emphasis on money and ceaseless fund raising. In order to avoid giving the wrong impression, teachers tried to present this lesson in a selfless, humanitarian light. Calling Sunday donations

48. "Five Japs Eating Rice," *Child's Gem*, October 1909; "The Lady Missionary," *Children's Friend*, 3 February 1883.

"benevolence" reflected this way of thinking. Pleas for donations were often couched in the guise of Christian enterprise. Methodist E. B. Chappell, for example, wrote that the aim of Sunday school benevolence was an effort "not to secure from the pupil as much money as possible, but to widen his sympathies and to develop in him a spirit of liberality."[49]

Lessons in benevolence may have seemed a rather fruitless endeavor in the South, since so many destitute families had little or nothing to give. Yet like so much about the Sunday school movement, this lesson was a bet on future rewards. "We should live for the future," declared a South Carolina Baptist. "If we train the children in this habit of giving, they will grow up to expect to give for God's cause." Sunday school leaders assumed that the lesson would leave an indelible mark on children's psyches, and that those who learned to give generously would continue to do so throughout their lives. Israel Black urged pupils to bring their pennies to class and give their toys and clothing to the less fortunate. "Upon these little ones will one day rest the responsibility of carrying forward the great benevolent and missionary work of the church," he affirmed. Southern Baptist J. S. Allen was thrilled with his Sunday school's interest in benevolence. "Nothing will bring a better return than money invested in a Sunday school. It is worth more than the same amount invested in a Railroad stock or Bank stock of any kind," he stated. A writer for the *Baptist Courier* was clear-cut on this subject: "Fix the habit now in the children."[50]

In rural southern Sunday schools, benevolence might mean something other than dropping a penny or nickel into a collection basket. Here, teachers developed creative means of giving, since the poor usually had no coins to give away. Presbyterian R. P. Smith visited a missionary teacher in a poor mountain Sunday school who encouraged his pupils to

---

49. E. B. Chappell, "Benevolence in the Sunday School," *Encyclopedia of Sunday Schools,* vol. 1, 89–90 (quote, 89). According to Christopher Owen, many southerners resented the "new ecclesiastical appreciation for the benefits of raising cash." Owen, *Sacred Flame of Love,* 153.

50. "Sunday School Convention, Edgehill Baptist Sunday School," *Working Christian,* August 1875; Israel Putnam Black, *Practical Primary Plans for Primary Teachers of the Sunday School* (New York: Fleming H. Revell, 1903), 93; Jesse Lee Cuninggim and Eric M. North, *The Organization and Administration of the Sunday School* (Nashville: Smith and Lamar, 1919), 68; "Sunday School Work," *Minutes of the Baptist State Sunday School Convention of North Carolina* (Raleigh: Edwards, Broughton, 1874), 30; "On Sunday Schools," *Baptist Courier,* 24 March 1881.

bring fruit, nuts, potatoes, or any produce the family could spare. One Sunday, a young boy arrived with two ducks he had killed and placed them at his teacher's feet. Farm children often earned money by picking and selling berries, herding cows, and gardening. At a Sunday school in Union Point, Georgia, pupils each received twenty-four grains of corn that they planted, sowed, harvested, and eventually sold for a total of thirty dollars to aid church mission work. ASSU missionary Isaac Emory reported that hundreds of children in his Sunday schools gathered chestnuts and raised chickens, which they later sold, donating the profits to the Sunday school. Many schools owned a "missionary hen" whose eggs were sold and the money earmarked for mission work.[51]

Naturally, pupils from privileged families could afford to give more. Children in a Richmond, Virginia, Sunday school raised $550 to help build a new church, and they donated cast-off clothing to the poor. A Sunday school magazine, *Pearls for the Little Ones,* carried the story of six girls in a Presbyterian Sunday school who spent their summer in a creative and inspiring way; they announced that they were on a "missionary vacation," earning money to support church work overseas. One girl gathered eggs for her grandmother; another earned a dollar by not uttering the word "gracious"; a third was paid to read the Bible to a blind lady; a fourth wiped the dishes after family meals and fed the chickens; a fifth earned money for not scowling; and the sixth girl gathered and sold flowers. The purpose of describing such selfless holiday activity was to inspire other youngsters to do the same.[52]

Youthful benevolence apparently made a difference and helped churches advance various causes. Annie Armstrong promoted Children's Day, an annual celebration to foster interest in Sunday schools, as the most important event on the Baptist Sunday school calendar, since all money raised went to aid missionary work. Her relentless efforts paid off. In 1897, she announced that over a nine-year period, Baptist women

---

51. R. P. Smith, "Some Results of Mission Work in the Mountains of North Carolina," Asheville, N.C., 1905, 42, Union Theological Seminary Library, Richmond; "Sunday School Intelligence," *Earnest Worker,* 8 February 1872; Isaac Emory to Maurice A. Wurts, Knoxville, Tenn., 2 December 1869, ASSU Correspondence, PHS; "He Who Careth for the Sparrows Careth Also for the Missionary Hen," *Children's Friend,* 15 June 1889.

52. "Annual Meeting of the First Baptist Church Sunday School of Richmond," *Earnest Worker,* 30 January 1873; "A Missionary Vacation," *Pearls for the Little Ones,* 1893; "What a Sunday School Can Do," *Earnest Worker,* 2 March 1871.

and children had donated or raised more than $410,000 for missionary work. Donations might also help Sunday schools purchase class equipment and furniture. A black Sunday school was able to collect a penny each week from its pupils, which it used to purchase books for the Sunday school library. Children raised money to build new mission churches and Sunday schools at home and abroad. Baptist John Williams was thrilled with youngsters in his state who donated nearly $2,200 to help build five mission churches. Contributions aided day schools for indigent children and supplemented a minister's salary. A Sunday School in Enon, South Carolina, collected $18.10 for its minister and encouraged others to do the same. Not only would this money supplement his meager salary, but "it will bring the pastor and the children nearer to each other," stated one observer. Sometimes money collected in Sunday school seemed to have little relationship to church needs. In the 1880s, white children in Richmond Sunday schools raised money to fund that city's Confederate war memorial. While some may have questioned the suitability of this undertaking, historian Charles Reagan Wilson has argued that to many southerners, religion and defending the South's "Lost Cause" were one and the same. The importance of fund raising was obvious; children were learning to give to the "treasury of the Lord." Often, youthful enthusiasm for giving was contagious and had a positive impact on adults. "Oh, what a blessing there is in this children's money!" an excited Baptist emoted. "And they are working right on, and show no signs of getting tired. And they don't get tired quick, like the older folks." He equated Sunday schools to bee hives and children to busy worker bees. Generous, hard-working pupils inspired all.[53]

Gender issues rarely received special attention in Sunday school lessons and stories, which upheld traditional assumptions about appropriate male and female roles. Illustrations depicted girls wearing aprons and holding brooms or kitchen utensils. Boys had their own world of masculine games and sports. They were depicted playing roughhouse, sledding, or helping their father with outdoor chores. A tale in the *Religious Herald* told girls to "give up all hope" of engaging in sports because

53. Annie Armstrong to James Frost, 2 July 1897, Baltimore, Md., Annie Armstrong Papers, SBHLA; "Our Little Ones," *Working Christian,* 20 November 1879; John G. Williams, "The Impetus Given to Church-Building by the Work of the Children of Our State during the Past Three Years," *Baptist Courier,* 5 March 1891; Wilson, *Baptized in Blood.*

they could never throw a ball as well as boys. An article on missionary work among Native Americans urged young men to raise money for the cause, adding, "I don't know how it is with girls, but all boys are interested in Indians." A typical story described little Susy Baird, who dreamed of growing up to be just like her mother—a missionary wife, president of her sewing circle, Sunday school teacher, and head of a ladies' prayer meeting. In one story in *Good Tidings,* a magazine addressed to black children, a hotel held a splendid party to honor the departure of its favorite guest, Betty. A stranger who witnessed the celebration questioned the identity of this beloved woman. He asked if she was particularly beautiful, brilliant, witty, or rich, and received a negative to each inquiry. He finally learned that what made Betty so special was that she never thought of herself. "She simply forgot that there was such a person as Betty Gordon and with her warm heart and quiet sympathies threw herself into the lives of others." Apparently no celebration was too grand for a selfless female.[54]

However effective and inspiring the lessons and however well-staffed the Sunday school, teachers could not count on regular attendance. Schools had to do more than instruct and uplift; they had to attract children and ensure that they learned their lessons. Public schools faced a similar problem, for effective compulsory school attendance laws did not exist in the South for decades after the Civil War. Youthful participation needed encouragement and rewards; attendance and performance could not be left to chance. To this end, Sunday schools used praise, social activities, and prizes to motivate and inspire students. A child's stellar attendance might earn special accolades in a Sunday school magazine, such as the notice of sixteen-year old Annie Perley's attending 312 successive Sunday school classes. A Baptist Sunday school in Prattville, Alabama, announced that 66 of its pupils had perfect attendance during a three-month period. A class of females "budding into womanhood" received praise for being present the entire year. Four boys in Paris, Kentucky, re-

---

54. "Why a Girl Cannot Throw," *Religious Herald,* 8 May 1902; "The Fifth Sunday," *Children's Friend,* 29 May 1910; "Self Consciousness," *Good Tidings,* 19 May 1883; "Susy and Her Mother," *Kind Words,* 22 May 1873. For a discussion of the separate world of male activity, see Ownby, *Subduing Satan,* and E. Anthony Rotundo, "Boy Culture: Middle-Class Boyhood in Nineteenth Century America," in *Meanings for Manhood: Constructions of Masculinity in Victorian America,* ed. Mark C. Carnes and Clyde Griffin (Chicago: University of Chicago Press, 1990), 15–36.

ceived public commendation as examples of "determination and punctuality" for walking four miles to Sunday school and arriving on time for morning class. Some superintendents posted an honor roll listing students with perfect attendance, who then earned a decorative certificate at the end of the year.[55]

Sunday school officers and teachers rewarded those children who excelled at memorization and completed their weekly Bible assignments. Church publishing houses sold an array of prizes and books to honor their brightest and most faithful pupils. A popular inducement was the five-gold-star honor system, with a star given to outstanding pupils for being present and punctual, bringing their weekly donation and Bible to class, and reciting the lesson perfectly. Pupils who excelled at memorizing special verses often received a prize for exceptional performance, as well as public notice in a church publication heralding their accomplishments. At a concert of sacred music at St. Stephen's AME Church in Wilmington, North Carolina, a young girl and boy received "two handsome sets of crockery" for reciting the most Bible verses. A Sunday school in Marietta, Georgia, awarded prizes to its two brightest pupils; a boy received a copy of *The Plantation Home,* while a girl earned a silver cup. In North Carolina, teachers at the Cane Creek Church Sunday school bragged that their students memorized 5,215 Bible verses in a single year. Dispensing praise and awarding prizes for such feats served as positive reinforcement for pupils. The goal was to get children to attend class, become familiar with the Bible, and embrace Jesus as their savior, whatever it might take. Teachers hoped that youngsters who memorized Bible verses would remember them and turn to them for spiritual guidance as adults.[56]

---

55. G. M. J., "312 Successive Sabbaths," *Sunday School Magazine,* 1874; "The Quarterly Review of the Baptist Sunday School, Prattville, Alabama," 1910, p. 1, Frost-Bell Papers, SBHLA; "A Good Example," *Earnest Worker,* 30 January 1873; "An Active Mission Sunday School," *Missionary Survey* (October 1913): 968. For background, see Wayne Flynt, "Dissent in Zion: Alabama Baptists and Social Issues, 1900–1914," *Journal of Southern History* 35 (November 1969): 523–42. For common school attendance, see Link, *A Hard Country,* 46–54. Historians debate the use of Sunday school incentives, some seeing it as social control, others as a recognition of childhood desires and needs. See Boyer, *Urban Masses and Moral Order in America,* 50; Boylan, *Sunday School,* 156–7.

56. Moore, *Country Sunday School,* 7–8; "Notes from Wilmington, N.C.," *Christian Recorder,* 14 December 1872; Phillips, *From the Farm to the Bishopric,* 27–8; Helen Mason, *Bill's Creek Baptist Church 200 Year History, 1782–1982* (Dallas, Tex.: n.p., 1984), 101.

Superintendents and teachers depended on pupils to recruit new class members, often turning this into a competitive game. They might divide a class into two teams, which then competed to attract the most newcomers to school. At one mission Sunday school, the designated purple team and gold team received a point for every new child or visitor who attended class, and ten points for individuals who joined the Sunday school. In urban areas, a Sunday school in one church might compete with another for the best attendance or the greatest number of new pupils. Sometimes students earned a prize for bringing in the most new pupils, such as a young boy who won a silver dollar for attracting thirteen of the school's eighteen new students. Sunday school alone was not a natural draw; it took ongoing effort to find new pupils.[57]

To more serious-minded southern evangelicals, however, the practice of awarding incentives and playing competitive games was upsetting. Critics found some prizes totally inappropriate, such as a series of dancing lessons that one Sunday school offered as a prize. In critics' eyes, attending Sunday school and getting to know and love God should be reward enough. Prizes, stars, and competitive games were a purely superficial means to attract and motivate students. H. Lee Finklea of Pineville, Alabama, was upset by what he deemed artificial entrapments. "Many Sunday school teachers are so unwise as to offer improper motives for attendance as offering prizes for regularity," he complained, "thus hiding and failing to impress upon their minds the fact that the highest motive for attendance is a sense of our obligations to God." Some Methodists feared that their Sunday schools were becoming a setting for pure entertainment. A Virginia Baptist denounced prizes and placards, insisting that "patient, persevering, prayerful instruction in the truth of the gospel" should be enough to draw pupils to the classroom. Another decried "superficial and flashy" artifices, likening prizes to a "system of bribery and corruption worse than the Credit Mobelier disgrace of Congress."[58]

57. "An Active Mission Sunday School," *Missionary Survey* (October 1913): 968; Henry Rainey, "Work of the Bethel," newspaper clipping, 29 January 1899, Frost-Bell Correspondence, SBHLA.

58. H. Lee Finklea, "Influence of the Christian in the Sunday School," *Proceedings of the Ninth Annual Session of the Monroe County Sunday School Convention, July 14 and 15, 1892* (Monroe, Ala.: Monroe Journal Job Print, 1892), 7; J. M. P. Otts, "Proselytism in the Sabbath School Work," *Kind Words,* 22 May 1873; "Annual Report of the Sunday School and Publication Board of the General Association of Virginia," *Religious Herald,* 21

Hymn singing—of growing importance in nineteenth-century American culture—was an important attraction for Sunday schools. Children testified to its appeal, and many admitted that hymn singing was their favorite part of class. Music enlivened the proceedings and added variety to the weekly schedule. Historian Paul Harvey suggests that Baptist church officials in particular welcomed singing because they believed it could channel "folk enthusiasm" and "rural excesses" into a meaningful experience and make the Sunday school more appealing. Singing allowed for a certain level of emotionalism within a controlled setting, without giving rise to excessive outbursts of sentiment that middle-class Sunday school workers decried. An exuberant North Carolina Baptist was thrilled with the singing he heard. "Many long-deserted school-houses wrapt in silence, have, within the past few months, become vocal with the melody of happy voices!" he exclaimed. Hymn singing became a regular feature of nearly every Sunday school gathering. Music opened and closed each Sunday school, and special choirs often entertained delegates at Sunday school conventions. Annie Armstrong recalled the delights of Sunday school singing, writing "I for one can testify that numbers and numbers of times a verse of hymns learned in childhood has in latter [sic] years brought to mind some blessed truth in times of need." AME minister Jonathan Taylor called Sunday hymns "one of the essential and potent agencies" and the "most powerful means" of enticing children into Sabbath school. Methodists described singing as a "delightful and successful method of imparting and impressing religious truths" and appointed a special committee to study plans for publishing a new hymnal.[59]

June 1866; "Address of the Bishops," *Journal of the General Conference of the Methodist Episcopal Church, South* (Nashville: Publishing House of the MECS, 1890), 37; Rev. J. M. P. Otts, "Proselytism in the Sabbath School Work," *Earnest Worker,* 22 May 1873. Elizabeth Hayes Turner argues that the prizes and awards used by Sunday schools introduced a sense of competition into young girls' lives, with a "masculine" emphasis on achievement and success. I sense that girls relished these competitive opportunities in Sunday school and did not see this as masculine. See Turner, *Women, Culture, and Community,* 71.

59. Harvey, *Redeeming the South;* "Report on Sabbath Schools," *Minutes of the 12th Annual Western North Carolina Baptist Convention, 1868,* 11; Annie Armstrong to James Marion Frost, 13 July 1896, Baltimore, Md., Frost-Bell Correspondence, SBHLA; Jonathan M. Taylor, "Requirements of the Sabbath School," *AME Church Review,* July 1900; R. M. Heriges, comp., "Report of the Special Committee on Sunday School Hymns and Tune Book," *Sunday School Legislation by the General Conference, MEC, South,* 19. For histories of church and Sunday school music, see Leonard Ellinwood, *The History of American Church Music* (1953; reprint, New York: Da Capo Press, 1970); William Jensen Reynolds

Evangelicals waxed enthusiastic over the benefits of singing. Sunday school lyrics served a serious purpose by underscoring the lesson and celebrating God. To observers, children's voices lifted in song suggested a happy, uplifting classroom experience. As a visiting bishop to Georgetown, South Carolina's AME Sunday school class remarked, "Forsooth, it made one feel transplanted to some ethereal abode as their lively young voices rang out." With similar hyperbole, another AME writer described Sunday school hymn singing as "one of those sacred lyrics that makes the Sabbath school minstrelsy of our country surpass that of the world." Singing was an easy means to teach youngsters Scripture and religious truths, for many lyrics came directly from the Bible. It also exposed children to many hymns that were sung in regular church services. Despite the simple lyrics and platitudes in many children's hymns, supporters insisted that memorizing sacred lyrics helped youngsters distinguish good music from bad. Only a few "lighter" songs should ever be sung, urged Baptist A. T. Robertson; "let the bulk of them be hymns of character and power."[60]

Teaching youngsters to sing usually fell to the Sunday school teacher, although superintendents often led singing in class assemblies. To aid the shy or untrained, music instructors traveled across the South to teach voice and choral conducting to superintendents and teachers. Aldine Kieffer, J. H. Ruebush, and others ran well-known music institutes where they taught Sunday school teachers and officers the basics of singing. Most volunteers could not afford special lessons, however, turning instead to the musical instructions which were a standard feature in children's hymnals. David Dortch's *Tidings of Joy* provided a few pages of musical instruction, "constructed so simply that almost anyone, by a little study, may become a good reader of music in a very short time." Some

---

and Milburn Price, *A Joyful Sound: Christian Hymnody*, 2nd ed. (New York: Holt, Rinehart, and Winston, 1978); Grace W. Conant, "Hymn Writers and Composers of Sunday-School Music," *Encyclopedia of Sunday Schools*, vol. 2, 540–2; Paul K. Conkin, *The Uneasy Center: Reformed Christianity in Antebellum America* (Chapel Hill: University of North Carolina Press, 1955), 197–209. Bill C. Malone argues that by 1900, religious hymns had become an integral part of American culture. See Malone, *Southern Music: American Music* (Lexington: University of Kentucky Press, 1979), 67.

60. E. C. R. "South Carolina Correspondence," *Christian Recorder*, 26 June 1869; "Our Sunday Schools," *Christian Recorder*, 6 March 1869; A. T. Robertson, "Sunday School Hymns," *Baptist Courier*, 20 August 1891.

editors created a question and answer section in the preface to their hymnals, covering topics such as the representation of pitch and the definition of a measure—in short, everything volunteers needed to become proficient in musical instruction.[61]

This explosion of interest in singing led to the creation of a system known as shape-note singing, which appeared in hymn books before the Civil War. To help inexperienced vocalists read music, song writers designated a distinct shape (a "shape note"), such as a triangle or circle, to represent each note of the musical scale. Initially there were only four shapes, but by the 1860s song writers popularized a universal system with a uniform shape for each of the seven notes. Many southern Sunday school hymnals typically included both round and shape notes. The system remained popular well into the twentieth century in parts of the rural South, where many children could not read the alphabet, much less music.[62]

Sunday school hymns addressed themes that paralleled the weekly lesson and taught children important biblical truths. Some hymns, such as the "Sunday-School Battle Song," had openly militaristic overtones in order to underscore the institution's serious purpose and lend a masculine touch to the Sunday school. One popular theme of hymns was praise of the Sunday school and celebration of happy pupils who shared their lives with God. The chorus of one song echoed, "I love to go, I love to go, I love to go to Sabbath School." Hymns glorified children's eventual entrance into heaven, where they learned they would meet God. The invitational hymn encouraged children to attend Sunday school. As one song emoted, "Will you come to our Sunday School? I really wish you would; O come and join our Bible class, And learn how to be good." Another hymn celebrated children who attended class: "Open the door for the

---

61. David Elijah Dortch, *Tidings of Joy: A Choice Collection of Sacred Songs for Sunday Schools* (Columbia, Tenn.: for the author, 1878), preface. For questions and answers on singing lessons, see J. H. Hall, John McPherson, and J. H. Ruebush, "Musical Notation," *Fountain of Praise, for Sunday Schools, Prayer, Praise and Revival Meetings* (Dayton, Va.: Ruebush, Kieffer, 1892), 2–10.

62. On shape-note singing, see Reynolds and Price, *A Joyful Sound,* 102; R. A. Glenn and Aldine Silliman Kieffer, eds., *New Melodies of Praise: A Collection of New Tunes and Hymns, for the Sabbath School and Praise Meeting* (Dayton, Va.: Ruebush, Kieffer, 1877), 2; Malone, *Southern Music: American Music,* 7; Buell E. Cobb Jr., *The Sacred Harp: A Tradition and Its Music* (Athens: University of Georgia Press, 1978).

children; See! they are coming in throngs; Bid them sit down to the banquet, Teach them your beautiful songs." Since the children singing these songs were already in Sunday school, the intent of these hymns must have been positive reinforcement. Temperance songs like "Waifs of the Drunkard's Sad Home" and "Beware of the Wine" urged youngsters to drink water and avoid this evil temptation.[63]

Despite the relevant messages they conveyed, Sunday school hymns had their critics. Some evangelicals complained about the very act of singing and the worldly, trivial nature of the lyrics of many songs. There was some truth in the observations of those who saw song lyrics as uninspired, nonsensical, or too secular. One Baptist dismissed all modern Sunday school songs, insisting that children learn only the classics. He believed that hymns should always elevate youngsters' thoughts toward heaven. Another Baptist writer deemed music a "dangerous" evil, especially hymns that tried to "profess too much." He felt that religious music had become pure "twaddle." Northern missionary Joanna Moore denounced singing, claiming that it detracted from Bible study and children's opportunity to focus directly on God. She deplored the fact that African Americans had incorporated music into their Sunday schools and churches as eagerly as whites. Traditionalists regarded singing as frivolous entertainment, producing theatrics and amusement rather than pious, sacred contemplation.[64]

The Sunday school also provided children with wholesome social activities, which testified to its efforts to entertain as well as uplift youngsters. Especially in rural areas, the church served as the center of

63. R. Lowry, "Sunday-School Battle Song," *Amaranth,* 111; Margaret C. Brown, "Our Sunday Song," *Child's Gem,* January 1910; Stevenson, *The Story of Southern Hymnology* (Roanoke, Va.: Stone Printing and Manufacturing, 1931), 104; Wyatt Marshall, "Gather Them In," in *The New Starry Crown: For the Sabbath School,* ed. Aldine S. Kieffer (Dayton, Va.: Ruebush, Kieffer, 1877), 72–3; D. E. Dortch and W. G. E. Cunnyngham, "Happy Child," *Grace and Glory: A Choice Collection of Sacred Songs, Original and Selected, for Sabbath-Schools, Revivals, etc.* (Nashville: Southern Methodist Publishing House, 1882), 91; William Thomas Dale, ed., *Children's Hosannas: A Sabbath-School Music Book* (Nashville: Cumberland Presbyterian Church, 1880), 154–5, 158–9. For background on temperance songs, see Samuel J. Rogal, "The Evolution and Demise of the American Temperance Hymn," *The Hymn* 42 (July 1991): 5–9.

64. "Sabbath Music," *Working Christian,* 4 September 1879; Joanna Moore, *"In Christ's Stead": Autobiographical Sketches* (Chicago: Woman's Baptist Home Mission Society, 1902), 85.

community life. The Sunday school expanded this role, offering additional activities that focused on children. Sunday schools tried to be appealing and attractive, and to that end their supporters organized special social events and celebrations. Superintendents, teachers, pupils, and parents all savored opportunities to show off a lively, well-mannered Sunday school. Holiday celebrations, parades, and social outings became popular in southern Sunday schools, filling a niche in rural southerners' lives and becoming a powerful attraction to join Sunday classes.[65]

Those who participated in Sunday school activities often had never before engaged in organized outings, parades, or pageants, and they were thrilled by the opportunity to do so. G. W. Ryan held a Sunday school celebration for fifteen hundred Mississippians, for which he had engaged the "best talent in our county." He reported that he had never witnessed anything comparable to the excitement generated by his event. Isaac Emory commented that a "new epoch" dawned for young mountain residents after youngsters enjoyed a train ride and Sunday school picnic organized for several hundred pupils. Sunday school attractions generated excitement and positive responses from everyone involved. The astonishing number of people participating in these activities certainly suggests their appeal.[66]

It is impossible to do justice here to the enthusiasm expressed in literally thousands of reports describing these events in denominational newspapers. Superintendents submitted lengthy reports of their school activities to church newspapers, with endless details about each event and the spirit that it generated. At least one editor finally stopped publishing every submission, claiming that his paper had little room for other news if he printed all the Sunday school reports that he received.

Settings for these special events varied. Sunday school dinners and bazaars might be held in a church sanctuary; picnics convened at local parks, beaches, or in the mountains. Lakewood Park in Charlotte, North Carolina, proved a perfect place for Sunday school picnics, with its roller coaster, launch pad and boats, tables, chairs, and "pure spring water," for "colored people only." Some Sunday schools held temperance meet-

---

65. Lyon, *The Sunday School and Its Methods*, 58, 60; Axtell, *The Organized Sunday School*, 55. Beth Schweiger sees entertainment as increasingly important to church life. See Schweiger, "Transformation of Southern Religion," 336–9.

66. G. W. Ryan, 28 July 1870, Rose Hill, Miss., and Isaac Emory, 13 October 1869, Knoxville, Tenn., both to Maurice A. Wurts, ASSU Correspondence, PHS.

ings, often preceded by "grand charades," in which pupils performed musicals and dramatic skits before appreciative audiences. A charade presented by a Virginia Sunday school included simple skits and musical performances such as "Rumpus in a Shoe-maker's Shop" and "A Cure for Obstinacy."[67]

Train and carriage excursions and all-day picnics were favorites during spring and summer; participants benefited from reduced rates offered by local railroad companies. These trips were eye-opening events for children and adults who had never before traveled by train. Some five hundred citizens of Walhalla, South Carolina, enjoyed a train ride into the mountains for their Sunday school celebration, which included a parade, Scripture reading, prayers, and speeches. "You do not often hear from us here in the mountains and we are glad to report the Sunday school cause progressing," noted a happy participant following the event. "The fields are already ripe for the harvest and the reapers are entering in to reap." Sometimes, familiar words failed to do justice to the occasion; one Mississippi Sunday school picnic was dubbed a "splendiferous magnificence." Sunday school–sponsored athletic events generated enthusiasm as well. The Young Ladies Society of the Tryon Street Methodist Sunday School of Charlotte, North Carolina, organized a picnic excursion and bicycle race to Statesville in June 1883. "A dashing race between the Charlotte and Statesville Bicyclists will be an interesting feature of the occasion," promised its promotional broadside. Another school offered a moonlight hayride, games, and running races for older pupils. These events never skirted their ultimate purpose, for they all included hymn singing, prayers, and speeches to celebrate the importance of Sunday school.[68]

The Sunday school parade was a favorite in southern communities. This event resembled a royal cavalcade, with an appointed king, queen, and ladies- and men-in-waiting, bedecked in robes and crowns. Members of the court rode through town atop wagons, followed by well-dressed

---

67. "Lakewood Park," *Star of Zion,* 7 September 1911; "Grand Charade for the Pleasant Grace Church," (Norfolk, Va.: W. M. Hicks, 1883); Paul Boyer, *Urban Masses and Moral Order in America, 1820–1920* (Cambridge: Harvard University Press, 1978), 34–53.

68. "Walhalla Picnic," *Working Christian,* 26 August 1880; "Pic Nic of the First Baptist Church Sunday School," *Religious Herald,* 14 June 1883; Statesville circular in the William Woods Holden Collection, Duke; letter to *Kind Words,* 1908.

pupils, church choirs, and perhaps even a band. After each parade, participants and observers enjoyed a picnic, with home-cooked food prepared by church women. Speeches, sports, games, singing, and lively entertainment completed the day's activities. A typical parade held in Little Rock, Arkansas, included a queen from each AME Sunday school in the city, who rode on a decorated chariot surrounded by her court, a band, scores of students, and "hacks, buggies, carriages, and throngs of people afoot, followed by parents and friends—then wagons filled with food." Reported one observer of the mile-long procession, "This display is said to be the finest ever witnessed in this city." Sunday school pupils were not only celebrating and socializing; these public events served as an effective advertising tool, making bystanders undoubtedly wish that they, too, belonged to a Sunday school.[69]

While participants relished such occasions, those who organized them derived immense satisfaction in having overseen such uplifting and exciting events. Probably no one wrote with more emotion about Sunday school celebrations than Fenner Pigott, a Methodist minister and Sunday school supervisor, who in old age fondly reminisced about a pageant that he and his wife had organized. Even the name of the pageant queen remained fresh in Pigott's mind. For the event, he constructed a carpeted platform and a throne covered with gold paper. Around the throne was a homemade arch covered with greenery. Mrs. Pigott designed and sewed the queen's gown and fashioned white outfits for the royal court's foreign ministers and maids of honor. During the ceremony, a chief justice crowned the queen and handed her a scepter. According to Pigott, each participant then recited his or her lines perfectly. As Pigott recalled, "This will forever linger on my memory as the grandest epoch in my history—it was an oasis in the desert." He stated that "it was the crowning and most satisfactory performance I ever conceived and executed in my life."[70]

In towns and cities across the South, Sunday schools representing different churches jointly sponsored events, suggesting that despite the competition for young souls, churches could cooperate when it came to socializing. ASSU missionary Isaac Emory reported that fifteen Sunday

---

69. J. T. Jennifer, "News from the Churches," *Christian Recorder*, 24 June 1871; "First of May Celebration, Georgetown, South Carolina," *Christian Recorder*, 18 May 1867. See also Robert Wood Lynn, "Last of the Great Religious Movements," 155.

70. Levi Woodbury Pigott, *Scenes and Incidents in the Life of a Home Missionary*, 92–8 (quote, 98).

schools and more than 3,000 people in Greenville, Kentucky, attended a joint jubilee. A celebration in De Kalb County, Alabama, attracted 6,000 to 8,000 participants from twenty-six different Sunday schools. Adults and children gathered on the lawn of a local mansion for singing, Bible reading, praying, and listening to a speech by former Confederate vice president Alexander Stephens. In 1867, Baptists and Methodists of Franklinton, North Carolina, held a joint picnic. Well-dressed children carried garlands of roses as they paraded through town. According to one report, "Nothing more beautiful could have been conceived." A spirit of cooperation was evident; as an observer noted, it was "peculiarly pleasing to behold the unity which characterized their meeting, where all seemed to join in fraternal union."[71]

Christmas, Easter, and the Fourth of July provided other social opportunities for Sunday schools, and enhanced the festive nature of these holidays. With fried chicken and sweet potato pies, African American women fêted Sunday school pupils at Easter. Santa Claus visited Sunday schools at Christmastime, and class members gathered to decorate the church Christmas tree and sing carols. The Presbyterian publishing firm printed special cards that teachers and supervisors could purchase and send to each pupil on his or her birthday. Some events had a serious purpose and gave youngsters an opportunity to reach out to others. The Sunday school of Richmond, Virginia's Third Street AME Church held a Thanksgiving Day Parade that involved some five hundred students and teachers who marched two miles to the Orphan Home, where parade participants fed the young residents a sumptuous feast.[72]

Celebrations were created specifically for the Sunday school, such as Children's Day, Rally Day, Decision Day, and Missionary Day. Children's Day was held each spring to raise money for missionary activities and generate excitement for the Sunday school. Most publishing houses produced an official program for the event so that all denominational schools could follow the same schedule. A typical Children's Day program included songs, prayers, responsive readings, and discussion topics.

71. Isaac Emory to Maurice A. Wurts, 8 September 1870, Knoxville, Tenn., ASSU Correspondence, PHS; "Sunday School Celebration," *Kind Words,* 3 September 1874; Eoline, "United Celebration of Sabbath Schools," *Biblical Recorder,* 15 May 1867.

72. L. C. V., "Christmas in the Newbern Sabbath School," *Earnest Worker,* 11 January 1872; "Birthday Greeting" in "Sunday School File," Presbyterian Historical Society, Montreat, N.C.; "A Letter from Richmond," *Christian Recorder,* 23 December 1865.

Generous contributions were a critical part of these events, and Sunday school workers kept an exact tabulation of what each child and class donated.[73]

Generally, Sunday school celebrations elicited positive responses. The *Encyclopedia of Sunday Schools,* though employing language that might have stifled any sense of the frivolous, defended their importance. "The discovery which wise Sunday-school leaders have made, that it is not practicable to separate the religious from the other natural elements which make up the life of a girl or boy, has led to the realization that the Sunday school must relate itself to all phases of youthful interest, and not alone to the spiritual side." Supporters argued that youngsters needed the wholesome, lively entertainment that Sunday school activities provided. AMEZ bishop George Clinton believed that such events "keep up and heighten the superior social influences" and had a positive impact on everyone involved. Others claimed that spelling bees, bazaars, and games sponsored by the Sunday school fostered friendliness and enhanced a sense of community. To parents, the benefits of their children participating in church-sponsored activities far outweighed the dire possibility of their being attracted to more sinful temptations, such as dancing, playing cards, or gambling.[74]

Youngsters were especially enthusiastic about the competitive games and special outings that were part of the Sunday school experience. In a world far simpler than our own, it is hard to imagine how these celebrations and planned activities loomed so large in young lives. Some children never forgot the awards or attention they received for their exceptional performance or perfect attendance. Many relished the opportunity to compete and excel. A determined Mary Howard proudly announced her intention to earn the solid gold cross that her Sunday school awarded students with perfect Sunday school attendance for five years. CME bishop Charles Henry Phillips never forgot the copy of *The Runaway, or Pride Punished* that he won when he was eleven for faithful Sunday school attendance and excellent memorization of his lessons. The fact that he referred to the volume as his "dear little book" suggests his real

73. "Programme for Children's Day, Sunday May 18, 1890," *Sunday School Magazine,* May 1890.

74. E. C. Foster, "Amusements and the Sunday School," *Encyclopedia of Sunday Schools,* vol. 1, 26–8 (quote, 26); George W. Clinton, "The Sabbath School—Its Advantages," part 2, *Star of Zion,* 1 May 1885.

joy in earning such a prize. The attention and accolades Benjamin Mays received in Sunday school had a similarly positive impact. Mays described his recital of portions of the Sermon on the Mount for Children's Day. When he finished, Mays recalled, the "house went wild: old women waved their handkerchiefs, old men stamped their feet, and the people generally applauded long and loud. It was a terrific ovation, let alone a tremendous experience for a nine-year-old boy." Everyone predicted that Mays would go places, and he never forgot the support and confidence he gained in Sunday school.[75]

Yet these social events also elicited criticism, especially from white evangelicals who either had no use for Sunday schools or who regarded them solely as sacred institutions. Several Southern white Baptists denounced Sunday school festivities. An 1869 article in the *Working Christian* warned all Sunday schools to avoid frivolity, insisting that children focus on Scripture rather than on picnics, concerts, and parades. Youngsters should need no inducement to attend Sunday school. Others declared social activities to be sacrilegious, for they failed to put God at the center of the day and encouraged an unbecoming competitiveness. W. C. Pierce of Cartellsburg, Kentucky, objected to Baptists participating in Children's Day because its exercises superseded the regular worship of God. "It is one in which the children vie with each other to excel in theatrical or stage performance and the friends of the children watch with anxiety to see if the children acquit themselves creditably," he complained. An event became entertainment rather than worship when "it dishonors God, his house, his day" and "brings women and girls before large mixed assemblies in a performance that claims to be religious." Some felt that donations collected at such events were inappropriate; "money for the lord that is gathered by improper means or by appeals to improper notions" should never be accepted. Others claimed that these events played upon youthful emotion, undermined purposeful Christian education, and could have deleterious lifelong effects. Some white Methodists decried the sense of fun generated by social activities, fearing that "foundations be laid for habitual and ruinous self-indulgence in the later years of life."

75. Mary Chamberlain Howard, "Six Little Ponies," *Presbyterian Standard*, 24 July 1912; Phillips, *From the Farm to the Bishopric*, 27–8; Benjamin Mays, *Born to Rebel: An Autobiography* (New York: Scribner, 1971; reprint, Athens: University of Georgia Press, 1987), 16–7.

To earnest, tradition-minded southern evangelicals, the Sunday school was a place for purposeful, pious activities. Yet these critics had little impact, for the events continued, proof of their popularity.[76]

What is clear in looking into the Sunday classroom—its personnel, lessons, and social activities—is that it was a place where, above all, evangelicals conveyed Christian and moral instruction to the young. Sunday schools brought church, pupils, and community together in purposeful activity. Most organizers insisted that the Sunday school create a warm and welcoming environment to attract children, yet also set a serious tone so that pupils would learn the lessons that would serve them for life. The Bible stories and moral tales that children learned in Sunday school taught them important middle-class virtues, such as obedience, sobriety, punctuality, and generosity. Pupils were taught to understand the need to engage in service to God. Of course the Sunday school did not appeal to everyone. Disruptive and bored students could aggravate the most patient teacher. Lessons could be regarded as manipulative as instuctors used them to shape young citizens according to evangelical, middle-class ideals. But in a world far simpler than our own, Sunday classes, under the guidance of a capable teacher and a dedicated superintendent, could give children a sense of belonging and uplift through Christian lessons, stories, and hymns, through the task of memorizing Scripture, and for some, the reward for doing well. For many black and white children, especially in the rural South, attending Sunday school might have been the most exciting, joyful moment of their week. Officials and teachers tried to fashion a classroom setting that served the needs of the church and the region, teaching lessons and values that southerners saw as critical for the next generation. The classroom experience gave adults a golden opportunity to raise each child according to the moral guidelines and scriptural dictates that they held dear.

76. "The Sabbath Schools," *Working Christian,* 7 August 1869; W. C. Pierce to James Marion Frost, 14 September 1897, Cartellsburg, Ky., in Frost-Bell Correspondence, SBHLA; "Address of the Bishops," *Journal of the Methodist Episcopal Church, South* (Nashville: Publishing House of the MECS, 1890), 37.

6

RACE AND THE SUNDAY SCHOOL

"What you make of the young people, you make of the race," announced a National Baptist supporter of Sunday schools. As African American church officials contemplated the future prospects of their race, many expressed the need for self-help, respectability, and racial uplift. Youngsters were key. Many blacks believed that in the Sunday school, adults could instill in children a sense of dignity and self-worth. By inculcating such values in African American youth, the next generation would be able to take its rightful place in a white world. "The children of today will be the men and women of tomorrow," declared the Reverend R. C. O. Benjamin. "The children of our Sunday schools are to form the working forces of our church; therefore, it is important that they be taught to be noble, good and loyal to virtue and to God." Church leaders wanted youngsters to absorb values that ultimately would advance the entire race. If children learned and then lived by Sunday school lessons, the future of the race seemed assured. Black leaders dreamed of a better world—and they pinpointed the Sunday school as one place to achieve their dream.[1]

1. C. L. Fisher, "Sunday School Literature—Its Preparation and Publication," *National Baptist Union,* 4 November 1904; R. C. O. Benjamin, "The Relation of the Sunday School to the Church," *Star of Zion,* 9 February 1893.

Certainly the Sunday school offered one of the better possibilities for African Americans in the late-nineteenth-century South. The outlook for blacks, which had momentarily brightened at the end of the Civil War, had darkened within a few years. The political and social opportunities promised under federal Reconstruction, a period that historian Leon Litwack has called one of "unparalleled hope," began to dissipate long before the last federal troops withdrew from the South in 1877. The federal government (and many northerners, for that matter) began to lose interest in the region. Left to their own devices, in the late nineteenth century southern states enacted laws that all but eliminated black male voters and opportunities for black political participation. Jim Crow laws legally segregated the races to keep African Americans separate and subordinate. Episodes of white violence against blacks, including the lynching of black men, also proved a brutally effective means of keeping blacks in their place; white perpetrators of race crimes rarely suffered any consequences for their actions. Historians have rightfully labeled the late nineteenth and early twentieth centuries as the nadir of African American history.[2]

Denied access to a white world, most blacks tried to stay out of harm's way and turned inward to their own communities and institutions, especially to home and church. The Sunday school became an important part of black community life, a place where adults could ensure that their children received a solid grounding in Christian education and sound moral values. Without it, the consequences could be dire. Satan was always waiting, as Baptist Silas Floyd warned parents; it was imperative that children attend Sunday school and embrace its "spiritual culture." In a less apocalyptic vein, CME bishop Charles H. Phillips urged people in his denomination to focus less on political concerns and more on "those pursuits that profit [their] family and build up the race." He believed that Sunday school could help teach young people how to do just that.[3]

Though southern Sunday schools welcomed children from varied backgrounds and faiths, the institution was racially segregated. Black and white southerners preferred to have their own churches and Sunday

---

2. Litwack, *Trouble in Mind*, xiii. See also Gaines, *Uplifting the Race*, 12–22; Beverly Guy-Shaftall, *Daughters of Sorrow: Attitudes toward Black Women, 1880–1920*, vol. 11, *Black Women in United States History*, ed. Darlene Clark Hine (Brooklyn: Carlson Publishing, 1990), introduction; Higginbotham, *Righteous Discontent*.

3. Floyd, *Floyd's Flowers*, 323–5; quote in Owen, *Sacred Flame of Love*, 174.

schools, and experiments in integrated Sunday schools rarely succeeded. ASSU missionary G. W. Ryan of Enterprise, Mississippi, had observed two integrated schools that broke apart over the race issue. Knowing that the "two races can not agree in school," he organized separate schools for black children. Northern Methodists discovered that the biracial churches and Sunday schools they organized rarely worked and ultimately alienated local whites. Certainly, Sunday school celebrations and holidays sometimes included black and white pupils who paraded, sang, and prayed together. Whites occasionally volunteered as superintendents or teachers in black Sunday schools. Black preachers might speak at white Sunday school conventions, and white ministers did so at black conferences. But overall, both races chose to run and attend their own Sunday schools.[4]

Thanks to northern agents who came South, some black Sunday schools began to thrive shortly after the Civil War. A few became models of efficiency and success. St. John's AME Chapel Sunday School in Norfolk, Virginia, was one such Sunday school. Every Sunday, its supervisor or pastor rang a bell to assemble the pupils. As the children filed into the building, the supervisor greeted each one and rewarded prompt students with a special blue ticket. Youngsters sang an opening hymn, roll was taken, and the superintendent welcomed the entire school. Pupils then separated by age into partitioned rooms for the weekly lesson. The teacher discussed a Bible passage or read from a Sunday school paper. Following this, children reassembled for closing exercises that included singing, a lesson review, the weekly offering, announcements, closing words from the superintendent, and a prayer.[5]

Though the overall structure and personnel of black and white Sunday schools were similar, some differences were evident. Race may have been a factor in the meeting time and length of class. By the late nineteenth century, morning was the most popular and convenient meeting time for white Sunday schools to convene, but afternoon was the time of choice for black schools. According to J. B. Tynes, afternoon classes "favor the condition of our people generally," perhaps because black church services could last two or three hours. One Sunday school leader felt that

4. G. W. Ryan to Maurice A. Wurts, 18 and 28 July 1870, Rose Hill, Enterprise, Miss., ASSU Correspondence, PHS.
5. "Our Sunday School," *Christian Recorder*, 6 March 1869.

afternoon sessions ensured higher attendance, since Sunday was the one day when children could sleep late. While most white Sunday schools met no longer than sixty to ninety minutes, many black Sunday schools had longer classes. An AME official suggested ninety-minute sessions for young pupils and two-hour classes for adolescents. One black Baptist Sunday school association limited the meeting time to three hours.[6]

Records show that black Sunday schools were more likely than white ones to have a female superintendent in charge. As many historians and black leaders have shown, black women played a significant role in racial and religious uplift, as well as in outreach efforts to improve community and family life. They founded civic and social clubs, supported issues such as prohibition, raised money to improve public schools, and were actively involved in church activities and Sunday school. By the 1870s, AME church doctrine officially recognized this situation, proclaiming that an ideal Sunday school should have both a male and female superintendent. The woman would assist the man, maintain order among female pupils, and keep tabs on female teachers. And though the black clergy may have preferred subservient females, women often took charge. Kate L. Smith, described as a "zealous Christian worker," was a one-woman show in the Zion Chapel AMEZ church in Natchez, Mississippi. Smith led the choir, served as president of the board of deaconesses, and for years was superintendent of the Sunday school. "[N]o more zealous and faithful one can be found," declared an admirer.[7]

African American women were much more visible at Sunday school conventions than white women. Despite the personal expense they in-

6. J. B. Tynes, "How Can We Increase the Number and Influence of Our Sunday Schools?" *Minutes of the Richmond, Virginia, District Conference and Sunday School Convention of the AME Church* (Staunton, Va.: Soneburner and Paufer Steam Printers, 1886), 11–2; "Report on Sabbath Schools," *Minutes of the 14th Annual Meeting of the Roanoke Missionary Baptist Association (Negro), 1879*, 7; J. H. Murphy, "Sunday-School Work," *AME Church Review* 6 (1889–1890): 430.

7. N. H. Downing to Maurice A. Wurts, 25 November 1868, Warrenton, N.C., ASSU Correspondence, PHS; "Report on Sabbath-Schools," *15th Quadrennial General Conference of the AME Church, 1872* (Philadelphia: AME Church Concern, 1872), 136; Dorothy Salem, *To Better Our World: Black Women in Organized Reform, 1890–1920*, vol. 14, *Black Women in United States History,* ed. Darlene Clark Hine, 9; Adams, *Cyclopedia of African Methodism in Mississippi,* 186. See also Higginbotham, *Righteous Discontent;* Greenwood, *Bittersweet Legacy;* Turner, *Women, Religion, and Community in Galveston, Texas;* Gaines, *Uplifting the Race;* Jones, *Labor of Love, Labor of Sorrow.*

curred to attend these meetings, including lost work days, black women comprised a higher percentage of delegates than their white counterparts. They often played a significant role in the convention proceedings, serving on special committees that studied a particular Sunday school issue and delivering many—sometimes all—of the speeches featured at these conferences. At the 1895 Baptist State Sunday School Convention of North Carolina, for instance, participants set aside an hour each day to hear women read their original essays. These recitations invariably elicited positive responses from the audience. After hearing various papers, a male listener observed, "This convention has caused us to feel that our young women are not at all behind in the great march of intellectual progress." At an AMEZ Sabbath school convention in Florida, delegates complimented female speakers on their "brilliant" and "bright and charming" talks. One pastor was so impressed that he offered financial assistance to the young women in his denomination who wished to attend Shaw University in Raleigh, North Carolina. Glowing accounts of these speeches in church publications suggest that black opinion felt women reflected positively on the entire race.[8]

The need to teach reading continued to be a more critical issue in black Sunday schools than in white ones because black illiteracy remained high, even by 1900. Though common schools offered African American children at least a limited education, blacks were taking nothing for granted. The Reverend S. N. Vass, an American Baptist Publication Society (ABPS) missionary working in the late-nineteenth-century South, despaired over the widespread racism and violence that he observed. He feared a time when no black child would have access to public schooling, due to "Negro hating politicians," and he saw the Sunday school as black youngsters' only hope. "If that day should ever come, here is a most practical means of spreading general intelligence among the masses, for already it does service to those of us who are too poor to attend the public schools," Vass commented. He warned fellow blacks to "begin to prepare for the worst."[9]

---

8. *Minutes of the Baptist State Sunday School Convention of North Carolina (Negro) 1895* (Raleigh: Edwards and Broughton, 1896), 16, 18. See also "Florida Notes—Sabbath School Convention," *Star of Zion*, 26 September 1889.

9. Rev. S. N. Vass, "Systematic Sunday School Work and Its Relation to the Denomination," *National Baptist Union*, 16 January 1904. For background on the wave of terror against black common schools, see Litwack, *Trouble in Mind*, 487.

Black ministers seemed more uncomfortable with the presence of a Sunday school in their church than did white preachers, though the fact that African Americans often expressed bold sentiments in their religious publications may skew the picture. Blacks showed little hesitancy in exposing tensions within their church community or airing negative comments about ministers' indifference or outright opposition to the Sunday school. As the most influential member in most black communities, a minister could make or break a Sunday school; for a number of reasons, he frequently chose the latter course. Sometimes ministers objected to Sunday schools on grounds of race. Several African American ministers in Louisville, Kentucky, objected to the children in their congregations attending a Sunday school that had been established by white Presbyterians. Yet this does not explain why so many other black preachers had no use for a Sunday school in their church. Ardent supporters of the institution lashed out at its adversaries. A Virginia Baptist called any preacher who stood in the way of the Sunday school "wholly unworthy of the great honor with which he has been clothed." Others blamed apathetic ministers for the sorry condition of Sunday schools in their area. "One reason why our Sunday schools are not more successful is because our preachers do not take interest in them," the Reverend O. L. Fisher wrote sadly. A Virginian wasted no time in expressing his sentiments. Any minister who impeded efforts to uplift the next generation was an "enemy to our race, a hindrance to prosperity, and an impediment to the onward march of our Zion."[10]

Various other factors suggest why some black ministers disliked or ignored the Sunday school. Some preachers had reason to regard it as an internal competitor of sorts, rather than as something that would enhance their own position and the status of their church. Many black Sunday schools profited from outside advice, financial assistance, and free literature, which afforded them a degree of independence and effectively put them beyond a minister's control. Black ministers with little or no education may have felt threatened by the pedagogical activities of many Sunday schools. Sometimes, school officials blamed ministers for poorly

10. Rev. O. L. Fisher, "Reports," *Minutes of the 23rd Annual Alabama Baptist State Convention, 1890,* 16, 14; "Committee on Sabbath Schools," *20th Annual Roanoke Missionary Baptist Association (Negro) (1885),* 7; "Report on Sabbath Schools," *Journal of the Virginia Annual Conference of the AME Church* (1874). See also W. J. Sides, "Relation of the Pastor to the Sunday School," *Star of Zion,* 13 December 1900.

run or floundering Sunday schools, which could only have generated hostility from the scapegoated clergymen.[11]

It is also likely that uneducated and rural black preachers, like their white counterparts, resented the middle-class airs and goals of Sunday schools. Respectability was key to the middle-class image of uplift. It was the black middle class who seized the leadership in Sunday school work; they wanted to demonstrate that African Americans were sober, obedient, thrifty, responsible, and pious people. Saving souls was important, but black church leaders regarded the Sunday school as a place where children would also develop sound character and learn fine manners. Black children needed to absorb bourgeois standards of respectability in order to erase the negative stereotypes that whites often held of African Americans. Some blacks even held out the hope that elevating their children's moral behavior would end white oppression and replace it with white respect.[12]

This emphasis on respectability and middle-class values suggests how class issues affected Sunday school endeavors. Sunday school leaders represented a "better class" of African Americans, who wanted to ensure a prosperous and godly future for every child. "If the American Negro would prolong their race, if they wish to have their posterity come up and stand side by side with the great men of other races, they must direct the attention of the young people to something else besides idling away their time on the streets and at disreputable places," charged one Sunday school teacher. Yet some black preachers had little use for the notions of respectability and bourgeois values that permeated the Sunday classroom. Sunday school rhetoric was often laced with a heavy dose of self-righteous superiority, as instructors denounced impoverished, lazy, and irresolute blacks. Middle-class African Americans tried to separate themselves from those whom they saw as a blight on the race.[13]

Like white schools, black Sunday school lessons focused on the Bible

11. John Little, "The Presbyterian Colored Missions," in *An Era of Progress and Promise,* ed. Hartshorn, 233–47.

12. Gaines, *Uplifting the Race,* 76–9; Higginbotham, *Righteous Discontent,* 185–229. For thoughts on the importance of black respectability, see Tera Hunter, *To 'Joy My Freedom: Southern Black Women's Lives and Labors after the Civil War* (Cambridge: Harvard University Press, 1997), 68; Greenwood, *Bittersweet Legacy.*

13. Greenwood, *Bittersweet Legacy,* 1–7; "Our Young People," *Christian Index,* 15 March 1890.

and used uniform lesson plans, as well as supplemental texts and newspapers. Yet while the lesson outlines were the same for blacks as they were for whites, black teachers emphasized issues of importance to their race. As we have seen, respectability was a major topic. African Americans' experience under slavery had kept blacks from attaining Victorian standards of behavior, fine manners, and proper patterns of speech. Attending Sunday school would expose youngsters to these lessons, undo bad habits, and teach them to shun sinful behavior. "Religion will polish every lady or gentleman, regardless of their high standing; it is impossible for them to be a complete lady or gentleman without it," wrote Sunday school worker Winnie Wood. The Sabbath school was the "nearest way to respectability" claimed a writer for the *Christian Index*.[14]

Though black Sunday schools taught the virtues of benevolence, the issue seemed to generate less attention than in white schools. Certainly children's donations were critical to every church and ultimately were put to good use. As Leon Litwack has stated, the black church was "one of the leading agencies of capital accumulation in the South," and the Sunday school played an important role in church fund raising. Weekly collections supported numerous worthwhile causes, including the National Aged Ministers Home, orphanages, asylums, and the medical departments at Shaw University and Meharry Medical College. Some African American Sunday schools raised money for special causes through channels other than the weekly collection basket, holding special entertainments and holiday pageants that charged admission. Sunday schools gave money to support missionary work in Africa, to establish scholarships to train ministers, and to send young women to college.[15]

Despite their poverty, African Americans were generous when it came to fund raising and donating money and material goods to their church. Yet the grim economic plight of many black families meant that many youngsters had little or nothing to give. Ministers who anticipated generous contributions from Sunday school sometimes were called up short by poor results. In 1889, a CME official in Montgomery, Alabama, was

---

14. Winnie K. Wood, "Our Boys and Girls," *Christian Index*, 8 July 1893. For the importance of manners and middle-class values in the black church, see Higginbotham, *Righteous Discontent*, 14, 96–7, 185–92.

15. Litwack, *Trouble in Mind*, 387–8. For examples of benevolence, see Charles S. Smith, "Dr. Smith's Speech," in *Dedicatory Services*, ed. Smith, 32; Rev. J. T. Jenifer, "Notes from the Churches," *Christian Recorder*, 21 December 1872.

disheartened to discover that one Sunday School had collected only three dollars from its Children's Day celebration. Refusing to acknowledge poverty as a reason for the humble amount, he chided his brethren for not being well versed in benevolence. "The colored people are not but a few steps from where they were at Emancipation," he sighed. On the other hand, Sunday school benevolence sometimes outperformed expectations. Children's contributions from St. John's AME Sunday school in Richmond often exceeded those from the church.[16]

By the late nineteenth century, temperance was an important topic in black Sunday schools, just as it was in white ones. Both northern and southern whites saw the benefit of including temperance lessons in the black Sunday school curriculum. Excessive drinking was a widespread problem among southern men of both races, but whites often blamed African Americans for the social problems caused by too much drink. For whites, a sober black population ensured a more peaceful, civilized South. Missionaries urged African Americans to commit themselves to total abstinence; as one white warned, the passage of the Fifteenth Amendment meant not only that African American men could vote but could "frequent the bar rooms." Southern whites worried that drunken black men would create chaos throughout the region.[17]

Middle-class African Americans were equally passionate about alcohol's deleterious effect on their young men. Drunkenness belied the image of respectability that many blacks so eagerly sought. AME members were fervent on the subject. "O rum thou cursed evil, we have sworn eternal vengeance against thee stem headed monster," one wailed. "See his in-

---

16. G. W. Darden, "Children's Day," *Christian Index*, 15 June 1889; "Our Sunday School," *Christian Recorder*, 6 March 1869. For fundraising efforts, see Kathleen C. Berkeley, "'Colored Ladies Also Contributed': Black Women's Activities from Benevolence to Social Welfare, 1866–1896," in *The Web of Southern Social Relations: Women, Family, and Education*, ed. Watter J. Fraser Jr., R. Frank Saunders Jr., and Jon L. Wakelyn (Athens: University of Georgia Press, 1985), 181–203; Dolores E. Janiewski, *Sisterhood Denied: Race, Gender, and Class in a New South Community* (Philadelphia: Temple University Press, 1985), 127–8; Sharon Ann Holt, "Making Freedom Pay: Freedpeople Working for Themselves, North Carolina, 1865–1900," *Journal of Southern History* 40 (May 1994): 229–62, esp. 253–4, 249–54.

17. Franklin Howard Kerfoot, *The Home Mission Work of the Southern Baptist Convention* (Baltimore: Baptist Mission Rooms, 1900), 8, 33; A. K. Parker et al., "Report of the Committee on the Colored People," *Fifty-Fifth Annual Report of the ABHMS* (New York: ABHMS, 1887), 33. See also Ownby, *Subduing Satan*, 172–3.

fluence along our streets and in our homes, broken hearted wives, weeping children." Church leaders predicted the downfall of the entire race if black men turned to alcohol to drown their sorrows and ignored their responsibilities to home, church, and community. AMEZ officials urged that all their Sunday schools drill students in lessons on "scientific narcotics" to demonstrate the negative effects of alcohol and tobacco. African American denominations appointed committees to study the temperance issue and promote the message in all Sabbath schools. Teachers preached abstinence from all liquor, and black Sunday school newspapers fulminated against alcohol indulgence.[18]

The message apparently brought results. The Sunday schools in Wadesboro, North Carolina, welcomed the involvement of the WCTU in their temperance crusade. Of the town's two thousand black Sunday school pupils, more than five hundred children signed an abstinence pledge, promising to shun whiskey, tobacco, and profanity; many who did so apparently also converted. In 1888, Frances Willard penned a "Letter from the National WCTU to the Colored People of the U.S.," which appeared in several black religious newspapers. Some African Americans supported the passage of a constitutional amendment to rid the nation of alcohol. Only with abstinence could sober, hard-working African Americans achieve success in the South and push their race "to the highest possible standard of material development," claimed AME bishop Grant.[19]

Race pride and self-help were important topics also addressed in black Sunday schools. Seeing members of their race teach and manage Sunday schools delivered a positive message to youngsters about what enterprising, dedicated blacks could achieve. African American teachers exposed children to black history and culture, emphasizing the deeds of heroes like Frederick Douglass and Toussaint L'Ouverture. Black writers produced material for Sunday school newsletters and denominational newspapers such as the *Star of Zion* and the *National Baptist Union,* which emphasized black heritage.

18. Bishop T. M. D. Ward, "Introductory Address," *Virginia Annual Conference of the AME, 1889,* 8; "Report of the Committee on Temperance," *Proceedings of the General Conference of the AME Zion Church, 1888,* 266.

19. E. L. Watkins, "Sabbath School Convention of the Wadesboro District," *Star of Zion,* 25 May 1893; Frances Willard, "Letter from the National WCTU to the Colored People of the U.S.," *Christian Index,* 11 February 1888; Bishop Grant, "Bishop Grant's Speech in St. Paul Church," in *Dedicatory Services,* ed. Smith, 49.

A lively setting probably typified black Sunday schools, at least judging by the comments of those who visited classes and by the emotionally charged services in African American churches. In contrast to white classrooms, the atmosphere in black Sunday schools sometimes appeared truly animated. African American youngsters responded eagerly and often physically to the joys of singing in Sunday school; their responses to hymn singing were universally heartfelt and positive. Singing was seen as one of the best means to become closer to God, gain personal strength and inspiration, and celebrate spiritual and earthly happiness.[20]

African Americans reacted with equal enthusiasm to Sunday school parades and public celebrations. Unlike some conservative whites who deemed these events too secular, blacks were effusive about any opportunity to march, dress up, play, celebrate, and dine together. AME members in Limpkins, Georgia, were thrilled with their Sunday school parade. It outshone one being held at the same time by white citizens, who "were compelled to stop and look at the colored children," reported a proud participant. "We are rising as a people," he chirped. The Sunday school parade provided an opportunity for the black community to demonstrate pride in their religious institutions. It united black citizens and allowed African Americans—if only for a few hours—to occupy public space that southern whites denied them or restricted under Jim Crow laws. For black children and their parents, time spent with family, fellow students, and community was one of the most joyful aspects of Sunday school. Overall, blacks approached their faith and Sunday school activities with a degree of abandon; the social and physical aspects of pageants, parades, and picnics reflected their joy in communal worship and the opportunity to be free of white control.[21]

Sunday school events, like those in the black church, were more than

20. Melva W. Costen, "Singing Praise to God in African American Worship Contexts," in *African American Religious Studies: An Interdisciplinary Anthology*, ed. Gayraud Wilmore (Durham: Duke University Press, 1989), 393.

21. W. H. Harris, "Notes from the Churches," *Christian Recorder*, 24 July 1873. Little has been written on celebrations in the nineteenth-century black community. See Litwack, *Trouble in Mind*, 389–92. For an earlier period, see Shane White, "'It Was a Proud Day': African Americans, Festivals, and Parades in the North, 1741–1834," *Journal of American History* 81 (June 1994): 13–50; William H. Wiggins Jr., *O Freedom! Afro-American Emancipation Celebrations* (Knoxville: University of Tennessee Press, 1987); Sterling Stuckey, *Slave Culture: Nationalist Theory and the Foundation of Black America* (New York: Oxford University Press, 1987), 75–83.

religious activities; they often had a social or political agenda as well. Many ministers marched at political rallies and expressed political opinions in their sermons. Sunday school conventions sometimes undertook work that went well beyond Sunday concerns. The black Baptist State Sunday School Convention of North Carolina focused its efforts on education, especially the education of young women. Because the state did little to provide more than rudimentary schooling for black children, North Carolina county and district Sunday school conventions assumed the responsibility of founding and supporting black secondary schools—ultimately supporting four of every five in the state. When communities needed help in establishing a new school, they "invariably turn to the Sunday-school of their locality and they seldom turn away in vain," black Baptists explained. Church and Sunday school events were comfortable settings to air almost any concern. As the center of the black community, the church was a welcoming and relatively safe place for religious leaders and laypeople to discuss the political, social, and economic problems that blacks faced. In the late nineteenth century, only a few bold African Americans—such as Ida B. Wells, William Monroe Trotter, and W. E. B. DuBois—publicly denounced racial oppression and injustice. Yet within the confines of their own church and in the pages of their church papers, many blacks vented anger and frustration over the nation's worsening racial climate.[22]

Sunday school conferences were another safe haven for blacks. In this setting, often absent of whites, African Americans decried racial violence and oppressive Jim Crow laws. These issues had special relevance to convention delegates, many of whom had just experienced the personal humiliation of traveling to conferences in segregated, filthy train cars. Jim Crow laws also made it impossible for black delegates to stay overnight in most hotels or dine in restaurants; they were forced to depend on local residents and churches to house and feed them. Such indignities were especially galling as they gathered to discuss a Christian enterprise.[23]

22. "Report of the Executive Board," *Minutes of the 39th Annual Baptist State Sunday School Convention of North Carolina (Negro), 1895*, 21; Gaines, *Uplifting the Race*, 60–5; Stowell, *Rebuilding Zion*, 151–3. The CME was less political than the AME, AMEZ, and NBC churches.

23. "The Vanguard's Silence on the Sunday-School Congress Accounted For," *National Baptist Union*, 26 June 1909; Harvey, *Redeeming the South*, 232–4.

Convention reports and denominational newspapers testify to the outspoken views expressed by Sunday school officials and delegates. African Americans were anything but silent about racial injustice as they watched their rights disintegrate and violence against blacks spread. No topic or situation seemed off limits. Delegates to the 1894 Kentucky AMEZ Sunday School Convention deliberately acknowledged the convention as an appropriate setting for addressing larger concerns. "While we recognize this is not a political gathering yet we are none the less interested in the cause of our race and those which are desirable to the advancement of Christian men and women," they stated. They went on to condemn white southerners' definitions of justice that legalized segregation and eliminated black civil and political rights.[24]

Kentucky AMEZ leaders also censured the state's new separate coach law, "so pernicious in its enactment and enforcement reflecting upon Negro manhood and womanhood," and presented a resolution that no one use any public transportation until the laws were overturned. Other Sunday school conventions passed resolutions condemning convict labor, unjust prison sentences for blacks, the "diabolical lynch law," and disenfranchisement. At one Sunday school conference, delegates discussed the rape of a ten-year-old black girl by a white man and deplored the fact that the rapist escaped without being punished, while black women were continually "exposed to the insults of the foulest rake of the other race." In their annual "Report on the State of the Country," Virginia AME church members vented their outrage. One speaker denounced President Grover Cleveland for his expressions of sympathy toward the "heathen Chinese" on the West Coast while "*colored civilized citizens* in the South are being shot in cool blood in the very arms of Justice, in the open noonday . . . and their murderers allowed to escape . . . without a word of rebuke." Black Methodists condemned the white law officers who forcibly removed one of their bishops from a first-class railroad car as he was traveling to a Sunday school convention. Another AME member denounced the "condemnable, ubiquitous, and hell-deserving sin" of lynching, observing that foreign visitors to the United States never confronted the injustices that blacks faced each day. In their literature and at Sunday

---

24. "State Sunday School Convention, Kentucky Conference, AMEZ Church," *Star of Zion*, 19 July 1894.

school conventions, African Americans spoke out in protest of their dismal situation.[25]

Attending a Sunday school conference demanded financial sacrifices, which served to remind blacks of their tenuous economic position. Many African Americans scrimped and saved in order to attend an event that they anticipated eagerly all year. But most felt the sacrifices were worth it, for these conventions provided delegates with rare opportunities to relax, socialize, make new friends, and leave behind the grind of their daily existence. Conference reports reveal how much the participants relished the dinners, group singing, picnics, and boat rides—all part of the week-long proceedings.[26]

A strong political tone did not typify all black conventions. Some purposely avoided any hint of the political. Especially when a number of whites were present, African American church leaders made every effort to exhibit an air of optimism about their future. Instead of criticizing widespread injustice, Sunday school officials tried to put their best foot forward and gain the approval of the white community.

One of the largest and best known of these conferences was the Negro Young People's Christian and Educational Congress, held in Atlanta from August 6 to 11, 1902. The event was the brainchild of Irvine Garland Penn, a black Methodist educator from Virginia. Penn organized the conference because he felt that many blacks had not prospered socially or economically since the abolition of slavery, and he feared the deterioration of his people. Penn pinpointed the Sunday school as the place to uplift and redeem African Americans. His conference, "Reaching the Unreached: The Race for Christ," was billed as a forum to discuss past racial achievements and to speculate on what blacks could achieve in the future. Calling it a "great gathering," Penn and fellow organizers hoped to instill new energy into Sunday schools and youth organizations, examine why adolescents seemed to be "growing averse to piety," and discuss topics

25. "State Sunday School Convention, Kentucky Conference," 2; "Report on the State of the Country," *Minutes of the Virginia Annual Conference of the AME, 1886* (Richmond: J. W. Fergusson and Son, 1886), 38; "Statement on the State of the Country," *Minutes of the Virginia Annual Conference of the AME, 1888* (Richmond: J. W. Fergusson and Son, 1888), 56; "State of the Country," *Minutes of the Virginia Annual Conference of the AME, 1892* (Richmond: J. W. Fergusson and Son, 1892), 45.

26. "The Vanguard's Silence."

vital to elevating the race. With a printed program of more than two hundred pages, the event promised something for everyone.²⁷

The five-day conference attracted national attention. Laypeople, ministers, and Sunday school experts addressed a wide range of issues—the need to uplift young men, the importance of feminine virtue, effective teaching methods for Sunday school, rising crime against blacks, and women's duties in the church. Women such as Nannie H. Burroughs (activist and one of the founders and leaders of the Women's Convention of the NBC) delivered speeches, seeing themselves as responsible for the future of the next generation. At the end of the conference, the congress issued an official declaration that combined the approaches of Booker T. Washington and W. E. B. DuBois. This declaration urged black public schools and Sunday schools to provide an education that defended the dignity of manual labor, yet allowed exceptional blacks to pursue a course of demanding academics and to make the most of their lives.²⁸

While the Sunday school constituted the focus of the congress, the event gave participants an opportunity to herald the accomplishments of African Americans. Speakers encouraged the adoption of middle-class values and derided the "lower class of negroes," who they felt reflected poorly on their race. The majority of delegates wanted whites to judge the race by its best representatives—including the well-mannered convention crowd—and not by hopeless, lazy, or unambitious blacks. Participants lived up to the high standards they had set for themselves. The crowd was praised for its "quiet and orderly manner"; the police reported not a single arrest for drunkenness or rowdy behavior. These Christian blacks demonstrated the best the South had to offer.²⁹

The congress achieved the attention Penn desired. The event attracted thousands of participants representing forty-one different denominations. Whites were present on the podium and in the audience. The *Atlanta Constitution* and a number of denominational newspapers gave the

---

27. Gaines, *Uplifting the Race,* 23; John Michael Mathews, "The Dilemma of Negro Leadership in the New South: The Case of the Negro Young People's Congress of 1902," *South Atlantic Quarterly* 73 (1974): 130–44.

28. "Declaration of Negro Congress Addressed to American People," *Atlanta Constitution,* 11 August 1902; Mathews, "The Dilemma," 141. See also Guy-Shaftall, *Daughters of Sorrow,* 74.

29. "Booker T. Washington to Address Congress," "Declaration of Negro Congress," and "Negro Visitors Well Behaved," *Atlanta Constitution,* 10 August 1902.

congress wide coverage, even printing some speeches in their entirety. While the event had a serious purpose, optimism and harmony prevailed. According to the *Atlanta Constitution,* the Congress was the "greatest meeting that colored people have ever held"; the *Southern Workman* said it represented the "best in personnel, character and purpose." Despite such accolades, though, Penn's dream of a triennial event went unfilled; the conference never met again. Four years later, Atlanta was the setting of a bloody race riot.[30]

African Americans' overall desire for autonomous Sunday schools concerned some white evangelicals, who worried about their inability to influence blacks' spiritual uplift. A few had watched anxiously when blacks exited their churches in droves after the Civil War—an action that they feared would not only lead to the downfall of the black race but would bring serious social disorder to the region. Like this handful of troubled whites, the Reverend Girardeau feared that blacks who left his Presbyterian church "will be exposed to fanatical, licentious, and superstitious influences which will tend to ruin them, and to injure the interest of society in general." He warned that without white guidance, blacks would lapse into a "condition of baptized heathenism." In an attempt to maintain their spiritual sway over African Americans, some whites looked to the Sunday school as a place where they could continue to oversee blacks' moral and Christian instruction. Teaching black youngsters how to behave and exposing them to Scripture and moral values were important if blacks were to become purposeful, respectable citizens. Southern whites wanted to fashion a docile, law-abiding black population, and the Sunday school offered them this possibility. Its lessons could be an effective, benevolent means to influence black behavior. Youngsters could perhaps even pass lessons on to parents who never had had the opportunity to attend Sunday school. As William Hartshorn wrote, working on behalf of black Sunday schools was a worthwhile endeavor, for the "Negro is naturally religious. He craves leadership; he loves to teach; the Sunday school and the church furnish the opportunity." To Hartshorn and like-minded whites, involvement in black Sunday schools

---

30. "A Great Gathering," *Christian Index,* 19 July 1902; "Young Negroes Ready for Work," *Atlanta Constitution,* 5 August 1902; "The Atlanta Congress," *Southern Workman* 31 (September 1902): 470.

was not only desirable but essential. White evangelicals began to discuss the amount of time, money, and energy they could devote to black Sunday schools and how best to become involved.[31]

Of the three major southern white denominations, Southern Presbyterians wrestled most profoundly—or at least most vocally—with the role they could and should play in black Sunday schools. This interest evolved in part from the Presbyterian antebellum plantation mission movement, in which some slaveholders tried to Christianize, uplift, and even educate their slaves. They paternalistically believed that slaves, like children, needed white guidance. After the war, many whites saw no reason to question this historical "truism" merely because blacks were now free. Other whites saw African American children heading in the wrong direction, and they urged immediate action before the situation became hopeless. Youngsters, especially young men, were loitering on city streets, gathering in gangs, gambling, and drinking. By imparting scriptural truths and Christian morals, whites believed they could save black children from a dire future and from the "calamities by which they are threatened." Presbyterians convinced themselves that such gestures would be welcome, for they believed that blacks were now willing "to be guided and controlled by their old and true friends."[32]

In this context, Southern Presbyterians developed an understandable approach to black Sunday schools. They concluded that all such schools should be organized and taught by whites. According to Southern Presbyterians, religious education was too important to be left in the hands of what they regarded as an inherently inferior race. Some whites were appalled by what they witnessed in black Sunday schools. "Heretofore, the disorderly conduct and unmanageable disposition of the pupils were even a greater hindrance to the prosecution of the work than their profound ignorance," wrote a discouraged Presbyterian. From a white vantage point, black Sunday schools seemed inefficient, disorganized, and poorly attended. "We cannot view their present deplorable, and, in many quar-

---

31. J. L. Girardeau, "Our Ecclesiastical Relations to Freedmen," *Southern Presbyterian Review* 18 (1868): 6; William N. Hartshorn, "Negroes, Sunday-School Work among the," *Encyclopedia of Sunday Schools*, vol. 2, p. 713. See also "The Colored Man in the South," *Southern Presbyterian Review* 28 (January 1877): 83–101.

32. "Instruction of Colored People," *Minutes of the General Assembly of the Presbyterian Church in the United States, 1866* (page torn, [1866]), 60.

ters, increasing ignorance of divine truth, and their lapse into deeper moral degradation and ruin, without sincere sorrow, nor without putting forth renewed efforts for their salvation," groaned an Alabama Presbyterian in 1878. Southern Presbyterians believed that if they had charge of black Sunday schools, classes would become purposeful and effective. Through the lessons they selected, whites could influence future generations, instill valuable scriptural guidelines, create an educated black race, and ultimately ensure a peaceful, orderly South.[33]

The debate among Presbyterians over what role they should play in black Sunday schools lasted for decades. Until nearly the end of the nineteenth century, however, this debate produced no substantive plan of action. In its absence, a handful of ministers, women, and theology students acted on their own to organize Sunday schools for African American youngsters. With little more than denominational rhetoric to support their efforts, white Presbyterians struggled to establish Sunday schools and teach their reluctant charges.[34]

In 1890, the church finally implemented an official plan with the establishment of its Committee on Home Missions. The idea was that the denomination and individual churches would organize mission Sunday schools for blacks and the less fortunate. Two years later, a newly formed Executive Committee of Colored Evangelism began to work on behalf of black Sunday schools. A white minister, the Reverend Alexander L. Phillips of Birmingham, Alabama, became the committee's first Executive Secretary for Colored Evangelistic Work. His mission was to promote and organize black Presbyterian Sunday schools, recruit white instructors and supervisors, and introduce modern techniques into the classroom. Despite Phillips's dedication and enthusiasm for the cause, he and his staff organized only ten schools during his first five years in office. By 1901, however, the number of Sunday schools rose to forty. Presbyterians boasted that "we stand almost alone in the South in our devotion and liberality to this cause."[35]

---

33. T. L. P., "Colored Sabbath Schools," *Earnest Worker*, 16 February 1870; "Colored Population," *Minutes of the Synod of Alabama* (Montgomery: Barrett and Brown, 1878), 13.

34. An issue that also undermined black-white cooperation was Presbyterians' insistence on an educated ministry. On the other hand, a growing number of middle-class black leaders saw this as important for racial uplift.

35. Thompson, *Presbyterians in the South,* vol. 3, 92–4; S. P. Verner, "Sunday Schools for Colored People," *Presbyterian Standard,* 1 July 1903, 19.

A few of these schools did enjoy some success, from the perspective both of white volunteers and of participants. In 1898, under the direction of John Little, students at the Presbyterian Theological Seminary in Louisville, Kentucky, created what white Presbyterians called a model black Sunday school. Although it started as a traditional mission Sunday school, it soon began to resemble a community center, offering sewing, cooking, industrial arts, and reading classes, as well as Bible study, cultural activities, lectures, and medical care. The practical training courses became so popular that officials had to select eager pupils based on their regular Sunday school attendance. John Little waxed enthusiastic about his school's accomplishments, claiming that the "hearts of the colored people are longing for something which will deliver them from the power of sin." He felt his school did just that, despite the enticements that obviously helped his cause. A paternalistic Little saw such outreach efforts as essential, for the "colored man is still in need of the careful and sympathetic training by the white man."[36]

Yet overall, Presbyterian efforts to influence black youngsters through the Sunday school proved frustrating. Presbyterians discovered that few black churches and families welcomed Sunday schools supervised and taught by whites, few black children wanted to attend classes, and—perhaps most revealing—few white Presbyterians wanted to teach black children. As Phillips wrote gloomily early in his tenure, "We have been pained beyond expression that our brethren of the church at large have not responded to what they had themselves taken for the call of God to duty in behalf of the colored people." He conducted his work in the midst of "indifference and hostility, where we had every reason to expect sympathy and help." Limited funds and few volunteers caused him to become increasingly disheartened. By 1906, the Committee on Home Missions counted only 1,965 black pupils and 201 white teachers in these Presbyterian Sunday schools. Three years later, the committee had to report that no new black Sunday schools had been organized. "They are maintained only by great perseverance and tact," it concluded. The church did not

36. Executive Committee of Colored Evangelization, *Fifteenth Annual Report, 1905–1906* (Richmond: Presbyterian Committee of Publication, 1906), 7; John Little, "Colored Sunday Schools in the South," *Presbyterian Standard*, 5 October 1904; J. G. Snedecor, "Sabbath-Schools with White Teachers," *Fourteenth Annual Report of the Executive Committee of Colored Evangelism* (Richmond: Presbyterian Committee of Publication, 1905), 7.

give up its efforts, however; in 1915, it redirected its focus to educating and training African American ministers.³⁷

White Southern Baptists and Methodists harbored fewer illusions about being as directly or as paternalistically involved in black Sunday schools—or at least they discussed the issue less often and with less passion than Presbyterians. In part this had to do with the fact that blacks had their own Baptist and Methodist denominations (though Southern Presbyterians established a small African American synod in 1898), and Baptists held fast to their belief that local churches should retain a degree of independence. Neither the Baptists nor the Methodists adopted a universal hands-off policy; both offered advice and financial assistance to black Sunday schools. White Southern Methodists prided themselves on their close relationship with CME Sunday schools, even after that denomination and its publishing house stood on firm ground. The SBC helped Richard Boyd's NBC publishing firm by giving advice and lending its book plates. Nonetheless, paternalism also infused the attitudes and actions of these white denominations. Methodist Atticus Haygood, regarded as a racial moderate whose popular treatise *Our Brother in Black* was considered by whites to be a sensitive, fair portrayal of blacks, echoed typical sentiments in calling most blacks "very ignorant." They needed education, elevation, and the "guidance and protection of a stronger people," Haygood claimed. He preached racial tolerance but, like most southern whites, abhorred the thought of race mixing. Baptist F. L. Law believed that blacks could not think for themselves and thus had to remain dependent on whites. It was fortunate, to his thinking, that white southerners understood that black children needed "mental and moral elevation" and could help African Americans organize their Sunday schools.³⁸

37. Executive Committee of Colored Evangelization, *Fifteenth Annual Report*, 1; "Mission Sabbath Schools," *Eighteenth Annual Report of the Executive Committee of Colored Evangelism* (Richmond: Presbyterian Committee of Publication, 1909), 7. See Thompson, *Presbyterians in the South*, vol. 3, 81–8, 142–6; Andrew E. Murray, *Presbyterians and the Negro—A History* (Richmond: Presbyterian Historical Society, 1966), 145–54; A. L. Phillips, *The Call of the Home Land: A Study of Home Missions* (Richmond: Presbyterian Committee of Publication, 1906), 75–87; R. E. Magill, "A Mighty Man Is Fallen," *Earnest Worker*, May 1915.

38. Atticus Haygood, *Our Brother in Black: His Freedom and His Future* (1889; reprint, Miami: Mnemosyne Publishers, 1969), 14, 34, 129; Law quote in J. M. Carroll, *A History of Texas Baptists, Comprising a Detailed Account of Their Activities, Their Progress, and Their Achievements* (Dallas: Baptist Standard Publishing, 1923), 340. For background on Haygood, see H. Shelton Smith, *In His Image, But . . .*, 232; Owen, *Sacred*

Even after Reconstruction ended in 1877, a number of northern religious organizations and denominations remained in the South and continued to engage in black Sunday school work. Many were horrified by the situation that African Americans faced, which only seemed to worsen over time. In their eyes, black public schools, churches, and Sunday schools all seemed to function below acceptable standards. Northern agents fretted about their perception of a decline in the spiritual condition of African Americans; they worried that it could bring about the downfall of the race, with a deleterious effect on the entire nation. They fervently believed that black children should attend well-run Sunday schools and common schools in order to absorb lessons in social and moral improvement.

In the late nineteenth and early twentieth centuries, several northern religious and educational foundations were founded that targeted the South as an object of their work. The Slater Fund, begun in 1882, provided funds to aid blacks through Christian education. (Atticus Haygood served as its southern agent until appointed a bishop in 1890.) The General Education Board, founded in 1902, held conferences throughout the South to discuss how best to promote and improve black education.[39]

The International Sunday School Association (ISSA), a Chicago-based organization, also became increasingly involved in black Sunday school work. William N. Hartshorn, chair of the ISSA Executive Committee, played a key role in this endeavor. His travels throughout the South convinced him that black Sunday schools were too few in number and poorly run, and he pressed his organization to commit resources to help found new Sunday schools and upgrade existing ones. In 1895, the ISSA initiated a new outreach program in the South by hiring an African American minister, L. B. Maxwell of Georgia, as its official missionary. When Maxwell died in 1902, the ISSA appointed two other men to continue his work. Yet after a decade of effort and expenditures of more than $24,000, the results proved disappointing.[40]

Flame of Love, 149; Joel Williamson, *The Crucible of Race: Black-White Relations in the American South since Emancipation* (New York: Oxford University Press, 1984), 88–93.

39. Louis D. Rubin Jr., *Teach the Freeman: The Correspondence of Rutherford B. Hayes and the Slater Fund for Negro Education,* vol. 2 (Baton Rouge: Louisiana State University Press, 1959), xx–xxiii.

40. William Newton Hartshorn, "The Sunday School and the Negro," in ISSA, *Organized Sunday School Work in America, 13th International Sunday School Convention, 1908–1911* (Chicago: ISSA, 1911), 515–21; G. R. Merrill, "Hartshorn, William Newton," *Encyclopedia of Sunday Schools,* vol. 2, 514–5.

ISSA officials decided that they needed to involve more African Americans in Sunday school work. The organization offered $450 to help pay the salary and expenses of any "suitable" black Sunday school missionary employed by a black nondenominational Sunday school association, if the state association matched that amount. Although blacks in five southern states responded positively, they never raised the necessary matching funds. The ISSA then scrapped this idea and met with black ministers in several southern cities. Still convinced that the greatest problem facing African Americans was a lack of proper moral and religious training, ISSA officials called a meeting in 1907 with field secretaries and Sunday school officials from ten southern states. The officials finally seemed to understand that blacks were intensely denominational and had little desire to engage in nondenominational Sunday school work. Moreover, blacks preferred to support their own churches rather than a project run by a white northern organization. ISSA evangelicals decided that the best approach would be to help educate African Americans, and to offer courses in Sunday school pedagogy, missionary work, and Christian education.[41]

Determined to put a plan into effect, Hartshorn and his wife invited seventy guests to their home in Clifton, Massachusetts, for a three-day conference in August 1908. These men and women were renowned in Sunday school and church circles from various states, denominations, and religious organizations. A third of the delegates were black; the majority of the guests were southern. Since the sponsoring agent was the ISSA, it is not surprising that all participants agreed on the worth of the Sunday school and celebrated the fact that it had already saved "millions of adults." Delegates saw the meeting, later called the Clifton conference, as history in the making. Hartshorn later compiled an illustrated book, *An Era of Progress and Promise,* with excerpts from conference papers and discussions. Summing up the event, Bishop George Clinton claimed the conference was the "best thing that has been done for the race" since Lincoln's Emancipation Proclamation.[42]

41. Hartshorn, "The Sunday School and the Negro," 515–21. For additional information on the 1907 conference, see David Henry Bradley Sr., *A History of the AME Zion Church,* vol. 2, *1872–1968* (Nashville: Parthenon Press, 1970), 74–6; Tyms, *The Rise of Religious Education among Negro Baptists,* 158.

42. Merrill, "Hartshorn," 514–5. The book is Hartshorn, ed., *An Era of Progress and Promise.* For quote, see Clinton, in *An Era of Progress,* ed. Hartshorn, frontispiece. Hartshorn was called the "promoter of conferences."

The Clifton proceedings offer fascinating insights into perceptions of Sunday school education for southern blacks, at least from the perspective of white and black leaders who were active in the movement. Participants focused entirely on black spiritual and educational welfare. They first looked to the past, observing that southern whites had once assumed responsibility for blacks' spiritual needs. Now, while a few whites still were actively working in this area, sentiment had shifted and commitment had waned. The conference participants concluded that southern whites were uncertain how to act toward African Americans and extended little assistance to uplift them. Because of this, they resolved that the ISSA had to play a greater role in racial uplift through black Sunday schools. The best means to do this was by establishing and strengthening teacher-training programs in southern black institutes and colleges. Self-help, under white guidance, was the best approach. To elevate the race and improve Christian and moral education, the quality of black Sunday school teaching had to improve.[43]

Though it was admittedly a small and exclusive gathering, the issues discussed at the Clifton conference are instructive. The problems that delegates tackled—such as the shortage of trained black teachers, the lack of order and structure in black Sunday school classes, and the failure of black academies and institutes to offer teacher training and Bible study—had worried Sunday school leaders and educators for years. Yet delegates also trumpeted the achievements of black Sunday schools and their positive influence on the race. H. L. McCrorey of Biddle University in Charlotte, North Carolina, concluded that Sunday schools were more important to African American children than to whites because the former often had no one at home to teach them Scripture and proper behavior. As one editorial summed up the proceedings, the "Sunday school is the instrumentality best adapted to impart to them the cultivation and discipline that they require."[44]

In the wake of the Clifton conference, the ISSA began to conduct southern Sunday school work through black colleges and schools. After a committee studied the best approach to black religious instruction, it appointed Reverend H. C. Lyman, a white teacher from South Carolina,

---

43. William N. Hartshorn, "The Clifton Conference," W. B. Mathews, "The Present Needs of the Negro," and H. L. McCrorey, "A Great Opportunity," all in *An Era of Progress and Promise,* ed. Hartshorn, 63, 59, and 202, respectively.

44. Hartshorn, "Clifton Conference," in *An Era of Progress,* ed. Hartshorn, 63.

as the ISSA Superintendent of Sunday School Work among the Colored People. In 1911, the ISSA launched its pedagogical experiment in several Atlanta black seminaries and colleges, and the plan soon spread to other institutions. By 1922, some 35,000 African American students had taken at least one ISSA teacher training class, though what impact these classes ultimately had is unknown.[45]

Home mission work was another way for whites to engage in black Sunday school work. Some evangelicals noticed the many volunteers and large sums of money that supported foreign outposts and lamented the fact that mission ventures too often ignored the needy at home. As a white Baptist insisted, it was time to focus attention on creating a "Christian civilization in America." By the late nineteenth century, more churches and individuals became interested in what many saw as "this godless people at the back door." Southern blacks offered a unique opportunity for mission endeavors, James Snedecor argued, for churches could combine both home and foreign work by uplifting millions of southerners of African ancestry. Women proved eager missionaries at home and abroad, for this work, like Sunday school teaching, was an acceptable and meaningful outlet for their energies. The founding of women's home mission organizations gave women another opportunity to labor beyond the confines of the domestic sphere.[46]

Founding black Sunday schools was an important aspect of home mission work and promised numerous benefits to everyone involved in them. In a sense, the home mission movement merely formalized ongoing efforts to establish outreach Sunday schools, an activity begun long before the Civil War. To thrifty evangelicals, this was an appealing endeavor. As a pragmatic A. B. Curry concluded, mission Sunday schools offered an "opportunity of maximum service to the Negroes at minimum cost." Unlike foreign missionary work, no new languages had to be learned, the needy were close at hand, and Sunday schools were easier and less expen-

---

45. H. C. Lyman, "Work among the Negroes," in ISSA, *Organized Sunday School Work in America, 14th International Sunday School Convention, 1911–1914* (Chicago: ISSA, 1914), 418; Tyms, *The Rise of Religious Education,* 160; Bradley, *History of the AME Zion Church,* vol. 2, 78.

46. "Christian America," *Minutes of the Jacksonville Baptist Association, 1911,* 16–7; James G. Snedecor, *Missionary Aspects of our Negro Population* (Richmond: L. D. Sullivan, 1906), 2. See also E. E. Bomar, "Religious Welfare of the Southern Negro," *Seminary Magazine* 2 (May 1889): 142–7.

sive to organize than churches or foreign missionary outposts. Church officials were convinced that the work would bring positive rewards, uplifting the South's most destitute people. Missionaries could reap personal blessings by working for such a grand, benevolent purpose. To some denominations, financial rewards were another incentive. African American pupils would "create a large and steady demand for books and school publications," claimed a hopeful Presbyterian, Edward Bromfield.[47]

Denominational home mission boards saw Sunday schools as the answer to black destitution and sin. Board leaders claimed that racial uplift would occur when blacks could absorb and live by white middle-class values. The SBC Home Mission Board saw black children as ideal subjects, for "with justice and kindness" from whites, they displayed a "perfect willingness to accept a subordinate place." The SBC Board hired its first evangelists in 1912 and later appointed dozens of volunteers to work among southern blacks. Eventually it had some 1,200 individuals working in the South, many of them student volunteers who organized mission Sunday schools and tried to teach Baptist doctrine. In a unique project, the SBC and NBC jointly hired missionaries; and by 1914, they had 47 men in the field. Southern Methodists also engaged in home missionary programs, establishing mission Sunday schools for blacks throughout the South, as well as schools for Cuban immigrants in Florida and for Germans and Mexicans in Texas.[48]

It is interesting that southern whites—who deemed blacks inferior, ignored many of their social and economic problems, and had no desire to welcome them into their homes or churches—expressed an interest in their Sunday schools. But this made sense. For some whites, Sunday school work helped assuage guilt over past injustices. In addition, it was

47. A. B. Curry Sr., "Sunday-School for the Negroes," *Missionary Survey* (November 1911): 18. "Missionary Aspects of Our Negro Population," (Richmond: L. D. Sullivan, 1906), 2; Edward C. Bromfield, *A Review of the Sabbath-School Mission Work of the Presbyterian Church, 1887–1893* (Philadelphia: Lane and Scott's Printing House, 1893), 10, 21, 28. See also Executive Committee of Colored Evangelization, *Fifteenth Annual Report, 1905–1906;* D. Clay Lilly, "The Attitude of the South to the Colored People," *Union Seminary Magazine* 16 (February–March 1905): 282–4. For mission Sunday schools see Boylan, *Sunday School,* 32–40; Turner, *Women, Culture, and Community,* 69–70.

48. Edward L. Wheeler, "An Overview of Black Southern Baptist Involvement," *Baptist History and Heritage* 16, no. 3 (1981): 3–11, 40.

easier to influence the faith and upbringing of children than to tackle adult problems. African American Sunday schools had more opportunities for white involvement than black churches, where whites had little opportunity to dictate religious messages and found black ministers difficult to handle. Missionaries often could circumvent a preacher and conduct Sunday school work on their own.

Southern whites' excessive worries about what they labeled the "Negro problem" (their term to describe the region's social ills) resonated in their discussions of black Sunday schools. To solve the "Negro problem," many whites felt they had to tighten existing laws, legally segregate the races, and mete out swift punishment to alleged perpetrators. Random violence against blacks remained an option; a single lynching viscerally reminded blacks that whites were in control. As historian Joel Williamson has argued, however, by the late nineteenth century some liberal southern whites were distressed by the level of violence used to address racial problems and ensure black subordination. Some white evangelicals sought more humane solutions to the South's social and racial problems. One meaningful and effective response, they believed, was to engage in religious uplift through the Sunday school. Christian benevolence could help resolve the "Negro problem." As Southern Presbyterians candidly admitted, their purpose in organizing black Sunday schools was not merely an act of Christian charity and saving souls. Under white tutelage, a "temper of docility would be engendered in the rising generation among them, the antagonisms of race would be mollified and amicable relations would be established." As another Presbyterian admitted, their work in black Sunday schools resulted from the highest of motives—serving Jesus Christ—as well as from the lowest—self-protection. "We must try to make better men and women of our colored population, or they will ruin our civilization," he wrote.[49]

Working with black Sunday school pupils also seemed natural to whites because it reinforced their traditional view of proper race relation-

---

49. Williamson, *A Rage for Order*, 152–205; "Report of the Standing Committee on Sabbath Schools," *Minutes of the General Assembly of the Presbyterian Church in the U.S.* (Richmond: Presbyterian Committee of Publication, 1896), 616; S. P. Verner, "Sabbath Schools for Colored People," *Presbyterian Standard* 45 (1 July 1903): 19. See George Allen Mebane, *"The Negro Problem" As Seen and Discussed by Southern White Men in a Conference at Montgomery, Alabama* (New York: Alliance Publishing, 1900); Lillian Smith, *Killers of the Dream* (New York: Norton, 1949).

ships—that of adult to child. Whites assumed that they possessed the capability and brain power to lead; African Americans did not. Black people simply were not "competent to take part in the conduct of colored Sunday schools," claimed missionary William Paxson.

White southerners' interest in African American Sunday schools also reflected their growing suspicion of outsiders and desire to rid the region of Yankees. Influencing and even controlling black schools was another step toward redeeming the South and putting race issues in the hands of southern whites. In 1900, delegates attending the Southern Society for the Promotion of the Study of Race Conditions and Problems in the South meeting in Montgomery articulated this very point. "Leadership of southern opinion has been too largely attempted merely from the North," asserted the executive committee. The South had to solve its own problems. Harmonious coexistence of the races was only possible, white southerners argued, if they were responsible for educating and uplifting blacks. The horrors of Reconstruction might be past, but religious meddling by northern missionaries continued. In public pronouncements, if not in their actions, southern evangelicals demonstrated a degree of possessiveness over the spiritual lives of blacks. If anything was to be done, they insisted, it should be undertaken by those who understood and could best serve the black population.[50]

It is hardly coincidental that as southern whites established their own Sunday school boards and publishing firms, they began to resent northern involvement in black Sunday schools. To their thinking, religious redemption involved eliminating northern influences in any southern enterprise, black or white. "The people of the North, as a mass, are utterly ignorant of the true character of the average freedman at the South," concluded W. P. Harrison, in typical parlance. "They understand his good points as little as they do his evil ones." Another insisted that the "African must be elevated if he is elevated at all, by that portion of the white race who are thoroughly acquainted with the weakness and the strength of his race character."[51]

50. Executive Committee, The Southern Society for the Promotion of the Study of Race Conditions and Problems in the South, *Race Problems of the South: Report of the Proceedings of the First Annual Conference* (1900; reprint, New York: Negro Universities Press, 1969), 10.
51. W. P. Harrison, "The Southern Methodist Church," *Southern Review* 25 (January 1879): 39, 42; E. E. Bomar, "Religious Welfare of the Southern Negro," *Seminary Magazine* 2 (May 1889): 145.

Economic concerns also motivated southern white interest in black religious uplift. By the late nineteenth century, the promise of better job opportunities and a better life in the Northeast had tempted some African Americans to migrate northward. Though this was only a minor phenomenon compared to the Great Migration that took place before and during World War I, some southern landowners and industrialists were already concerned about the loss of cheap labor. In his 1889 book, *The Prosperity of the South Dependent upon the Elevation of the Negro,* Lewis Harvie Blair, a prescient white Virginia reformer, advanced the radical argument that whites had to concern themselves with destitute blacks or else the South would lose its labor force from farms, mines, and factories. They needed to pay more attention to the South's primary workers and find the means to encourage them to stay. The region's economic future was threatened unless everyone enjoyed a decent life.[52]

If the region's laborers were to function effectively in a growing industrial and consumer economy, whites believed, they had to understand the importance of responsibility, sobriety, and hard work. Black Sunday schools offered a venue where whites could ensure that the right lessons were taught to future workers. African American youngsters could mature into productive workers by learning values that would best serve the white South. As a report for the Southern Society for the Promotion of Race Conditions and Problems in the South argued, whites had to transform black people into "industrious, self respecting Negroes." Molding a working class of "docile Negroes" would "place the South in the foreground among the industrial countries of the World." Industrious black workers were a resource "of untold value to the White population if they are educated in the right way," the report concluded.[53]

Racial and economic issues surrounding the Sunday school unleashed misunderstandings. Nowhere was this more evident than in the creation of Richard Boyd's NBC publishing firm in 1896. Eager to establish a profitable company, a savvy Boyd requested immediate assistance from the ABPS, wanting to borrow its printing plates until his business could

---

52. Lewis Harvie Blair, *The Prosperity of the South Dependent upon the Elevation of the Negro* (Richmond: E. Waddley, 1889); Charles E. Wynes, "Lewis Harvie Blair, Virginia Reformer: The Uplift of the Negro and Southern Prosperity," *Virginia Magazine of History and Biography* 72 (January 1964): 1–2.

53. Wynes, "Lewis Harvie Blair," 1–2; Executive Committee of the Southern Society for the Promotion of Race Conditions, *Race Problems,* 88.

stand on its own. ABPS editor A. J. Rowland refused his request because Boyd would not give credit to the ABPS for borrowed material, and because Rowland feared increased business competition. Boyd then turned to James Frost of the SBC, who was more than happy to assist. Rowland lashed out, calling Frost's gesture an act of "betrayal." Frost's generosity was doubly insulting, for it meant that not only would the new NBC publishing business compete with the ABPS, but that it had the assistance of white Southern Baptists.[54]

Rowland carried on a chilly correspondence with Frost, calling his action duplicitous. He tried to gain the support of NBC members by writing and then distributing a leaflet, "A Word to Negro Baptists," to remind them of the ABPS's long and generous support of their churches and Sunday schools. Rowland predicted that a black publishing firm would undermine the healthy relationship between the ABPS and NBC, incite racial antagonism, and alienate northern whites. If African Americans remained loyal to the ABPS and continued to purchase its literature, he promised that they could count on inexpensive Sunday school publications, skilled writers and editors, and an absence of racial or sectional bias. Should black Baptists move ahead with their publishing venture, he threatened, the NBC "cannot expect that the Society will be able to continue its favors" to a "people who show their hostility to it by refusing to support it."[55]

The dispute became public. From all over the South, white Baptists wrote to advise Frost on an appropriate course of action. In Jackson, Mississippi, John Buck believed that black Baptists had every right to use SBC book plates. "I think we ought to help these people all we can and hope you will understand that I am heartily in favor of doing that," he wrote. D. S. Snodgrass of San Antonio, Texas, concluded that the ABPS had no claim to superior literature. "I hope you and all those brethren who have helped Bro Boyd so far will not suffer him to be outdone by Dr. Rowland nor [sic] any other agency engaged against his enterprise," he wrote. Having seen samples of NBC literature, he concluded, "I desire to commend Bro R. H. Boyd to the confidence and cooperation of all

54. See the many letters exchanged between Frost and Rowland in Frost-Bell Correspondence, 1896–97, SBHLA.
55. "A Word to Negro Baptists" (n.d., n.p.), in Frost-Bell Correspondence, SBHLA. Although anonymous, the language and contents strongly suggest that Rowland wrote it.

Southern Baptists." Annie Armstrong found her friend Rowland upset with all blacks. "He seemed to think that they were not capable of taking charge of their own work . . . he regards them almost in the light of a forlorn hope," she observed. SBC members viewed this controversy as a ready-made opportunity to eliminate their most powerful publishing competitor in the region and to expand markets for both the SBC and NBC publishing houses. Boyd's business and the SBC Sunday school board began to turn a healthy profit, and the ABPS—though not yet ready to yield—began to lose influence in the South. By 1910, the ABPS had withdrawn from the region, leaving the market to Southern Baptists.[56]

Overall, whites in the North and South had only limited success in their efforts to take charge of black Sunday school education. Some of this was due to white attitudes. Both northern missionaries and southern whites often exhibited a paternalistic, superior air; it seemed impossible for them to shed racist attitudes. Most whites never consulted African Americans about Sunday school issues to discuss what, if any, white involvement might be welcome. In their correspondence and in published essays, whites often categorized blacks as lazy, ignorant, and sinful. In white eyes, aiding and organizing black Sunday schools was a duty worth the effort, and one which ultimately would benefit both races.[57]

Most importantly, southern and northern whites' failure to work effectively with black Sunday schools reflected blacks' desire to control their own lives, communities, and institutions, and to reap the benefits of their own enterprises. Though the going was difficult, many black churches were less needy by the turn of the century than they had been right after the Civil War, when any help had been welcome. Admittedly, a number of black Sunday schools continued to accept and even solicit outside advice, financial assistance, and free or inexpensive classroom literature. But generally, African Americans were determined to run their

---

56. John T. Buck, 19 March 1897, Jackson, Miss.; D. S. Snodgrass, 23 February 1897, San Antonio, Tex.; Annie Armstrong, 13 May 1897, Baltimore, Md.; all to James Marion Frost, in Frost-Bell Correspondence, SBHLA. See also Sernett, *Bound for the Promised Land*, 97–8.

57. "Sunday Schools for Colored Persons," *Religious Herald*, 5 April 1866; Homer McMillan, *"Unfinished Tasks" of the Southern Presbyterian Church* (Richmond, Va.: Presbyterian Committee of Publication, 1922).

own institutions, and when they welcomed white assistance, it was more likely on their terms.

The issue of race touched everything in the South; certainly this was true of the Sunday school. Whites tried to address the "Negro problem" by encouraging the formation of black Sunday classes and making some effort to oversee them. They believed that through proper Christian lessons, a docile, well-behaved, and hardworking black population would accept its place in the southern hierarchy. Southern whites wanted to aid those in need, eliminate northern competition, and ensure that black children absorbed Christian beliefs and learned to live according to middle-class values. The black Sunday school gained whites' attention because it served their ends.

But Sunday schools were important to African Americans on a more fundamental level. Sunday schools helped strengthen and expand African American churches and communities, and gave blacks additional resolve and strength to stand on their own. The institution became a place where lessons in racial uplift and race pride were taught. Good manners, respectability, and moral improvement were important if African American children were to occupy a significant place in the region's and the nation's future. Numerous Sunday schools, conferences, and religious publications provided a forum for African Americans to vent their anger and frustration at the inequities they faced, and to seek solutions to growing oppression. The Sunday school was an institution that allowed blacks to shape the contours of their lives and look ahead to a brighter future.

7

The Modern Southern Sunday School

In 1904, a Presbyterian considered how modernization might be affecting the condition of southern Sunday schools and breathed a sigh of relief to discover that only a few schools made light of religious tradition. Sunday school officers and teachers in a "southern latitude," he observed, embraced an old-fashioned view of Biblical doctrine. He celebrated the "fact that we are something like 150 years behind the time." Yet this Presbyterian believed that many turn-of-the-century Sunday school officials could also boast of their "progressive" approach, running "up-to-date," efficient Sunday schools, with skilled teachers and relevant lessons—but schools that always put the Bible and conversion center stage. Southern Sunday schools employed modern techniques even as they sought traditional ends.[1]

This vision, however exaggerated, did reflect the situation of many southern Sunday schools around the turn of the century. In 1915, Sunday schools looked very different than they had in the aftermath of the Civil War. For one thing, there were more of them. Sunday schools now dotted

1. "Editorial," *Earnest Worker,* November 1904, 371.

the landscape, and had become a fixture in most mainstream Protestant churches. Denominational boards had centralized the management of their schools and oversaw thousands of teachers and hundreds of thousands of pupils. Denominational publishing houses were supplying much of the literature for their church Sunday schools. Supervisors and teachers depended on standardized lessons and fixed routines. Officials encouraged the use of modern management techniques to organize and run Sunday classes, believing that efficient Sunday schools would uplift southern children and reflect positively on everyone involved.[2]

However, much work remained to be done. Though evangelicals had labored hard to put a Sunday school in every southern church, many still lacked one. Rural Sunday schools in particular were often poorly housed and managed, where they existed at all. Despite their growing popularity, Sunday schools had little impact on many poor, rural southerners, who clung to traditional folkways and rejected the seemingly pretentious, middle-class values that Sunday schools tried to encourage.

Yet for millions of southerners, the Sunday school was as important at the turn of the century as it had been in the aftermath of the Civil War. Both in Sunday school and in the church, individuals found hope and strength as they faced a modern world. Myriad problems plagued the region. The South's agrarian economy—dependent upon cash crops, sharecropping, and tenant farming—meant that for many people, life remained virtually unchanged since the Civil War. Though cotton prices had fallen, landowners remained wedded to this crop that had once brought the region so much wealth. In many areas, soils were exhausted; increasing debt and crop lien meant a tenuous existence for farm families. The depression that began in 1893 heightened the region's economic woes, as did the nation's dwindling money supply. Railroads and powerful corporations gained more control over the economy, leaving farmers and workers feeling powerless. A weak federal government did little to correct the precarious economic situation. Black and white farmers turned to cooperative alliances to help them deal with the crisis. The rise and rapid demise of the Populist Party in the 1890s left many with unrealized dreams of a changed social and political landscape.

2. Paul Harvey also argues that evangelicals were agreeable to modernization because they used business-oriented agencies to conduct their affairs and approached Sunday school work in a modern, rational manner. The SBC adopted the "technologies, if not the theology, of modernity." Harvey, *Redeeming the South,* 31, 78 (quote, 31).

The emergence of a modern, fast-paced world troubled many southerners and aroused intense fears that are difficult to fathom today. "The earth around is fraught with the inspiration of progress," wrote a worried Alabama Baptist. "Society is moved by a dashing and heaving and a confused whirl of elements hitherto unknown." Many evangelicals equated a modern world with a more sinful one. Presbyterians, for example, urged active resistance to the icy winds of modernity. "Everything that wealth and worldliness and godlessness can do to hinder and harm the church is being done, and we have a great and arduous struggle before us," they explained. Methodists were equally alarmed, citing the presence of a "subtle, alluring, materialistic spirit that is affecting our homes." Cities were producing a "moral stupor" that was the "breeding grounds of anarchy and vice." Problems that had once been confined to the urban Northeast have "recently become acute in the South," they noted. Nearly everyone was affected by the consequences of industrialization. Railroads penetrated small towns, expanding the boundaries of rural communities; national markets, rather than local merchants, influenced product demand and price. Some families abandoned farming and gravitated to southern towns or mill villages, seeking paid employment and better opportunities for their children. Men desperate for jobs left their families to work in mining or timber camps. The lure of city and town life enticed young people from home. Southern cities faced the problems inherent in a burgeoning population. Though the most profound changes of the late nineteenth century—immigration, urbanization, and industrialization—had less impact overall on the South than on the Northeast, southerners witnessed significant change, responding with alarm as they tried to make sense of their new world.[3]

Southerners were not the only ones concerned about the state of their country. By the 1890s, a number of Americans began actively to confront the nation's ills. Groups of middle-class, progressive reformers battled urgent, large-scale issues, such as monopolistic business practices, government corruption, excess alcohol consumption, the inferior status of

3. "Report on Periodicals," *Minutes of the 69th Annual Session of the Alabama Baptist Association* (Montgomery: Baptist Job Print, 1888), 7; *Annual Conference of the Methodist Episcopal Church, South, 1906;* "Narrative of the State of Religion," *General Assembly of the Presbyterian Church in the U.S., 1891* (Richmond: Presbyterian Committee of Publication, 1891), 263; Ownby, *Subduing Satan*, 210–1; Ayers, *Promise of the New South*, 413–22.

women, exploitative child labor, squalid urban housing, and prostitution. Muckrakers worked passionately to alert Americans to the dangers of unhealthy food, urban corruption, unethical corporate practices, and hazardous working conditions. Progressive reformers set up organizations, gathered statistics and information, held conferences to study particular problems, aired their findings, and took action. No problem avoided their sharp eye. The dangers of gambling, dance halls, and even merry-go-rounds caught their attention.[4]

In some sense, the southern Sunday school paralleled the goals of progressive reform as it sought to uplift the nation's number one progressive concern—its children. Like so many progressive endeavors, Sunday school work often began at a grassroots level. Like progressive reformers, Sunday school workers had well-defined goals and often adopted an interventionist approach to educate and uplift individuals. Increasingly, Sunday schools engaged in a form of "social Christianity," encouraging members to address some of the same social concerns that progressive reformers did, such as temperance and outreach programs for the poor. On the other hand, the ultimate concern of both black and white Sunday schools was to bring children to God—not political, economic, or social issues. Sunday school officials fervently hoped that by saving souls and improving personal behavior, social reform would come as a matter of course.[5]

Evangelical southerners were all too aware of what they perceived as a growing "spiritual sterility" or religious decline throughout the region. A sinful, modern world seemed to be spinning out of human control. Defiant youngsters, a "city craze," and temptations such as the automobile lured young people away from the spiritual joys of Sunday school and church. As disheartened black Baptists despaired, "The average young men and women are not as religious as in former years. They care less about Sunday school, less about the church, less about any kind of reli-

---

4. For background on the late-nineteenth-century South, see Ayers, *Promise of the New South;* Wilson, *Baptized in Blood;* Richard L. McCormick, "Public Life in Industrial America, 1877–1917," in *The New American History,* ed. Eric Foner (Philadelphia: Temple University Press, 1990), 93–117; Nell Painter, *Standing at Armageddon: The United States, 1877–1919* (New York: W. W. Norton, 1987); Silber, *Romance of Reunion;* Lears, *No Place of Grace,* xvii; Foster, *Ghosts of the Confederacy,* 6, 79–80.

5. See Robert Wiebe, *A Search for Order, 1877–1920* (New York: Hill and Wang, 1967), vii; Ayers, *Promise of the New South,* 171.

gious meeting." Sunday school volunteers now had to work harder than ever to ensure the weekly attendance at church and Sunday school that would strengthen every family's faith. Youngsters needed to learn and live by Scripture in order to save themselves from a world run amok.[6]

Theological debates in northern seminaries and churches also generated uneasiness among southern evangelicals. AME bishop H. M. Turner called his era an "age of the most dare-devil skepticism . . . a mass of philosophical abstractions." Nearly all southerners recoiled at the dangerous doctrines of nihilism and socialism; but to evangelicals, worse was yet to come. Liberal scholars in the Northeast began to dissect and question the Bible, pondering its meaning and analyzing its content. Scientific, rational thinking based on Darwin's theory of evolution challenged scriptural views that many southerners took as fact. Horrified that anyone would challenge the inerrancy of the Bible, evangelicals castigated such intellectual endeavors as misguided challenges to the fundamentals of faith. A white Southern Methodist lamented that a "materialistic and Godless idea of education" had done incalculable harm to his church. Though he and others bemoaned the rising tide of religious skepticism, the thorny issue of the inerrancy of the Bible had little direct impact on Sunday schools—or on most southerners, for that matter. Intellectual issues were ill suited for Sunday lessons. Troubled evangelicals might denounce these religious, scholarly debates and use them as another argument for simple, straightforward Bible instruction: Scripture should always be the guide for a child's future. Fears surrounding the potential impact these issues might have on one's faith may have motivated individuals to work even harder for the Sunday school cause.[7]

Though the South never experienced first hand the flood of immigrants who came to America around the turn of the century (and who mostly settled in the Northeast), southerners worried nonetheless about foreigners inundating the region. A number of Europeans gravitated to southern cities like St. Louis, New Orleans, Galveston, and Birmingham, which to some degree began to resemble the crime-ridden, filthy, crowded cities in the Northeast. Yet southerners were not of one mind about for-

6. "Report of the Executive Board," *Minutes of 38th Annual Session of the Baptist State Sunday School Convention of North Carolina (Negro)* (n.p., 1910), 22.

7. Bishop H. M. Turner, "Letter," *AME Church Review* 1 (1884): 46; Washington Conference and Mattawskeet Circuit Conference, *Minutes of the North Carolina District Conference Reports of the Methodist Episcopal Church, South*, 1897, Duke.

eigners. Some regarded them as a blight on the landscape. AME member J. Allen Viney saw foreigners "filling up our country, bringing ideas and customs detrimental and uncongenial to the healthy growth of our civil, political and religious institutions." Like many African Americans, Viney viewed immigrants as competitors in a limited job market. Other southerners exhibited more sympathy, seeing immigrants as God's children who needed nurturing and exposure to evangelical Protestantism. They encouraged churches to expand their home mission programs, teach Scripture and middle-class values to foreigners, and expose them to a "Christian civilization in America." Mission Sunday schools for immigrant children were widely seen as the best means to convey Protestant ideals, in the hope that young pupils would become good Christians and good Americans, passing on what they learned to their parents.[8]

Another nationwide issue incorporated into the Sunday school curriculum was the "boy problem." Dramatic rhetoric expressed in sermons, essays, books, and newspapers expanded this concern to one of epidemic proportions by the turn of the century. Americans concluded that males seemed to be an endangered, almost pitiful species, headed for certain ruin. Statistics indicated that young men under twenty committed more than two-thirds of all crimes nationwide. Scholarly studies on young men (a field called "boyology") showed that military recruits in the Spanish-American War were a weak, sickly lot. Experts partly blamed soldiers' underperformance on the deleterious effects of tobacco, alcohol, and fast living, "wrecking their constitution, destroying their intellects and damning their souls." To serious, self-disciplined evangelicals, such behavior was reckless self-indulgence. In recognition of the crisis, Florida Baptists labeled the intermediate male department the "death pit" of their Sunday schools. By the age of fifteen or sixteen, many boys left Sunday school and church altogether. Males at the prime age for conversion were thus lost, and there seemed to be little chance to save young men and resurrect

---

8. William P. Paxson to George Graves, 1868, St. Louis, ASSU Correspondence, PHS; J. Allen Viney, "Sunday-Schools," *AME Church Review* 7 (1891): 314; "Christianize America," *Minutes of the 33rd Annual Session of the Jacksonville (Fla.) Baptist Association* (Jacksonville: Baptist Association, 1911): 16–7. See also Samuel Tyndale Wilson, *The Southern Mountaineers* (New York: Presbyterian Home Missions, 1906), 97–102; Silber, *Romance of Reunion*, 142; Deborah V. McCauley, *Appalachian Mountain Religion: A History* (Urbana: University of Illinois Press, 1995); "The American Outlook," *Tennessee Outlook*, 25 February 1897.

the South. Clergy were especially upset, because without young men they would be hard pressed to fill the ranks of the ministry. Boys were the nation's future hope, but also one of its greatest concerns.[9]

Males seemed to have fallen victim to a host of sins. According to popular thought, alcoholism, masturbation, and a loss of masculinity threatened young men and portended disaster for the nation. Heightened fears over homosexuality—due in part to a more visible gay culture in northern cities—shook a nation that prided itself on its masculine identity. The "feminization" of public and Sunday schools was also worrisome. Americans now took note of surveys and reports that confirmed the overwhelmingly female membership in churches and Sunday schools. "In many of them not a single young man was to be seen," noted one black Baptist. African Americans despaired over their young men, whom they counted on to uplift the race. "The hope of a race, of a nation, is the boys," asserted Bishop George Clinton. Those like Reverend J. W. Smith abandoned all hope for male adolescents who deserted family and church, drifted to cities, lived dissolute lives, and became "rampant infidels who doubt everything and profess to believe in nothing." Alarmists pointed to the fact that boys spent their childhood almost exclusively in the company of women. With few male teachers, boys lacked mentors who could help them assert their masculinity. To many Americans, the nation's feminine identity had reached crisis proportions.[10]

The "boy problem" demanded an explanation. Some blacks attributed it to wider social problems, such as the paucity of jobs, low wages, and the ongoing battle for existence. Bishop Clinton urged his church members to live simply, telling Christian mothers to raise their children right by sending them to church and Sunday school. He blamed parents who favored daughters over sons. Males seemed to be shortchanged at

---

9. See William Byron Forbush, *The Boy Problem*, 6th ed. (Boston: Pilgrim Press, 1907); Ownby, *Subduing Satan*, 21–102; Silber, *Romance of Reunion*, 167–8; E. Anthony Rotundo, "Boy Culture: Middle-Class Boyhood in Nineteenth Century America," and Clyde Griffin, "Reconstructing Masculinity from the Evangelical Revival to the Waning of Progressivism: A Speculative Analysis," both in *Meanings for Manhood*, ed. Carnes and Griffin, 15–36 and 191–200; Kimmel, *Manhood in America*, esp. 81–188.

10. "Presidential Address," *Minutes of the 37th Annual Baptist State Sunday School Convention of North Carolina (Negro)* (n.p., 1909), 22; J. W. Smith, "Growing Evils," *Star of Zion*, 7 November 1889; "Editorials," *Christian Index*, 31 August 1889. See also Avery, *Behold the Child*, 184.

home, in Sunday school, and in church—a response that in part reflected women's growing involvement in volunteer activities, benevolent reform efforts, and church work. Articles in church publications such as "Are We Threatened by a Feminine Christianity?" fed such fears.[11]

Sunday schools dealt with the "boy problem" by focusing more attention on males. Weekly lessons featured male heroes who behaved well and rejected sinful temptations. Boys were featured in stories such as "The Child Colporteur" and "A Good Sabbath School Boy," and they invariably displayed ideal traits such as integrity, honesty, and humility. Sunday school stories showed young men pursuing sports and boys' games, working hard, reading their Bibles, and shunning alcohol and tobacco. Tales adopted a military tone to suggest the compatibility of masculinity with Christianity. Rarely, though, did these stories exhibit the rough-and-tumble hyper-masculinity found in popular westerns and dime novels. Instead, Sunday lessons encouraged boys to become teachers, pastors, and fathers when they grew up.[12]

This focus on young men was part of a movement that came to be known as Muscular Christianity. At issue was the need to present a more vigorous, manly image of Christianity and Jesus. Boys needed to learn that there was nothing sissy about emulating him. Emma Sasser urged young men to imitate Jesus and other men in the Bible. "If our young men would be truly great, let them follow these illustrious men," she exhorted. "The world is calling for men of brain and power to remember that the past is shouting to them to be noble and great." A Methodist urged the formation of classes where boys could discuss their bodies with a "conservative Christian physician." Advisors urged Sunday schools to build gymnasiums, and they suggested more classroom competitions and games so that boys would beg to come to Sunday school. Male interests needed to be center stage.[13]

---

11. "Presidential Address," *Minutes of the 37th Annual Session,* 20; Clinton, "Extracts from Talk," 2; "Are We Threatened by a Feminine Christianity?" *Current Literature* 42 (1907): 420.

12. "To the Boys," *Children's Friend,* 4 September 1886; "A Boy's Religion," *Children's Friend,* 4 June 1887; S. Walter McGill, "How to Retain Our Hold upon the Boys?" *Proceedings of the 32nd Annual Conference of the Kentucky Sunday School Union* (Louisville: KSSU, 1897), 51.

13. Emma W. Sasser, "Where Are Our Young Men?" *Minutes of the 23rd Annual Session of the Baptist State Sunday School Convention of North Carolina (Negro), 1895* (Ra-

Part of the "boy problem" in Sunday school was not a male issue at all, but the fact that Sunday schools traditionally were associated with young children; they had trouble attracting and retaining adolescents and young adults, especially males. To woo them, in the late nineteenth century denominations began to found youth organizations and Bible study groups. National organizations such as Christian Endeavors, Epworth Leagues, Baracas, and Varick Christian Endeavor Societies established southern chapters and gained a youthful following. These groups were the next logical step in Christian education and offered activities that appealed to a more mature audience. Groups met weekly for prayer sessions and Bible study and sponsored coeducational social activities such as picnics, hayrides, and holiday dinners. Members engaged in service projects by tutoring, teaching at mission Sunday schools, or preparing monthly meals for orphaned children. By the early twentieth century, several Sunday school boards had altered their names and expanded their responsibilities to include young adult societies.

Denominational loyalty, which had been increasing for decades, began to define southern religious life by the turn of the century. The dwindling number of northern missionaries in the South lessened the regional competition that had motivated missionaries and laypeople to work hard for the Sunday school cause. Southern denominational Sunday school boards and publishing houses still competed with one another and maintained their pace of recruitment, keeping volunteers busy and sustaining growth. But churches now began to focus inward to locate potential Sunday scholars, and officials expanded the boundaries of Sunday school membership. Everyone, not just children, needed what the Sunday school had to offer.[14]

Significant changes in the Sunday school population thus occurred by the early twentieth century. Adult pupils were recruited; special classes and separate Sunday school departments were organized for them. The inclusion of older pupils was not new; some adults had attended Sunday school for years. After the Civil War, freedmen of all ages came to Sunday

---

leigh: Edwards and Broughton), 34; Henry F. Cope, "The Man in the Sunday School," *Sunday School Magazine* 39 (January 1909): 7; "More about the Boy's Body," *Sunday School Magazine* 30 (April 1910): 131. See also E. Anthony Rotundo, *American Manhood: Transformations in Masculinity from the Revolution to the Modern Era* (New York: Basic Books, 1993), 224; Kimmel, *Manhood in America,* 175–9.

14. Schweiger, "Transformation of Southern Religion," 354.

school in order to learn to read, and some grown-ups attended because they wanted to participate in programmed Bible study or to enjoy the company of young people. A few classes included a wide range of ages, such as the Reverend William L. Johnson's Sunday school, which included pupils from five to sixty years of age. Overall, though, adults had not been a focus of Sunday school recruitment nor a significant percentage of school membership before the 1880s.[15]

Sunday school leaders encountered some problems as they began to reach out to adult pupils. It was one thing to meet youngsters' needs; grown-ups offered a greater challenge. Adult classes had to appeal to a wide range of mature tastes and varied backgrounds. Adult minds were less pliable than a child's; they tended to be more critical and demanding. Determining what lessons would best meet adult needs and how to keep them interested were not easy tasks for Sunday school teachers.[16]

The inclusion of adult students meant that the definition of Sunday school and the justification for its existence had to change. In their zeal to attract children, Sunday school leaders often had depicted adults as hopeless, beyond salvation, and lacking the innocence of youth. Grown-ups seemed too worldly, too scarred by life to open their hearts and minds to Sunday lessons. Such attitudes had to be discarded. In addition, the inclusion of adult students necessitated alterations in the language of church doctrine and Sunday school constitutions. A Sunday school could no longer be called a "nursery" of the church. For example, instead of "children," Sunday school officials now referred to "persons," "individuals," or "scholars"—terms that avoided any hint of age. Denominational leaders went out of their way to encourage their Sunday schools to open their doors to all ages. The southern Sunday school, declared one official, had "ceased to be a child's institution" and now embraced everyone.[17]

---

15. William L. Johnson comments in a report by T. H. Legare to Maurice A. Wurts, 12 April 1880, Orangeburg, S.C., ASSU Correspondence, PHS. For background on adult Sunday schools, see Charles W. Brewbaker, *The Adult Program in the Church School* (New York: Fleming H. Revell, 1925); William E. Niblette, "The Adult Sunday School Movement: History with Design," *Christian Education Journal* 5 (1984): 29–36.

16. W. C. Barclay, "Adult Department," *Encyclopedia of Sunday Schools*, vol. 1, 11.

17. Leftwich, *Child in the Midst*, 9–10; "Report of Committee on Sunday Schools," *Proceedings of the 33rd Annual Session of the Baptist Convention of Western North Carolina, 1889* (Asheville: Randolph-Kerr, 1890), 20.

Indeed, evangelicals believed that adults needed Biblical instruction as much as children did. Since children who attended Sunday school often went to church, there was a certain reciprocal logic to the idea that church-going adults should attend Sunday school. No one ever outgrew Sunday school lessons, insisted Georgia Baptists, for "none are so wise that they have no need to be taught, and we are never too old to learn." Some officials saw adults as an exciting new field for evangelical work that could reinvigorate the Sunday school movement, offering eager volunteers something else to do. As self-satisfied National Baptists admitted in 1908, their work among children had "almost reached its limits"; and many grown-ups who had never attended Sunday school in their youth now desired the Christian education they lacked. Other evangelicals argued that the opportunity to pursue Bible study gave grown-ups an exposure to scriptural knowledge they could not acquire in church. After all, preachers did not teach or discuss; they exhorted. Adult Sunday classes also could address topics inappropriate for the worship service, such as child nurturing, home economics, and community uplift. Many evangelicals believed that domestic life and individual behavior would improve if families spent their Sundays engaged in religious activities. Even devout, church-going adults should be in Sunday school, for though the sinner needed saving, the saved should never be ignored. Moreover, unlike public schools, Sunday schools offered eternal messages. At every age and stage in life, proponents argued, one needed to be in touch with God.[18]

Church officials soon recognized the benefits that adult pupils brought to Sunday school. Parents could better assist their offspring with weekly Bible assignments and help them improve performance. A parent's presence could inspire (or enforce) attendance from the young, especially from those adolescents who liked to slip out of class or who never showed up in the first place. Mothers would know exactly where their children were every Sunday and what they were studying. Youngsters whose parents attended Sunday school allegedly were better behaved. "By their own behavior they afford the only proper example for the conduct of their tender offspring who is to come after them," insisted Baptist James Harvey Joiner. The financial benefits of adult pupils were obvious.

18. Quote in Gardner et al., *History of the Georgia Baptist Association,* 228; "The Development of the Adult Department," *National Baptist Union,* 11 January 1908.

Every new Sunday school member meant additional monetary contributions and more readers of denominational publications.[19]

Though the level of adult participation in Sunday schools by 1915 is unknown, it is likely that a larger percentage of adults in the South attended Sunday school than in other areas of the country, especially considering the popularity of adult Sunday schools in the region today. Then as now, these classes emphasized the importance of family religion and reinforced a family model that often typified the southern social structure. Like the family labor system of cotton mill workers and farmers, in which men, women, and children all worked, adult Sunday schools preserved family cohesion, allowing an entire family to participate in a similar religious activity each week. In addition, adult classes also were a social outlet that rural southerners must have relished. And since many country churches still did not hold regular weekly worship services, the Sunday school became an acceptable substitute. Volunteers provided Bible instruction, with or without a minister present.[20]

Adults were not the only target for evangelicals; Sunday school officials also reached out to attract the very young. Formerly, infants and toddlers had seemed too restless and immature to attend class, much less absorb the Bible or learn Scripture. Southerners generally assumed that children under four should stay at home; any mother who sent her very young children to Sunday school was criticized as merely wanting a respite from her brood. The best age to begin Sunday school, officials believed, was five or six. Propelled by the fear that youngsters or their parents might be attracted to a rival faith, however, church officials began to insist that young children and infants be enrolled in Sunday school. They reasoned that to wait until a child reached a particular age could mean that he or she was lost to another denomination or, worse yet, lost forever. Though Sunday school teachers rightly questioned young children's ability to learn Scripture, they became convinced that a commitment at birth made sense.[21]

The Cradle Roll Department, created specifically for newborns, be-

---

19. Joiner, "Speech to the Sunday School Meeting."
20. McHugh, *Mill Family*, 97; Hall et al., *Like a Family*.
21. J. L., "Infant Classes in Sunday School," *Sunday School Magazine* 4 (1874): 228. Some of this interest reflected the nation's growing interest in educating young children in kindergarten.

came a regular feature of southern Sunday schools by the turn of the century. To enroll, a mother merely placed her infant's name on a special roll sheet and received a certificate symbolizing the baby's membership in Sunday school. The department had no specific meeting time or place. Its volunteers visited homes and sometimes worked with mothers to ensure sound parenting and home worship. Yet even infants and toddlers generated new money-making opportunities for denominational publishing firms. For instance, Southern Presbyterians sold birthday gifts, post cards, and greeting cards aimed at one-, two- and three-year-olds. Special teaching tools geared toward toddlers included lesson leaflets with simple illustrations from the Bible. Here was another bet on future rewards, since the department served as a feeder to the main Sunday school. Sometimes even present rewards were forthcoming. One Arkansas man was so impressed to see his infant's name on the Cradle Roll that he and his wife promptly joined the church.[22]

The Home Department was another innovation. Its purpose was to serve individuals physically unable to attend Sunday school, such as housebound mothers, the physically challenged, the sick, the elderly, prisoners, nurses, and household servants—anyone who could not make it to class. The Reverend C. O. Jones of Louisville, with a bit of levity, claimed that it reached out to those who suffered from the disease "*morbus sabbaticus.*" But most Sunday school workers took this endeavor seriously. Volunteers canvassed neighborhoods and followed up on referrals to locate potential members. Again, this department brought financial benefits to the denomination. Homebound pupils purchased church literature in order to keep up with the weekly lesson, thus assisting the publishing firm. Pupils made a weekly donation. The department allowed members to remain at home each Sunday with a clear conscience. No one escaped the lengthening arm of the Sunday school.[23]

22. W. H. Dodd, "The Infant Class in the Sabbath School," *Baptist State Sunday School Convention of North Carolina, 1874* (Raleigh: Edwards, Broughton, 1875), 37; Cuninggim and North, *Organization and Administration*, 136–7; Black, *Practical Primary Plans for Primary Teachers,* 121; "Cradle Roll," *Earnest Worker,* June 1906.

23. C. O. Jones, "What Can the Sunday School Do for Those Who Must Stay at Home?" *Minutes of the 28th Annual Session of the Kentucky Sunday School Union* (Louisville: John P. Morton, 1893), 77; Annie Armstrong to James Marion Frost, 17 September 1896, Baltimore, Md., Frost-Bell Correspondence, SBHLA. See also E. A. Fox, *The Pastor's Place of Privilege and Power in the Sunday School* (Nashville: Publishing House of the

Around the turn of the century, Sunday schools also began to adopt a number of new methods in order to become more efficient and successful. The improved and streamlined Sunday school operations were a far cry from the more casual approach to organizing classes decades earlier. Sunday school boards began to employ modern business and scientific management practices and to mimic some of the organizational methods used in public schools and society at large. This approach was not lost on volunteers. One man equated the Sunday school of twenty-five years ago to an old-time country store, with everything stocked on one shelf "in mixed confusion." He likened the modern Sunday school to a department store, with a perfect assortment of goods found in well-ordered departments, under competent management, and "running like clock work."[24]

One important step toward improving efficiency was to quantify every activity. Running a successful Sunday school, like a successful corporation, meant that keeping accurate statistics was essential. As E. N. Woodruff queried, "If, then, statistics can be and is [sic] used with profit in the affairs of the world, why may not we use it with equal, yes, with greater profit in the work of the Sunday School?" In their popular Sunday school advice manual, Jesse Cuninggim and Eric North stressed the need for careful recordkeeping. Like modern companies, a Sunday school had to know where it stood and where it was headed. Statistics could highlight a school's shortcomings and help determine where new schools were needed. Publishing houses could gain a better sense of the bottom line, know which publications sold well and which ones did not, and identify new markets. Supervisors and editors were held accountable for quantifying every Sunday school activity.[25]

Recording statistics was not a new undertaking; some superintendents and teachers had kept track of weekly proceedings for years. However, previous efforts had been haphazard and depended on individual initiative. Some teachers scrupulously recorded attendance, the lesson topic,

---

MECS, 1907), 152; Lilian Stevenson Forbes, *The Home Department of the Sunday School* (Nashville: Sunday School Board of the SBC, 1916), 7–8.

24. Walter N. Vernon et al., *The Methodist Excitement in Texas: A History* (Dallas: Texas United Methodist History Society, 1984), 248.

25. E. N. Woodruff, "The Great Importance of Statistics," *Kentucky Sunday-School Union Reporter* 2 (May 1894): 5; Cuninggim and North, *Organization and Administration*, 109, 135.

and even the weather. Others did nothing. Inconsistency was no longer acceptable; the collecting of information had to be reliable and systematic. Every event demanded precise tabulation if the Sunday school was to thrive.

To make this task easier for Sunday school officials, publishing firms produced and sold special ledgers in which supervisors responded to a standard set of questions, filling in the blanks and submitting data to their Sunday school board. A uniform approach helped officials identify which schools were not doing well and encourage better performance. Sunday school boards came down hard on schools that ignored this task. Southern Presbyterians were continually frustrated by incomplete or nonexistent statistics from their Sunday schools. Year after year, officers complained when schools and synods failed to submit the required data. Finally, the Presbyterian Sunday school board took action; it began to publish the names of individual schools that ignored their recordkeeping responsibilities. Perhaps unsurprisingly, more complete information was forthcoming. From the array of collected data, publishing firms annually began to print detailed figures revealing attendance and donation records. Church members were now better informed about denominational Sunday school work, and Sunday school officials could compare their accomplishments to others.

Another step that led to more efficient Sunday schools was the introduction and standardization of graded classes, separating pupils by age. Large Sunday schools had been dividing pupils by age into manageably sized sections for years. By the late nineteenth century, segregating students by age became standard procedure in all but the smallest Sunday schools. Officers studied how public schools separated classes by age and began to do the same. This step met with some resistance by critics who saw it as yet another effort to standardize and homogenize Sunday schools. Yet officials argued that graded classes fulfilled orders from above, for "Sunday Schools must be graded because God has graded human life."[26]

Sunday school boards established departments and committees to oversee graded classes. A modern Sunday school was divided vertically into the following categories, with someone in charge of each department:

26. Cuninggim and North, *Organization and Administration*, 26.

> Cradle Roll, infants to 3 years old
> Beginner, children 4 to 5 years old
> Primary, 6 to 8 years old
> Junior, 9 to 12 years old (separated by gender)
> Intermediate, 13 to 16 years old (separated by gender)
> Senior, 17 to 20 years old
> Adult, 21 and older.

This plan increased the bureaucratic character of Sunday school operations. But it delivered the hopeful message that pupils could be happily ensconced in Sunday school their entire lives.[27]

Graded classes and departments demanded standardized graded lessons, "to meet the spiritual needs of the pupil at each stage of his development." The uniform lesson plan used for years would no longer suffice. In fact, a graded plan had been considered during the debate over uniform lessons in the 1870s but apparently had been set aside in the interests of national uniformity and harmony. Sunday school officials and teachers began to insist that in order for lessons to fit the structure of graded classrooms, they had to be written to suit various age groups.[28]

Critics charged that the problem with uniform lessons was that they lived up to their name, failing to accommodate the wide range of students now in Sunday school. Teachers of primary classes found the material too difficult for their youngest pupils. Older students found the lessons elementary and boring. Some teachers adjusted lessons to fit their class, perhaps rewriting them in their entirety and inventing new questions. Some denominations, frustrated by the uniform system, had already begun preparing and printing a supplemental lesson plan, graded questions, and Bible commentaries.

In 1908, the ISSA officially adopted a graded lesson plan for Sunday schools nationwide, a new approach that created seventeen different lessons, each geared to a different age. This step elicited intense controversy

---

27. James Alexander Mitchell, *The Normal Manual of Modern Sunday School Method*, vol. 1, *Method in Management* (Memphis: Memphis Sunday School Publishing, 1919), 29–36.

28. Edwin Barfield Chappell, *Introduction and Use of the Graded Lessons: International Series, General Manual* (Nashville: Publishing House of the MECS, 1914), 16. See also Ira M. Price, "Graded Lessons, International, History of the," *Encyclopedia of Sunday Schools*, vol. 2, 469–71.

in the South and led to, as the *Encyclopedia of Sunday Schools* dryly noted, "serious difficulties" in southern Sunday school ranks. Although some of its members objected, the National Baptists were largely accepting of the plan, reasoning that they could prepare a supplemental outline that allowed teachers to adapt the week's lesson to church doctrine. White Baptists, Methodists, and Presbyterians were far more critical. They objected to the absence of doctrine, the inclusion of extra-biblical lessons, the failure to include topics they felt were important, and the attempts to interpret Scripture. Some teachers, especially in small schools, found the seventeen new categories far too complicated. Others saw the age divisions as artificial. Some southerners complained that in the rush to create this new system, lessons were hastily written and poorly structured. Publishing firms objected to the expense of printing so many different lessons in their magazines. Southern Presbyterians, who had already begun producing their own graded supplements, had no use for the new version.[29]

With their longstanding concerns over denominational and regional loyalty, southern evangelicals seemed likely to complain about anything that northerners promoted and produced. Southern Methodists, who were especially interested in social issues, complained that the lessons slighted important concerns such as church history, temperance, and dance hall reform. "The social plagues which threaten our very life should have their proper treatment in our lesson courses," insisted Methodist William Mouzon Brabham. He ranted, "The places where our young people spend their spare time, the things which make them dissatisfied, the conditions of health, roads, public schools, and such matters is [*sic*] not beyond the scope of our study in connection with the Sunday School." But regional issues were not the problem for Southern Methodists, who soon entered a cooperative venture—a "Graded Lesson Syndicate"—with northern Protestants to prepare suitable graded courses. Complaints from the South did force the ISSA to modify its original program. In an attempt to please all parties, the ISSA lesson committee met

29. Price, "Graded Lessons," 471; "Baptist Doctrines and the Sunday School," *National Baptist Union*, 17 April 1909; Benson, *Popular History of Christian Education*, 211; Alexander Leroy Phillips, ed., *The Westminster Standard Teacher Training Course. First Standard Course* (Richmond: Presbyterian Committee of Publication, 1912), 160; Frank Glenn Lankard, *A History of the American Sunday School Curriculum* (New York: Abingdon Press, 1927), 201–2, 276.

and drew up a supplemental plan. Yet this new plan also proved unacceptable to many. In 1911, Southern Baptists appointed a committee to produce their own graded lessons.[30]

Around this time, Sunday school boards also began to draft standards of excellence by which to assess each of their Sunday schools. The sheer number of Sunday schools made it impossible for denominations to rely on traveling ministers and missionaries to keep an eye on every school, as they had done in the past. Instead, churches outlined expectations, established written standards, and insisted that Sunday schools strive to achieve them. Every school had to be held accountable to the highest ideals.

In 1910, Alexander L. Phillips produced "A Model Presbyterian Sunday School," which outlined the steps necessary to forming an excellent school. His checklist covered twenty areas, including the condition of the library, the level of giving, the use of denominational literature, and the amount of time a class spent on Bible study. In an ideal school, according to Phillips, each grade should have a separate room, which should be supplied with maps, charts, a blackboard, and musical instruments. A volunteer librarian should be on staff. Pupils also were to attend church faithfully. Harvey Beauchamp introduced a similar concept in his "AA–1 Standards of Excellence" for white Southern Baptist Sunday schools. Many Sunday school officers used Beauchamp's standards to rate their own schools, and the SBC publishing house awarded certificates and banners to those that measured up to his ideals. This approach not only improved classroom conditions but fostered a more uniform approach in all denominational Sunday schools and encouraged students to work together to achieve special recognition for their school.[31]

---

30. Brabham, *Sunday School Work in Town and Country,* 78–9. See also James Roger Skelton, "The Development of the Grading Program in Southern Baptist Sunday Schools" (Ph.D. diss., Southwestern Baptist Theology Seminary, Fort Worth, Tex., 1957), 91–9; Grant, "The Sunday School Movement in America," 34–6; Chappell, *Introduction and Use of the Graded Lessons,* 41, and *Recent Development of Religious Education,* 77–8; Executive Committee of Publication, General Assembly of the Presbyterian Church in the U.S., *Concerning the International Graded Sunday School Lessons* (Richmond: Presbyterian Publishing House, 1910), 3–10, esp. 8.

31. Alexander Leroy Phillips, "A Model Presbyterian Sunday School" (Richmond: Presbyterian Committee of Publication, 1910), 3; Harvey Beauchamp, *The Advanced, or AA–1 Standard of Excellence for Sunday Schools in Baptist Churches* (Nashville: Southern Baptist Sunday School Board, 1916).

Sunday school manuals insisted on the highest standards for teachers. Supervisors were to scrutinize each teacher's character and personal life; instructors were expected to set a good example for their students. Humility was essential. As Henry Cope advised, "We want Sunday school teachers who are blameless before God in love, in fidelity, and in good works." Yet Sunday schools could hardly afford to be as exacting as advisors and officials wished. Judging by the endless lamentations of Sunday school officials, the most serious problem the institution faced continued to be a dearth of good teachers, a shortage that worsened each year. In 1890, the KSSU complained of its host of incompetent teachers. "You can find more unskilled teachers in the Sunday school ranks than in any other similar body," it moaned. The very success of the Sunday school was partly responsible for this crisis; the continued growth of Sunday schools and the introduction of graded classes had increased the demand for instructors. But it wasn't only a question of numbers; Sunday school officials' expectations rose as well. Having to meet the new standards of excellence pressured schools to find exceptional volunteers. Compared to public school instructors, Sunday school teachers fell short. Unlike public school teachers, who were trained for their profession, few Sunday school teachers had ever even taken a course in basic pedagogy. How many had read a manual outlining the best methods to conduct a class? How many teachers had read the Bible? North Carolina National Baptists struggled to find good teachers, but by 1915, they complained that 90 percent of their Sunday school instructors lacked adequate mental or spiritual training. They concluded that exhaustion, poverty, or illiteracy kept many hardworking adults from volunteering to teach Sunday classes. Sunday schools could no longer accept anyone who professed familiarity with the Bible; knowledgeable, skilled teachers—and plenty of them—were required.[32]

32. Henry Frederick Cope, *The Great Evil and Its Remedy, or Parental Responsibility in the Moral and Religious Training of Children* (Nashville: MECS Publishing House, 1889), 89; Kentucky Sunday School Union, 1890; "Report of the Corresponding Secretary," *Minutes of the 43rd Annual Session of the Baptist State Sunday School Convention of North Carolina (Negro)* (n.p., 1915), 14. See also Tillett, *Theological Seminaries and Teacher Training*, 10. William A. Link shows a similar emphasis on educated public school teachers that was often more rhetoric than reality. In 1885 in Virginia, only 27 percent of all teachers had at least a high school degree. Only 6 percent had earned a college degree. See Link, *A Hard Country and a Lonely Place*, 58–9.

Some officials tried to attract capable teachers and retain their best ones by trumpeting the rewards of the job. Methodists extolled the virtues of keeping busy, working hard, and improving one's character through such meaningful work. Southern Presbyterians praised the "zeal and energy" of their female teachers who, they claimed, bore responsibility for the "future prosperity and success" of their church. NBC officials also used positive reinforcement and enticements to attract and retain volunteers. "No field affords such grand opportunities for Christian men and women, and especially young men and women, to aid in the uplift of the people as the Sunday-school," insisted one member. Officials urged young women to pursue normal studies for a career in teaching, hoping they would also use their skills in Sunday school. To this end, some African American Sunday schools donated a portion of the weekly collection to fund scholarships to send young women to college. Sunday schools deserved the best and brightest; teaching was the Lord's work and too important to slight.[33]

Given the need to retain teachers, Sunday school officials had to cater to those who volunteered. Negative comments and unreasonable demands could discourage volunteers, so officials began to eliminate criticism and devise methods to aid novices. They urged superintendents to hold weekly teacher meetings to study the week's lesson and discuss its meaning—a suggestion that a good number of superintendents apparently adopted. A less appealing idea was to professionalize the job and attract qualified instructors by paying them a salary, as public schools did. Not surprisingly, this idea generated no enthusiasm from church officials; denominations could not afford to pay their thousands of teachers and superintendents. One of the celebrated glories of the Sunday school was its volunteer basis. Besides, officials argued, volunteers received adequate compensation by selflessly serving God and seeking the conversion and salvation of all.[34]

Sunday school boards turned to experts in pedagogy to help solve their teaching problems. By the early twentieth century, denominational Sunday school boards had established teaching institutes and hired ex-

---

33. *Presbyterian Standard*, 1903; "President's Annual Report," *Minutes of the 39th Annual Session of the North Carolina Baptist State Sunday School Convention (Negro)* (n.p., 1911), 28.

34. See W. B. Carothers, "Report," *Minutes of the 28th Annual Session of the Kentucky Sunday School Union* (Louisville: John P. Morton, 1893), 27.

perts to hold special training courses for volunteers. The idea was to attract more teachers, improve their methods of instruction, and ensure that they met minimum standards. These experts traveled nationwide, organizing conferences, delivering speeches, and presenting special classes on various aspects of teaching and Sunday school work.

Southern Methodists were especially enthusiastic about this approach. As early as 1882, a Methodist official suggested the idea of teacher-training courses, though nearly two decades passed before this became a reality. In 1902, the MECS set up a Department of Teacher Training and hired the Reverend Howard M. Hamill, an Alabama native and former field secretary of the ISSA, as its first superintendent. Hamill saw Sunday school teaching as an art. His wife, Ada, had charge of primary teaching and labored without pay. The two became pioneers in the field. In the manuals that Hamill wrote on Sunday school pedagogy, he promoted "old-time methods" in class, such as rote memorization of Scripture. Mindful of his denomination's ongoing worries about a balanced budget, Hamill emphasized the economic benefits of his work, which "from a financial point of view, is more than paying its way." Training classes increased the demand for Sunday school literature and classroom aids, and ultimately improved the economic standing of the church.[35]

The Hamills held seminars, institutes, and workshops throughout the South, often in conjunction with a Sunday school convention. Texas Methodists invited Hamill to lead their first teaching institute a year after he began his work; some five hundred volunteers attended the three-day course. In March 1907, the Florida Training School for State Sunday School Workers held its week-long conference in Tampa with Hamill in charge. Advertisements promised that the event would be both "exciting and useful." A local resident, Will Pegram, predicted that the Sunday school conference "will mean a great deal for Sunday schools here and I hope to attend every night." After hearing Hamill's lecture on "The Big Boy," Pegram pronounced it a "fine talk." The Hamills also lectured on Sunday school music, Bible study, primary and junior work, and missionary work. In the evenings, conference participants heard papers on "The

35. Heriges, "From the Bishop's Address," and "Sunday School Legislation," 86; Howard M. Hamill, *The Sunday-School Teacher* (Nashville: Publishing House of the MECS, 1906), ii; Hamill, *Sunday-School Teacher-Training* (Philadelphia: Sunday School Times, 1904), 93; Chappell, *Recent Development of Religious Education*, 122–4. Newspapers and convention programs reveal the Hamills' extremely busy schedule until they retired in 1915.

Negro Problem," "The Baby and Its Friends," "World Wide Sunday Schools," and "Service of Song." Participants like Pegram felt rewarded and informed, and Florida Methodists must have been pleased. Hamill's endeavors in the United States were so successful that the MECS sent him and his wife to Korea and Japan to work with Sunday school teachers there.[36]

Southern Baptists made a similar commitment to a teaching department. Bernard Washington Spilman of the North Carolina Baptist State Sunday School Convention became its first field secretary. Spilman's book, *Normal Studies for Sunday School Workers,* was recommended for all Baptist teachers. After reading it, instructors took an exam on its contents and received a certificate testifying to their mastery of the material. In a shift away from the denomination's emphasis on independent local churches, white Southern Baptists encouraged their Sunday school teachers to use similar instructional methods and purchase only denominational literature. Uniformity of thought and loyalty to the church and publishing house were paramount.[37]

To introduce future ministers to Sunday school work and foster enthusiasm for the institution, theological seminaries began to offer courses and establish departments in Sunday school pedagogy. In 1904, Southern Methodists began a fundraising drive to raise $50,000 to endow a chair in the field of Sunday school pedagogy at Vanderbilt University. They turned to their 15,000 Sunday schools to contribute liberally. Similarly, the Baptist Theological Seminary in Louisville established a Chair of Sunday School Pedagogy in 1906 to expose future Baptist ministers to Christian education and Sunday school work. Both denominations understood the significant role that ministers could play in Sunday school education.[38]

---

36. "State Sunday School Convention," *Tennessee Methodist,* 8 December 1896; "Sunday School," *Minutes of the 37th Annual Methodist Episcopal Church, South, North West Texas Conference* (Bowie: North Texas Conference, 1902), 35, Duke; "Florida International Training School Program, 1907," and Will Pegram to Irene Pegram, 5 and 12 March 1907, Tampa, Fla., both in Craven-Pegram Family Papers, Duke.

37. Bernard Washington Spilman, *Normal Studies for Sunday School Workers* (Nashville: Sunday School Board, SBC, 1901); Frost, *Sunday School Board,* 61; Fitch, "Major Thrusts," 17–30.

38. Heriges, "Sunday School Legislation," 72; Chappell, *Recent Development,* 141; Heriges, "Sunday School Legislation," 76; Tillett, *Theological Seminaries,* 6. By 1906, Southern Methodists had raised $17,000 for the chair. It took ten years to raise the $50,000, and during the effort, Vanderbilt became alienated from the MECS. The denomination turned to Emory College and Southern Methodist University and split the money

By the turn of the century, the attention and resources given to the physical setting and appearance of Sunday schools reflected their elevated status in the church and community. In part, this reflected an overall upgrading of church structures throughout the South as churches gained a stronger financial footing. Many of the faithful wanted to celebrate God in grand style and display the wealth of their congregation. "When architecture is made beautiful, cathedrals spacious, and financial systems are extensive and flourishing," wrote Methodist Wilbur F. Glenn, "all for the uplifting of mankind and the promotion of the kingdom of righteousness, then we may look for enrichment in the lives of our citizens." Erecting large, handsome buildings was a means to attract and retain followers. Only a few decades earlier, teachers had often scrambled to find a decent place to hold Sunday class. Now, black and white Sunday school officials wanted impressive, comfortable spaces that demonstrated the institution's significance and met pupils' needs. Church leaders were willing to raise and spend money for a worthy Sunday school structure that would reflect well on the denomination and attract public attention.[39]

Accordingly, the field of Sunday school architecture burgeoned in the late nineteenth century, and dozens of books and manuals appeared on the subject. One expert, Marion Lawrance, defined the church as a religious temple and the Sunday school as its "workshop." A top-notch setting for this workshop would foster better learning and provide visible evidence of what a church could achieve. "Build yourself a good Sunday school, and by and by your Sunday school will build you a good church," Lawrance wrote. To his thinking, a modern Sunday school in an inspiring setting, with well-equipped, commodious classrooms, would attract the attention and the members it deserved.[40]

Reflecting this interest in religious architecture, the 1893 Chicago World's Fair held a competition for the best modern Sunday school design. From dozens of entries, Lewis Miller, supervisor of a Methodist Sunday school in Akron, Ohio, submitted the prize-winning plan. His design, which came to be known as the Akron plan, had classrooms radiating out from a central assembly area. Sliding doors or curtains separated

---

for the chair between the two. Most of the money ultimately went to train preachers in Sunday school work rather than laypeople. Chappell, *Recent Development,* 144.

39. Quote in Owen, *Sacred Flame of Love,* 154.

40. Marion Lawrance, *Housing the Sunday School, or A Practical Study of Sunday School Buildings* (Philadelphia: Westminster Press, 1911), 11–2.

the spaces. Sunday school advisor J. A. Lyon was thrilled with the possibilities that Miller's scheme offered pupils. "When the pie is opened and the birds begin to sing," he chirped, "they are practically all together and nearly in a semicircle." The Akron plan allowed for expansiveness, flexibility, and an intimacy that were absent in earlier Sunday school settings.[41]

Southern Sunday schools began to adopt architectural plans, such as the Akron plan, that were popular nationwide. Two southern churches that followed the Akron model were Nashville's Tulip Street Methodist Church and the First Presbyterian Church of Greensboro, North Carolina. Both had a semicircular auditorium that doubled as the church sanctuary, with classrooms radiating outward and panels dividing one classroom space from another. Greensboro Presbyterians boasted that their modern Sunday school included the "most perfect possible facilities," with windows, maps, blackboards, electric bells, and outlets for stereopticon equipment in every classroom. Steam heat ensured year-round comfort; a kitchen allowed the Sunday school to hold dinners and holiday celebrations on site. A 1904 church report boasted that this design was the "most modern Sunday school building in the country."[42]

Within a decade, however, the Akron plan proved less than ideal. With the growth of Sunday schools and the inclusion of older and younger pupils and graded classes, a single auditorium for common worship no longer sufficed. Classrooms seemed too cramped for the number of projects now undertaken in modern religious education. The scheme allowed little space for the actitivies of restless primary and beginner pupils. New architectural schemes situated the Sunday school in a separate space, behind the pulpit or adjacent to the sanctuary. The First Baptist Church of Mobile, Alabama, positioned its Sunday school behind the sanctuary, with two floors for classrooms and a library, a rendering that Lawrance described as "one of the most complete buildings I know of in this style." The Tabernacle Baptist Church of Richmond was well known in Sunday school circles for its unique arrangement, with the Sunday

---

41. H. F. Evans, "Architecture, Sunday School," in *Encyclopedia of Sunday Schools*, vol. 1, 29–54; Lyon, *The Sunday School and Its Methods*, 478.

42. For a description of the Greensboro church, see Meta Louise Beall, "A Model Sunday School Building," *Presbyterian Standard* 45 (12 August 1903): 18–9. The Tulip Street Methodist Church reflects my observation of this Nashville neighborhood.

school and auditorium next to each other, and good lighting and ventilation.[43]

Southern churches also hired architects like Lawrance to design spaces for their Sunday school. By the early twentieth century, many Sunday schools were housed in a separate building on church property, with features such as a dining area, kitchen, gymnasium, nursery, and playground. Churches invested significant amounts of money in these structures. The Presbyterian Sunday school in Greensboro cost $30,000. In 1894, the Calvary Baptist Church in Washington, D.C., erected its three-story building at a cost of $100,000; it was regarded by an admirer as the "finest Sunday-school building in the world." Even churches in small towns began to house their Sunday classes in splendor. In 1917, the Purity Presbyterian Church of Chester, South Carolina, dedicated its new $22,000 Sunday school building. The Sunday school used its new spaces to hold conferences and conventions that addressed specific social concerns, echoing the reform conventions that met during the Progressive Era. Sunday school conventions and conferences met at the local, state, and regional level.[44]

The new chautauqua movement also helped prompt interest and enthusiasm for Sunday school conferences. This began when two Northern Methodists, John H. Vincent and Lewis Miller, organized a summer institute at Lake Chautauqua in upstate New York in 1874. They called this a "Sunday-School Teachers' Assembly," held to advance Sunday school work by offering training sessions, adult classes, and lectures for teachers, superintendents, and ministers. The institute soon attracted hundreds of people each summer, with well-known personalities invited as featured speakers. Similar summer camps opened in various locations nationwide,

43. Cuninggim and North, *Organization and Administration,* 122; Herbert Francis Evans, *The Sunday-School Building and Its Equipment* (Chicago: University of Chicago Press, 1914), 10–2; James Floyd White, *Protestant Worship and Church Architecture: Theological and Historical Considerations* (New York: Oxford University Press, 1964), 127–8; Lawrance, *Housing the Sunday School,* 50.

44. Quote in Greene, *The Twentieth Century Sunday School,* 8; James Dudley, *History of the Purity Presbyterian Church,* 149. See also Christopher H. Owen, "By Design: The Social Meaning of Methodist Church Architecture in Nineteenth-Century Georgia," *Georgia Historical Quarterly* 75 (summer 1991): 221–53. Members of St. Johns Chapel Sunday School in Norfolk noted that "our southern church architecture differs from that of the North." However, in looking at photographs of classrooms nationwide, it is hard to detect regional differences. See "Our Sunday School," *Christian Recorder,* 6 March 1890.

and the word "chautauqua" became a part of church vocabulary and synonymous with Christian conferences. A few southerners were eager participants. Laura Haygood of Atlanta attended New York's Chautauqua in the summer of 1881, returning home with a renewed commitment to Sunday school teaching. Inspired by what she had learned, she began to offer teacher-training classes in her home and helped found two Atlanta Sunday schools that eventually developed into full-fledged churches. The chautauqua movement peaked in the early twentieth century with some three hundred institutes throughout the United States.[45]

Southerners adopted the chautauqua concept and established scores of retreats and summer camps throughout the region. Those founded by individuals and state Sunday school organizations usually welcomed all Protestants; denominational camps confined their programs to church members only. Unlike the New York model, which soon included an array of social and cultural offerings, most southern chautauquas retained a serious, religious focus. North Carolina Baptists purchased a thousand acres in the mountains near Asheville and opened Ridgecrest Baptist Assembly. They boasted that their chautauqua would provide a "spiritual and an instructive feast" for workers and promised that all participants would depart with "special spiritual preparation." Presbyterians opened a mountain chautauqua that they named Montreat, also near Asheville. African American denominations convened traveling chautauquas that met in a different location each year, perhaps because they had difficulty raising enough money to purchase land for a permanent retreat or because they met white resistance when they tried to do so. The NBC held its first chautauqua in Nashville in 1906, its second in New Orleans, and its third in Jacksonville, Florida, in 1908.[46]

Nondenominational state Sunday school associations also established

45. R. Michael Harton, "Early Chautauqua Institution As a Model Lifelong Learning Enterprise," *Review and Expositor* 84 (summer 1987): 487–506; Benson, *Popular History*, 199; Victoria Case and Robert Ormond Case, *We Called It Culture: The Story of Chautauqua* (New York: Doubleday, 1948), v, 12–3; Joseph E. Gould, *The Chautauqua Movement: An Episode in the Continuing American Revolution* (Albany: State University of New York Press, 1961); Brown and Brown, *Life and Letters of Laura Haygood*, 67.

46. "Second Annual Meeting, North Carolina Baptist Sunday School Chautauqua, August 28–September 2, 1894," Frost-Bell Papers, SBHLA; "National Baptist Sunday School Congress and Young People's Chautauqua," *National Baptist Union*, 6 July 1907; J. W. Jenkins, "The Coming Congress," *National Baptist Union*, 21 March 1908.

summer chautauquas. The Kentucky Sunday School Union purchased twenty acres of land outside Lexington, land that had been part of Ashland, Henry Clay's home. This family-oriented camp was a bit more frivolous than most in the South, promising "recreation, amusement and instruction, all in one." As a promoter noted, "It combines the popular with the technical; it affords entertainment for the little children and instruction for the teacher; it has its secular schemes and its Biblical schools." Activities included picnics, scheduled addresses, group singing, and discussions of Sunday school issues. Founders promised to provide any activity that "will suit your purse." Should such claims create the wrong impression, they insisted that the "convention is neither a picnic nor a debating society, but an assembly of serious persons aiming to promote the efficiency of Sunday schools."[47]

The Monteagle Sunday School Assembly in Tennessee was another successful southern chautauqua, founded by an energetic Scottish immigrant, John Moffat. A plateau northwest of Chattanooga was the perfect setting for his Christian camp, and local businessmen helped him purchase the land. The Monteagle Assembly opened in 1883. Though it was purportedly ecumenical, Methodists and Baptists predominated; Jews and Catholics were banned. Leaders carefully scrutinized the behavior of participants; liquor and card playing were forbidden and wholesome pursuits were encouraged. Entire families attended, supporting one Methodist's assessment that Monteagle was the "happiest place for children" that he knew. Some members built their own cottages on land leased from the assembly. Various communities also built and furnished homes for their delegates. A 2,500-seat amphitheater was completed the first year, and a twenty-sided assembly hall with 3,600 seats was unveiled in 1889.[48]

Monteagle tried to live up to its motto, "The advancement of science, literary attainment, Sunday school interest, and the promotion of the broadest popular culture in the interest of Christianity." It held a special training school for Sunday school teachers that attracted individuals nationwide. It invited well-known speakers to address participants, includ-

---

47. J. R. Deering, "Kentucky Chautauqua," *Minutes of the 25th Annual Session of the Kentucky Sunday School Union* (Louisville: John P. Morton, 1890), 28–9.

48. Ridley Wills II, "The Monteagle Sunday School Assembly—A Brief Account of Its Origin and History," *Tennessee Historical Quarterly* 44 (1985): 3–26.

ing Atticus Haygood and William Jennings Bryan. Monteagle started a music festival in 1905, a summer event which survives to this day. Eventually fire destroyed several buildings, and Monteagle gradually disappeared, as did southerners' interest in chautauquas.[49]

Less impressive than the chautauqua concept—but far more popular—were the periodic Sunday school conferences and conventions convened to discuss Sunday school issues. Volunteer workers, church officials, and selected delegates gathered to study Sunday school issues, present papers on common problems, share new ideas, and engage in lengthy discussions to further the cause. State and regional Sunday school boards encouraged the convening of volunteers from every county, conference, district, or presbytery to meet at regular intervals. Though such meetings were not a new concept, by the turn of the century the sheer number of these conferences was striking, reflecting the commitment of those engaged in Sunday school work. Better transportation throughout the region now made it easier for delegates to attend the meetings, and railroad companies often gave delegates discounted rates. Judging by the scheduled programs, conferences also provided a welcome social outlet where delegates enjoyed picnics, boat rides, and community dinners. These conferences lasted from two days to two weeks and gained a life of their own in the late-nineteenth-century South.

These conferences sought to generate interest and renew commitment to Sunday school work. Standing committees studied and reported on particular issues, such as teacher training, the paucity of men in Sunday school, primary education, and the Sunday school library. Conventions also generated publicity for the Sunday school; each one advertised widely before and after it met. Denominational newspapers often printed the program, speeches, and committee reports in their entirety. Attendance figures show that more male delegates than females participated, probably because more men than women served in official positions and because men felt more comfortable traveling alone and interacting in a public setting. Though Sunday school conventions apparently began to decline in the Northeast by the late nineteenth century, nothing suggests this was true in the South before 1915. They continued to attract Sunday school volunteers who welcomed the opportunity to share their concerns, learn new pedagogical methods, and socialize.[50]

49. Ibid.
50. Higginbotham, *Righteous Discontent*, 164–5.

Despite the enthusiasm that surrounded efficient, up-to-date southern Sunday schools, it is important to remember that many rural southerners remained untouched by the institution or repudiated it outright. Many rural southerners rejected modernization, progressive ideas, and anything that challenged their traditional culture and well-established habits. Some had no use for a Sunday school and what it represented. In fact, Sunday school mission work and church publishing were sometimes the very reasons that individuals rejected mainstream Protestantism and joined sects such as the Landmarks, Pentacostals, or Primitive Baptists. Many rural southerners had no use for respectability, urban affectations, high fashion, elitism, fund raising, and crafted Christian education—all of which seemed to typify the modern Sunday school. They also opposed the centralization that characterized many southern Protestant denominations, as well as the materialism and competition that defined their work.[51]

Rural southerners often had no use for a programmed approach to children's religious education, especially one dictated by others. Agencies like the Home and Foreign Mission Boards were also suspect, for they seemed to be moving denominations toward greater bureaucratization and a loss of control for local churches. Critics detected a corporate mentality of church-goers and officials who seemed to be in love with money. In their eyes, conversion should always be more important than outreach efforts or raising money. Rural and marginalized southerners demonstrated their faith in a more emotional, expressive manner at church and revivals. The modern church and Sunday school, with their bureaucratic structure and organized, rational approach to Christian education, had no place in the lives of these people or the upbringing of their children.[52]

Yet despite resistance or indifference, the southern Sunday school had come into its own by the early twentieth century. It played an important part in southern culture in addressing certain problems that had become part of a rapidly modernizing world. At the same time, however, it highlighted the traditional, seeking to reform individual behavior and save souls. While some Sunday lessons addressed the social problems plaguing the region and nation, other lessons focused on Scripture, for southerners knew that the basis of a good life was found in the Bible. They were con-

51. Harvey, *Redeeming the South*, 8, 86–95.
52. Ibid., 78; Litwack, *Trouble in Mind*, 395–8; Owen, *Sacred Flame of Love*, 160–3.

vinced that a population of morally sound citizens who lived by scriptural dictates would ultimately raise up the South. The Sunday school sought to accomplish its tasks by employing modern techniques used by businesses and institutions. A centralized, bureaucratic approach, vertically organized departments, trained teachers, and graded classes and lessons seemed to promise success. Southern evangelicals now recruited new members both within and outside the denomination, determined that the Sunday school could touch the lives of everyone.

8

AN INCOMPLETE CURE

"No movement of modern times has a more inspiring history than the Sunday school," exclaimed Methodist minister Edgar Alonzo Fox in 1907, looking back at more than four decades of hard work. "It has braved the opposition of the clergy, the indifference of the laity, and the sneers of the wiseacres, and to-day numbers in its ranks the largest standing army in the world," he wrote. Dean Wilbur Tillett of Vanderbilt University was equally fervent, calling the Sunday school the "mightiest, perhaps, of all modern agencies to be employed in the future by the church on saving men from sin." With so many southerners converting and living according to scriptural dictates and middle-class values, both Fox and Tillett felt that the southern Sunday school had much to celebrate.[1]

By 1915, the Sunday school was a well-established institution. Its impact on individuals, churches, and the South was, in many respects,

---

1. Edgar Alonzo Fox, *The Pastor's Place of Privilege and Power in the Sunday School* (Nashville: Publishing House of the MECS, Smith and Lamar, 1907), 138; Tillett, *Theological Seminaries and Teacher Training*, 5.

profound. It could take credit for much of the growth of southern denominations; millions of young people joined a church in part because of the Christian education they had received in Sunday classes. From the ranks of Sunday school pupils, denominations reaped new ministers, missionaries, and lay volunteers. Sunday school officials were convinced that Sunday lessons enriched the lives of both pupils and volunteers. They were equally certain that the moral and social values taught in Sunday school helped southerners lead more purposeful lives. To forward-thinking individuals, well-run Sunday schools—schools that focused attention on the Bible—reflected the spirit of the New South. Had he been alive in 1900, Henry Grady, Atlanta journalist and famed spokesman of the New South philosophy, would have heralded the southern Sunday school as an institution that served the region well.

Certainly by 1915 there was a widely held perception that every church and southern community needed a Sunday school. AMEZ member J. A. Bass gushed over a scene he witnessed in South Mills, North Carolina. "The chiming of the bells upon a Sabbath morning, and the tramp of many little feet, making their way to the Sunday-School, impress the visitor that he is in the midst of christian civilization," he proclaimed. To Bass, South Mills represented "one of the coming towns" in the state. The existence of a Sunday school reassured individuals like Bass that the citizens of South Mills were fixed on a course of right living. Any community without a Sunday school seemed to put its future at risk.[2]

Southerners' commitment to Sunday schools reflected a nationwide trend. The steady stream of books written about the Sunday school was one measure of its importance. An impressive work, the *Encyclopedia of Sunday Schools and Religious Education,* published in 1915, testified to the fact that the Sunday school had become a fixture in American religious life—and on library reference shelves as well. Editors of the three-volume encyclopedia hired experts in their field to write scholarly, informative articles on every aspect of the Sunday school. Equally important was the federal government's four *Surveys of Religious Bodies,* first undertaken by the Bureau of the Census in 1906, which was also the first national census to focus on religion and to devote pages to Sunday school statistics. Widespread interest in Sunday schools was also evident at the

---

2. J. A. Bass, "How Children's Day Was Observed, &c.," *Star of Zion,* 20 September 1888.

local level, as numerous officials and teachers became self-proclaimed experts in the field, publishing pamphlets and advice manuals on how to run effective schools. The very title of one such manual—*The Sunday-School in Ten Red-Hot Chapters*—exemplified one southern minister's enthusiasm for the institution and his insight into successful Sunday school work. Scores of similar volumes appeared annually. The number of volumes on Sunday school topics found in library collections today suggests that the institution was, indeed, "red-hot."[3]

Assessing the impact of the southern Sunday school deserves consideration from several perspectives. One approach is to examine quantitative data to assess Sunday school growth in the region. The best sources are the *Surveys of Religious Bodies* of 1906 and 1916. Statistics from these two surveys reveal remarkable growth in southern Sunday schools even in the early twentieth century (Table 1). In 1906, the number of pupils attending Sunday school in the seven southern Protestant denominations stood at 3,662,120, with 414,302 adult volunteers working in 60,655 Sunday schools. Ten years later, those numbers had risen to 4,463,023 pupils, 551,699 volunteers, and 69,588 Sunday schools.[4]

The two censuses also show that the number of pupils and Sunday schools in the South rose at a faster rate than the national average (Table 2). Between 1906 and 1916, the number of Sunday school pupils nationwide increased by 35.7 percent, while every southern state but three exceeded that number. Texas experienced the most rapid growth; the number of new pupils in its Sunday schools increased by nearly twice the national average. Similarly, while the number of new Sunday schools nationwide grew by 9.3 percent, all but five southern states exceeded that rate. The number of Sunday schools in Florida rose by 38.5 percent, while those in Arkansas, Kentucky, North Carolina, and Texas rose by more than 20 percent. Among the seven largest southern denominations, all but one also made noteworthy advances in founding new Sunday schools. Four of them—the SBC, the MECS, the CME, and the PCUS—

3. McFarland et al., eds., *Encyclopedia of Sunday Schools;* P. L. Stanton, *The Sunday-School in Ten Red-Hot Chapters* (Fairmont, Ga.: by the author, 1898).

4. U.S. Department of Commerce, Bureau of the Census. *Special Reports: Religious Bodies, 1906,* vol. 1 (Washington, D.C.: Government Printing Office, 1910); U.S. Department of Commerce, Bureau of the Census. *Special Reports: Religious Bodies, 1916,* vol. 1 (Washington D.C.: Government Printing Office, 1919), 60–4. Religious censuses were also taken in 1926 and 1936.

TABLE 1
Numbers of Sunday Schools, Officers and Teachers, and Pupils, 1906 and 1916

Denomination	SUNDAY SCHOOLS 1906	1916	OFFICERS/ TEACHERS 1906	1916	PUPILS 1906	1916	% GAIN, PUPILS	% GAIN, SCHOOLS
Southern Baptist	15,035	18,162	106,017	160,171	1,014,690	1,665,996	64.2	20.8
National Baptist	17,910	20,099	100,069	123,817	924,665	1,181,270	27.8	12.2
MECS	14,306	16,690	113,328	152,177	1,040,160	1,688,559	62.3	16.7
AME	6,285	6,277	41,941	45,350	292,689	311,051	6.3	−0.01
AMEZ	2,092	2,544	16,245	18,982	107,692	135,102	25.5	21.6
CME	2,328	2,543	12,375	18,890	92,457	167,880	81.6	9.2
PCUS	2,699	3,273	24,327	32,312	189,767	313,165	65.0	21.3
Totals	60,655	69,588	414,302	551,699	3,662,120	5,463,023		

Sources: U.S. Department of Commerce, Bureau of the Census, *Special Reports: Religious Bodies, 1916* (Washington, D.C.: GPO, 1919), Table 18, p. 59.

witnessed more than 60 percent growth in new Sunday schools over the decade.[5]

Even more important was the growth of the Sunday school population compared to population increases in southern states (Table 3). Although the Census Bureau figures for Sunday schools and for the general population overlap, making exact comparisons impossible, the general population figures from the 1900, 1910, and 1920 censuses can be related at least approximately to the 1906 and 1916 surveys of religious bodies. In doing so we see that, for instance, the Sunday school populations in Kentucky and Arkansas grew roughly three to four times faster than the overall state populations in this general time frame. In North Carolina and Texas, Sunday schools grew at least two to three times faster than the general population. Indeed, in every case, the percentage of new Sunday

---

5. The reasons for this reflect both the popularity of Sunday schools in the South and the fact that the North was well ahead in Sunday school work by 1906 and therefore experienced a lower percentage increase. Bureau of the Census, *Religious Bodies, 1916*, 59.

TABLE 2
Denominational Sunday Schools and Pupils, 1906 and 1916

State	SUNDAY SCHOOLS 1906	SUNDAY SCHOOLS 1916	PUPILS 1906	PUPILS 1916	% GAIN, PUPILS	% GAIN, SCHOOLS
United States	178,214	194,759	14,685,997	19,935,890	35.7	9.3
Alabama	6,808	7,847	361,279	524,935	45.3	15.3
Arkansas	4,398	5,302	230,238	342,947	49.0	20.6
Florida	2,603	3,605	124,592	205,980	65.3	38.5
Georgia	8,052	8,619	460,769	613,947	33.2	7.0
Kentucky	4,723	5,704	314,667	476,566	51.5	20.8
Louisiana	3,320	3,399	177,739	221,326	24.5	2.4
Maryland	2,606	2,797	261,440	329,629	26.1	7.3
Mississippi	5,911	6,569	286,257	388,608	35.8	11.1
North Carolina	7,293	8,930	487,261	739,215	51.7	22.4
South Carolina	5,020	5,413	328,829	452,047	37.5	7.8
Tennessee	6,101	6,884	355,550	523,681	47.3	12.8
Texas	8,678	11,174	535,535	918,374	72.1	28.8
Virginia	5,965	6,461	430,452	598,379	39.0	8.3

Sources: U.S. Department of Commerce, Bureau of the Census, *Special Reports: Religious Bodies, 1916* (Washington, D.C.: GPO, 1919), Table 19, p. 61.

school pupils far exceeded the percentage growth in overall population. Clearly, the Sunday school reached many needy southerners.

The expansion of southern Sunday schools gave southern evangelicals cause to rejoice. Redefining and broadening the concept of Sunday school membership in the late nineteenth century by including adults, homebound pupils, and infants were important steps in increasing membership. The two federal censuses suggest the impact of these changes. Between 1906 and 1916, the percentage increase in pupils attending Sunday school exceeded the growth in the number of new Sunday schools, indicating that larger attendance had more to do with internal expansion and more inclusive membership than with the founding of new schools.

TABLE 3
Population Growth of Southern States by Decade, 1890–1920 (in 000s)

STATE	1900	1910	% GAIN	1920	% GAIN
Alabama	1,829	2,138	16.9	2,348	9.8
Arkansas	1,312	1,574	19.9	1,752	11.3
Florida	529	753	42.3	968	28.5
Georgia	2,216	2,609	17.7	2,896	11.0
Kentucky	2,147	2,290	6.6	2,417	5.5
Louisiana	1,382	1,656	19.8	1,799	8.6
Maryland	1,188	1,295	10.7	1,450	11.9
Mississippi	1,551	1,797	24.6	1,791	−0.3
N. Carolina	1,894	2,206	16.5	2,559	16.0
S. Carolina	1,340	1,515	13.0	1,684	11.1
Tennessee	2,021	2,185	8.1	2,338	7.0
Texas	3,049	3,897	27.8	4,663	19.7
Virginia	1,854	2,062	11.2	2,309	12.0

Source: U.S. Department of Commerce, Bureau of Census, "Populations of States," *Historical Statistics of the United States: Colonial Times to 1790,* part 1 (Washington, D.C., 1970), 24–35.

Quantitative evidence, however, is only one means to measure success. The issue of how much impact the southern Sunday school had on pupils, families, and volunteer workers is equally important to consider. Statistics do not reveal how often individual pupils attended class and whether they benefited by the experience. How Sunday lessons affected students' lives and what satisfaction volunteers gained from their work are questions that have significant implications for the influence of Sunday school.

While attendance records do not necessarily reflect pupils' response to Sunday school, adults regarded attendance as a yardstick by which to measure their success. Dutiful pupils who faithfully went to class and actively participated were the ideal. A Georgia mother could not hide her joy when reporting, "We have a flourishing Sabbath School at Mt. Zion. Jimmie attends regularly. He hasn't missed a lesson." ASSU missionary William Self was equally thrilled by children in his East Tennessee district who walked two to three miles to attend school, "climbing around cliffs, over rocks, and wading creeks to learn something about Jesus and his love." James Mallory reported that the "huge attendance" at his Sunday school made mornings there a "pleasant occasion." Adults set great store by pupils who showed up each week.[6]

Southern parents who wanted their children to become pious, upstanding citizens felt increasingly obligated to send their offspring to Sunday school—and perhaps to attend themselves as well. Though church leaders fretted that the Sunday school might usurp domestic religious instruction and encourage mothers to neglect their duty, southern parents did not see it that way. In a typical example, widow Margaret McCullough of Galveston, Texas, enrolled all her children in Sunday school and felt deep satisfaction by "pointing [them] to the 'lamb of God.'" Both she and at least one of her daughters taught a Sunday class. A good Christian family meant that members attended both church and Sunday school.[7]

The experiences of Mahala Roach and two of her children show in more detail the importance of Sunday school to one southern family. Roach, a devout Methodist and wealthy Vicksburg, Mississippi, widow, raised her five children alone after her husband died. As a cooperative eight-year-old, her son Jim faithfully attended Sunday school, read his weekly lesson, and memorized Scripture. For several years, he went to class each week. When he turned thirteen, Roach noted that Jim learned his lesson and "went pleasantly to Sunday school—then to church." But by the time he was fourteen, Jim developed a mind of his own. Roach now expressed frustration when he failed to learn his weekly lesson or skipped Sunday school entirely. He "got the old mule," she wrote when Jim stubbornly refused to attend class. One Sunday he headed for school but apparently changed his mind, and his mother despaired, "I am sorry he is so unruly." The following year was a repeat of the previous one. Yet when he turned sixteen, Jim had either grown up and accepted Sunday school as an important part of his life or had decided that continuing to defy his mother and the minister was too much work. Roach described

---

6. E. A. Gray to her son, 17 May 1877, Bolingbrook, Ga., Burge-Gray Family Letters, Emory; "Three Orphans," *Kind Words*, 8 June 1872; William Self, "Who Will Help Them," 1870, ASSU Correspondence, PHS; Mallory, *"Fear God and Walk Humbly"*, 454.

7. Turner, *Women, Culture, and Community*, 65; Avery, *Behold the Child*, 6.

Jim's moment of recognition as one of the happiest days of her life. "First, my precious Jim arose early, dressed himself neatly, and declared that Dr. Sansom had conquered him and he was going to Sunday school. My heart bounded with joy, and when the dear boy started off, a fervent 'God bless my darling' went with him." Problems from that point forward were either minimal or Roach failed to record them.[8]

At sixteen, Roach's daughter Hala also had a mind of her own, though in different ways from her brother Jim. Hala won first prize in Sunday school for memorizing the most verses. She began to teach Sunday school. Yet her willful spirit and sense of fun elicited reprimands from the minister, once for attending a masquerade ball and another time for failing to sing the church creed in Sunday school. At one point, Hala was so angry when the minister scolded her that she refused to attend either church or Sunday school. But when she turned nineteen, she accepted a permanent position to teach Sunday school and also joined a temperance society. These activities ceased the following year when Hala got married and resigned her Sunday school post.[9]

Mahala Roach's interest in Sunday school education reflected the sentiments of many southern parents: their children needed to attend in order to become well-mannered, devout Christians. Roach never expressed uneasiness about the role this institution played in her children's upbringing or worried that it might be usurping Christian nurturing at home. In fact, she welcomed the Sunday school, convinced that her youngsters were better off for attending it. Their attendance and accomplishments in class reflected her success as a mother. Yet we must bear in mind that parents who were devout Christians or as vigilant as Roach were those most likely to send their offspring to Sunday school. At home, these youngsters probably received assistance with their lessons and were encouraged—if not forced—to go to class. As might be expected, the most faithful pupils tended to be from religious homes, where attending church and Sunday school was an obligatory part of childhood.

Personal comments in letters and memoirs show that Sunday school often left an indelible imprint on children and, in some cases, permanently changed their lives. Some who attended Sunday school reminisced

---

8. Mahala Roach Diaries, 31 March 1872, 6 July 1873, and 29 August 1875, Vicksburg, Miss., SHC.
9. Ibid.

fondly about a particular class, a beloved teacher, or an inspiring lesson. Children's letters to Sunday school newspapers or to a favorite teacher often expressed joy in learning the Bible or participating in a Sunday school event. They mentioned the thrill of reading stories about Jesus that celebrated righteous living, and the role that Scripture played in teaching them to behave. Sunday school workers tried to make the day a pleasant experience for children, with frequent success. Many southern youngsters discovered a sense of place and purpose there. Sunday school comprised a significant part of their life beyond the home.[10]

A Sunday school teacher often made a profound impression on youngsters. In letters and comments in church newspapers, pupils expressed admiration—even adoration—for a special teacher. One Presbyterian called his Sunday school instructor a "dear, saintly mother in Israel." Julia Rankin of Guilford County, North Carolina, adored her teacher, Mr. Alexander, and her Sunday class. "I love to go because I love our teacher dearly," she confessed. Rankin found Alexander's method of testing pupils on the Bible and their questioning him in return especially stimulating, and she was astonished that he never missed an answer. Pupils in a Wilmington, North Carolina, AMEZ Sunday school so admired their teacher, Georgia Mask, that when she suddenly died, they put their classroom chairs "in mourning" for thirty days. Ermine McGaha wrote a former teacher, James Harvey Joiner, "When quite young, Providence placed me in your Sabbath School Class. Your unwavering faith, so manifest in your zeal—and your correct understanding of the Scriptures, commanded my love and reverence." This teacher, like many others, made an indelible imprint on a youngster. As McGaha wondered, "What would my life have been like without such teachings?" James Wright recalled that the most important person in his childhood, besides family members and the pastor, was "Miss Mamie Brown, my Sunday school teacher, who gave me a beautiful Sunday school card with the words, 'keep thyself pure' printed on it." Wright could not yet read, but his mother explained what the passage meant. "I kept the card for many years, and it had much influence on my life," he reminisced. In his memoir, James H. Robinson remembered the reassuring words of his Sunday school superintendent and preacher, both of whom inculcated in him the idea of racial equality and the importance of hard work. He took comfort in those

10. Avery, *Behold the Child*, 93.

thoughts, hoping that the future would be better than what his family endured in the Jim Crow South.[11]

Sunday school lessons and classroom experiences gave added meaning to many pupils' lives. A sense of order and well-defined expectations, which were the norm in well-run Sunday schools, provided children with a sense of direction and motivated many to excel. Charles Phillips claimed that his book prize always inspired him, with its straightforward message about the negative consequences of excessive pride. "No book ... that I ever read during my childhood impressed me" like the story of Ralph Rattler and his pride, Phillips recalled. "It helped and stimulated me to shun a course that meant ruin and degradation. . . . Young as I was, I was determined by God's help to pursue a different course from that chosen by Ralph Rattler." The routine of memorizing Scripture had a positive impact as well. Phillips claimed that the catechism and Bible verses he memorized for Sunday school were his salvation. The Reverend Hight Moore recalled that he struggled to memorize the most Bible verses in his class, determined to win a red leather testament. Though he never earned the top prize, Moore later acknowledged the importance of memorizing Scripture; as an adult, he quoted Bible passages to good effect. To Benjamin Mays, church and Sunday school were a refuge, a place where he could "be free and relax from the toil and oppression of the week" and escape the carping and fighting that went on in his home.[12]

A few individuals even credited the Sunday school with permanently changing their lives. ASSU missionary Adam Reeder related the story of a man who swore and broke the Sabbath until friends finally convinced him to attend Sunday school. This experience altered his life forever. He converted and reportedly prayed twice a day, hoping to "get his children to quit the eavels he once encouraged." Another man "forty someod [sic] years old who could not read" began to attend Sunday school after friends pleaded with him to become literate. After a teacher taught him

11. Julia Rankin to William Henry Wills, 16 June 1870, n.p., William Henry Wills Collection, SHC; "Resolutions," *Star of Zion*, 25 January 1894; Ermine McGaha to James Henry Joiner, n.p., n.d., James Henry Joiner Papers, SHC; Richard R. Wright Jr., *87 Years behind the Black Curtain: An Autobiography* (Philadelphia: Rare Book Company, 1965), 60; James H. Robinson, *Road without Turning: The Story of Reverend James H. Robinson, An Autobiography* (New York: Farrar, Straus, 1950), 60.

12. Phillips, *From the Farm to the Bishopric*, 28; Moore, *The Country Sunday School*, 5–9; Mays, *Born to Rebel*, 9, 16.

to read the Bible, "I heard him say he would not take $500,000 for what he had learned," reported a pleased Reeder.¹³

Although skeptics might question whether an institution that met only once a week and for an hour or two at best could have had much influence on children (let alone adults), the above examples suggest that it did. While the amount of time a child committed to Sunday school may seem limited, these precious moments could be significant, especially in a period when many southern children had little free time or opportunity to attend any type of school. Comments scattered throughout church publications suggest that the average pupil attended Sunday school for three or four years. Attendance books show that while some children left after a couple of weeks, the faithful continued well into their teen years. This rather limited time spent in Sunday school also typified some southern children's attendance at weekday school. Without the existence or enforcement of compulsory school attendance laws, many southern children attended public school sporadically or not at all. In 1880, the average American attended public school for four years. In 1890, the average North Carolinian had 2.6 years of public schooling; in Alabama and South Carolina, the figure was 2.5 years. At the turn of the century, Edgar Gardner Murphy lamented that only 60 percent of southern children enrolled in weekday school; among them, the average daily attendance was 70 percent. African American children received even less education. In Virginia, 45 percent were enrolled in day school but only 26 percent kept up daily attendance. In other words, many southern children had only a limited exposure to day school, just as they did to Sunday school; others never attended either institution.¹⁴

And then there were youngsters who made it all too apparent that they hated Sunday school and remained untouched by its influence. We

13. Adam Reeder to John McCullagh, 19 January 1875, Barboursville, Ky., ASSU Correspondence, PHS.

14. Edgar Gardner Murphy, *Problems of the Present South* (New York: Macmillan, 1904), 229; Coontz, *Social Origins of Private Life*, 275. School attendance in Virginia was a problem, according to William Link. Approximately one-fifth of all white children and two-fifths of all black children in the state did not attend public school in 1890. See Link, *A Hard Country and a Lonely Place*, 53. Thomas D. Clark claims that 60 percent of Virginia's white children were enrolled in public school but only 37 percent maintained daily attendance. See Clark, *Three Paths to the Modern South: Education, Agriculture, and Conservation* (Athens: University of Georgia Press, 1965), 17.

can assume that discontent or bored pupils were common, although records are sparse; disaffected students were unlikely to submit written complaints to a church newspaper or a Sunday school teacher. Children who hated the idea of attending class each week left after one visit; others never showed up in the first place and thus do not appear in any extant records. Some children did their best to disrupt the proceedings, creating a nightmare for teachers. These pupils may have resembled "Tommy," a friend of James Robinson's, who attended Sunday school but "only because he had to." According to Robinson, Tommy arrived late and left early, showed no interest in the weekly lesson, and stole money from the collection plate. The fact that Tommy belonged to a gang that stole and destroyed property lent credence to the warnings of Sunday school advisors that young people who disliked or avoided Sunday school were likely troublemakers.[15]

Adults involved in Sunday school work reaped benefits as well. Many superintendents saw their role as inspiring and important, and they worked hard to succeed. Each week a North Carolina Methodist walked seven miles round-trip to oversee his school. An equally dedicated man supervised one Sunday school in the morning and a second one in the afternoon. ASSU missionary William Bulkley described an energetic superintendent who had "his whole heart in the Sunday school work." Another superintendent, John Pepper, served for fifty years and claimed to give as much attention to the Sunday school as he gave to his paid job. These men seemed to relish the personal rewards of working for such a benevolent cause, as well as the status and authority associated with their position.[16]

Sunday school missionaries and colporteurs were also enthusiastic about their work and delighted in each success. Henry Hartzog was thrilled when he discovered a "Baptist sentiment" in the Appalachian and Piedmont regions, where residents welcomed him with open arms. He identified mountaineers as the very people whom the Sunday school should reach—"plain, clear-headed, independent people who love the

---

15. Robinson, *Road without Turning*, 54–5.
16. Alamance Circuit, *Minutes of the North Carolina Quarterly Conference Reports of the Methodist Episcopal Church, South, 1884*, Duke; William H. Bulkley to Maurice A. Wurts, 15 March 1870, Louisville, Ky., ASSU Correspondence, PHS; John Robertson Pepper, *Well-Nigh 50 Years at the Superintendent's Desk* (Memphis: Press of Early-Freeburg, 1929), 7.

old-fashioned religion," he wrote. Baptist missionaries were in such demand there that the denomination requested more volunteers, turning to seminary students to help spread the "old fashioned religion" in the mountains. Hartzog gave a decidedly romantic spin to this work, probably to attract volunteers. Not only would students aid the destitute, he claimed, but they could trek through the mountains, learn to preach, and eat "wild honey, fried chicken, butter milk, spring-water." The bracing air and liberal exercise would "fill out the gothic and angular proportions of the pallid student with rosy mountain flesh." From Hartzog's perspective, nothing seemed more idyllic than the daily life of a Sunday school missionary.[17]

Faith inspired hundreds of thousands of southern women to become Sunday school teachers, but other reasons motivated them as well. Black Baptists in Tennessee distributed a questionnaire to determine why their teachers volunteered. The most common response (78 percent) was a desire to serve the church. The second most frequent reason was a love of children (68.5 percent), followed by an interest in youngsters' moral and religious education (49.7 percent) and the joy of teaching (40.3 percent). Well down the list were more pragmatic responses, including the fact that no one else could be found (19.9 percent), a desire to please the superintendent (17.4 percent), having no valid excuse to refuse (16.2 percent), and improving the standing of the church (4.9 percent). A larger sense of duty propelled others. One woman, though frustrated by the challenges she faced as the only teacher in a school for African American children, continued her effort, for "being the child of a slaveowner, and so taught to feel my responsibility to those whom God put among us, I shall keep up teaching all children who will come."[18]

Many white teachers also responded enthusiastically to their work. Mrs. D. S. Watson of Anderson, South Carolina, loved her job because she felt she could "fill the young and tender minds with love for Jesus, so that our sons may grow up God-fearing men and our daughters 'polished after the similitude of a palace.'" Most instructors took their task seri-

17. Henry S. Hartzog, "Missions in Kentucky Mountains," *Seminary Magazine* 1 (December 1888): 250–1.

18. T. O. Fuller, *History of the Negro Baptists of Tennessee* (Memphis: Haskins Print, 1936), 178; "Sunday-Schools with White Teachers," *14th Annual Report of the Executive Committee of Colored Evangelism, 1905* (Richmond: Presbyterian Publishing House, 1905), 6.

ously, spending hours preparing the weekly lesson and attending teacher review sessions. Some instructors seemed to devote their entire lives to the Sunday school. Miss Battie Shropshire of Rome, Georgia, taught Sunday school faithfully for more than fifty years; a Hartsville, South Carolina, woman taught for sixty-five years. Others claimed that teaching Sunday school was the brightest moment of their week. A dedicated Mabel Kennedy conducted two Sunday classes, one in the morning with eighty-five young women and another in the afternoon with fifty-two pupils. A North Carolina teacher called her duties "heavenly work" and celebrated her commitment. "The good God raises good teachers to lead [children] to Heaven," she wrote. When an elderly woman finally agreed to teach Sunday school despite her "nervous and excitable" nature, her initial reluctance turned to joy. She discovered that she loved the job, and felt that her life had a renewed purpose. Bessie Dewey Lacy of Raleigh delighted in her class of young men, writing, "Oh! how I do enjoy it." Such optimistic responses make sense, since those who disliked teaching Sunday school gave it up or never volunteered in the first place. Nevertheless, Sunday school teaching was a job that many women genuinely enjoyed.[19]

But teaching Sunday school was also a challenge. Controlling unruly children and inspiring apathetic pupils were demanding tasks for even the most able instructors. A teacher's most onerous duty was probably disciplining ill-behaved students. Mary Ogilve simply washed her hands of them and expelled naughty children so that she could focus attention on the most "teachable." Yet by doing this, Ogilve cast out the very children most likely in need of what the Sunday school had to offer. Some

---

19. Mrs. D. S. Watson, "Woman's Work in the Church," *Baptist Courier*, 25 June 1885; letter from Beaverdam, N.C., in the *Baptist Courier*, 19 March 1885; Georgia Hamlet, *A History of the First Baptist Church, Anderson, S.C.* (Anderson, S.C: privately printed, 1979), 57; Malcolm Stuart Sweet, *Unto Everlasting Life: The History of the Hartsville Presbyterian Church, 1867–1952* (Hartsville, S.C.: Hartsville Presbyterian Church, 1954), 121; "1905 Centenary Methodist Church Sunday School, St. Louis," *19th Annual Report of the Woman's Home Mission Society of the Methodist Episcopal Church, South* (Nashville: MECS Publishing House, 1905); Mabel Kennedy, "Mabel Kennedy, St. Louis Centenary Methodist Church," *22nd Annual Report of the Woman's Mission Society of the Methodist Episcopal Church, South* (Nashville: Publishing House of the MECS, 1908), 149; "The Experience of an Elderly Lady As a Sunday School Teacher," *Earnest Worker*, 27 February 1873; Bessie Lacy Dewey to Fred Lacy, 18 April 1888, Charlotte, N.C., Drury Lacy Collection, SHC. See also Susan Thistlethwaite, "The Feminization of American Religious Education," *Religious Education* 76 (July–August 1981): 391–402.

instructors found the duty daunting. "The thought that, to some extent, as a teacher, I was responsible for the eternal happiness or misery of the little ones under my instruction," one elderly man admitted, "was almost overwhelming." Bessie Lacy Dewey admitted that her male Sunday school class required extensive preparation and even then, did not always go well. A white Presbyterian in charge of a black Sunday school found her task somewhat dispiriting. "I am the sole teacher. To teach them seems to me a more hopeless task each year," she sighed. Sethelle Boyd of North Carolina was discouraged after taking over her sister's class. "I always feel so helpless when I'm trying to teach children the Bible—it is so easy, and so hard for them to understand." She felt uncomfortable when answering children's questions. After one pupil asked her whether it was a sin to drink and dance, Boyd confessed, "I don't think it's a sin to do either—I like wine and I like to dance—but when it comes to teaching a Sabbath school class, I hardly know what to say." It was one thing for a sociable young woman to accept her own weaknesses and desires, but another to serve as a shining example to youngsters.[20]

Southern women proved to be dedicated Sunday school teachers; their influence on the institution was profound. Hundreds of thousands of them quietly made their mark there. Without their voluntary participation, it is likely the southern Sunday school would have enjoyed only limited success. Assessing the impact that Sunday school teaching had on southern women, however, is more difficult. Historian Jean Friedman's argument that family and religion confined southern women to an "enclosed garden" offers one perspective on this issue. In her view, southern women had few opportunities to expand their activities beyond home and church. The Sunday school fell within acceptable parameters of female activity. Friedman suggests that the opportunities provided by the Sunday school, and the endless pronouncements praising female instructors for their work, created an environment where women felt comfortable and rewarded for their efforts. Of course, leadership roles in the church structure, decent paid jobs, and an effective political voice still

20. Estelle Haskin, "Dallas, Tex., Settlement House," *18th Annual Report of the Woman's Home Missionary Society of the MECS* (Nashville: Publishing House of the MECS, 1904), 44; "An Old Man's Pleas," 1; Bessie Lacy Dewey to Fred Lacy, 18 April 1888, Raleigh, N.C., Drury Lacy Collection, SHC; *14th Annual Report of the Executive Committee of Colored Evangelism, 1905,* 106; Sethelle Boyd Diary, c. 1880, privately held by Scott and Scottie Lindsay, Charlotte, N.C.

were unavailable to women. Sunday school teaching provided one opportunity to make the best of the limitations they faced.[21]

Other scholars have seen Sunday school teaching as a golden opportunity for women, at least at this juncture. John Boles has called the church an important "incubator for women's culture" and Elizabeth Hayes Turner has shown that through their church, urban southern women engaged in benevolent service projects that took them out into the public realm, well beyond the domestic sphere. Through church-related activities, she argues, women gained confidence and self-respect. Evelyn Brooks Higginbotham also sees the church as enhancing black Baptist women's influence and power as they worked collectively through local, state, and national associations. In her view, these religious activities helped to transform "unknown and unconfident women into leaders and agents of social service and racial self-help."[22]

Teaching Sunday school offered a different type of experience for southern women than many other organized volunteer activities. Associational activities often fostered a sense of female bonding and provided leadership opportunities. Women established their own organizations, elected leaders, raised money, and tackled various concerns. Sunday school teaching, on the other hand, was an individualized activity, usually without a female support system. Teachers might participate in weekly review sessions and attend periodic Sunday school conferences, but otherwise they acted on their own. They had charge of their own classroom and their own pupils and employed their own teaching style. Females who wrote for Sunday school publications also worked independently, usually writing in the privacy of their homes. Such pursuits, nevertheless, must have helped many southern women develop a sense of confidence and self-worth. Female Sunday school teachers often expressed immense satisfaction in having charge of an entire class and imprinting faith and good behavior on their young charges. Many were thrilled when youngsters converted as a result of their teaching. With limited scholarly research on the personal lives of women in the New South,

21. Jean E. Friedman, *The Enclosed Garden: Women and Community in the Evangelical South, 1830–1900* (Chapel Hill: University of North Carolina Press, 1985). See also Salem, *To Better Our World*, 9, 14, 65–100; Scott, *Natural Allies,* 182.

22. John Boles, *Irony of Southern Religion,* The Rockwell Lecture Series (New York: Peter Lang, 1994), 34; Turner, *Women, Culture, and Community;* Higginbotham, *Righteous Discontent*, 1, 17.

one can only suggest how important Sunday school teaching was to many southern women.

Mixed messages about female roles were evident in Sunday school lessons. On the one hand, religious stories and poems upheld traditional assumptions about women's secondary place in society and celebrated their domestic, maternal duties. Lessons and pictures often depicted girls as pious and self-sacrificing. Yet at the same time, Sunday school lessons taught that Christian women could be assertive and strong. Girls learned that if they were good, loved God, and lived according to the Bible, they could be universally admired and influential. Though excluded from elevated positions within the church, females could be confident and bold—powers that derived from being children of God. Stories written for Sunday school classes often described daughters teaching irreligious parents the importance of faith and encouraging them to attend church. In real life, female pupils earned accolades and won prizes for sterling classroom attendance and memorization of Scripture. As contemporary studies suggest, the preponderance of females in Sunday classes must have given girls a place where they could participate actively—and excel—in a fairly safe environment. Sunday lessons upheld traditional gender stereotypes but elevated females who faithfully served God. How such messages ultimately affected southern women deserves further study.[23]

One issue historians have debated is how purposefully adults used Sunday school lessons to fashion a captive, vulnerable population that would serve their needs and those of the larger society. As we have seen with Sunday schools in mill villages, there is no doubt that officials and volunteers sought to shape young people into pious, responsible adults. Scholars such as E. P. Thompson and Paul Boyer have taken this argument a step farther, stating that businessmen and church officials in England and the United States purposely used Sunday school lessons to control children's social development and educate them to fit the needs of an urbanizing, industrializing society. The Sunday school gave churches a subtle but effective means to mold young members.[24]

What Thompson and Boyer suggest has some truth to it. Southern church and Sunday school leaders had an agenda when it came to uplift-

23. Smith, *Killers of the Dream*, 66; Boles, *Irony of Southern Religion*, 34.
24. See E. P. Thompson, *The Making of the English Working Class* (New York: Pantheon, 1964), 375–9; Boyer, *Urban Masses and Moral Order in America*, 47–53.

ing children. Because adults created the lessons, they could control what pupils learned in class. Through mission Sunday schools, evangelicals reached out to educate and assimilate those on the fringes of society. They believed that Sunday lessons grounded in middle-class values would impress upon less fortunate children important ideals, such as responsibility, punctuality, and good manners. A Sunday lesson about the need to work hard, for example, may have encouraged some children to become more productive laborers. Weekly messages on systematic benevolence stressed the need for youngsters to give generously throughout their lives, and these lessons may have affected the future financial soundness of a church. Whites who taught or ran black Sunday schools admitted that their efforts were, in part, undertaken to benefit the South by teaching African American youngsters how to behave according to a white value system. Manipulating children to do right was part of the Sunday school agenda.[25]

But such manipulation is not the entire story. Many individuals who engaged in Sunday school work saw their endeavors in a purely humanitarian and Christian light. Their motivation was faith; they were involved because they believed in the goals of Sunday schools and wanted children to live according to the Bible. Most Sunday school workers deeply believed in the superiority of the Protestant Christian faith. They believed every youngster's conversion was critical because it was the heart of their faith. Sunday school education, in their eyes, would benefit each pupil and ultimately create stronger southern families, churches, and communities. These opinions rarely met opposition from southern parents or their children, at least among mainstream Protestants. Southerners usually welcomed the Sunday school because they embraced its values and expectations for their own children. They did not regard missionaries and volunteers as interlopers delivering a manipulative message. They wanted and needed what Sunday school agents offered their children. Southerners accepted Christian, value-laden messages because they believed in them.

Despite the Sunday school's positive impact on the South and on southern denominations, no institution could accomplish all that its supporters envisioned. One sharp disappointment, at least from the perspective of northern missionaries, was the failure of the idea that the Sunday

25. Coontz, *Social Origins of Private Life*, 263.

school could reunite North and South, heal national wounds, and end the division among the Baptists, Methodists, and Presbyterians. Although northerners hoped that the nation's shared approach to children's Christian education and the use of similar lessons would help restore national unity, it did not.[26]

To a large degree, of course, regional differences were absent in the southern Sunday classroom. From the perspective of the daily schedule, weekly lessons, and the beliefs of pupils and parents, Sunday schools nationwide had much in common. All of them taught children similar Christian lessons and middle-class values. Most classes centered each lesson on the Bible and encouraged childhood conversion. For years, many black and white southern Sunday schools purchased or borrowed literature that was produced and used in the North. Parents—North and South, black and white—believed that the Sunday school could help their children become pious, well-behaved citizens. Denominations across America established Sunday school boards with similar functions and saw publishing as a lucrative business. The values taught in Sunday school and the steps undertaken to achieve its success were similar for most Protestants nationwide.

From the perspective of those at the top, though, the southern Sunday school movement intensified, rather than mitigated, denominational and regional loyalty. Denominational differences began to assume greater importance as southern churches became stronger and focused more attention on Sunday school organization and publishing. Church officials encouraged members' loyalty because they needed more pupils and more converts. Differences among various denominations became an increasingly serious matter, because the success of their church and the viability of the publishing business depended on the creation of more Sunday schools. Sunday school officials made a point to differentiate their church from the opposition.

A unique sense of vitality characterized the southern Sunday school movement; competition for pupils was intense during the latter third of the nineteenth century and undoubtedly helped to promote interest in the institution. Black and white missionaries working in the South proved relentless in trying to outdo the competition. Publishing houses vied with one another to sell the most Sunday school literature and reap the largest

---

26. See Stowell, *Rebuilding Zion*.

profits. Denominations competed with one another to attract the most pupils and claim the greatest number of converts. While such rivalry often resulted in uncharitable comments flung between adveraries, this heightened level of activity invigorated the movement and ultimately benefited needy southerners.

The Sunday school gave southerners another opportunity to redeem their region and reclaim their space. Southern denominations began to streamline and upgrade Sunday school operations in order to compete effectively. By the 1880s, many northern religious organizations began to lose interest in the South or were troubled by the region's growing sectarianism and turned to more promising fields elsewhere. Northern organizations like the ABPS ultimately abandoned the South after book sales declined due to competition from black and white Southern Baptists.

An unanticipated result of the southern Sunday school movement was the increased attention that churches paid to economic issues. The emphasis on material concerns was probably inevitable, considering the nation's fixation on business and economic interests in the late nineteenth century. Many churches had always displayed an acquisitive nature, making significant investments in real estate and engaging in efforts to solicit donations. Sunday school publishing imparted an even greater competitive and materialistic character to southern denominations. Editors now joined church officials and missionaries in urging the expansion of Sunday schools, anticipating that each new pupil would purchase denominational publications and help fill church coffers. A profitable publishing house became critical to the success of every denomination.

The Sunday school movement also amplified churches' attention to money by drawing children into their fundraising schemes. From their first day in school, youngsters learned the importance of systematic benevolence and the need to work selflessly to enhance the financial standing of their church. Officials urged pupils to bring large contributions to every special Sunday school celebration. Leaders set monetary goals for events such as Missionary Day and Children's Day, and students exerted themselves to ensure that their own class reached its goal. Young people learned to purchase denominational literature for classroom and home use. By the turn of the century, Sunday schools were not merely an institution to serve God and help children lead Christian lives; pupils were critical fund raisers and consumers.

This acquisitive character generated negative responses among traditionalists and caused some to question the purpose of the Sunday school. An AME member feared the Sunday school was becoming "mere machinery" for fund raising and collecting money. Likewise, Methodist minister George Smith objected to the attention paid to material concerns. "Money covers many sins," he warned, "the anxiety of all classes to get money leads the church to depend too largely upon wealth without reference to the way in which it is gathered." But churches and Sunday schools needed money, and emphasizing children's benevolence and expanding denominational publishing to improve a balance sheet showed no sign of abating.[27]

An examination of the Sunday school offers a few insights into the issue of southern exceptionalism. The idea of southern Sunday schools preserving and even enhancing regional identity often appeared to be more rhetoric than real. In his study of religious reconstruction, historian Daniel Stowell argues that regional Sunday school periodicals upheld the unique ideals of southern denominations and evoked strong memories of the Confederacy. My research suggests that pro-southern comments were rare in the decades covered in this study. Rather than feeling deep-seated antagonism toward the North, southern church leaders and editors seemed bent upon emphasizing loyalty to their own Sunday schools in order to drive northerners out of the region, attract more pupils to their faith, and ensure loyalty to church publications. Southern church officials may have denounced underhanded tactics by Yankee missionaries and rivals' unorthodox literature, but they shared similar lessons and Protestant ideals with northerners.[28]

The southern Sunday school movement reinforced, rather than mitigated, the region's racial divide. Indeed, it is hardly surprising that each race wanted to organize and run its own Sunday schools. Northern whites who tried to establish biracial classes discovered that they satisfied neither race and sometimes stirred up white racial sensitivities. Southern whites did little to welcome African Americans into their churches, refusing to elevate black men to positions of authority or treat them with respect. African Americans had no desire to support Sunday schools organized and taught by whites. Sunday schools, like the region's churches, upheld a racially segregated South.

27. Jonathan M. Taylor, "Requirements of the Sabbath School," *AME Church Review* 17 (October 1900): 164; George G. Smith Diary, 4 January 1887, Emory.
28. Stowell, *Rebuilding Zion*, 120–2.

Black and white southern Sunday schools nonetheless shared similarities in their overall structure and written lessons. In part this was because for years, African American Sunday schools had depended upon whites' advice, financial support, and publications. Yet black Sunday school lessons and activities also adopted a somewhat different approach from white schools. The classroom focused on children's need to acquire dignity and respectability. African American parents insisted that their children hold their heads high and summon up their best behavior, the better to fit into a white world. At the same time, African American Sunday schools strengthened a sense of community and gave blacks an institution to help them endure white oppression and racism. Black children attended classes run and taught by members of their own race, absorbing lessons in race pride and racial uplift. Sunday school teachers gave youngsters the strength to confront a dismal present and good reason to hope for a brighter future. The Sunday school had a far-reaching influence in the black community.[29]

In order to attract and retain a following, Sunday schools could never stray far from teaching the beliefs and values that were acceptable to pupils and parents. It is hardly surprising, therefore, that white Sunday schools at this juncture did little to confront or alter white southerners' racial attitudes and behavior. Southern clergy—and Sunday school officials—never thought about the church as a place to challenge racism and violence. Rather, they were "unintentional defenders of the status quo," as historian John Boles has claimed. Boles sees this as the central tragedy of southern white Protestantism in the century following the Civil War.[30]

In fact, a central paradox of the southern Sunday school movement relates to its timing. The institution enjoyed enormous popularity during the very period that the region experienced intense turmoil in race relations. The Sunday school's phenomenal growth occurred during decades of heightened racial violence, an increase in lynchings, and the passage of Jim Crow and other laws that legalized black subordination and racial segregation. Nearly all white southerners repudiated African Americans who demanded an equal place in society. Some whites responded to such

---

29. Higginbotham, *Righteous Discontent*, 186–8.
30. Boles, *Irony of Southern Religion*, 101. See also Owen, *Sacred Flame of Love*, 168. In the antebellum South, ministers supported slavery or ignored the topic altogether. A century later, Martin Luther King Jr. took white Protestant clergy to task for avoiding civil rights issues and hiding behind their pulpits.

claims with violence or by supporting new laws that denied black rights. These developments seemed a direct contradiction to Sunday lessons that taught youngsters about Christian love and human understanding.

It is unclear whether southern whites who engaged in racist acts or supported Jim Crow laws had been dutiful Sunday school pupils and churchgoers. It would be wishful thinking to assume that racists never went to Sunday school or church, or never had parents who set an example of Christian charity. Doubtless some of the region's most virulent racists saw themselves as good Christians, seeing no contradiction between bad behavior and strong faith. Nearly all southern whites indirectly tolerated racist actions by their silence, and did not see racism as undermining Christian ideals. Antebellum southern whites had used the Bible to defend slavery as an institution sanctioned by God. Southern Sunday school lessons may not have used the Bible to defend racist attitudes and acts, but they did not use Scripture to challenge them. To white thinking, the world had to function the way God—and they—had ordered it.

The Sunday school attracted children from a broad spectrum of the population; yet children raised with strong religious convictions and sent off to Sunday school did not necessarily develop into tolerant, charitable adults. As adults, some former pupils almost certainly supported or joined organizations such as the Ku Klux Klan, which preached white superiority and engaged in violence against blacks. Theodore Bilbo, a racist demagogue, had parents who apparently felt a "reverence" for Baptist teachings. As a teenager, he was active in his church. The mother of another southern demagogue of the early twentieth century, James Vardaman, was a devout Methodist and allegedly strict in teaching her son right from wrong. The father of Thomas Dixon, author of *The Clansman,* was a Baptist preacher. These three men may have attended Sunday school as children; all seemed to have parents who identified themselves as good Christians. Yet as adults, these men employed racist rhetoric to great effect and gained a popular following as "Negro baiters" and white supremacists. Religious exposure in childhood did not necessarily alter white thinking on race.[31]

31. A. Wigfall Green, *The Man Bilbo* (Baton Rouge: Louisiana State University Press, 1963), 10–1; William F. Holmes, *The White Chief: James Kimble Vardaman* (Baton Rouge: Louisiana State University Press, 1970), 5; Raymond Allen Cook, *Fire from the Flint: The Amazing Careers of Thomas Dixon* (Winston-Salem, N.C.: John F. Blair, 1968), 3.

A better understanding of how southern white children were socialized during the postbellum years can give historians a better grasp on how young people learned about race and the kind of behavior that upheld a segregated South. Childhood experiences in white Sunday schools, like those in public schools, were deeply influential. Segregated institutions such as the Sunday school delivered an unspoken message about racial distinctions and who held power in the South. By their silence on human equality, white Sunday schools failed to challenge white youngsters' understanding about race. African Americans, on the other hand, found freedom in their Sunday classroom to teach ideals important to their race. Here, more so than in state-supported public schools, blacks could control the messages delivered to their children. Their Sunday schools taught youngsters to believe in God and in the promise of a brighter future. While black churches, Sunday schools, and publications often attacked racial oppression, white children heard only silence. Apparently the idea that all humans were equal in society and in the eyes of God were lessons that adult whites assumed did not need learning. They envisioned a well-ordered world in which blacks occupied the bottom rung. Sunday lessons erased blacks from the white mind.

With great eloquence, the southern writer Lillian Smith, in her unforgettable memoir *Killers of the Dream*, has offered insight into how southern white youngsters learned about race. As she wrote:

> From the time little Southern children take their first step they learn their ritual, for Southern Tradition leads them through its intricate movements. And some, if their faces are dark, learn to bend, hat in hand; and others, if their faces are white, learn to hold their heads high. Some step off the sidewalk while others pass by in arrogance. Bending, shoving, genuflecting, ignoring, stepping off, demanding, giving in, avoiding. . . . Children, moving through the labyrinth made by grown-ups' greed and guilt and fear. So we learned the dance that cripples the human spirit, step by step by step, we who were white and we who were colored, day by day, hour by hour, year by year, until the movements were reflexes and made for the rest of our life without thinking. Alas, for many white children, they were movements made for the rest of their lives without feeling.[32]

32. Smith, *Killers of the Dream*, 66.

To white youngsters, a belief in racial superiority was normative from birth; it was continually reinforced by custom, behavior, and daily experience. Few whites in the South—or in the nation, for that matter—considered the need to teach human equality or bring together the races to share ideas and experiences. White superiority was imbedded in the American mindset, and, whether spoken or unspoken, was reinforced in white Sunday schools. In white minds, raising up the South did not include challenging the racial status quo.

This study of the southern Sunday school movement ends before the United States entered World War I. Though not a particularly significant year in the southern Sunday school movement, 1915 marked the official split in the National Baptist Convention—a move sparked by controversy over Richard Boyd's publishing firm. That same year, Southern Presbyterians officially gave up efforts to oversee and teach African American Sunday schools. A year later, the federal government undertook its second survey of religion. More meaningful, perhaps, is that 1915 marked a half century since emancipation and the end of the Civil War. During those five decades, the Sunday school came into its own and became an important institution in a majority of the South's mainstream Protestant churches. Though it would continue to alter and expand throughout the twentieth century, at no other time in the region's history was the Sunday school so influential and so important to the South's very existence.

The Sunday school was significant because it placed children center stage and gave them a defined space within the church. As churches came to accept modern ideas about childhood, they acknowledged their responsibility to uplift youngsters. The Sunday school redirected Christian thought about the role of children in a number of ways, such as the importance of conversion and how it was achieved, Christian education, and qualifications for membership in the church community. Adults believed that a sound Christian upbringing would shape and improve each pupil's life and ultimately enhance the future of the South. Evangelicals looked ahead with both fear and optimism, wanting to create a brighter future based on the promise of a new generation.

We can never know what the region—or the nation, for that matter—might have been like without Sunday schools. During a half century of enormous social, political, and economic change, the Sunday school became an institution that gave hope and strength to millions of southerners. Sunday schools helped the South recover from a devastating war, clarify southern society's expectations for future generations, define young people's proper behavior, and offset the uncertainty of a modern, changing world. Sunday schools reinforced the importance of religion by bringing young people into the church and extending the influence of faith to church members, ultimately strengthening church and family ties.

Overall, though, the Sunday school offered an incomplete cure to many problems that the South faced during the latter decades of the nineteenth century. Most significantly, the Sunday school did not improve race relations in any meaningful way. Southern whites were unable to understand—much less identify as a problem—the devastating effects of racial oppression and white supremacy. In spite of this, however, the Sunday school occupied a significant place in the lives of millions of black and white southerners and in thousands of the region's churches and communities. It was responsible for much of the growth of southern churches, as well as an increased emphasis on denominational loyalty. Pupils and volunteers involved in the Sunday school were touched by it and, in many cases, found their lives brightened by their experience.

An understanding of the Sunday school's significant role in raising up the New South can help to reshape our thinking as we explore those critical decades and investigate how institutions began to reach out to future generations. A historical understanding of the southern Sunday school also helps us better comprehend the role of parents and institutions, present and past, as we raise our own children in an equally chaotic world.

BIBLIOGRAPHY

PRIMARY SOURCES

Manuscript Collections

American Bible Society Archives, New York, N.Y.

William F. Baird Collection.
E. A. Bolles Collection.
S. R. Chadwick Collection.
S. P. Whitten Collection.
Calvin H. Wiley Collection.

*James P. Boyce Centennial Library Archives,
Baptist Theological Seminary, Louisville, Ky.*

John Albert Broadus Correspondence.

*Rare Book, Manuscript, and Special Collections Library,
William R. Perkins Library, Duke University, Durham, N.C.*

Edmund Blum Papers.
Craven-Pegram Family Papers.

Robert Paine Dick Papers.
Gaines Chapel Sunday School Record Book.
Frances Louisa Goodrich Papers.
Grant County Sunday School Association Records.
Hatchett Family Papers.
William Woods Holden Papers.
Brooks Iverson Papers.
Annie Fouch Jennings Papers.
North Carolina Conference, District Conference Reports, MECS.
Cornelius Miller Pickens Papers.
Robert Nirwana Simms Papers.
Washington Varner Papers.
Carrie Weadon Papers.
Sidney W. Wilkinson Papers.

North Carolina State Archives, Raleigh, N.C.

G. Wilson McPhail Papers.

Special Collections, Emory University Libraries, Atlanta, Ga.

John W. Baker Collection.
Burge-Gray Family Letters.
Samuel Porter Jones Letters.
Log-Cabin Community Sunday School: Memories of Twenty-Five Years.
James V. M. Morris Diaries.
George G. Smith Papers.

Presbyterian Historical Society, Philadelphia, Pa.

American Sunday School Union Annual Reports.
American Sunday School Union Correspondence, 1865–1880.

Southern Historical Collection, Wilson Library, University of North Carolina, Chapel Hill

Anderson-Thornwell Papers.
Algernon Barbee Address.
Beale and Davis Family Papers.
Alexander Davis Betts Papers.
Emily Morrison Bondurant Papers.

D. A. Brigham Books.
Julian Shakespeare Carr Papers.
Cobb Family Papers.
Goelet and Buncombe Family Papers.
Pleasant Daniel Gold Papers.
John Lipscomb Johnson Papers.
James Harvey Joiner Papers.
Louise Rigsbee Jones Papers.
Drury Lacy Papers.
William Parson McCorkle Papers.
Basil Manly Jr. Papers.
Rangeley Family Papers.
Joseph Rennie Papers.
Roach and Eggleston Family Papers.
Wheelers Baptist Church Minute Books.
Ferdinand Hannon Whitaker Papers.
Calvin Henderson Wiley Papers.
William Henry Wills Papers.
Norvell Winsboro Wilson Papers.

Southern Baptist Historical Library and Archives, Nashville, Tenn.

Annie Armstrong Correspondence.
Lansing Burrows Papers.
Frost-Bell Correspondence, 1891–1904.
Una Roberts Lawrence Collection.

Tennessee State Archives, Nashville

Church Records.

Baptist Historical Collection, Wake Forest University Library, Winston-Salem, N.C.

Fannie E. S. Heck Papers.

CHURCH AND SUNDAY SCHOOL PROCEEDINGS

Southern Baptists

Minutes of the Alabama Baptist Association, 1867–1905.
Minutes of the Florida Baptist State Convention, 1903–1905.

Minutes of the Annual Sesson of the Jacksonville (Fla.) Baptist Association, 1911.
Minutes of the Georgia Baptist State Convention, 1867–1883.
Minutes of the Sunday School Convention of the State of Georgia.
Minutes of the Mississippi Baptist State Convention, 1888–1911.
Minutes of the Baptist Association of North Carolina, 1876–1884.
Minutes of the Baptist State Convention of South Carolina, 1871–1897.
Minutes of the Baptist General Association of Virginia, 1865–1898.
Proceedings of the Alabama Baptist State Convention, 1871–1897.
Proceedings of the Arkansas Baptist State Convention, 1892–1900.
Proceedings of the Baptist State Convention of North Carolina, 1874–1890.
Proceedings of the Baptist Convention of Western North Carolina, 1895.
Proceedings of the Southern Baptist Convention, 1872–1892.
Proceedings of the Baptist Convention of Tennessee, 1875–1898.

Black Baptists and National Baptist Convention

Journal of the Annual Session of the National Baptist Convention, 1899.
Minutes of the Alabama Colored Baptist State Convention, 1892–1897.
Minutes of the Baptist State Sunday School Convention of North Carolina (Negro), 1881–1910.
Minutes of the Reedy Creek Missionary Baptist Association (Negro), 1881, 1914.
Minutes of the Roanoke Missionary Baptist Association (Negro), 1879, 1885, 1916.
Minutes of the Wake (N.C.) Baptist Association (Negro), 1879–1894.

African Methodist Episcopal Church

Journal of the General Conference of the AME Church, 1872–1888.
Journal of the Proceedings of the Annual Session of the Western North Carolina Conference, 1910–1912.
Journal of the Virginia Annual Conference of the AME Church, 1874–1914.
Minutes of the Richmond (Va.) District Conference and Sunday School Convention, 1886.

African Methodist Episcopal Zion Church

Doctrines and Disciplines of the African Methodist Episcopal Zion Church in America, 1872, 1892, 1901.
Proceedings of the General Conference of the AME Zion Church, 1888–1904.
Official Journal of the Quadrennial Session of the General Conference of the AMEZ Church, 1880–1908.
Minutes of the North Carolina Annual Conference of the AMEZ, 1865, 1896.
Minutes of the Virginia Annual Conference of the AMEZ, 1885–1912.

Bibliography 255

Presbyterian Church in the United States

Executive Committee of Colored Evangelization, *Reports*, 1892–1909.
Executive Committee of Publication, "Concerning the International Graded Sunday School Lessons," 1910.
Minutes of the General Assembly of the Presbyterian Church in the United States, 1865–1915.
Minutes of the Synod of Alabama, 1865–1900.

Presbyterian Church in the United States of America

Correspondence of the Board of Publication. Colportage Department.
Executive Committee of Southern Evangelization, 1892–1910.

Methodist Episcopal Church, South

Annual Report of the Woman's Home Missionary Society of the MECS, 1898–1909.
Doctrines and Discipline of the MECS, 1866–1914.
Journal of the General Conference of the Methodist Episcopal Church, South, 1866–1918.
Minutes of the Alabama Conference of the MECS, 1873–1914.
Minutes of the Kentucky Annual Conference of the MECS, 1870–1891.
Minutes of the Louisiana Annual Conference of the MECS, 1884–1913.
Minutes of the Mississippi Annual Conference of the MECS, 1867–1873.
Minutes of the Northwest Texas Annual Conference of the MECS, 1866–1909.
Minutes of the Virginia Annual Conference of the MECS, 1890–1897.

Others

American Baptist Home Mission Society, *Annual Report*, 1866–1908.
American Baptist Missionary Convention (Black), *Annual Report*, 1869–1915.
American Baptist Publication Society, *Annual Report*, 1868–1907.
American Tract Society, *Annual Report*, 1866–1872.
Annual Report of the Sunday School Union of the Methodist Episcopal Church, 1866–1889.
Colored Methodist Episcopal Church. *The Doctrines and Discipline of the Colored Methodist Episcopal Church in America*. Byhalia, Miss.: E. Cottrell for the CMEC, 1883.
Minutes of the Sunday School Convention of the State of Georgia, 1873–1882.

Minutes of the Annual Session of the Kentucky Sunday School Union, 1867–1897.
Proceedings of the North Carolina State Sunday School Convention, 1878–1894.
Minutes of the South Carolina State Sunday School Convention, 1891.

Periodicals

Alabama Baptist, 1877–1893.
Advanced Quarterly, ABPS.
AME Church Review, 1884–1903.
AME Teachers' Quarterly, 1886, 1893.
Atlanta Constitution, 1902.
The Baptist, 1870.
Baptist Courier (Greenville), 1881–1894.
Baptist Home Mission Monthly, 1878–1880.
Biblical Recorder, 1867–1871.
Blue Ridge Baptist, 1882–1886.
Central Christian Advocate, 1872–1882.
The Children's Friend, 1862–1914.
Christian Advocate, 1876–1906.
Christian Index, 1885–1905.
Christian Recorder, 1865–1876.
The Colporter, 1898.
The Earnest Worker, 1870–1915.
Good Tidings, 1884–1893.
Kentucky Sunday School Union Reporter, 1891–1900.
Kind Words, 1871–1901.
Kind Words Teacher, 1887.
Methodist Advocate, 1869–1874.
Methodist Quarterly Review, 1874–1878.
Missionary Survey, 1911–1914.
National Baptist Union, 1901–1909.
North Carolina Baptist, 1891.
North Carolina Sunday School Beacon, 1901–1911.
Our Home Field, 1888–1904.
Our Little People, 1889–1915.
Pearls for Little Ones, 1893–1914.
The Presbyterian Quarterly, 1889–1896.
Presbyterian Standard, 1902–1906.
Religious Education, 1904–1907.
Religious Herald, 1865–1902.

The Seminary Magazine, 1888–1899.
Southern Christian Recorder, 1902–1903.
The Southern Presbyterian Review, 1867–1877.
The Southern Review, 1867–1879.
The Southern Workman, 1903.
Star of Zion, 1884–1915.
Sunday School Magazine, 1871–1908.
Sunday School Missionary, 1911.
Sunday School Monitor, 1902–1906.
Sunday School Visitor, 1893–1898.
Superintendent's Quarterly, SBC, 1910.
Tennessee Advocate, 1869–1874.
Tennessee Methodist, 1892–1893.
Tennessee Outlook, 1897.
Texas Christian Advocate, 1872–1881.
The Working Christian, 1869–1880.

PRINTED SOURCES

Adler, Felix. *The Moral Instruction of Children*. New York: D. Appleton, 1893.

Alexander, John L. *The Boy and the Sunday School: A Manual of Principle and Method for the Work of the Sunday School with Teen Age Boys*. New York: Association Press, 1915.

ABPS Executive Committee. "Facts Which Should Be Known by Southern Baptists." Philadelphia: ABPS, [1896].

AME Church. *Hymn and Tune Book; Adapted to the Doctrines and Usages of the Church*. Philadelphia: AME Book Concern, 1941.

ATS. *The American Tract Society Documents, 1824–1925*. New York: Arno Press, 1972.

Anthony, Bascom. *Fifty Years in the Ministry*. Macon, Ga.: J. W. Burke, 1937.

Anthony, James D. *Life and Times of Rev. J. D. Anthony: An Autobiography*. Atlanta: C. P. Byrd, 1896.

Arnett, Benjamin W., ed. *The Budget of the AME,C*. Xenia, Ohio: Torchlight Printing, 1881.

——— . *The Centennial Budget*. Philadelphia: AME Book Concern, 1888.

——— . *Fourth Annual Budget of the AME*. Xenia, Ohio: Torchlight Printing, 1884.

Atkins, James. *The Kingdom in the Cradle*. Nashville: Publishing House of the MECS, 1905.

Atkins, James, and William J. Kirkpatrick. *The Young People's Hymnal No. 2;*

Adapted to the Use of . . . Sunday Schools, Epworth Leagues, Prayer Meetings, and Revivals. Nashville: Publishing House of the MECS, 1901.

Atkinson, William E., comp. *The Value of the Sunday School*. New York: Fleming H. Revell, 1922.

Axtell, James Wickleff. *Grading the Sunday School: The Outcome of Organization*. Nashville: Cumberland Press, 1904.

———. *The Organized Sunday School: A Working Manual for Officers*. Nashville: Publishing House of the MECS, 1902.

———. *The Superintendent's Handbook*. Nashville: Cumberland Press, 1903.

———. *The Teaching Problem: A Message to Sunday School Workers*. Nashville: Cumberland Press, 1902.

Bain, Donald W. *Edenton Street Sunday School of the MEC,S, Raleigh, N.C.*. Raleigh: Edwards, Broughton, 1881.

Baird, E. T., and Karl Reden. *The Voice of Praise: A Selection of Hymns and Tunes, for the Sabbath School, Prayer Meeting, and Family Circle*. Richmond, Va.: E. Thompson Baird, 1872.

Baldwin, Maud Junkin. *The Juniors: How to Teach and Train Them*. Nashville: Baptist Sunday School Board, 1924.

Barclay, Wade Crawford. *The Pupil, the Teacher, and the School: First Standard Manual of Teacher Training*. Nashville: Publishing House of the MECS, 1914.

Beauchamp, Harvey. *The Advanced, or AA-1 Standard of Excellence for Sunday Schools in Baptist Churches*. Nashville: Baptist Sunday School Board, 1916.

———. *The Graded Sunday School*. Nashville: Sunday School Board, SBC, 1910.

Bentley, John H. *After Eight Decades: The Story of the American Baptist Publication Society*. Philadelphia: ABPS, 1908.

Black, Israel P. *Practical Primary Plans for Primary Teachers of the Sunday School*. New York: Fleming H. Revell, 1903.

Blackall, C. R. *Our Sunday School Work and How to Do It: A Manual for Baptist Sunday School Teachers*. Philadelphia: ABPS, 1901.

Boyd, Richard H., ed. *The National Baptist Hymnal, Arranged for the Use of Churches, Sunday Schools, and Young People's Societies*. 4th ed. Nashville: National Baptist Publishing Board, 1903.

Boyd, Sethelle. *Diary*. Privately owned by Scott and Scottie Lindsay, Charlotte, N.C.

Boykin, T. C. *Friendly Suggestions about Sunday-School Work*. Atlanta: James P. Harrison, 1877.

Boyle, Anna M. *Cradle Roll Stories for the Sunday School and Home*. Nashville: Sunday School Board of the SBC, 1918.

Brewbaker, Charles W. *The Adult Program in the Church School*. New York: Fleming H. Revell, 1925.

Brittain, M. L. *History and Methods of Sunday School Work; an Address . . . to the Stone Mountain Association, Sept. 6, 1900.* Nashville: Sunday School Board, SBC, 1900.

Bromfield, Edward C. *A Review of the Sabbath School Mission Work of the Presbyterian Church, 1887–1893.* Philadelphia: Allen, Lane and Scott's Printing House, 1893.

Brown, Marianna Catherine. *How to Plan a Lesson, and Other Talks to Sunday-School Teachers.* New York: Fleming H. Revell, 1904.

———. *Sunday-School Movements in America.* New York: Fleming H. Revell, 1901.

Brown, Oswald Eugene, and Anna Muse Brown, eds. *Life and Letters of Laura Askew Haygood.* Nashville: Publishing House of the MECS, 1904.

Browne, Henry Bascom. "Methodist Sunday Schools: After a Hundred Years." Address delivered to the History Society of the South Carolina Conference, MECS. Bennettsville, S.C., Nov. 28, 1911.

Bunbury, Selina. *A Visit to the Catacombs, or, First Christian Cemeteries at Rome and a Midnight Visit to Mount Vesuvius.* Nashville: Publishing House of the MECS, 1890.

Burke, J. W. *Burke's First Catechism for Little Folks.* 8th ed. Macon, Ga.: J. W. Burke, 1870.

Burkhead, L. S. *Centennial of Methodism in North Carolina, Containing the History and Addresses . . . Delivered at North Carolina Annual Conference, Raleigh.* Raleigh: John Nichols, 1876.

Burroughs, Prince Emanuel. *A Complete Guide to Church Building.* Nashville: Sunday School Board of the SBC, 1923.

Bushnell, Horace. *Christian Nurture.* 1847. Reprint, New Haven: Yale University Press, 1950.

Camp, Elias Morris. *Sermons, Addresses, and Reminiscences and Important Correspondence.* Nashville: National Baptist Publishing Board, 1901.

Campbell, Robert F. "Mission Work among the Mountain Whites in Asheville Presbytery, N.C." Asheville, N.C.: The Citizen, 1899.

———. "Some Aspects of the Race Problem in the South." 2nd ed. Asheville, N.C.: The Citizen, 1899.

Case, Carl Delos. *The Masculine in Religion.* Philadelphia: ABPS, 1906.

Chappell, Edwin Banfield. *Building the Kingdom: The Educational Ideal of the Church.* Nashville: Publishing House of the MECS, 1914.

———. *Evangelism in the Sunday School.* Nashville: Publishing House of the MECS, 1925.

———. *Introduction and Use of the Graded Lessons; International Series, General Manual.* Nashville: Publishing House of the MECS, 1914.

———. *Recent Development of Religious Education in the MEC, South: An Interpretation.* Nashville: Cokesbury Press, 1935.

Cope, Henry Frederick. *Efficiency in the Sunday School.* New York: Hodder and Stoughton, 1912.
———. *The Evolution of the Sunday School.* New York: The Pilgrim Press, 1911.
———. *The Modern Sunday School and Its Present Day Task.* New York: Fleming H. Revell, 1916.
———. *Religious Education in the Church.* New York: Scribners, 1918.
———. *Religious Education in the Family.* Chicago: University of Chicago Press, 1915.
Cope, Samuel W. *The Great Evil and Its Remedy, or Parental Responsibility in the Moral and Religious Training of Children.* Nashville: Publishing House of the MECS, 1889.
Corey, Charles H. *A History of the Richmond Theological Seminary, with Reminiscences of Thirty Years' Work among the Colored People of the South.* Richmond, Va.: J. W. Randolph, 1895.
Cowan, E. P. "A Sketch of the Origin and Work of the Presbyterian Board of Missions for Freedmen." Pittsburgh: Presbyterian Board of Missions for Freedmen, 1888.
Craig, J. N. *A Brief History of the General Assembly's Home Missions, Presbyterian Church in the U.S., 1861–1898.* Atlanta: Franklin Printing and Publishing, 1898.
Cronk, E. C. *The Kingdom of the Child Mind.* Augusta: Richards and Shaver, 1903.
Cuninggim, Jesse Lee. *A Plan for Better Religious Instruction in the Southern Methodist Church.* Nashville: Publishing House of the MECS, 1901.
Cuninggim, Jesse Lee, and Eric M. North. *The Organization and Administration of the Sunday School.* Nashville: Methodist Book Concern, 1919.
Cunnyngham, W. G. E. *The Sunday School: Its History and Management.* Nashville: Barbee and Smith, 1902.
Cunnyngham, W. G. E., and R. M. McIntosh. *Living Songs: for the Sunday School, the Epworth League, Prayer Meetings, Revivals, and All Special Occasions of Christian Work and Worship.* Nashville: Publishing House of the MECS, 1892.
———. *New Life without Notes.* Nashville: Southern Methodist Publishing House, 1886.
Dabney, R. L. "The New South: A Discourse." Raleigh: Edwards, Broughton, 1883.
———. "Speech Against the Ecclesiastical Equality of Negro Preachers in Our Church and Their Right to Rule over White Christians." Richmond: n.p., 1868.
Dale, William Thomas, ed. *Children's Hosannas: A Sabbath School Music Book.* Nashville: Cumberland Presbyterian Church, 1880.

Davis, Frank M. *Always Welcome: A Choice Collection of Song Gems for the Sunday School, Prayer and Praise Meetings and the Home Circle*. Savannah, Ga.: Ludden and Bates, n.d.

———. *Brightest Glory: A Collection of Choice Original Hymns and Tunes*. Vicksburg, Miss.: Frank M. Davis, 1896.

DesBrunner, Edmund. *Church Life in the Rural South*. New York: George H. Doran, 1923.

Doane, W. H. *Glorious Praise*. Louisville, Ky.: Harvey and Burnett, 1904.

Dortch, D. E. *Tidings of Joy: A Choice Collection of Sacred Songs for Sunday Schools*. Columbia, Tenn.: by the author, 1878.

Dortch, D. E., and W. G. E. Cunnyngham. *Grace and Glory: A Choice Collection of Sacred Songs, Original and Selected for Sabbath Schools, Revivals, etc.* Nashville: Southern Methodist Publishing House, 1882.

Doub, William C. "Methodism As Related to the History of Sunday Schools." Greensboro, N.C.: J. S. Hampton, 1884.

Douglass, Harlan Paul. *Christian Reconstruction in the South*. Boston: Pilgrim Press, 1909.

Drury, Belle Paxson. *A Fruitful Life: A Narrative of the Experiences and Missionary Labors of Stephen Paxson*. Philadelphia: ASSU, 1882.

DuBois, W. E. B. *The Negro Church*. Atlanta: Atlanta University Press, 1903.

Duncan, R. S. *The History of Sunday Schools, from the Most Ancient Times to the Present*. Memphis: Southern Baptist Publication Society, 1876.

Edwards, Gus Callaway. *The Country Town Sunday School*. Clarksville, Ga.: Legal Publishing, 1915.

Evans, Herbert Francis. *The Sunday-School Building and Its Equipment*. Chicago: University of Chicago Press, 1914.

Executive Board of the Baptist General Convention of Texas. *Centennial Story of Texas Baptists*. Dallas: Baptist General Convention of Texas, 1936.

Floyd, Silas X. *Floyd's Flowers, or Duty and Beauty for Colored Children*. Atlanta: Hertel, Jenkins, 1905.

Forbes, Lilian S. *The Home Department of the Sunday School*. Nashville: Sunday School Board of the SBC, 1916.

Forbush, William Byron. *The Boy Problem*. 6th ed. Boston: The Pilgrim Press, 1907.

Foster, Sarah Jane. *Sarah Jane Foster, Teacher of the Freedmen: A Diary and Letters*. Ed. Wayne E. Reilly. Charlottesville: University Press of Virginia, 1990.

Fox, E. A. *The Pastor's Place of Privilege and Power in the Sunday School*. Nashville: Publishing House of the MECS, 1907.

Frost, James Marion. *The School of the Church: Its Pre-eminent Place and Purpose*. New York: Fleming H. Revell, 1911.

———. *The Sunday School Board: Southern Baptist Convention, Its History and Work*. Nashville: Sunday School Board, 1914.

———. *The Sunday School Problem and What Can Be Done with It.* Nashville: n.p., n.d.

———. *A Word and a Plea Made with Those Not Using the Sunday School Periodicals Issued by the Southern Baptist Convention.* Nashville: n.p., 1903.

Fuller, Thomas O. *Twenty Years in Public Life, 1890–1910.* Nashville: National Baptist Publishing Board, 1910.

Gaines, Wesley J. *African Methodism in the South, or 25 Years of Freedom.* 1890. Reprint, Chicago: Afro-American Press, 1969.

The General Education Board. *An Account of Its Activities, 1902–1914.* New York: General Education Board, 1915.

Glenn, R. A., and Aldine Silliman Kieffer, eds. *New Melodies of Praise: A Collection of New Tunes and Hymns for the Sabbath School and Praise Meeting.* Dayton, Va.: Ruebush, Kieffer, 1877.

Gordon, E. C. *The Sunday-School Teacher's Work: What It Is and How to Do It.* Richmond, Va.: Whittet and Shepperson, 1887.

Grabs, W. F. *Sunday School Speeches for the Young Folks.* Randleman, N.C.: W. C. Phillips, 1888.

Grado, Pedro. *Pequena coleccion de himnas: escogidos y adaptados con especialidad a las reuniones de las ligas Epworth.* Laredo, Tex.: El Paso Printing, 1908.

Grady, Henry. *The New South: Writings and Speeches of Henry Grady.* Savannah, Ga.: Beehive Press, 1971.

Greene, Samuel H. *The Twentieth Century Sunday School.* Nashville: Sunday School Board of the SBC, 1904.

Greene, Samuel H., and Horace Kephart. *Our Southern Highlanders: A Narrative of Adventure in the Southern Appalachians and a Study of Life among the Mountaineers.* New York: Macmillan, 1916.

Hall, J. H., John McPherson, and J. H. Ruebush. *Fountain of Praise, for Sunday Schools, Prayer, Praise and Revival Meetings.* Dayton, Va.: Ruebush-Kieffer, 1892.

Hamill, Howard Melancthon. *The Sunday School Teacher.* Nashville: Publishing House of the MECS, 1906.

———. *Sunday-School Teacher-Training.* Philadelphia: Sunday School Times, 1904.

Hamilton, Alice McGuire. *Blue Ridge Mountain Memories: The True Story of a Mountain Girl at the Turn of the Century.* Atlanta: Conger, 1977.

Hardin, John Wesley. *The Life of John Wesley Hardin As Written by Himself.* Norman, Okla.: University of Oklahoma Press, 1961.

Harris, Hugh Henry. *The Organization and Administration of the Intermediate Department.* Nashville: Publishing House of the MECS, 1924.

Hartshorn, William Newton. *An Era of Progress and Promise, 1863–1910: The Religious, Moral and Educational Development of the American Negro since His Emancipation.* Boston: Priscilla, 1910.

Bibliography

Hartzell, J. C. *Methodism and the Negro in the United States.* Cincinnati: Cranston and Curtis, 1894.

Hatcher, William E. *The Pastor and the Sunday School.* Nashville: Sunday School Board of the SBC, 1902.

Haygood, Atticus G. *The Amaranth: A Book of Songs, Hymns, Anthems, Chants, and Concert Pieces for the Sunday-School.* Nashville: Publishing House of the MECS, 1877.

———. *Our Brother in Black: His Freedom and His Future.* 1889. Reprint, Miami: Mnemosyne, 1969.

———. *Our Children.* St. Louis: Advocate Publishing House, 1884.

———. *The Sunday School.* Atlanta: Atlanta Intelligence Book and Job Office, 1868.

Haygood, Atticus G., and R. M. McIntosh. *Five Songs for Sunday-Schools.* Macon, Ga.: J. W. Burke, 1890.

Heriges, R. M. *History of the Publishing House, MEC, South.* Nashville: MECS, n.d.

———. "Sunday School Legislation by the General Conference, MEC, South, 1846–1926." Typescript. Pitts Theology Library, Emory University.

Holland, D. B. *Primary Lessons in Vocal Music Designed for Sabbath Schools and Other Classes Learning to Sing.* Raleigh, N.C.: Thomas M. Hughes, 1868.

Home Mission Board of the Southern Baptist Convention. *Handbook of the Home Mission Board.* Atlanta: James P. Harrison, 1892.

Hooker, Elizabeth R. *Religion in the Highlands: Native Churches and Missionary Enterprise in the Southern Appalachian Area.* New York: Home Missions Council, 1923.

Hughson, Walter, comp. *The Church's Mission to the Mountaineers of the South.* Hartford, Conn.: Church Missions Publishing, 1908.

Hull, Asa, and D. R. M'Anally Jr. *The Royal Favorite. A Choice Collection of Original and Selected Hymns and Tunes Suitable for Sunday-Schools, Bible Classes and the Home Circle.* St. Louis: Advocate Publishing House, 1877.

Iden, Susan Franks. *Historical Sketch Commemorating the Opening of the New Sunday School Building, Edenton Street Methodist Sunday School, April 28, 1912.* Raleigh: Edwards and Broughton, n.d.

International Sunday School Association. Executive Committee. 11th International Sunday School Convention. *The Development of the Sunday School, 1780–1905.* Boston: ISSA, 1905.

———. *Half a Century of Growth and Service: The Story of the ISSA.* Chicago: ISSA, 1916.

———. 12th International Sunday School Convention. *Organized Sunday School Work in America, 1905–1908.* Chicago: ISSA, 1908.

———. 13th International Sunday School Convention. *Organized Sunday School Work in America, 1908–1911.* Chicago: ISSA, 1911.

———. 14th International Sunday School Convention. *Organized Sunday School Work in America, 1911–1914.* Chicago: ISSA, 1914.

Jackson, Nannie Stillwell. *Vinegar Pie and Chicken Bread: A Woman's Diary of Life in the Rural South, 1890–1891.* Ed. Margaret Jones Bolsterli. Fayetteville: University of Arkansas Press, 1982.

James, J. A. *The Sunday School Teacher's Guide.* Philadelphia: ASSU, n.d.

Johnson, Anna. *The Primary Class.* Nashville: Publishing House of the MECS, 1890.

Jones, A. M. *Quaint Characters, or Colportage Sketches.* Nashville: Publishing House of the MECS, 1890.

Kerby, M. S., and D. P. Airhart. *The Song Gem for Sunday-Schools, Revivals and Religious Meetings.* Temple, Tex.: M. S. Kerby, 1888.

Kerfoot, Franklin Howard. *The Home Mission Work of the Southern Baptist Convention.* Baltimore: Baptist Mission Rooms, 1900.

Kieffer, Aldine S., ed. *The New Starry Crown: For the Sabbath School.* Dayton, Va.: Ruebush, Kieffer, 1877.

Kirkland, W. D., James Atkins, and William J. Kirkpatrick. *The Young People's Hymnal. Adapted to the Use of Sunday Schools, Epworth Leagues, Prayer Meetings, and Revivals.* Nashville: Publishing House of the MECS, 1899.

Lane, Bishop Isaac. *Autobiography of Bishop Isaac Lane, LL.D., with a Short History of the CME Church in America and of Methodism.* Nashville: Publishing House of the MECS, 1916.

Lawrance, Marion. *Housing the Sunday School: or, A Practical Study of Sunday School Buildings.* Philadelphia: Westminster Press, 1911.

Leavell, Landrum Pinson. *The Intermediate Department of the Sunday School.* Nashville: Sunday School Board of the SBC, 1918.

———. *Pupil Life, with Hints to Teachers.* Nashville: Sunday School Board of the SBC, 1919.

Leftwich, William M. *The Child in the Midst: or, The Sunday-School of To-Day.* Nashville: Southern Methodist Publishing House, 1882.

LeGuin, Magnolia Wynn. *A Home-Concealed Woman: The Diaries of Magnolia Wynn LeGuin, 1901–1913.* Ed. Charles A. LeGuin. Athens: University of Georgia Press, 1990.

Lewis, Hazel Asenath. *Methods for Primary Teachers.* St. Louis: Front Rank Press, 1921.

Link, William A., ed. *The Rebuilding of Old Commonwealths and Other Documents of Social Reform in the Progressive Era South.* New York, Boston: St. Martin's Press, 1996.

Linton, G. W. *Twilight Zephyrs for the Sunday School: A New Collection of*

Hymns and Tunes for Sunday Schools, Missionary Meetings, Anniversaries, Temperance Meetings. and the Social Circle. St. Louis: John Burns, 1881.

Lyon, G. W., and J. L. Moore. *Pearls of Praise: A Collection of New Hymns and Tunes for Sunday-School and Song Service.* Atlanta: J. B. Vaughan, 1891.

Lyon, J. A. *The Sunday School and Its Methods.* Nashville: MECS Publishing House, 1895.

McIntosh, R. M., and W. G. E. Cunnyngham. *New Life, or Songs and Tunes for Sunday-Schools, Prayer Meetings, and Revival Occasions.* Nashville: Southern Methodist Publishing House, 1880.

McKinney, A. H. *The Pastor and Teacher Training. The Sunday School Board Seminary Lectures. Course #4.* Nashville: Sunday School Board of the SBC, 1905.

McMillan, Homer. *"Unfinished Tasks" of the Southern Presbyterian Church.* Richmond, Va.: Presbyterian Committee of Publication, 1922.

Mallory, James. *"Fear God and Walk Humbly": The Agricultural Journal of James Mallory, 1843–1877.* Eds. Grady McWhiney, Warren O. Moore Jr., and Robert F. Pace. Tuscaloosa: University of Alabama Press, 1997.

Manly, Basil, Jr. *Little Lessons for Little People.* St. Louis: National Baptist Publishing, 1867.

———. *Sunday School Questions on the Four Gospels, together with a Condensed Harmony.* Vol. 1. Raleigh: Baptist Sunday School and Publication Board of North Carolina, 1864.

Masters, Victor I. *Baptist Home Missions: A Manual for Mission Study Classes.* Atlanta: Home Mission Board of the SBC, 1914.

———. *Country Church in the South.* Atlanta: Home Mission Board of the SBC, 1916.

———. *The Home Mission Task: Its Fundamental Character, Magnitude and Present Urgency.* Atlanta: Home Mission Board of the SBC, 1912.

Mayo, Amory D. *Southern Women in the Recent Educational Movement in the South.* 1892. Reprint, Baton Rouge: Louisiana State University Press, 1978.

Mays, Benjamin E. *Born to Rebel: An Autobiography.* New York: Charles Scribner's Sons, 1971. Reprint, Athens: University of Georgia Press, 1987.

Mebane, George Allen. *"The Negro Problem" As Seen and Discussed by Southern White Men in a Conference at Montgomery, Alabama.* New York: Alliance Publishing, 1900.

Miller, Minor C. *These Things I Remember.* Philadelphia: Dorrance, 1968.

Mitchell, James Alexander. *The Normal Manual of Modern Sunday School Method.* Memphis: Memphis Sunday School Publishing, 1919.

Moore, Hight C. *The Country Sunday School.* Philadelphia: ABPS, 1906.

———. *Normal Studies for Sunday School Workers.* Vol. 2, *The Books of the Bible.* Nashville: Sunday School Board of the SBC, 1902.

Moore, Joanna P. *In Christ's Stead: Autobiographical Sketches*. Chicago: Woman's Baptist Home Mission Society, 1902.

Morris, E. C. *Sermons, Addresses and Reminiscences and Important Correspondence*. Nashville: National Baptist Publishing Board, 1901.

Morris, Samuel L. *At Our Door: A Study of Home Missions with Special Reference to the South and West*. New York: Fleming H. Revell, 1904.

———. *The Task that Challenges: Home Mission Text Book*. Richmond: Presbyterian Committee of Publication, 1917.

Murphy, Edgar Gardner. *Problems of the Present South*. New York: Macmillan, 1904.

Murray, E. C. "The Sunday-School: Its True Nature and Mission, and Relation to the Church." *Presbyterian Quarterly* 3 (1889): 114–8.

Musselman, H. T. *The Baptist Teacher-Training Manual. Introductory Book*. Philadelphia: Griffith and Rowland, 1909.

National Baptist Convention Sunday School Board. *Gospel Pearls*. Nashville: NBC, 1921.

National Sunday-School Convention of the United States. Yearbooks, 1869, 1872. Newark, N.J.

Oslin, S. J., and L. G. McClendon. *Pearls of Truth in Song for Sabbath Schools, Prayer and Praise Meetings*. Dayton, Va.: Ruebush, Kieffer, 1890.

Payne, Daniel Alexander. *The History of the AMEC*. 1891. Reprint, New York: Johnson Reprint, 1968.

Pearce, William C. *The Adult Bible Class: Its Organization and Work*. Philadelphia: Westminster Press, 1909.

Penn, Irvine Garland. *The Afro-American Press and Its Editors*. 1891. Reprint, New York: Arno Press, 1969.

———, ed. *The United Negro: His Problems and His Progress, Containing the Addresses and Proceedings of the Negro Young People's Christian and Educational Congress, August 6–11, 1902*. Atlanta: D. E. Luther, 1902.

Pepper, John Robertson. *Some Tried Plans of Sunday School Work*. N.p: privately published, N.d.

———. *The Sunday-School Teacher*. Nashville: Southern Methodist Publishing House, 1887.

———. *Thirty Years at the Superintendent's Desk, Lessons Learned and Noted*. New York: Fleming H. Revell, 1910.

———. *Well-Nigh Fifty Years at the Superintendent's Desk*. Memphis: Press of Early-Freeburg, 1929.

Phillips, Alexander Leroy. *The Call of the Home Land: A Study in Home Missions*. Richmond: Presbyterian Committee of Publication, 1906.

———. "A Model Presbyterian Sunday School." Richmond: Presbyterian Committee of Publication, 1910.

———. "Sabbath-Schools and the Southern Presbyterian Church." Richmond: Whittet and Shepperson, 1902.

———. *The Westminster Standard Teacher Training Course. First Standard Course.* Richmond: Presbyterian Committee of Publication, 1912.

Phillips, Charles Henry. *From the Farm to the Bishopric: An Autobiography.* Nashville: Parthenon Press, 1932.

———. *The History of the Colored Methodist Episcopal Church in America, Comprising Its Organization, Subsequent Development, and Present Status.* Jackson, Tenn.: Publishing House of the CME, 1925.

Pigott, Levi Woodbury. *Scenes and Incidents in the Life of a Home Missionary, with a Biographical Sketch of Fenner S. Pigott.* Norfolk, Va.: n.p., 1901.

Read, C. H. "Sabbath Schools: Their Relation to the Church and the Obligations of the Church in the Management of Them." Richmond: Presbyterian Committee of Publication, n.d.

Rhyne, Jennings J. *Some Southern Cotton Mill Workers and Their Villages.* Chapel Hill: University of North Carolina Press, 1930.

Robertson, Archibald Thomas. *Life and Letters of John Albert Broadus.* Philadelphia: ABPS, 1901.

Robinson, James H. *Road without Turning: The Story of Reverend James H. Robinson, An Autobiography.* New York: Farrar, Straus, 1950.

Robinson, R. L. *History of the Georgia Baptist Association.* Union Point, Ga.: n.p., 1928.

Rubin, Louis D., Jr., ed. *Teach the Freeman: The Correspondence of Rutherford B. Hayes and the Slater Fund for Negro Education.* 2 vols. Baton Rouge: Louisiana State University Press, 1959.

Schauffler, Adolphus. *Pastoral Leadership in Sunday School Forces.* Nashville: Sunday School Board of the SBC, 1903.

Showalter, Anthony. *The Highway to Heaven—A New Collection of Gospel Songs.* Dalton, Ga.: n.p., 1899.

Showalter, Anthony, J. L. M. Evilsizer, and Joseph B. Moon. *The Glad Evangel, No. 2 for Sunday Schools, Christian Endeavor Societies.* Powder Springs, Ga.: Joseph B. Moon, 1890.

Smith, Charles Spence. *Dedicatory Services at the Publishing House of the A.M.E. Church Sunday School Union.* Nashville: Publishing House of the AME Church Sunday School Union, 1894.

Smith, George. *Childhood and Conversion.* Nashville: Publishing House of the MECS, 1891.

Snedecor, James G. *Missionary Aspects of Our Negro Population.* Richmond: L. D. Sullivan, 1906.

The Southern Society for the Promotion of the Study of Race Conditions and Problems in the South. *Race Problems of the South: Report of the Proceedings of the First Annual Conference.* Richmond: B. F. Johnson, 1900.

Spilman, Bernard Washington. *Normal Studies for Sunday School Workers.* Nashville: Sunday School Board of the SBC, 1901.

Spilman, Bernard Washington, L. P. Leavell, and Hight C. Moore. *Convention Normal Manual for Sunday School Workers.* Nashville: Sunday School Board of the SBC, 1909.

Stanton, P. L. *The Sunday-School in Ten Red-Hot Chapters.* Fairmont, Ga.: by the author, 1898.

Stuart, George Rutledge. *What Every Methodist Should Know.* Nashville: MECS Publishing House, 1923.

Summers, Thomas O. *Sabbaths with My Class, with an Introduction on Bible-Class Teaching.* Nashville: Southern Methodist Publishing House, 1886.

Thompson, Samuel Hunter. *The Highlanders of the South.* New York: Eaton and Mains, 1910.

Tillett, Wilbur Fiske. *Theological Seminaries and Teacher Training: A Discussion of the Preacher's Relation to the Sunday School and the Young Life of the Church.* Nashville: MECS Publishing House, 1910.

Trumbull, Henry Clay. *The Origin and Expansion of the Sunday-School.* Philadelphia: Sunday School Times, 1906.

———. *The Sunday-School: Its Origin, Mission, Methods and Auxiliaries.* Philadelphia: John D. Wattles, 1888.

U.S. Department of Commerce, Bureau of the Census. *Special Reports: Religious Bodies, 1906.* Washington, D.C.: GPO, 1910.

———. *Special Reports: Religious Bodies, 1916.* Washington, D.C.: GPO, 1919.

Whitted, J. A. *A History of the Negro Baptists of North Carolina.* Raleigh, N.C.: Edwards and Broughton, 1908.

Williams, Annie L. *Plans and Programs for Cradle Roll, Beginners and Primary Workers.* Nashville: Sunday School Board of the SBC, 1918.

Wilson, Samuel Tyndale. *The Southern Mountaineers.* New York: Presbyterian Home Missions, 1906.

Witherspoon, T. D. "The Sunday-School: Its Present Peril." *Presbyterian Quarterly* 11 (1897): 175–89.

Wright, Richard R. *Centennial Encyclopedia of the AMEC.* Philadelphia: Book Concern of the AME Church, 1916.

Wright, Richard R., Jr. *87 Years behind the Black Curtain: An Autobiography.* Philadelphia: Rare Book, 1965.

SECONDARY SOURCES

Books

Abell, Aaron I. *The Urban Impact on American Protestantism, 1865–1900.* Cambridge: Harvard University Press, 1943.

Adams, Revel Alcorn. *Cyclopedia of African Methodism in Mississippi*. Natchez, Miss.: n.p., 1902.

Anderson, James D. *The Education of Blacks in the South, 1860–1935*. Chapel Hill: University of North Carolina Press, 1988.

Angell, Stephen Ward. *Bishop Henry McNeal Turner and African-American Religion in the South*. Knoxville: University of Tennessee Press, 1992.

Ariès, Philippe. *Centuries of Childhood: A Social History of Family Life*. New York: Random House, 1962.

Avery, Gillian. *Behold the Child: American Children and Their Books, 1621–1922*. Baltimore: Johns Hopkins University Press, 1994.

Ayers, Edward L. *The Promise of the New South: Life after Reconstruction*. New York: Oxford University Press, 1992.

Bailey, Hugh C. *Edgar Gardner Murphy, Gentle Progressive*. Coral Gables, Fla: University of Miami Press, 1968.

Bailey, Kenneth K. *Southern White Protestantism in the Twentieth Century*. New York: Harper and Row, 1964.

Baker, Robert Andrew. *The Southern Baptist Convention and Its People, 1607–1972*. Nashville: Broadman Press, 1974.

———. *The Story of the Sunday School Board*. Nashville: Convention Press, 1966.

Bardaglio, Peter W. *Reconstructing the Household: Families, Sex, and the Law in the Nineteenth-Century South*. Chapel Hill: University of North Carolina Press, 1995.

Barnes, Lemuel Call, Mary Clark Barnes, and Edward M. Stephenson. *Pioneers of Light: The First Century of the American Baptist Publication Society, 1824–1924*. Philadelphia: ABPS, n.d.

Barnes, William Wright. *The Southern Baptist Convention, 1845–1953*. Nashville: Broadman Press, 1954.

Bederman, Gail. *Manliness and Civilization: A Cultural History of Gender and Race in the United States, 1880–1917*. Chicago: University of Chicago Press, 1995.

Bell, Sadie. *The Church, the State, and Education in Virginia*. 1930. Reprint, New York: Arno Press, 1969.

Benardete, Jane, and Phyllis Moe, eds. *Companions of Our Youth: Stories by Women for Young People's Magazines, 1865–1900*. New York: Frederick Ungar, 1980.

Benson, Clarence Herbert. *A Popular History of Christian Education*. Chicago: Moody Press, 1943.

Bode, Frederick. *Protestantism and the New South: North Carolina Baptists and Methodists in Political Crisis, 1894–1903*. Charlottesville: University Press of Virginia, 1975.

Boles, Donald E. *The Bible, Religion, and Public Schools*. Ames: Iowa State University Press, 1961.

Boles, John B. *The Irony of Southern Religion*. Rockwell Lecture Series. New York: Peter Lang, 1994.

Booth, Charles Octavius. *The Cyclopedia of the Colored Baptists of Alabama: Their Leaders and Their Work*. Birmingham: Alabama Publishing, 1895.

Bordin, Ruth. *Woman and Temperance: The Quest for Power and Liberty, 1873–1900*. Philadelphia: Temple University Press, 1981.

Bowen, Cawthon A. *Child and Church: A History of Methodist Church-School Curriculum*. New York: Abingdon Press, 1960.

Boyer, Paul. *Purity in Print: The Vice Society Movement and Book Censorship in America*. New York: Charles Scribner's Sons, 1968.

———. *Urban Masses and Moral Order in America, 1820–1920*. Cambridge: Harvard University Press, 1978.

Boylan, Anne M. *Sunday School: The Formation of an American Institution, 1790–1880*. New Haven: Yale University Press, 1988.

Brabham, Mouzon William. *A History of Sunday School Work in the North Carolina Conference, MEC,S*. Greensboro: North Carolina Christian Advocate, 1925.

———. *Planning Modern Church Buildings*. Nashville: Cokesbury Press, 1928.

———. *The Sunday School at Work in Town and Country*. New York: George H. Doran, 1922.

Braden, Beulah B. *When Grandma Was a Girl*. Oak Ridge, Tenn.: Oak Ridge and Clinton-Carrier News, 1976.

Bradley, David Henry, Sr. *A History of the AME Zion Church*. Vol. 2, *1872–1968*. Nashville: Parthenon Press, 1970.

Buck, Paul H. *The Road to Reunion, 1865–1900*. Boston: Little, Brown, 1937.

Bucke, Emory Stevens, ed. *The History of American Methodism*. 3 vols. New York: Abingdon Press, 1964.

Bullock, Henry Allen. *A History of Negro Education in the South from 1619 to the Present*. Cambridge: Harvard University Press, 1967.

Bullock, Penelope L. *The Afro-American Periodical Press, 1838–1909*. Baton Rouge: Louisiana State University Press, 1981.

Burroughs, Prince Emanuel. *Fifty Fruitful Years, 1891–1941: The Story of the Sunday School Board of the Southern Baptist Convention*. Nashville: Broadman Press, 1941.

Burton, Joe W. *Road to Nashville*. Nashville: Broadman Press, 1977.

Candler, Warren A. *Bishop Charles Betts Galloway: A Prince of Preachers and a Christian Statesman*. Nashville: Cokesbury Press, 1927.

Carlton, David L. *Mill and Town in South Carolina, 1880–1920*. Baton Rouge: Louisiana State University Press, 1982.

Carnes, Mark C., and Clyde Griffin, eds. *Meanings for Manhood: Constructions of Masculinity in Victorian America*. Chicago: University of Chicago Press, 1990.

Carpenter, Marie Elizabeth. *The Treatment of the Negro in American History School Textbooks*. Menasha, Wis.: George Banta, 1941.

Carroll, J. M. *A History of Texas Baptists; Comprising a Detailed Account of Their Activities, Their Progress, and Their Achievements*. Dallas: Baptist Standard Publishing, 1923.

Case, Victoria, and Robert Ormond Case. *We Called It Culture: The Story of Chautauqua*. New York: Doubleday, 1948.

Christian, John T. *A History of the Baptists of Louisiana*. Shreveport: Executive Board, Louisiana Baptist Convention, 1923.

Clark, Elmer T. *Methodism in Western North Carolina*. Nashville: Western North Carolina Conference of the Methodist Church, 1966.

Clark, Thomas D. *Three Paths to the Modern South: Education, Agriculture, and Conservation*. Athens: University of Georgia Press, 1965.

Cobb, Buell E., Jr. *The Sacred Harp: A Tradition and Its Music*. Athens: University of Georgia Press, 1978.

Cook, Raymond Allen. *Fire from the Flint: The Amazing Careers of Thomas Dixon*. Winston-Salem, N.C.: John F. Blair, 1968.

Coontz, Stephanie. *The Social Origins of Private Life: A History of American Families, 1600–1900*. London: Verso, 1988.

Cox, Norman Wade, ed. *Encyclopedia of Southern Baptists*. 2 vols. Nashville: Broadman Press, 1958.

Cutt, Margaret Nancy. *Ministering Angels: A Study of Nineteenth-Century Evangelical Writing for Children*. Wormley, Eng.: Five Owls Press, 1979.

DeBerg, Betty A. *Ungodly Women: Gender and the First Wave of American Fundamentalism*. Minneapolis: Fortress Press, 1990.

Degler, Carl N. *At Odds: Women and the Family in America from the Revolution to the Present*. New York: Oxford University Press, 1980.

Detweiler, Frederick K. *The Negro Press in the United States*. 1922. Reprint, College Park, Md.: McGrath, 1968.

Dill, Jacob Smiser. *Isaac Taylor Tichenor: The Home Mission Statesman*. Nashville: Sunday School Board, SBC, 1908.

Dittmer, John. *Black Georgia in the Progressive Era, 1900–1920*. Urbana: University of Illinois Press, 1977.

Duren, William Larkin. *The Trail of the Circuit Rider*. New Orleans: Chalmers' Printing House, 1936.

Dvorak, Katharine L. *An African-American Exodus: The Segregation of the Southern Churches*. New York: Carlson, 1991.

Eighmy, John Lee. *Churches in Cultural Captivity: A History of the Social Attitudes of Southern Baptists*. Knoxville: University of Tennessee Press, 1972.

Ellinwood, Leonard. *The History of American Church Music.* 1953. Rev. ed., New York: Da Capo Press, 1970.

Elson, Ruth Miller. *Guardians of Tradition: American Schoolbooks of the Nineteenth Century.* Lincoln: University of Nebraska Press, 1964.

Farish, Hunter Dickinson. *The Circuit Rider Dismounts: A Social History of Southern Methodism, 1865–1900.* Richmond, Va.: Dietz Press, 1938.

Fergusson, Edmund Morris. *Historic Chapters in Christian Education in America: A Brief History of the American Sunday School Movement.* New York: Fleming H. Revell, 1935.

Finke, Roger, and Rodney Stark. *The Churching of America, 1776–1990: Winners and Losers in Our Religious Economy.* New Brunswick, N.J.: Rutgers University Press, 1992.

Fitts, Leroy. *A History of Black Baptists.* Nashville: Broadman Press, 1985.

Flynt, J. Wayne. *Poor but Proud: Alabama's Poor Whites.* Tuscaloosa: University of Alabama Press, 1989.

Foner, Eric, ed. *The New American History.* Philadelphia: Temple University Press, 1990.

———. *Reconstruction: America's Unfinished Revolution, 1863–1977.* New York: Harper and Row, 1988.

Foster, Gaines M. *Ghosts of the Confederacy: Defeat, the Lost Cause, and the Emergence of the New South, 1865–1913.* New York: Oxford University Press, 1987.

Frederickson, George. *The Black Image in the White Mind: The Debate on Afro-American Character and Destiny, 1817–1914.* New York: Harper and Row, 1971.

Friedman, Jean. *The Enclosed Garden: Women and Community in the Evangelical South, 1830–1900.* Chapel Hill: University of North Carolina Press, 1985.

Fuller, Thomas O. *History of the Negro Baptists of Tennessee.* Memphis: Haskins Print, 1936.

Gaines, Kevin K. *Uplifting the Race: Black Leadership, Politics, and Culture in the Twentieth Century.* Chapel Hill: University of North Carolina Press, 1996.

Gardner, Robert G. *A Decade of Debate and Division: Georgia Baptists and the Formation of the Southern Baptist Convention.* Macon, Ga.: Mercer University Press, 1995.

Gardner, Robert G., et al. *A History of the Georgia Baptist Association, 1784–1984.* Atlanta: Georgia Baptist Historical Society, 1988.

Garrett, Mary Lou Stewart. *History of Fairview Presbyterian Church of Greenville County, S.C.* N.p.: A Press, 1986.

Gaston, Paul M. *The New South Creed: A Study in Southern Mythmaking.* New York: Alfred A. Knopf, 1970.

Gilmore, Glenda. *Gender and Jim Crow: Women and the Politics of White Supremacy in North Carolina, 1896–1920*. Chapel Hill: University of North Carolina Press, 1996.

Ginzberg, Lori D. *Women and the Work of Benevolence: Morality, Politics, and Class in the Nineteenth-Century United States*. New Haven: Yale University Press, 1990.

Goen, C. C. *Broken Churches, Broken Nation: Denominational Schisms and the Coming of the American Civil War*. Macon, Ga.: Mercer University Press, 1985.

Goodenow, Ronald K., and Arthur O. White, eds. *Education and the Rise of the New South*. Boston: G. K. Hall, 1981.

Gould, Joseph E. *The Chautauqua Movement: An Episode in the Continuing American Revolution*. Albany: State University of New York, 1961.

Graff, Harvey J. *Conflicting Paths: Growing Up in America*. Cambridge: Harvard University Press, 1995.

Grantham, Dewey W. *Southern Progressivism: The Reconciliation of Progress and Tradition*. Knoxville: University of Tennessee Press, 1983.

Green, A. Wigfall. *The Man Bilbo*. Baton Rouge: Louisiana State University Press, 1963.

Greenwood, Janette Thomas. *Bittersweet Legacy: The Black and White "Better Classes" in Charlotte, 1850–1910*. Chapel Hill: University of North Carolina Press, 1994.

Guy-Shaftall, Beverly. *Daughters of Sorrow: Attitudes toward Black Women, 1880-1920*. Vol. 11 of *Black Women in United States History*, ed. Darlene Clark Hine. Brooklyn: Carlson Publishing, 1990.

Gwin, Minrose C. *Black and White Women of the Old South: The Peculiar Sisterhood in American Literature*. Knoxville: University of Tennessee Press, 1985.

Hahn, Steven, and Jonathan Prude, eds. *The Countryside in the Age of Capitalist Transformation: Essays in the Social History of Rural America*. Chapel Hill: University of North Carolina Press, 1985.

Hall, Jacquelyn, et al. *Like a Family: The Making of a Southern Cotton Mill World*. Chapel Hill: University of North Carolina Press, 1987.

Hamlet, Georgia. *A History of the First Baptist Church, Anderson, S.C., 1821–1979*. N.p., n.d.

Handy, Robert T. *A Christian America: Protestant Hopes and Historical Realities*. New York: Oxford University Press, 1971.

———. *Undermined Establishment; Church-State Relations in America, 1880–1920*. Princeton: Princeton University Press, 1991.

Harlan, Louis R. *Separate and Unequal: Public School Campaigns and Racism in the Southern Seaboard States, 1901–1915*. Chapel Hill: University of North Carolina Press, 1958.

Harmon, Nolan B., ed. *The Encyclopedia of World Methodism.* 2 vols. Nashville: United Methodist Publishing House, 1974.

Harvey, Paul. *Redeeming the South: Religious Cultures and Racial Identities among Southern Baptists, 1865–1925.* Chapel Hill: University of North Carolina Press, 1997.

Higginbotham, Evelyn Brooks. *Righteous Discontent: The Women's Movement in the Black Baptist Church, 1880–1920.* Cambridge: Harvard University Press, 1993.

Hildebrand, Reginald E. *The Times Were Strange and Stirring: Methodist Preachers and the Crisis of Emancipation.* Durham, N.C.: Duke University Press, 1995.

Hill, Sam S., ed. *Encyclopedia of Religion in the South.* Macon, Ga.: Mercer University Press, 1984.

———. *Religion in the Southern States: A Historical Study.* Macon, Ga.: Mercer University Press, 1983.

———. *The South and the North in American Religion.* Athens: University of Georgia Press, 1980.

———. *Varieties of Southern Religious Experience.* Baton Rouge: Louisiana State University Press, 1982.

Himmelfarb, Gertrude. *The De-Moralization of Society: From Victorian Virtues to Modern Values.* New York: Alfred A. Knopf, 1995.

Hiner, N. Ray, and Joseph M. Hawes, eds. *Growing Up in America: Children in Historical Perspective.* Urbana: University of Illinois Press, 1985.

Hinson, E. Glenn. *A History of Baptists in Arkansas, 1818–1978.* Little Rock: Arkansas Baptist State Convention, 1979.

Holder, Ray. *The Mississippi Methodists, 1799–1983: A Moral People "Born of Conviction".* Jackson, Miss.: Maverick Prints, 1984.

Holmes, William F. *The White Chief: James Kimble Vardaman.* Baton Rouge: Louisiana State University Press, 1970.

Hopkins, Charles H. *The Rise of the Social Gospel in American Protestantism, 1865–1915.* New Haven: Yale University Press, 1940.

Hunter, Tera W. *To 'Joy My Freedom: Southern Black Women's Lives and Labors after the Civil War.* Cambridge: Harvard University Press, 1997.

Jackson, Joseph Harrison. *A Story of Christian Activism: The History of the National Baptist Convention, USA, Inc.* Nashville: Townsend Press, 1980.

James, F. C. *African Methodism in South Carolina: A Bicentennial Focus.* Tappan, N.Y: Custombook, 1987.

Joiner, Edward Earl. *A History of Florida Baptists.* Jacksonville: Florida Baptist Convention, 1972.

Jones, Jacqueline. *The Dispossessed: America's Underclasses from the Civil War to the Present.* New York: Basic Books, 1992.

———. *Labor of Love, Labor of Sorrow: Black Women, Work, and Family from Slavery to the Present*. New York: Basic Books, 1985.

———. *Soldiers of Light and Love: Northern Teachers and Georgia Blacks, 1865–1873*. Chapel Hill: University of North Carolina Press, 1980.

Joyce, Donald Franklin. *Gatekeepers of Black Culture: Black-Owned Book Publishing in the United States, 1817–1981*. Westport, Conn.: Greenwood Press, 1983.

Kasson, John F. *Rudeness and Civility: Manners in Nineteenth Century Urban America*. New York: Hill and Wang, 1990.

Kealing, H. T. *History of African Methodism in Texas*. Waco, Tex.: C. F. Blanks, 1885.

Kelly, R. Gordon, ed. *Children's Periodicals of the United States*. Westport, Conn.: Greenwood Press, 1984.

Kendall, W. Fred. *A History of the Tennessee Baptist Convention*. Brentwood: Executive Board, Tennessee Baptist Convention, 1974.

Kennedy, William Bean. *The Shaping of Protestant Education, 1789–1860: An Interpretation of the Sunday School and the Development of Protestant Educational Strategy in the United States*. Ed. C. Ellis Nelson. New York: Association Press, 1966.

Kiefer, Monica. *American Children through Their Books, 1700–1835*. Philadelphia: University of Pennsylvania Press, 1948.

Kimmel, Michael. *Manhood in America: A Cultural History*. New York: Free Press, 1996.

Knight, Edgar Wallace. *The Influence of Reconstruction on Education in the South*. 1913. Reprint, New York: Arno Press, 1972.

———. *Public Education in the South*. New York: Ginn, 1922.

Knoff, Gerald E. *The World Sunday School Movement: The Story of a Broadening Mission*. New York: Seabury Press, 1979.

Kolchin, Peter. *First Freedom: The Responses of Alabama Blacks to Emancipation and Reconstruction*. Westport, Conn.: Greenwood Press, 1972.

Kuykendall, John W. *Southern Enterprize: The Work of National Evangelical Societies in the Antebellum South*. Westport, Conn.: Greenwood Press, 1982.

Lakey, Othal Hawthorne. *The Rise of "Colored Methodism": A Study of the Background and the Beginnings of the Christian Methodist Episcopal Church*. Dallas: Crescendo Book Publishers, 1972.

Lankard, Frank Glenn. *A History of the American Sunday School Curriculum*. New York: Abingdon Press, 1927.

Laqueur, Thomas Walter. *Religion and Respectability: Sunday Schools and Working Class Culture, 1780–1850*. New Haven: Yale University Press, 1976.

Lasch, Christopher. *Haven in a Heartless World: The Family Besieged*. New York: Basic Books, 1977.

Lears, T. Jackson. *No Place of Grace: Antimodernism and the Transformation of American Culture, 1880–1920.* New York: Pantheon Books, 1981.

Leavell, Roland Q. *An Unashamed Worker: The Biography of Landrum Pinson Leavell.* Richmond: Sunday School Board of the SBC, 1932.

Leloudis, James L. *Schooling in the New South: Pedagogy, Self, and Society in North Carolina, 1880–1920.* Chapel Hill: University of North Carolina Press, 1996.

Lincoln, C. Eric, and Lawrence H. Mamiya. *The Black Church in the African-American Experience.* Durham, N.C.: Duke University Press, 1990.

Link, J. B. *Texas Historical and Biographical Magazine Designed to Give a Complete History of the Baptists of Texas.* 2 vols. Austin, Tex.: J. B. Link, 1892.

Link, William A. *A Hard Country and A Lonely Place: Schooling, Society, and Reform in Rural Virginia, 1870–1920.* Chapel Hill: University of North Carolina Press, 1986.

———. *The Paradox of Southern Progressivism, 1880–1930.* Chapel Hill: University of North Carolina Press, 1992.

Litwack, Leon F. *Been in the Storm So Long: The Aftermath of Slavery.* New York: Random House, 1979.

———. *Trouble in Mind: Black Southerners in the Age of Jim Crow.* New York: Alfred A. Knopf, 1998.

Loveland, Anne C. *Southern Evangelicals and the Social Order, 1800–1860.* Baton Rouge: Louisiana State University Press, 1980.

Lovett, Bobby L. *A Black Man's Dream: The First 100 Years. Richard Henry Boyd and the National Baptist Publishing Board.* N.p.: Mega Corporation, 1993.

Luker, Ralph E. *The Social Gospel in Black and White: American Racial Reform, 1885–1912.* Chapel Hill: University of North Carolina Press, 1991.

Lynn, Robert Wood. *Protestant Strategies in Education.* Ed. C. Ellis Nelson. New York: Association Press, 1964.

Lynn, Robert Wood, and Elliott Wright. *The Big Little School: Two Hundred Years of the Sunday School.* 2nd ed. Birmingham, Ala.: Religious Education Press, 1980.

MacLeod, Anne Scott. *American Childhood: Essays on Children's Literature of the Nineteenth and Twentieth Centuries.* Athens: University of Georgia Press, 1994.

MacLeod, David I. *The Age of the Child: Children in America, 1890–1920.* New York: Twayne, 1998.

McAfee, Sara S. *History of the Woman's Missionary Society in the Colored Methodist Episcopal Church.* 1934. Reprint, Phenix City, Ala.: Phenix City Herald, 1945.

McBeth, Leon. *Women in Baptist Life.* Nashville: Broadman Press, 1979.

McCauley, Deborah Vansau. *Appalachian Mountain Religion: A History*. Urbana: University of Illinois Press, 1995.
McCullagh, Joseph H. *"The Sunday-School Man of the South": A Sketch of the Life and Labors of the Rev. John McCullagh*. Philadelphia: ASSU, 1889.
McDowell, John Patrick. *The Social Gospel in the South*. Baton Rouge: Louisiana State University Press, 1982.
McFarland, John T., et al., eds. *The Encyclopedia of Sunday Schools and Religious Education*. 3 vols. New York: Thomas Nelson and Sons, 1915.
McHugh, Cathy L. *Mill Family: The Labor System in the Southern Cotton Textile Industry, 1880–1915*. New York: Oxford University Press, 1988.
McLaughlin, Henry W. *The Gospel in Action*. Richmond: John Knox, 1944.
McLemore, Richard A., and Nannie P. McLemore. *The History of the First Baptist Church of Jackson, Mississippi*. Jackson: Hederman Bros., n.d.
Magruder, Edith Clysdale, and Judith Brigham. *A Historical Study of the Educational Agencies of the Southern Baptist Convention, 1845–1945*. New York: Columbia University Teachers' College, 1951.
Malone, Bill C. *Southern Music, American Music*. Lexington: University of Kentucky Press, 1979.
Mangan, J. A., and James Walvin, eds. *Manliness and Morality: Middle-Class Masculinity in Britain and America, 1800–1940*. New York: St. Martin's Press, 1987.
Mann, Harold W. *Atticus Greene Haygood: Methodist Bishop, Editor, and Educator*. Athens: University of Georgia Press, 1965.
Mariner, Kirk. *Revival's Children: A Religious History of Virginia's Eastern Shore*. Salisbury, Md.: Peninsula Press, 1979.
Marsden, George M. *Fundamentalism and American Culture: The Shaping of Twentieth-Century Evangelism, 1870–1925*. New York: Oxford University Press, 1980.
Marten, James. *The Children's Civil War*. Chapel Hill: University of North Carolina Press, 1998.
Marty, Martin E., ed. *Protestantism and Regionalism*. Vol. 7 of *Modern American Protestantism and Its World*. Munich: K. G. Saur, 1992.
Mason, Helen. *Bill's Creek Baptist Church: 200 Year History, 1782–1982*. Dallas: n.p., 1984.
Mathews, Don. *Religion in the Old South*. Chicago: University of Chicago Press, 1977.
May, Henry Farnham. *Protestant Churches and Industrial America*. 1949. Reprint, New York: Octagon Books, 1963.
Meigs, Cornelia, et al., eds. *A Critical History of Children's Literature: A Survey of Children's Books in English*. London: Macmillan, 1969.
Miller, Randall M., and Jon L. Wakelyn, eds. *Catholics in the Old South: Essays on Church and Culture*. Macon, Ga.: Mercer University Press, 1983.

Mintz, Steven, and Susan Kellogg. *Domestic Revolutions: A Social History of American Family Life*. New York: Free Press, 1988.

Monteagle Sunday School Assembly. *Mountain Voices: The Centennial History of Monteagle Sunday School Assembly*. Nashville: Parthenon Press, 1982.

Montgomery, William Edward. *Under Their Own Vine and Fig Tree: The African-American Church in the South, 1865–1900*. Baton Rouge: Louisiana State University Press, 1992.

Morris, Robert C. *Reading, 'Riting, and Reconstruction: The Education of Freedmen in the South, 1861–1870*. Chicago: University of Chicago Press, 1981.

Morrison, Theodore. *Chautauqua: A Center for Education, Religion and the Arts in America*. Chicago: University of Chicago Press, 1974.

Morrow, Ralph E. *Northern Methodism and Reconstruction*. East Lansing: Michigan State University Press, 1956.

Moseley, James G. *A Cultural History of Religion in America*. Westport, Conn.: Greenwood Press, 1981.

Mott, Frank Luther. *A History of American Magazines*. Vol. 3, *1865–1885*, and Vol. 4, *1885–1905*. Cambridge: Harvard University Press, 1938 and 1957.

Murray, Andrew E. *Presbyterians and the Negro—a History*. Philadelphia: Presbyterian Historical Society, 1966.

Nieman, Donald G., ed. *The African-American Family in the South, 1861–1900*. Vol. 8 of *African-American Life in the Post-Emancipation South, 1861–1900*. New York: Garland Publishing, 1994.

———. *African Americans and Education in the South, 1865–1900*. Vol. 10 of *African-American Life in the Post-Emancipation South, 1861–1900*. New York: Garland Publishing, 1994.

———. *Church and Community among Black Southerners, 1865–1900*. Vol. 9 of *African-American Life in the Post-Emancipation South, 1861–1900*. New York: Garland Publishing, 1994.

Noble, M. C. S. *A History of the Public Schools of North Carolina*. Chapel Hill: University of North Carolina Press, 1930.

Owen, Christopher H. *The Sacred Flame of Love: Methodism and Society in Nineteenth-Century Georgia*. Athens: University of Georgia Press, 1998.

Ownby, Ted. *Subduing Satan: Religion, Recreation, and Manhood in the Rural South, 1865–1920*. Chapel Hill: University of North Carolina Press, 1990.

Painter, Nell Irvin. *Standing at Armageddon: The United States, 1877–1919*. New York: W. W. Norton, 1987.

Parker, Alison M. *Purifying America: Women, Cultural Reform, and Pro-Censorship Activism, 1873–1933*. Urbana: University of Illinois Press, 1997.

Pelt, Owen D., and Ralph Lee Smith. *The Story of the National Baptists*. New York: Vantage Press, 1960.

Pitchford, B. W. *They Named the Church Zion*. Baton Rouge: Louisiana State University Press, 1968.

Pivar, David J. *Purity Crusade, Sexual Morality, and Social Control, 1868–1900*. Westport, Conn.: Greenwood Press, 1973.

Posey, Walter Brownlow. *Religious Strife on the Southern Frontier*. Baton Rouge: Louisiana State University Press, 1965.

Prather, H. Leon. *Resurgent Politics and Educational Progressivism in the New South: North Carolina, 1890–1913*. Rutherford, N.J.: Fairleigh Dickinson University Press, 1979.

Reid, Avery Hamilton. *Baptists in Alabama: Their Organization and Witness*. Montgomery: Alabama Baptist State Convention, 1967.

Reiner, Jacqueline S. *From Virtue to Character: American Childhood, 1775–1850*. New York: Twayne, 1996.

Reynolds, William Jensen. *A Survey of Christian Hymnody*. New York: Holt, Rinehart, and Winston, 1963.

Reynolds, William Jensen, and Milburn Price. *A Joyful Sound: Christian Hymnody*. 2nd ed. New York: Holt, Rinehart, and Winston, 1978.

Rhyne, Jennings J. *Some Southern Cotton Mill Workers and Their Villages*. Chapel Hill: University of North Carolina Press, 1930.

Rice, Edwin Wilbur. *The Sunday School Movement, 1780–1917, and the American Sunday-School Union, 1817–1917*. 1917. Reprint, New York: Arno Press, 1971.

Richardson, Harry V. *Dark Salvation: The Story of Methodism As It Developed among Blacks in America*. New York: Doubleday, 1976.

Richardson, Joe M. *Christian Reconstruction: The American Missionary Association and Southern Blacks, 1861–1890*. Athens: University of Georgia Press, 1986.

Ripley, C. Peter. *Slaves and Freedmen in Civil War Louisiana*. Baton Rouge: Louisiana State University Press, 1976.

Robinson, R. L. *History of the Georgia Baptist Association*. Union Point, Ga.: n.p., 1928.

Rogal, Samuel J., comp. *The Children's Jubilee: A Bibliographical Survey of Hymnals for Infants, Youth, and Sunday Schools Published in Britain and America, 1655–1900*. Westport, Conn.: Greenwood Press, 1983.

Rotundo, E. Anthony. *American Manhood: Transformations in Masculinity from the Revolution to the Modern Era*. New York: Basic Books, 1993.

Ryland, Garnett H. *The Baptists of Virginia, 1699–1926*. Richmond: Virginia Board of Missions and Education, 1955.

Salem, Dorothy. *To Better Our World: Black Women in Organized Reform, 1890–1920*. Vol. 14 of *Black Women in United States History from Colonial Times through the Nineteenth Century*, ed. Darlene Clark Hine. Brooklyn, N.Y.: Carloon Publishing, 1990.

Schweninger, Loren. *Black Property Owners in the South, 1790–1915.* Urbana: University of Illinois Press, 1990.

Scott, Anne Firor. *Natural Allies: Women's Associations in American History.* Urbana: University of Illinois Press, 1991.

Sensabaugh, L. F. *The Small Sunday School: Its Plan and Work.* Nashville: Cokesbury Press, 1929.

———. *The Sunday School Worker: His Life and Work.* Nashville: Cokesbury Press, 1926.

Sernett, Milton C. *Bound for the Promised Land: African American Religion and the Great Migration.* Durham, N.C.: Duke University Press, 1997.

Seymour, Jack L. *From Sunday School to Church School: Continuities in Protestant Church Education in the United States, 1860–1929.* Washington, D.C.: University Press of America, 1982.

Shapiro, Henry D. *Appalachia on Our Mind: The Southern Mountains and Mountaineers in American Consciousness, 1870–1920.* Chapel Hill: University of North Carolina Press, 1978.

Shurden, Walter B. *The Sunday School Board: Ninety Years of Service.* Nashville: Broadman Press, 1981.

Silber, Nina. *The Romance of Reunion: Northerners and Southerners, 1865–1900.* Chapel Hill: University of North Carolina Press, 1993.

Sims, Anastatia. *The Power of Femininity in the New South: Women's Organizations and Politics in North Carolina, 1880–1930.* Columbia: University of South Carolina Press, 1997.

Slocum, Stephen Elmore, Jr. *The American Tract Society, 1825–1975: An Evangelical Effort to Influence the Religious and Moral Life of the United States.* New York: New York University Press, 1975.

Smith, H. Shelton. *In His Image, But . . . Racism in Southern Religion, 1780–1910.* Durham, N.C.: Duke University Press, 1972.

Smith, Lillian. *Killers of the Dream.* New York: Norton, 1949.

Smith, Mark M. *Mastered by the Clock: Time, Slavery, and Freedom in the American South.* Chapel Hill: University of North Carolina Press, 1998.

Snay, Mitchell. *Gospel of Disunion: Religion and Separatism in the Antebellum South.* Cambridge: Cambridge University Press, 1993.

Sokolosky, Barbara. *ASSU Papers, 1817–1915: A Guide to the Microfilm Edition.* Sanford, N.C.: Microfilming Corporation of America, 1980.

Spain, Rufus B. *At Ease in Zion: A Social History of Southern Baptists, 1865–1900.* Nashville: Vanderbilt University Press, 1967.

Sparks, Randy J. *On Jordan's Stormy Banks: Evangelicalism in Mississippi, 1773–1876.* Athens: University of Georgia Press, 1994.

Startup, Kenneth Moore. *The Root of All Evil: The Protestant Clergy and the Economic Mind of the Old South.* Athens: University of Georgia Press, 1997.

Stephenson, William. *Sallie Southall Cotten: A Woman's Life in North Carolina.* Greenville, N.C.: Pamlico Press, 1987.

Stevenson, Arthur L. *The Story of Southern Hymnology.* Roanoke, Va.: Stone Printing and Manufacturing, 1931.

Stowell, Daniel W. *Rebuilding Zion: The Religious Reconstruction of the South, 1863–1877.* New York: Oxford University Press, 1998.

Street, T. Watson. *The Story of Southern Presbyterians.* Richmond: John Knox Press, 1960.

Stuckey, Sterling. *Slave Culture: Nationalist Theory and the Foundations of Black America.* New York: Oxford University Press, 1987.

Sweet, Malcolm Stuart. *Unto Everlasting Life: The History of the Hartsville Presbyterian Church, 1867–1952.* Hartsville, S.C.: Hart Presbyterian Church, 1954.

Swint, Henry Lee. *The Northern Teacher in the South, 1862–1870.* Nashville: Vanderbilt University Press, 1941.

Synan, Vinson. *The Holiness-Pentecostal Movement in the United States.* Grand Rapids, Mich.: William B. Eerdmans, 1971.

Tamke, Susan S. *Make a Joyful Noise Unto the Lord: Hymns As a Reflector of Victorian Social Attitudes.* Athens: Ohio University Press, 1978.

Tapia, John E. *Circuit Chautauqua: From Rural Education to Popular Entertainment in Early Twentieth-Century America.* Jefferson, N.C.: McFarland, 1997.

Thomas, Mary Martha, ed. *Stepping out of the Shadows: Alabama Women, 1819–1990.* Tuscaloosa: University of Alabama Press, 1995.

Thompson, Edward Palmer. *The Making of the English Working Class.* London: Victor Gollancz, 1965.

Thompson, Ernest Trice. *Presbyterian Missions in the Southern United States.* Richmond: Presbyterian Committee of Publication, 1934.

———. *Presbyterians in the South.* Vol. 2, *1861–1890*, and Vol. 3, *1890–1972*. Richmond: John Knox Press, 1963–1973.

Tindall, George Brown. *South Carolina Negroes, 1877–1900.* Columbia: University of South Carolina Press, 1952.

Tucker, David M. *Black Pastors and Leaders: Memphis, 1819–1972.* Memphis: Memphis State University Press, 1975.

Turner, Elizabeth Hayes. *Women, Culture, and Community: Religion and Reform in Galveston, 1880–1920.* New York: Oxford University Press, 1997.

Tyms, James D. *The Rise of Religious Education among Negro Baptists: A Historical Case Study.* New York: Exposition Press, 1965.

Vaughn, William Preston. *Schools for All; The Blacks and Public Education in the South, 1865–1877.* Lexington: University Press of Kentucky, 1974.

Vernon, Walter N., et al. *The Methodist Excitement in Texas: A History.* Dallas: Texas United Methodist Historical Society, 1984.

Waldrop, Frank C. *Mountain Voices: The Centennial History of the Monteagle Sunday School Assembly.* Monteagle, N.C.: Sunday School Assembly, 1982.

Walker, Clarence E. *A Rock in a Weary Land: The African Methodist Episcopal Church during the Civil War and Reconstruction.* Baton Rouge: Louisiana State University Press, 1982.

Walls, William J. *The African Methodist Episcopal Zion Church: Reality of the Black Church.* Charlotte, N.C.: AME Zion Publishing House, 1974.

Washington, James Melvin. *Frustrated Fellowship: The Black Baptist Quest for Social Power.* Macon, Ga.: Mercer University Press, 1986.

Weatherford, W. D., and Earl D. C. Brewer. *Life and Religion in Southern Appalachia: An Interpretation of Selected Data from the Southern Appalachian Studies.* New York: Friendship Press, 1962.

West, Elliott, and Paula Petrik, eds. *Small Worlds: Children and Adolescents in America, 1850–1950.* Lawrence: University Press of Kansas, 1992.

Wharton, Vernon Lane. *The Negro in Mississippi, 1865–1890.* Chapel Hill: University of North Carolina Press, 1947.

Wheeler, Edward L. *Uplifting the Race: The Black Minister in the New South, 1865–1902.* Lanham, Md.: University Press of America, 1986.

White, Charles Lincoln. *A Century of Faith.* Philadelphia: Judson Press, 1932.

White, James Floyd. *Protestant Worship and Church Architecture: Theological and Historical Considerations.* New York: Oxford University Press, 1964.

Wiebe, Robert H. *The Search for Order, 1877–1920.* New York: Hill and Wang, 1967.

Wiener, Jonathan. *Social Origins of the New South: Alabama, 1860–1885.* Baton Rouge: Louisiana State University Press, 1978.

Wiggins, William H., Jr. *O Freedom! Afro-American Emancipation Celebrations.* Knoxville: University of Tennessee Press, 1987.

Williamson, Joel. *A Rage for Order: Black-White Relations in the American South since Reconstruction.* New York: Oxford University Press, 1986.

Wilson, Charles Reagan. *Baptized in Blood: The Religion of the Lost Cause.* Athens: University of Georgia Press, 1980.

——, ed. *Religion in the South.* Jackson: University Press of Mississippi, 1985.

Wishy, Bernard. *The Child of the Republic: The Dawn of Modern American Child Nurture.* Philadelphia: University of Pennsylvania Press, 1968.

Woodbridge, John D., Mark A. Knoll, and Nathan O. Hatch. *The Gospel in America: Themes in the Story of America's Evangelicals.* Grand Rapids, Mich.: Zondervan, 1979.

Woodson, Carter Godwin. *The History of the Negro Church.* 2nd ed. Washington, D.C.: Associated Publishers, 1921.

Woodward, C. Vann. *Origins of the New South, 1877–1913.* Baton Rouge: Louisiana State University Press, 1951.

Wright, George C. *Life behind a Veil: Blacks in Louisville, Kentucky, 1865–1930.* Baton Rouge: Louisiana State University Press, 1985.
Wright, Richard R., Jr. *The Bishops of the AMEC.* Nashville: AMEC Sunday School Union, 1963.
Wyckoff, D. Campbell, ed. *Renewing the Sunday School and the CCD.* Birmingham, Ala.: Religious Education Press, 1986.
Zelizer, Vivana A. *Pricing the Priceless Child: The Changing Social Value of Children.* New York: Basic Books, 1985.

Theses, Dissertations, and Unpublished Secondary Sources

Bell, Hazel Ruth. "Why Adults Attend Sunday School in Southern Baptist Churches." Ph.D. diss., University of Oklahoma, 1988.
Clemmons, William Preston. "The Development of a Sunday School Strategy in the Southern Baptist Convention, 1896–1926." Ed.D. diss., Southern Baptist Theological Seminary, 1971.
Correll, Emily Clare Newby. "Woman's Work for Woman: The Methodist and Baptist Woman's Missionary Societies in North Carolina, 1878–1930." M.A. thesis, University of North Carolina, 1977.
Crandall, Robert A. "The Sunday School As an Instructional Agency for Religious Instruction in American Protestantism, 1872–1922." Ph.D. diss., Notre Dame University, 1977.
Gardner, W. A. "Kentucky Baptist Sunday School History." Ms. in Southern Baptist Theological Seminary, Louisville, n.d.
Grant, Edward D. "The Sunday School Movement in America (from the Beginning until 1928): A Study of the Development of Organization and Curricula in the Growth of the Religious Education Movement in America." Typed ms. at the Presbyterian Historical Society, Philadelphia.
Grice, Ethel Harrison. "The History of the Sunday School Work in the Southern Baptist Convention." M.A. thesis, Vanderbilt University, 1929.
Haynes, Julietta. "A History of the Primitive Baptists." Ph.D. diss., University of Texas, Austin, 1959.
Huff, Ronald. "Social Christian Clergymen and Feminism during the Progressive Era, 1890–1920." Ph.D. diss., Union Theological Seminary, 1978.
Lawton, Alice Stockton. "The Development of the Curriculum of Southern Baptist Sunday Schools." M.A. thesis, George Peabody College for Teachers, 1932.
Lindley, Percy E. "Evolution of the Sunday School: A Study in the Development of Religious Education." M.A. thesis, Vanderbilt University, 1921.
McClellan, B. Edward. "Schools and the Shaping of Character: Moral Education in America, 1607–Present." Bloomington, Ind.: ERIC, 1992.

Martin, Patricia Summerlin. "Hidden Work: Baptist Women in Texas, 1880–1920." Ph.D. diss., Rice University, 1982.

Moose, J. L. Walter. "Sunday School Work As Promoted by the Baptist State Convention of North Carolina, 1830–1930." M.A. thesis, Wake Forest College, 1950.

Morton, Frances. "What Brought Us Together: The Women's Home Missionary Movement in Atlanta, 1880–1920." Honors thesis, Davidson College, 1993.

Mussina, Malcolm Vivian. "The Background and Origins of the American Religious Tract Movement." Ph.D. diss., Drew Theological Seminary, 1936.

Porter, Curt. "Chautauqua and Tennessee." M.A. thesis, Vanderbilt University, 1962.

Praytor, Robert E. "From Concern to Neglect: Alabama Baptists' Religious Relationship to the Negro, 1823–1870." M.A. thesis, Samford University, 1971.

Schweiger, Beth Barton. "The Transformation of Southern Religion: Clergy and Congregations in Virginia, 1830–1895." Ph.D. diss., University of Virginia, 1994.

Skelton, James Roger. "The Development of the Grading Program in Southern Baptist Sunday Schools." Ph.D. diss., Southwestern Baptist Theological Seminary, 1957.

Tatum, Charles Edward. "The CMEC, with Emphasis on Negroes in Texas, 1870 to 1970: A Study in Historical-Cultural Geography." Ph.D. diss., Michigan State University, 1971.

Williams, Gilbert Anthony. "The 'A.M.E. Christian Recorder': A Forum for the Social Ideas of Black Americans, 1854–1902." Ph.D. diss., University of Illinois, Urbana, 1979.

Wills, David Wood. "Aspects of Social Thought in the African Methodist Episcopal Church, 1884–1910." Ph.D. diss., Harvard University, 1975.

Articles

Anders, Sarah Frances. "Woman's Role in the Southern Baptist Convention and Its Churches." *Review and Expositor* 72 (winter 1975): 31–9.

Archibald, Helen A. "History of Religious Education, 1850–1950: A Documentary Trail." *Religious Education* 82 (summer 1987): 405–14.

Armstrong, Thomas F. "The Building of a Black Church: Community in Post Civil War Liberty County, Georgia." *Georgia Historical Quarterly* 66 (fall 1982): 346–67.

Bardaglio, Peter. "The Children of Jubilee: African American Children in Wartime." In *Divided Houses: Gender and the Civil War,* eds. Catherine Clinton and Nina Silber, 213–29. New York: Oxford University Press, 1992.

Bates, Barbara Snedeker. "Denominational Periodicals: The Invisible Literature." *Phaedrus* 7 (1980): 13–8.
Bell, John L. "The Presbyterian Church and the Negro in North Carolina during Reconstruction." *North Carolina Historical Review* 40 (1963): 15–36.
Berkeley, Kathleen C. "'Colored Ladies Also Contributed': Black Women's Activities from Benevolence to Social Welfare, 1866–1896." In *The Web of Southern Social Relations: Women, Family, and Education*, ed. Watter J. Fraser Jr., R. Frank Saunders Jr., and Jon L. Wakelyn, 181–203. Athens: University of Georgia Press, 1985.
Boylan, Anne M. "Sunday Schools and Changing Evangelical Views of Children in the 1820s." *Church History* 48 (September 1979): 320–33.
Briggs, F. Allen. "The Sunday School Library." In *Reader in American Library History*, ed. Michael H. Harris, 64–71. Washington, D.C.: NCR, 1971.
Burns, Sarah. "Barefoot Boys and Other Country Children: Sentiment and Ideology in Nineteenth-Century American Art." *The American Art Journal* 20 (1988): 24–50.
Chapman, Kathryn. "The Minister to Children in Southern Baptist Life." *Baptist History and Heritage* 25, no. 4 (1990): 13–20.
Clemmons, William Preston. "The Contributions of the Sunday School to Southern Baptist Churches." *Baptist History and Heritage* 18, no. 1 (1983): 31–43.
Costen, Melva W. "Singing Praise to God in African American Worship Contexts." In *African American Religious Studies: An Interdisciplinary Anthology*, ed. Gayraud Wilmore, 392–404. Durham, N.C.: Duke University Press, 1989.
Crumpler, Carolyn Weatherford. "The Role of Women in Baptist Missions." *Baptist History and Heritage* 27, no. 3 (1992): 25–33.
Finke, Roger. "Demographics of Religious Participation: An Ecological Approach, 1850–1980." *Journal for the Scientific Study of Religion* 28 (1989): 45–58.
Fitch, James E. "Major Thrusts in Sunday School Development since 1900." *Baptist History and Heritage* 18, no. 1 (1983): 17–30.
Flynt, J. Wayne. "Dissent in Zion: Alabama Baptists and Social Issues, 1900–1914." *Journal of Southern History* 35 (November 1969): 523–42.
———. "The Impact of Social Factors on Southern Baptist Expansion, 1800–1914." *Baptist History and Heritage* 17, no. 3 (1982): 20–31.
———. "Southern Baptists and Reform, 1890–1920." *Baptist History and Heritage* 7, no. 4 (1972): 211–24.
———. "Southern Baptists: Rural to Urban Transition." *Baptist History and Heritage* 16, no. 1 (1981): 24–34.
Forbes, Wesley L. "The Sunday School Board and Baptist Church Music." *Baptist History and Heritage* 19, no. 1 (1984): 17–26.

Gillespie, Joanna. "Schooling through Fiction." *Children's Literature* 14 (1986): 62–81.

Gladden, R. K., and G. W. Hanson. "American Baptist Church School Curriculum: A One Hundred and 54 Year Story." *Foundations* 17 (July 1974): 214–25.

Gravely, William B. "The Social, Political, and Religious Significance of the Formation of the Colored Methodist Episcopal Church (1870)." *Methodist History* 18 (1979): 3–25.

Hackett, David G. "Sociology of Religion and American Religious History: Retrospect and Prospect." *Journal for the Scientific Study of Religion* 27 (1988): 461–71.

Halbrooks, Thomas. "The Roots of Southern Baptist Relationships with Other Denominations." *Baptist History and Heritage* 25, no. 3 (1990): 3–13.

Hardesty, Nancy A. "'The Best Temperance Organization in the Land': Southern Methodism and the W.C.T.U. in Georgia." *Methodist History* 28 (April 1990): 187–94.

Harton, R. Michael. "Early Chautauqua Institution As a Model Lifelong Learning Enterprise." *Review and Expositor* 84 (summer 1987): 487–506.

Heisey, Terry. "Singet Hallelujah! Music in the Evangelical Association, 1800–1894." *Methodist History* 28 (July 1990): 237–51.

Hobbs, June Hadden. "His Religion and Hers in Nineteenth Century Hymnody." In *Nineteenth-Century Women Learn to Write,* ed. Catherine Hobbs, 120–44. Charlottesville: University of Virginia Press, 1995.

Holt, Sharon Ann. "Making Freedom Pay: Freedpeople Working for Themselves, North Carolina, 1865–1900." *Journal of Southern History* 60 (May 1994): 229–62.

Hulan, Richard Huffman. "The American Revolution in Hymnody." *The Hymn* 35 (October 1984): 199–208.

Kathan, Boardman W. "The Sunday School Revisited." *Religious Education* 75 (Jan.–Feb. 1980): 5–14.

Luker, Ralph E. "The Social Gospel and the Failure of Racial Reform, 1877–1898." *Church History* 46 (March 1977): 80–99.

Lynn, Robert Wood. "The Last of the Great Religious Movements." *The Duke Divinity School Review* 40 (fall 1975): 151–60.

McBeth, Leon. "The Changing Role of Women in Baptist History." *Southwestern Journal of Theology* 22 (fall 1979): 84–96.

Massaglia, Martin L. "Colporter Ministry: The Transitions of Power." *Foundations* 24 (Oct.–Dec. 1981): 328–41.

Mathews, John Michael. "The Dilemma of Negro Leadership in the New South: The Case of the Negro Young People's Congress of 1902." *South Atlantic Quarterly* 73 (1974): 130–44.

May, Lynn E., Jr. "The Emerging Role of Sunday Schools in Southern Baptist Life to 1900." *Baptist History and Heritage* 18, no. 1 (1983): 6–17.

———. "The Family in Baptist History." *Baptist History and Heritage* 17, no. 1 (1982): 1–59.

———. "Missions in the Southern Baptist Experience." *Baptist History and Heritage* 26, no. 1 (1991): 2–36.

———. "The Sunday School: A Two-Hundred-Year Heritage." *Baptist History and Heritage* 15, no. 4 (1980): 3–11.

Miller, Page Putnam. "Women in the Vanguard of the Sunday School Movement." *Journal of Presbyterian History* 58 (1980): 311–25.

Moore, David O. "The Withdrawal of Blacks from Southern Baptist Churches following Emancipation." *Baptist History and Heritage* 16, no. 3 (1981): 12–8.

Moore, Laurence. "Bible Reading and Nonsectarian Schooling: The Failure of Religious Instruction in Nineteenth-Century Public Education." *Journal of American History* 86 (March 2000): 1581–99.

Murrell, Irvin. "Southern Ante-Bellum Baptist Hymnody." *Baptist History and Heritage* 27, no. 2 (1992): 12–8.

Niblette, William E. "The Adult Sunday School Movement: History with Design." *Christian Education Journal* 5 (1984): 29–36.

Ognibene, Richard. "Catholic and Protestant Education in the Late Nineteenth Century." *Religious Education* 77 (Jan.–Feb. 1982): 5–20.

Osterman, Mary J. "The Two-Hundred Year Struggle for Protestant Religious Education Curriculum Theory." *Religious Education* 75 (Sept.–Oct. 1980): 528–38.

Owen, Christopher H. "By Design: The Social Meaning of Methodist Church Architecture in Nineteenth-Century Georgia." *Georgia Historical Quarterly* 75 (1991): 221–53.

Pearce, Larry Wesley. "The American Missionary Association and the Freedmen in Arkansas, 1863–1878." *Arkansas Historical Quarterly* 30 (1971): 123–44.

Porter, Ellen Jane. "The Sunday School Movement." *The Hymn* 35 (October 1984): 209–13.

Quist, John W. "Slaveholding Operatives of the Benevolent Empire: Bible, Tract, and Sunday School Societies in Antebellum Tuscaloosa County, Alabama." *Journal of Southern History* 62 (August 1996): 481–526.

Ray, Cecil A. "The Missionary Motif of the Southern Baptist Convention." *Baptist History and Heritage* 26, no. 1 (1991): 4–12.

Rogal, Samuel J. "The Evolution and Demise of the American Temperance Hymn." *The Hymn* 42 (July 1991): 5–9.

Schweninger, Loren. "The American Missionary Association and Northern Philanthropy in Reconstruction Alabama." *Alabama Historical Quarterly* 32 (fall/winter 1970): 129–56.

Siburt, James T. "Tennessee Colporteurs: Flatboat Evangelism." *Tennessee Historical Quarterly* 47 (1988): 227–33.

Siler, James. "Sunday Schools Remembered." *Appalachian Heritage* 4 (spring 1976): 49–54.

Sisk, Glenn N. "Churches in the Alabama Black Belt, 1875–1917." *Church History* 23 (June 1954): 153–74.

Smylie, James H. "The American Sunday School Union Papers, 1817–1915." *Journal of Presbyterian History* 58 (winter 1980): 372–76.

Thistlethwaite, Susan Brooks. "The Feminization of American Religious Education." *Religious Education* 76 (Jul.–Aug. 1981): 391–401.

Thomas, Mary Martha. "White and Black Alabama Women during the Progressive Era, 1890–1920." In *Stepping out of the Shadows: Alabama Women, 1819–1990*, ed. Mary Martha Thomas, 75–95. Tuscaloosa: University of Alabama Press, 1995.

Warner, R. Stephen. "Work in Progress toward a New Paradigm for the Sociological Study of Religion in the United States." *American Journal of Sociology* 98 (March 1993): 1044–93.

Warren, Katie C., and Jo M. Bevington. "The Contributions of Children to Southern Baptists." *Baptist History and Heritage* 25 (October 1990): 4–12.

Washburn, A. V. "Sunday-School: A Vehicle for Church Growth." *Baptist History and Heritage* 18, no. 1 (1983): 56–64.

Wheeler, Edward L. "An Overview of Black Southern Baptist Involvements." *Baptist History and Heritage* 16, no. 3 (1981): 3–11, 40.

White, Shane. "'It Was a Proud Day': African Americans, Festivals, and Parades in the North, 1741–1834." *Journal of American History* 81 (June 1994): 13–50.

Wills, Ridley, II. "The Monteagle Sunday School Assembly—A Brief Account of Its Origin and History." *Tennessee Historical Quarterly* 44 (1985): 3–26.

Wilson, Charles Reagan. "The Religion of the Lost Cause." *Journal of Southern History* 46 (1980): 219–38.

Wynes, Charles E. "Lewis Harview Blair, Virginia Reformer: The Uplift of the Negro and Southern Prosperity." *Virginia Magazine of History and Biography* 72 (January 1964): 3–18.

Zipf, Karen L. "'Among These American Heathens': Congregational Missionaries and African American Evangelicals during Reconstruction, 1865–1878." *North Carolina Historical Review* 74 (April 1977): 111–34.

INDEX

Adults, in Sunday school, 202–5, 233–4
Advice books, Sunday school, 5–6, 107–8
African Methodist Episcopal Church, 32, 46, 47, 166, 171, 175; and Connectional Sabbath School Union, 73; and publishing, 89, 96, 97–8, 105, 107, 108, 113–4; and Sunday school organization, 73
African Methodist Episcopal Zion Church, 32, 47, 172, 175; and Sunday School board, 73–4; and publishing, 98, 113, 117, 119; and uniform lessons, 136
Akron plan, 216–7
Alabama Baptist State Convention, 68
Alabama Negro Baptist Sunday School Convention, 33
Alcohol, 57, 141–2, 171–2, 200. *See also* Temperance
Allen, J. S., 146
Alvord, John W., 18
American Baptist Home Missionary Society, 31, 38, 46, 63
American Baptist Publication Society, 31, 32–3, 86, 94, 100, 101; and blacks, 21–2, 47, 96, 190–2; and publications, 32, 94, 119
American Bible Society, 14, 48, 53
American Missionary Association, 18, 46, 48
American Sunday School Union, 28–30, 33, 40, 46, 48, 49, 51, 54; history of, 28; and blacks, 41, 96; and fund raising, 41–3
American Tract Society, 17–8, 31, 43, 46, 48, 96
Ancott, J. J., 75
Andrews, A. S., 133
Antimission movement, 116, 117, 117n
Appalachia: conditions in, 35–6, 75; Sunday schools in, 85, 127–8, 146–7, 156, 157, 235–6
Architecture, Sunday school, 216–8, 218n
Arkansas Baptist State Convention, 131
Armstrong, Annie, 65, 113, 125, 147, 152, 192
Arnold, C. M., 67

Atlanta Constitution, 178
Attendance, 67, 84–6, 149, 151, 198, 229–31, 234; as Sunday school lesson, 139, 141; in public school, 149, 234, 234n
Avery, Gillian, 90
Axtell, James, 122, 123, 124

Baird, E. Thompson, 94, 108
Baker, John, 57
Baptist State Sunday School Convention of North Carolina (black), 167, 174
Baptist Theological Seminary, 215
Baptist Woman's Home Missionary Society, 125
Baptists, Southern
—white, 65, 68, 68n, 70–1, 78, 100, 116, 134, 144, 161; and black Sunday schools, 182. *See also* Southern Baptist Convention
—black, 32–3, 117, 197–8. *See also* National Baptist Convention
Baracas, 202
Barclay, Wade, 134
Bass, J. A., 225
Beauchamp, Harvey, 211
Behavior, 34–6, 40–1, 76, 93, 237–8; as Sunday school lesson, 24, 138–9, 140, 141, 143, 232; of blacks, 178–80, 190; of mill workers, 59
Benjamin, R. C. O., 22, 163
Biblical criticism, 198
Bilbo, Theodore, 246
Black Israel, 146
Black, W. C., 142
Blair, Lewis Harvie, 190
Boles, John, 239, 245
Bolles, Edwin, 30, 53
"Boy problem," 199–202
Boyd, Richard H., 102–3, 103n, 190–2, 248; response to, 102n
Boyd, Sethelle, 238
Boyer, Paul, 240
Boykin, Thomas Cooper, 68, 68n
Boylan, Anne, 11, 66n, 112n, 121, 128n
Brabham, William Mouzon, 210

Bradley, Mary, 104
Broadus, John, 137
Brown, Mamie, 232
Bruce, Robert Blair, 98
Bryan, William Jennings, 221
Buchanan, James C. 36, 48
Buck, John, 191
Buck, Paul H., 27–8 n. 2, 39 n. 20
Bulkley, William, 40–1, 65–6, 235
Burroughs, Nannie H., 177
Burrows, Lansing, 23, 130
Bushnell, Horace, 4

Calvary Baptist Church, Washington, D.C., 218
Campbell, J. P., 96
Carnahan, Mrs. C. M., 128
Catholics in South, 62–4
Chadwick, S. R., 37
Chappell, E. B., 146
Charlton, C. W., 30, 35, 49, 50–1
Chautauqua movement, 218–21
Childrearing, concepts of, 4–7, 79–80, 82, 247–8
Children: images of, 4–5; socialization of, 247–8
Children's Day, 147, 159–60, 161, 171, 243
The Child's Gem, 107, 112
Christian Endeavors, 202
Christian nurture, 4, 8, 188
Christian Recorder, 115
Civil War: effect of, 1, 6–7, 9–10, 14, 16, 52; and textbooks, 95; and missionaries, 49
Class issues, 169, 170, 177–8, 187, 195
Cleveland, Grover, 175
Clifton conference, 184–5
Clinton, George, 160, 184, 200
Colored Methodist Episcopal Church, 47, 64, 98–9, 182; and Sunday school, 74; and publishing, 98–9
Colporteurs, 29, 35, 36, 118, 235–6. *See also* Missionaries
Competition: among missionaries, 38, 46,

Index 291

47, 61, 71, 77–8; among denominations, 47, 65, 66, 71, 87–8, 120, 242–3; among children, 67, 151, 160; among Sunday schools, 86–7, 151, 152n; among publishers, 114, 120, 243; for Sunday school members, 151
Comstock, Anthony, 91
Conventions, Sunday school, 66, 66n, 152, 167, 174–78, 184–5, 221. *See also* Chautauqua movement
Conversion: in Sunday school, 12–4, 14n, 50, 132–4, 133n, 222, 241; statistics on, 13–5; as goal, 194. *See also* Decision Day
Coontz, Stephanie, 80
Cope, Henry, 16, 212
Cope, Samuel W., 82
Corporal punishment, 123
Cradle Roll Department, 205–6
Crowder, W. J. W., 51
Cuninggim, Jesse, 207
Cunnyngham, W. G. E., 125
Curry, A. B., 186
Cuyler, Theodore, 81

Decision Day, 13, 159
Denominationalism. *See* Sectarianism
Destitution in the South, 10–1, 34–6, 85
Dimmock, T. W., 50
Dixon, Thomas, 246
Doctrines and Discipline (MECS), 72–3, 105
Dortch, David, 153
Douglass, Frederick, 12, 172
Downing, N. H., 124
DuBois, W. E. B., 174, 177

Earnest Worker, 108, 117
Eastman, John, 48, 85
Economic issues: in South, 190, 195; in Sunday school, 41–4; in church, 243. *See also* Sunday school; Fund raising
Edmondson, Mrs. W. C., 104
Ellington, W. L., 30
Emory, Isaac, 35, 42, 43, 50, 54, 147, 156, 158–9

Encyclopedia of Sunday Schools, 160, 210, 225
Epworth Leagues, 202
An Era of Progress and Promise, 184
Evolution, theory of, 138, 198

Fairview Presbyterian Church, Greenville, S.C., 11
Family, 80–2; and worship, 16, 205; decline of, 16–7; and domestic violence, 82; ideal, 140
Fathers, 51
Finke, Roger, 87
Finklea, H. Lee, 151
First Baptist Church, Mobile, Ala., 217
First Presbyterian Church, Greensboro, N.C., 217, 218
First Presbyterian Church, Greenwood, S.C., 128
Fisher, O. L., 168
Florida Training School for State Sunday School Workers, 214–5
Floyd, Silas, 141, 164
Floyd's Flowers, 141
Foster, Gaines, 50n, 52, 53n
Foster, Sarah Jane, 19, 48
Fox, Edgar Alonzo, 224
Freedmen's Bureau, 17, 18
Friedman, Jean, 238
Frontier conditions, 39
Frost, James Marion, 71n, 100–1, 103, 115, 118, 144, 191
Fuller, Erasmus, 45
Fund raising, 41–4, 76–7, 146n, 160, 161, 170, 205, 243–4;

Gambling, 57
Gender roles, 9, 148–9, 239–40; in Sunday school, 148–9. *See also* Men; Women
General Education Board, 183
Gilmore, Glenda, 129n, 130n
Girardeau, J. L., 178
Glenn, Jane, 56
Glenn, Mrs. V. K., 57
Good Tidings, 96, 149

Goodrich, Frances Louisa, 124
Grady, Henry, 225
Grant, A., 89, 97
Gray, G. Harrison, 51
Gray, Robert, 25
The Great Evil and Its Remedy, 82
Great Migration, 190
Greene, Samuel, 8
Griffith, R. H., 60

Hall, J. N., 113
Hamill, Ada, 214–5
Hamill, Howard M., 125, 214–5, 214n
Hardshell Baptists, 51, 74
Harris, William and Robert, 50
Harrison, W. P., 189
Hartland, Alice, 104
Hartshorn, William N., 178, 183–4, 184n
Hartzog, Henry, 235–6
Harvey, Paul, 102n, 152, 195n
Hatcher, William, 13
Haygood, Atticus, 81, 86, 103, 110, 136, 182, 183, 221
Haygood, Laura, 57, 219
Hiden, J. C., 138–9
Higgenbotham, Evelyn Brooks, 239
Holden, W. W., 85
Home Department, 206
Home Mission movement, 144–5, 180–81, 186–7, 199
Homosexuality, fear of, 200
Hooker, Elizabeth, 127–8
Howard, Mary, 160
Hull, Asa, 106
Hymn singing, 105, 126, 142, 152–5, 173; critics of, 155. *See also* Hymnals; Music; Shape-note singing
Hymnals, 105–7, 107n, 113, 152, 153–4

Immigrants, 198–9
Infants, in Sunday school, 205–6
International Sunday School Association, 23, 66n, 183–6, 209, 210

Jacobs, Charles C., xi
Jackson, Stonewall, 12

Jenkins, A. E., 50
Jim Crow laws, 2, 164, 173, 174, 175, 233, 245, 246
Johnson, J. W., 75
Johnson, William L., 203
Joiner, James Harvey, xi, 204, 232
Jones, A. M., 31
Jones, C. O., 206
Jones, G. S., 51, 63

Kennedy, Mabel, 237
Kentucky AMEZ Sunday School Convention, 175
Kentucky Sunday School Reporter, 68
Kentucky Sunday School Union, 67–8, 67n, 83, 212, 220
Kieffer, Aldine, 153
Killers of the Dream, 247
Kimmel, Michael, 129n
Kind Words, 107
Kindergarten, 205n
Knight, Edgar, 19
Ku Klux Klan, 246

Lacy, Bessie Dewey, 237, 238
Lancaster, Aggrey, 143
Lancaster, L. J., 74
Law, F. L., 182
Lawrance, Marion, 216, 218
Leftwich, William, 92
Legare, John, 42
Legare, T. H., 36
Libraries, public, 109, 109n
Libraries, Sunday school, 109–11
Link, William, 212n, 234n
Literacy, 90; in South, 17–20, 21, 22, 93; among blacks, 22, 167
Literature, American, 90–2; response to, 91–5, 109–10
Little, John, 181
Little Lessons for Little People, 134
Litwack, Leon, 164, 170
Log Cabin Union Sunday School, 60
London Tract Society, 114, 114n

"Lost Cause," 148
Lyman, H. C., 185–6
Lynching, 164, 175, 188
Lyon, J. A., 24, 82, 86, 217

McAnally, D. R., Jr., 106
McCrorey, H. L., 185
McCullagh, John, 26, 28–9, 41–2, 49, 54, 63
McCullough, Margaret, 230
McGaha, Ermine, 232
McIntosh, R. M., 106
Mallory, James, 60, 230
Manly, Basil, Jr., 7, 34, 106, 134
Marsh, Jonathan, 42, 85
Marten, James, 9
Martindale, C. O., 25, 78
Mask, Georgia, 232
Mathews, Don, 128
Maxwell, L. B., 183
Mays, Benjamin, 109, 161, 233
Meharry Medical College, 170
Men: in Sunday school, 122; as teachers, 128, 129, as superintendents, 122–4; as missionaries, 57; problems involving, 200–1. *See also* "Boy problem"; Fathers
Methodist Episcopal Church, 31, 45–6, 46n, 96, 98, 165
Methodist Episcopal Church, South, 68–9, 72–3, 111, 135, 187, 210, 215n; and Sunday school, 68–9, 72–3; and publishing, 92–3, 99–100, 100n, 105, 107, 108, 111, 112, 114, 116, 117, 118, 119; and conversion, 133n; and uniform lessons, 136; and black Sunday schools, 182, 184; and teacher training, 214–5; response to literature, 92; fear of modernity, 196; and Sunday school pedagogy, 125
Mill villages: and Sunday school, 58–9, 196, 240; churchgoers in, 59n
Miller, Lewis, 216, 218
Ministers, 182; in Sunday school work, 57, 59, 69, 79; reaction to Sunday schools, 78–9, 168–9
Missionaries, 29, 33, 77, 87, 235–6, 243;

—northern: 2, 10, 21, 30, 31, 33, 38, 44–6, 48–9, 61–2, 183, 184, 189, 243; challenges facing, 36–7, 37n; complaints of, 37, 47; female, 48, 124; and freedpeople, 27n, 44–8, 53, 183, 184; goals of, 27n, 53n; influence of in South, 26–54; reactions of, 26n, 27, 30, 33–6, 45, 50–3, 235–6; requirements for, 36; resistance to, 30; response to, 38–9, 39n, 46–8, 50–3, 50n, 60–2; success of, 52–4. *See also* names of individual denominations and organizations
—southern: 62, 74–6, 118, 183–4, 187; reactions of, 74–6; hardships of, 75; resistance to, 74
Missionary Day, 144, 159, 243
Missionary hen, 147
Missionary work, 143–4, 145, 170
Mize, G. E., 65
Modernization, 196, 198; fear of, 116, 222; and Sunday schools, 194, 195n, 207–23
Moffatt, John, 220
Monteagle Sunday School Assembly, 220–1
Montreat, 219
Moore, Hight C., 14. 233
Moore, Joanna, 155
Moravian Female Mission Society, 11–2
Morehead, Lilly, 124–5
Morgan, Wallie M., 86
Mormons, 62, 64–5, 65n
Morris, Elias Camp, 96, 102
Morris, James V. M., 57
Morse, Mrs. E. H., 104
Moss, James, 90
Mothers: attitudes toward, 80–2, 140–1; role of, 80–2; and Sunday school, 204, 205, 230–1
Muckrakers, 197
Muscular Christianity, 201
Myers, Sarah, 104

National Baptist Convention, 96, 97, 111, 112, 187, 204, 210, 212, 248; and publishing, 102–3, 103n, 182, 190–2; and

chautauquas, 219; and Southern Baptist Convention, 182
National Baptist Hymnal, 107
National Baptist Union, 172
National Sunday School Association, 7–8, 135, 136
Native Americans, 144, 145, 149
"Negro Problem," 188–9, 193
Negro Young People's Christian and Education Congress, 176–8
Nelson, D. B., 85
Nihilism, 198
Nondenominational Sunday schools. *See* Union Sunday Schools; American Sunday School Union
Normal Studies for Sunday School Workers, 215
North, Eric, 207
North Carolina State Sunday School Convention, 66

Ogilve, Mary, 237
Our Brother in Black, 182
Our Little People, 105, 107
Owen, Christopher, 46n, 146n

Parades, Sunday school, 156, 157–9
Parents: role of, 16–7, 81, 82–3, 140; failings of, 17, 95–6; response to Sunday school, 230, 231; and Sunday school, 79–80, 83, 204; and home worship, 95. *See also* Fathers; Mothers; Family
Paxson, Stephen, 61
Paxson, William P., 122, 189
Pearson, W. A., 16
Pedagogy, Sunday school, 127–8, 214, 215, 215n
Pegram, Will, 214
Penn, Irvine Garland, 176, 177
Pentacostals, 222
Pepper, John, 235
Phillips, Alexander L., 72, 180, 181, 211
Phillips, Charles Henry, 15, 81, 160–1, 164, 233

Picnics, Sunday school, 156–7, 158, 159, 173
Pierce, W. C., 161
Pigott, Fenner, 124, 158
Plagiarism, 113–4
Plantation mission movement, 178
Pollard, R. T., 33
Populist Party, 195
Presbyterian Church in the United States, 14n, 39, 65, 72, 106, 111, 135, 182, 210; and black Sunday schools, 179–82, 180n, 188, 248; Committee on Home Missions, 180, 181; and modernity, 196; publishing, 94, 100, 105, 108, 112, 117, 118, 159; rate of conversion, 14n; response to literature, 91–2; and statistics, 208; and Sunday school, 72; and uniform lessons, 135–6, 137
Presbyterian Church in the United States of America, 31
Presbyterian Theological Seminary, 181
Primitive Baptists, 39, 78, 222
Progressivism, 196–7, 218
The Prosperity of the South Depends upon the Elevation of the Negro, 190
Public schools, 17, 20, 22–3, 83; and blacks, 174; condition of, 20–1; federal role in, 22–3; problems, 19–20; religion in, 22–3, 23n, 83–4; segregation of, 20–1; and Sunday schools, 83–4; and textbooks, 95, 97;
Punctuality, 59n, 139
Pupils, response to Sunday school, 226–32, 234, 235
Purity Presbyterian Church, Chester, S.C., 218

Quisenberry, H. N., 74

Racial uplift, 3, 96, 97, 102, 163, 169, 170, 177, 180n, 185, 187, 193, 245
Racism, 48, 175, 244–8, 245n
Rally Day, 159
Rankin, Julia, 232
Rape, 175

Index

Reading. *See* Literacy
Reconstruction, 1, 2, 3, 49, 52, 53, 54, 61, 95, 164
Reeder, Adam, 43–4, 233–4
Religious declension, 197–8
Religious destitution, 34–5
Revivals, 133
Rhyne, Jennings J., 59n
Ridgecrest Baptist Assembly, 219
Roach, Hala, 230–1
Roach, Jim, 230–1
Roach, Mahala, 230–1
Robertson, A. T., 153
Robinson, James H., 127, 232, 235
Robinson, Lidd, 120
Rowland, A. J., 191, 191n
Ruebush, J. H., 153
Ruffner, W. H., 46
Ryan, G. W., 39–40, 156, 165
Ryan, J. K., 130

Sabbath observance, 15–6, 141
St. John's AME Chapel Sunday School, 165, 218n
St. Stephen's AME Church, Wilmington, N.C., 150
Sasser, Emma, 201
Schweninger, Loren, 103
Sectarianism, 29–30, 87–8, 184; debate over, 112n; and Sunday school, 42, 60–1, 66, 67, 76, 202, 202n, 242; absence of, 112, 112n, 113, 114, 121, 127
Segregation, 2, 175, 188, 245, 247; of Sunday school, 164. *See also* Jim Crow laws
Self, William, 229
Self-help, black, 192–3
Shape-note singing, 154
Sharp, George, 34
Shaw University, 167, 170
Shropshire, Battie, 237
Silber, Nina, 26–7n
Slater Fund, 183
Smith, Charles, 89
Smith, Mrs. F. M., 104
Smith, George G., 5, 76, 81, 244
Smith, J. W., 200
Smith, Kate L., 166
Smith, L. W., 119
Smith, Lillian, 247
Smith, Mark, 60n
Smith, R. P., 146–7
Snedecor, James, 186
Snodgrass, D. S., 119, 191
Social Christianity, 197
Socialism, 198
Southern Baptist Convention, 71, 210–1; and Home Mission Board, 187; and National Baptist Convention, 182, 187, 191–92; and Sunday school pedagogy, 215; and teacher training, 215. *See also* Baptists, Southern (white)
Southern Baptist Sunday School Board, 86, 100–1, 182; founding of, 71n, 71–2; response to 70, 70n, 71; and publishing, 107, 107n, 108, 112
Southern exceptionalism, 244
Southern Society for the Promotion of the Study of Race Conditions and Problems in the South, 189, 190
Southern Workman, 178
Spearman, G. W., 16
Spilman, Bernard Washington, 15, 24, 215
Star of Zion, 117, 172
Stark, Rodney, 87
State conventions, 66–8, 68n. *See also* names of individual states
Stephens, Alexander, 159
Stevenson, Samuel, 48
Stowell, Daniel, 112n, 244
Stringer, Thomas W., 46
Summers, Thomas O., 114
Sunday observance, 141
Sunday school: attire, 85, 126, 139; boards, 68–71, 195; classroom aids, 111–2; condition of, 85, 86, 127–8, 179–80, 183, 194; critics of, 210; economic issues for, 76, 114–5, 205, 243–4; evaluation of, 224, 225, 231–49; evergreen, 84–6; failings of, 241–2; founding of, 55–6, 65;

goals of, 3, 23–5, 77, 82–3, 87, 211; graded classes in, 208–10; graded lessons in, 209–10; growth of, 226–9, 245; history of, 11–2; influence of, 240–1; and interracial efforts, 46n, 178–88, 192–3, 144; lessons in, 59, 112–3, 127, 132–3; 154, 240–2; 145–8, 170–1; literature for, 43, 112–3, 119; location of, 57–9, 173; meeting time of, 165–6; mission of, 57, 181, 186, 241; modernization of, 207–23; opposition to, 39–40, 70, 74, 76, 181, 222; organization of, 68, 195, 207; publications and, 31, 32, 86–7, 112; reading classes in, 17–9, 18n, 84, 167, 233; response to, 15, 161–2; rewards for achievements in, 149–51, 150n, 160–1, 233; role of, 5–8, 12–3, 15, 16, 23–5; rural, 84, 86, 195; significance of, 248–9; and social activities, 156–62, 173, 202; standards for, 211; statistics on, 207–8, 227–9; success of, 224–5

Sunday School Beacon, 66

The Sunday School in Ten Red-Hot Chapters, 226

Sunday School Magazine, 105, 108, 136

Sunday school parades, 156, 157–9, 173

Sunday school publishing, 89–120, 195, 244; advertising of, 104–5, 106, 115–6; authors, 103–4, 104n; and borrowed material, 113–4, 114n, 242; competition in, 94–5, 101, 104–5, 242–3; fiction, 108, 110; goals of, 90, 93, 95–7, 101, 102, 103, 115; history of, 97–8, 99; impact of, 120; magazines, 107, 112; marketing devices, 117–8; by northern firms, 118, 119; opposition to, 116–7, 119–20; problems of, 118–9; profits of, 114–5, 117, 119, 120; and record-keeping, 207–8; and white influence on blacks, 96–7, 97n

Sunday School Union of London, 134

Sunday School World, 49

Superintendents, 122–5, 235; duties of, 123, 124, 153, 156; gender of, 123–5, 166; qualifications of, 122; response of to role, 235

Survey of Religious Bodies, 225, 226–8

Swint, Henry, 52n

Systematic benevolence, 145–6, 147, 241, 243. *See also* Sunday school; Fund raising

Tabernacle Baptist Church, Richmond, Va., 217

Tanner, Benjamin, 73, 113

Taxation, 19–20

Taylor, Jonathan, 152

Teachers, northern, 27n

Teachers, public school, 129, 212n

Teachers, Sunday school, 83, 125, 153–5, 231; attire of, 126; enticements to, 213; gender of, 128–31; influence of, 232–3; marital status of, 129, 130n; problems, 212 of; qualifications of, 126–7, 212–3; response of pupils to, 232–3; responses of to job, 236–7; shortage of, 126–7, 212–3; standards for, 126, 127, 212; training of, 125, 213–5, 219–20; and uniform lessons, 137, 138

Temperance, as lesson, 128, 141–3, 155, 156–57, 171–2, 197

Temperance Sunday, 143

Tennessee Baptist State Convention, 32

Tenney, S. F., 110

Textbooks, in Sunday school, 21–2

Third Street AME Church, Richmond, Va., 159

Thompson, E. P., 240

Tichenor, I. T., 70

Tillett, Wilbur, 99, 224

Trapp, C. O., 110

Trevino, Esther, 56

Trotter, William Monroe, 174

Tryon Street Methodist Sunday School, Charlotte, N.C., 157

Tulip Street Methodist Church, Nashville, Tenn., 217

Turner, Elizabeth Hayes, 152n, 239

Turner, H. M., 198

Index

Tynes, J. B., 165
Tyson, James, 127

Uniform lessons, 103, 134–8, 142, 170; acceptance of, 135–7; resistance to, 135–6; and teachers, 137–8; failings of, 209
Union Methodist Church Sunday School, Goldsboro, N.C., 128
Union Sunday schools, 28, 39–40, 50, 60, 67. *See also* American Sunday School Union

Van Ness, I. J., 114
Vanderbilt University, 215, 215n
Vardaman, James, 246
Varick Christian Endeavor Society, 202
Vass, S. N., 167
Views of Christian Nurture, 4
Vincent, John H., 135, 218
Viney, J. Allen, 138–9, 199
Virginia Bible Society, 58
Virginia State Penitentiary, 58

Ware, George T., 123
Warner, R. Stephen, 87, 132
Washington, Booker T., 177
Washington, Mary, 140
Watkins, J. B., 10
Watson, Mrs. D. S., 236
Wells, Ida B., 174
Whildren, Frank, 37

Wiley, Calvin H., 34
Willard, Frances, 142, 172
Williams, John, 148
Williamson, Joel, 188
Wills, William Henry, 75
Wilson, Charles Reagan, 148
Washington, Booker T., 177
Women: role of, 8–9, 125, 129, 132, 148–9, 201, 238–40; in Sunday school, 9, 55–7, 86–7, 118, 131, 238–9; as authors, 104, 104n, 239; in church, 128–9, 131, 132, 239, 240; at conventions, 166–7, 177, 221; as editors, 104; as fund raisers, 148; as missionaries, 48, 186; as public school teachers, 129n; as Sunday school teachers, 128–32, 128n, 213, 236–9; as superintendents, 123, 124, 166
Women's Christian Temperance Union, 142, 143, 172
Women's Convention of the National Baptist Convention, 177
Wood, Winnie, 170
Woodruff, E. N., 207
Woodson, Carter, 19
Wright, James, 232

Yellow journalism, 91–2
Youth organizations, 202. *See also* names of specific organizations

Zelizer, Viviana, 4